BLOOMSBURY

BLOOMSBURY, BELSEN, OXFORD

Janet Vaughan – Medical Pioneer

Sheena Evans

University of Chester Press

First published 2024
by University of Chester Press
Parkgate Road
Chester CH1 4BJ

Printed and bound in the UK
by TJ Books
Padstow PL28 8RW

University of Chester
Cover designed by the LIS Graphics Team
University of Chester

A catalogue record of this book is available
from the British Library

ISBN 978-1-910481-26-4

For my family, and especially for Dai –

lusern i fi

Contents

LIST OF ILLUSTRATIONS

Cover photograph. Janet Vaughan, March 1945 (Elliott and Fry). © National Portrait Gallery, London.

PLATES

Plate 14: The Slough depot office at work, 1942. Oxford, Bodleian Libraries, MS. 13145.

Plate 15: Slough staff loading 2,000 bottles of dried serum for North Africa, 1942. Oxford, Bodleian Libraries, MS. 13145.

Plate 16: British, American and Australian experts in India, with Indian colleagues. Wellcome Collection, Sir Weldon Dalrymple-Champneys, Bart, GC/139 H.2/2.

Plate 17: The Gourlays and two friends of their children on holiday in Switzerland, 1946 (JP).

Plate 18: The family at Plovers Field, 1950s (JP).

Plate 19: Mary's wedding, 1955 (JP).

Plate 20: Janet Vaughan in her laboratory, late 1950s (Ray Cripps Witney Press Ltd, Witney, Oxon). Courtesy of the Principal and Fellows of Somerville College Oxford.

Plate 21: Portrait of Dame Janet Vaughan by Claude Rogers, 1957. © Crispin Rogers. Courtesy of the Principal and Fellows of Somerville College Oxford.

Plate 22: Vaughan and Gourlay on holiday, 1950s (JP).

Plate 23: Vaughan chairing a conference session in Italy, March 1970. Courtesy of Mary Sissons-Joshi.

Plate 24: Vaughan (on top step, right) at a conference in York, July 1976. Courtesy of Mary Sissons-Joshi.

Plate 25: Portrait of Janet Vaughan by Godfrey Argent Studio, 1979. © Godfrey Argent Estate/The Royal Society (IM/GA/JGRS/8149).

Plate 26: Vaughan canvassing as Labour Party candidate for the local council election, 1973 (JP).

Plate 27: Vaughan with family, including three great-grandchildren, in the 1980s (JP).

Plate 28: Vaughan speaking at the unveiling of the memorial to British and Irish volunteers who died in the Spanish Civil War, 1985 (JP).

Plate 29: Portrait of Dame Janet Vaughan, 1986. © Victoria Crowe. Courtesy of National Portrait Gallery, London.

SIMPLIFIED FAMILY TREES
Vaughan family

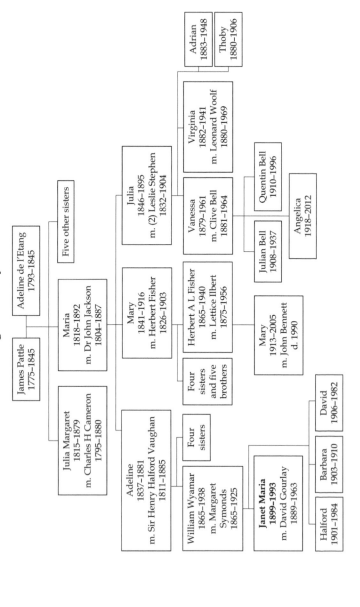

Symonds family

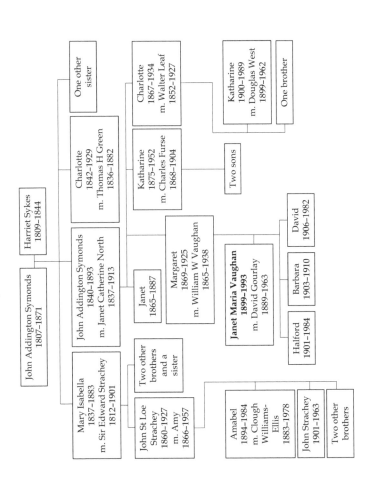

ABBREVIATIONS

AERE	Atomic Energy Research Establishment
AICL (BPMS)	British Postgraduate Medical School, by permission of Archives Imperial College London
ASM	Association of Senior Members, Somerville College (old Somervillians)
BL	British Library
BMA	British Medical Association
BMJ	*British Medical Journal, BMJ* and *The BMJ*
Br J Exp Pathol	*British Journal of Experimental Pathology*
Br J Radiol	*British Journal of Radiology*
BMIHT	British Motor Industry Heritage Trust
BPMS	British Postgraduate Medical School
BRO	Berkshire Record Office
CERN	European Organisation for Nuclear Research
CMO	Chief Medical Officer
CND	Campaign for Nuclear Disarmament
CP	Communist Party
CSC	The Commonwealth Scholarships Commission
CUF	Common University Fund
DBE	Dame Commander of the Order of the British Empire
DCL	Doctorate in Civil Law by Diploma
DM	Doctor of Medicine
EMS	Emergency Medical Service (Second World War)
FRCP	Fellow of the Royal College of Physicians
FRS	Fellow of the Royal Society
HRO	Hampshire Record Office
HHC	Hull History Centre
HMLC	Harvard Medical Library collection, Center for the History of Medicine in the Francis A Countway Library, Harvard University. Collections of letters: Minot: GA55, Box 3, f. 38–39; Lisco: Box 2, f. 2; Castle: Box 2, f. 27.

IAEA	International Atomic Energy Authority
ICRP	International Commission for Radiation Protection
IWMSA	Imperial War Museum Sound Archives
JA	Janet Vaughan, 'Jogging Along' (1979). Ironically titled unpublished personal memoir. Copy given to author by Mary Park.
JAS	John Addington Symonds (Janet Vaughan's maternal grandfather)
JBS	J B S Haldane
JP	Illustration used courtesy of James Park
JPP	James Park papers and interviews
J Pathol Bacteriol	*The Journal of Pathology and Bacteriology*
KCC	King's College Cambridge Modern Archives
LMA	London Metropolitan Archives
LMH	Lady Margaret Hall
LSF	Library of the Society of Friends
LSHTM	London School of Hygiene and Tropical Medicine
LULSC	Leeds University Libraries Special Collections
MML	Marx Memorial Library
MRC	Medical Research Council
MRCUW	Modern Records Centre, University of Warwick
NF	Nuffield Foundation
NPHT	Nuffield Provincial Hospitals Trust
NRPB	National Radiation Protection Board
OBE	Order of the British Empire
OBL	Oxford, Bodleian Libraries (other collections)
OBLUA	Oxford, Bodleian Libraries, University of Oxford Archives
OHC	Oxford History Centre
ORHB	Oxford Regional Hospital Board
POW	Prisoner of war
Proc R Soc Med	*Proceedings of the Royal Society of Medicine*

RAC	Rockefeller Archive Center
RCEP	Royal Commission on Environmental Pollution
RCN	Royal College of Nursing
RCP	Royal College of Physicians (YFC – Younger Fellows Club)
RCPL	Royal College of Physicians Library
RCS	Royal College of Surgeons
RLHA	Royal London Hospital Archives
RS	Collections of the Royal Society
RSA&SC	Rugby School Archives and Special Collections
RSL	Radcliffe Science Library, Oxford
SCA	Somerville College Archives
SCR	Senior Common Room (Somerville)
TA	Tate Archive
TML	Thorndike Memorial Laboratory
TNA	The National Archives
UCH	University College Hospital
UCLSC	University College London Special Collections
UGC	University Grants Committee
UOBLSC	University of Bristol Library Special Collections
UOH	United Oxford Hospitals
USSCK	University of Sussex Special Collections at The Keep
VW Diary	Virginia Woolf and Anne Olivier Bell, *The Letters of Virginia Woolf* Volume 1 (London, Hogarth Press, 1977); and also with Andrew McNeillie, Volumes 2–5 (London, Hogarth Press, 1978, 1980, 1982 and 1984)
VW Letters	Virginia Woolf and Nigel Nicolson, *The Letters of Virginia Woolf*, Volumes 1–6 (London, Hogarth Press, 1975, 1976, 1977, 1978, 1979 and 1980)
Wellcome Collection	Wellcome Trust: Wellcome Collection

ACKNOWLEDGEMENTS

I could not have produced such a rounded picture of Vaughan as a personality without the help, support and often the generous hospitality of Vaughan's family, and particularly of James Park, her grandson and the keeper of the papers still in her possession when she died, as well as some important collections of letters and many family photographs. James also very generously gave me copies of recorded interviews he had conducted with family members and friends. Her daughter Mary Park kindly gave me some very useful books, and she and Vaughan's nephew John showed me additional papers and family portraits. Vaughan's nieces Susan Aglionby and Ann Steadman, and her great-niece Julia, also shared their memories, papers and photograph albums. David Gourlay's nephews Brian and Colin gave me valuable help too. The family were also able to put me in touch with Maureen Owen, and so start the process of gathering memories of the Oxford lab.

Liz Cooke at Somerville College went the extra mile several times over in helping me to contact the many old Somervillians who shared their memories via interviews, phone conversations, emails and letters. I have used these to build a composite picture of Vaughan as Principal, quoting individuals only where it seemed particularly pertinent to do so. Professor Caroline Barron gave crucial help at various stages. Chance meetings have also played their part, for instance when a colleague of my husband turned out to be the godmother of Mike Davies, a technician in the Oxford lab from 1964–66 who provided me with some vivid memories.

Dr Kate Murphy generously shared her knowledge of early women at the BBC with me, before publication of her book on the subject; and Rosemary Seton's pertinent question and later conversations after a talk I gave on Vaughan prompted me to think more deeply about her changing attitude to Christianity over the course of her life. William Dalrymple kindly told me of the article which revealed the Indian contribution to Vaughan's (and also his own) family tree. And Victoria Crowe shared her memories of making friends with Vaughan while painting the portrait now in the National Portrait Gallery in London.

I am grateful too to my old college, now called Murray Edwards College, Cambridge, for making me a senior visiting fellow in 2013 in order to facilitate my research. Personal circumstances made it impossible for me to use the fellowship as I and they intended, but their action boosted my confidence and strengthened my resolve at a difficult time. Dr Amy Erickson also gave me valuable encouragement.

The many archives and libraries I visited are shown in the bibliography. All the staff I encountered showed me unfailing courtesy. I am particularly grateful to those at Somerville College, the Bodleian Library, Imperial College London, the London Metropolitan Archives, Rugby School, The National Archives, the British Library and the Wellcome Library and Collection, where I believe I spent the most time and caused the most work. The London Library was a source of rare books as well as lengthy loans on occasion, and at Dorich House Museum in Kingston, Brenda Martin and Jonathan Black kindly shared with me their research into Dora Gordine's life. The Harvard Medical Library Collection and the Rockefeller Archive Center were swift and efficient in sending me copies of key letters and papers.

I have been greatly helped in the writing process by my friend Ruth Cohen, who raised so many pertinent questions over cups of coffee in the Friends House café opposite Euston Station in London. Talks I gave at Somerville College, the Institute of Historical Research, the Centre for History in Public Health at the London School of Hygiene and Tropical Medicine, annual conferences of the Women's History Network and a small, enthusiastic women's history group meeting in Bloomsbury did much to help me shape individual chapters. Professor A V Hoffbrand kindly read and commented on a very early, long draft of the haematology story, and Professor Lorna Secker-Walker helpfully reviewed the draft chapters on radiation research. Professor Pat Thane's comments on a fuller draft of the Royal Commission on Equal Pay section, and Dr Patricia Fara's on the Belsen chapter and then the full draft, were invaluable, as has been their more general interest and support along the way. Gladstone's Library at Hawarden provided some peaceful thinking time.

Acknowledgements

Dr Pat Starkey of the University of Liverpool provided helpful comments on the near-final draft, and Hugo Rée and Robin Adams applied critical and knowledgeable eyes to the public health and other specialist aspects. Pauline Adams, whose history of Somerville College gave me so much essential background information, very kindly read through the Somerville chapters and made necessary factual amendments. Old Somervillians Margaret Clare and Patricia Baines read earlier drafts of the post-war Oxford chapters and also, especially as non-scientists, gave helpful comments and encouragement.

My editor at University of Chester Press, Sarah Griffiths, has been extraordinarily patient and encouraging whilst I finalised the text, and in guiding me through the final processes leading to publication. Any factual mistakes which remain in the text are down to me. My daughter Kathy, a writer herself, has acted as an invaluable 'lay' reader.

I cannot end without thanking all those others, too numerous to mention by name, who have helped me along the way; including faithful friends who often assumed that this 'Janet' I kept talking about was an aunt or cousin of mine.

Foreword

I first heard of Janet Vaughan when I saw her being interviewed as one of six *Women of Our Century*: a BBC series first broadcast in 1984, when Vaughan was 84, and repeated in 1988. The one-hour interview passed in a flash, and I kept wishing the interviewer would let her speak for longer on each topic. What a story. Early days in Bloomsbury as a pathologist who became a pioneering haematologist and expert on the anaemias, but also a socialist who worked for Spanish Medical Aid and for better nutrition for the British poor. The driving force in setting up and running the wartime blood transfusion service for London, while planning reforms to medical education in preparation for the National Health Service. Going to test a treatment for starvation in the Bergen-Belsen concentration camp soon after its liberation. Principal of Somerville College Oxford at the age of 45, but also entering a new research field and becoming a world authority on the effects of radiation on bone. As I listened, I thought 'Someone should be writing this woman's biography.'

At that time, I had a young family and a job, so might have forgotten about her, but for one thing. Her account of testing treatments for pernicious anaemia in the 1920s invoked my mother's story of her pregnancy with me in 1945. At four months she was (mis)diagnosed with pernicious anaemia and advised to have an abortion, which she refused. There followed a regime of eating raw liver twice a week, and injections of liver extract once a month – effective for the anaemia of pregnancy which she must have had. When I was born, I was paraded through the hospital as a miracle baby. Now I saw that she had not been exaggerating. When I was contemplating retirement some years later, I wrote to Somerville and, encouraged by the college and her family, started to research Vaughan's life.

I never dreamt that I would spend more than 20 years on this task, from the first interviews with people close to her, fitted in before I retired, until finally deciding that I must stop researching and write. Starting off with family papers and interviews, and a copy of Vaughan's brief personal memoir, ironically titled 'Jogging Along' (JA), there seemed at first to be more bread than filling in the sandwich of this story. The people I spoke to usually knew about only one or two aspects of her life, and even those not in much depth. Her appearances were peripheral at best in the biographies of her contemporaries, and in their published letters and diaries.

There was no shortage of information about Vaughan's fascinating family tree, peopled by medical men on both maternal and paternal sides, but also by a number of determined and influential women, some of whom were descended through one great-grandmother from an eighteenth-century Bengali woman who had converted to Roman Catholicism and married a French officer in Pondicherry. All this could have occupied a chapter in itself, but I yielded to the many friends who told me they hated 'ancestor' chapters, and also decided in the interest of brevity that I would only draw attention to those who had a direct influence on her. For those interested in finding out more about her family, I have included the main sources in the endnotes and bibliography and indicated key people in the simplified family trees on pp. xii and xiii.

My research took me to beautiful and interesting places, from Clifton in Bristol to Rugby School in Warwickshire, Giggleswick in Yorkshire to Wellington in Berkshire, Upton Castle in Pembrokeshire to Llantony Priory in the Black Mountains; and from Boston in the United States to the cities of India. The more I found out, the more I realised there was still to find; but I hope I have drawn the line in a reasonable place. The official and personal records of Vaughan's relations, friends and colleagues have not only shed much light on her story, but yielded insights into other lives, places and customs. Nearly always the events revealed in the records are far more intriguing – and often exciting – than I had ever expected them to be. She seemed to have an uncanny ability to find her way to the interesting action in what were certainly interesting times; and while she did not believe in keeping more than a small minority of her own letters and papers, her habit of writing frequent notes to friends and colleagues means that such notes are almost always to be discovered amongst the papers of those who kept their own.

One big lacuna I found at the beginning related to Vaughan's husband, David Gourlay. Some people from her post-war Oxford days implied that he was a nonentity compared to his wife, and could not understand why she had married him. I rejected that idea, knowing that such a strong and forthright character as Vaughan would never have chosen – and then stayed loyal to – a nonentity. Fortunately, I happen to live in Surbiton, where Gourlay's family settled from 1907 onwards. Knowing that he had been a conscientious objector in the First World War, I looked at the newspaper records in our local history centre, and soon found the accounts of his appearances before the local and appeal tribunals in the spring of 1916. The statements he gave in support of his case were clear, articulate and obviously based on well-founded personal convictions; and he had the courage and strength to refuse to be brow-beaten into accepting non-combatant service. This and the rest of his story up to 1930, as I was gradually able to piece it out, convinced me that I was right: the marriage was a love-match between two very different but complementary characters, who had been fortunate to meet when they did.

The more I found out, the more I liked and admired this woman who had dropped out of public memory, and the more astonished I was by how much she achieved. Although a good publicist for causes, she always downplayed her own contribution, so that even her own family had no idea of its breadth and depth. Once I had collected the evidence, the main problem became how to organise the material so as to do justice to each aspect without confusing readers. After many false starts I decided to arrange it chronologically but in parallel subject chapters, so as to keep at its core the science which Vaughan said was central to her life, whilst making links between this and the family matters (also central, by her own account) and work for social justice which she pursued outside the lab.

The subject areas multiplied during the Second World War, necessitating separate chapters dealing with her work on reform of medical education (including a trip to wartime India as an adviser), and on public bodies and charitable bodies such as the Royal Commission on Equal Pay and the Nuffield Foundation, in addition to her 'main' work in blood transfusion. Her time at the Belsen camp was short, but I decided to give it a separate chapter so as to explain her role and its context, and make clear the lasting emotional impact of this experience. In post-war Oxford Vaughan's energies were still widely distributed, leading me to create a separate chapter additional to those on Somerville and her new research field, covering her various contributions to Oxford medicine. These included a whirlwind stint on the new Oxford Regional Hospital Board as well as her devotion to the cause of developing medical education in Oxford.

I kept science at the core, but, as I am a non-scientist myself, I believe this story will be of great interest to general readers. I have therefore tried, while I hope doing justice to her achievements, to avoid so far as possible the kind of technical language which, especially in relation to her post-war work on radiation, would be off-putting and increasingly impenetrable to the general reader. I also thought those with no experience of scientific research would be interested in the kind of inside view of the lab which several of those who worked with her in the 1950s and 1960s kindly shared with me. So I have included these memories in separate sections in the relevant chapter. I hope, too, that these accounts convey something of what Vaughan meant by the 'fun' of doing research.

The biography is a rounded one, which tries to cover at least the central fields of her activity and convey her character, including its flaws. She taught her children that 'people come first', and lived out her own precept with all her formidable energy and talents. The result is I believe an engrossing story, which deserves to be properly and accurately told.

One last point concerns my choice of cover photograph. A number of people stressed that Vaughan was beautiful, but most available photographs of her convey little idea of this: she generally looks serious and preoccupied. Only this early 1945 picture, taken just after her appointment as Principal of Somerville College Oxford and just before she went to Belsen, shows her looking relaxed, attractive and still youthful. It seemed a good image with which to introduce her.

FINDING A VOCATION 1899–1925

CHAPTER 1
Who's afraid of Virginia Woolf?
1899–1918

Lively relations

When Virginia Woolf first met Janet Vaughan as an adult, her reactions were not complimentary. In February 1924, she commented that this medical student was 'a lady; large, gawky, will marry & breed'.[1] In May 1926, the recently qualified doctor was 'Good dull Janet Vaughan'.[2] Virginia would soon change her opinion. And for Janet as a child she held no terrors, but was simply an occasional and welcome visitor to the Vaughan family home. Virginia Stephen, as she was then, was her father's first cousin and a much-loved friend of her mother, with little sign as yet of the intimidating intellect for which she became famous.

Janet's parents, Margaret (Madge) Symonds and William Wyamar (Will) Vaughan had first met in the winter of 1889–90, when the 20-year-old Madge was visiting the Stephen family in London. She was the daughter of the writer John Addington Symonds, and had grown up with three sisters in an unconventional, bohemian household in Davos, Switzerland.[3] The Stephen sisters, Vanessa and Virginia, whose father Leslie was Symonds's friend, called her 'The Chief' because of her vivid, dark beauty and outspoken boldness of expression.[4] Will was good looking and athletic, but a far more conventional character, destined for a career as a school teacher. He was immediately smitten by Madge, and maintained his suit over the following years, undeterred by several refusals of marriage.

Will's father, Henry Halford Vaughan, had been a brilliant scholar and Regius professor of modern history at Oxford, but moved in 1867 (when Will, his third child, was two years old) to the rather tumbledown and isolated Upton Castle in West Wales, where he served as a circuit judge. His wife was one of the three beautiful daughters of a leading Calcutta surgeon, Dr Jackson. One of her sisters married the father of H A L (Herbert) Fisher, academic

1

historian and government minister, and the other became Leslie Stephen's second wife, the mother of Vanessa and Virginia. Will did not inherit his father's intellectual brilliance, but had great strength of character, and firm Christian principles nurtured at Rugby School.

The couple's courtship was long and troubled. Symonds's wife Catherine was an accomplished artist and the sister of Marianne North, whose paintings of trees and plants are now housed in a gallery at the Royal Botanic Gardens, Kew, in London. Neither Catherine nor her husband thought the match suitable, given Madge's mercurial temperament and wish to be a writer like her father. She suffered severe depression after his death in 1893, and her first full length book, *Days Spent on a Doge's Farm*, was dedicated to him, with the addition of a quote from Tennyson: 'O love, we two shall go no longer / To lands of summer across the sea.'[5] She had some success in 1897 with a guide book to Perugia, written jointly with a friend, but her mood swings continued. Eventually, both she and her family were won over by Will's determination and obvious sincerity.

Janet's heritage from these parents, on the one side love of the visual and literary arts and rebellious bohemianism, on the other practical acumen and stern devotion to the needs of others, especially the young, would be apparent in her own character throughout her life. Notably, too, the family fortunes on both sides had been founded by medical men.

A spirited child

Will Vaughan and Madge Symonds were married in London in July 1898, aged 33 and 29. After a honeymoon that included a visit to Davos, they went to live in Bristol, where Will was house tutor of School House, Clifton College. Number 4 Albert Road was a modest but substantial two-storey detached villa with basement, large enough to accommodate four servants as well as the family at the time of the 1901 census. It overlooked the school's athletic ground a few hundred yards from the College. The terraces and squares of Clifton, high above the city, had dignity and solidity, and the Avon Gorge and the Downs, offering invigorating walks, were close by. Madge had her house decorated with William

Morris wallpaper and fabrics, as her mother had done at Clifton Hill House, the former home of the Symonds family before their move to Switzerland. It was situated a short walk down the hill from Albert Road.[6]

By the spring of 1899, Madge was pregnant. Katharine, her youngest sister, came to stay in the summer, and accompanied Will and Madge on a holiday in Wiltshire. She wrote to their sister Lotta on 29 July that the day before had been 'the anniversary of that dismal day [the wedding, when Madge's mood was still low] last year. It found Madge in all the happiness and content which we hoped and dared not expect. She is different and gentler and easier to live with.'[7] Lotta, the most conventional of the sisters, had been happily married to a successful banker, Walter Leaf, since 1894.

Janet was born on 18 October – the physician St Luke's day, as she would later emphasise – and proved strong. She may have been named for Madge's eldest sister, praised by her as 'a perfect character'.[8] For her first few years, the new baby was known as Popsy – this time perhaps in memory of her great-aunt Marianne North, universally called 'Aunt Pop' in the Symonds's and their children's households. Madge asked Vanessa Stephen to be a godmother, but withdrew the request with some embarrassment when Vanessa, an agnostic, said she was willing but that Madge should know she had never been christened herself, or wished to be.[9]

The conventional Will is likely to have been behind the decision not to have Vanessa as godmother. Katharine became engaged to the artist Charles Furse early in 1900, and they married in October; but she thought Will would dislike her bohemian choice 'because he is that class and training'.[10] There seem, however, to have been few shadows on the Vaughans' relationship in these early days. Virginia Stephen noticed at the Furse wedding that 'Will and Madge looked both of them extremely well, and Will showed everyone photographs of the infant.' Again in April 1901 she found them 'very well and almost too happy, one never found Madge without Will or Will without Madge'.[11]

This halcyon period continued. Janet's brother Halford (pronounced Harford by the family) was born in September 1901, when Janet was almost two. On the day before his birth, Madge wrote thanking her mother for some flowers and longing for the Alps again:

> But England is very beautiful ... Every evening I go up on the Downs for a good tramp, and watch the sun set over the river ... There are lots of little harebells left in the grass ... and ... the Popsy ... says nearly everything now and is extremely attentive and intelligent – and appropriates all the new baby's belongings with stern and egotistical confidence. Will is very hard at work, but we nearly always get a walk together in the day.[12] [Underlining in source and in subsequent quotations.]

A second daughter, Barbara, was born in late January 1903. A few weeks before, over Christmas of 1902, the three-year-old Janet suffered a traumatic event. The family were staying with relatives in Tunbridge Wells when their young nursery maid was killed by a falling branch in the garden. Madge's mother wrote of this 'terrible blow' to Popsy, urging Madge not to let her cry in bed, but to soothe and pet her through the crying fits. Janet and Halford went to stay with their grandmother in Lyme Regis in January and February (presumably to be out of the way when the new baby was born and being settled), and she soon wrote that Janet had cried in bed the previous evening for 20 minutes, wanting Nanny to lie beside her.

> Janet is not a baby now, but an extra-intelligent child, and if [the nanny] reasoned with her in the right way and at the right time, she would show her the reason of things ... [when the children return home, Madge should accustom Janet to sleep in another room with the nursery-maid] ... it is not good ... for so nervous a child to be liable to wake with two crying babies at any time of night.[13]

However well the accident was explained, Janet was too young a child to understand fully what had happened, and why the maid had suddenly disappeared from her life; or why she should shortly afterwards be sent away from her own home to stay with her grandmother. The Vaughan children, like many others of their time and class, spent far more time with nanny and nursery maid than with their parents, and Katharine Furse made it clear that the Symonds family was not given to the physical expression of affection.[14] This nursery maid had probably been a major source of comfort and cuddles, and Janet must have formed some mental scar tissue as a result of her death. Her early childhood was, however, fundamentally secure and happy. Family photographs from this period show her as quite tall for her age, with an eager, open smile. There were walks around Clifton, visits to the zoological gardens opposite Clifton College and plenty of visits to and from relations and friends.[15]

***

Will was ambitious for a headship. At Clifton he was a house master and, from 1903, head of the 'modern side', with its emphasis on science and modern languages. He also had glowing references from his cousin Herbert Fisher, and from Virginia and Vanessa's father, Leslie Stephen.[16] At first, however, this was not enough. His academic career had been respectable rather than brilliant, and his success so far was founded on his strength and personality as a teacher. It mattered too that most public school headmasters at this time were in Anglican orders, but Will, whilst a committed Christian, had no such vocation. Applications for headships at Sedburgh and Bedford failed in 1900 and 1903 respectively.[17]

He soon benefited, however, from the rising tide of professionalism in late Victorian and Edwardian Britain, now spreading to the public schools and ushering in a period of reform and expansion.[18] Early in 1904, he applied successfully for the headship of Giggleswick School in the Yorkshire Dales, a long-established foundation serving mainly the professional classes of the northern industrial towns. It had modern dormitory houses, dedicated science and other facilities, and a beautiful late Victorian chapel: the gift of an old boy, in honour of Queen Victoria's diamond jubilee. Nonetheless pupil numbers had gone down and the school needed strong leadership to turn it around. The successful applicant would have free accommodation and £200 a year plus a yearly payment linked to the number of boys in the school. He must be aged under 45, in sympathy with the governors' stress on thoroughness of scientific instruction, and responsible for chapel services; but he need not be in orders.

The Vaughan family moved in over Easter 1904. The school was built on a hill overlooking the small town of Giggleswick, with views to the fells on every side. The headmaster's house was light, spacious and well-proportioned, with large windows and a pleasant garden to one side. Madge wrote to a friend in November that year that Yorkshire 'is a place – a climate! I cannot exaggerate my pleasure in it.'[19] Janet would remember particularly the

> strange red brick chapel topped by a ... green copper dome and lined with brilliant mosaics. [Madge] loved the Pennine Hills and the flowers ... I ... remember the excitement of finding grass of Parnassus, Primula Farinosa, Pinguicola grandiflora, and sundew. She grew to enjoy the Yorkshire people and their ways [and] had a great capacity for ... making every ordinary thing exciting. Every year we rode over Buckly Brow in a Wagonette to a special wood ... where wild lilies of the valley and Solomon's Seal grew, as well as primroses and wood anemones ... She taught us to toboggan in the winter ... the Giggleswick years were the happiest ... of my mother's later life ...[20]

Will set about reforming the school. Disregarding his own income, he immediately cut the number of boys by limiting the intake to those aged 14 and over. When the Oxford and Cambridge Examinations Board inspected the school in 1906 there were 118 boys (as against 145 in 1903), but they praised Vaughan as headmaster and teacher. He appointed well-qualified masters, offered more scholarships and enabled older boys to attend higher education extension lectures in nearby Settle. And – true to the tradition of outreach he knew from Clifton, with its mission in the poorer districts of Bristol – he opened a club for working boys in Leeds, which he visited frequently, as well as inviting the boys on visits to the school.[21]

Will was a Liberal in politics, and very conscious of the gap between rich and poor. The Boer War had ended in 1902, but the army's problems in recruiting enough able-bodied men to fight that war had shocked middle-class England. Experience in Manchester was typical of that in other industrial cities: of 12,000 men volunteering, only 1,200 were accepted as fully fit. Meanwhile Rowntree's work showed that nearly 30% of the nation were living at or below the poverty line: in other words, on the verge of hunger.[22] Will made sure that his pupils were aware of contemporary publications on the social and economic situation.[23]

Among the family's visitors, the 22-year-old Virginia Stephen came for about 10 days in November 1904, when she was recovering from the breakdown triggered by her father's death early in that year. She returned for nearly two weeks in April 1906, staying in a neighbouring house so as to be more independent. Shortly before the 1904 visit, the doctor had advised rest for Madge, and she was thinking of a holiday abroad, perhaps in Rome. Presumably she was showing signs of depression again.

Virginia wrote of her longing for a walk in the school's beautiful surroundings, of the difficulty of being alone with Madge, and Will's fears lest Madge might 'talk morbidly', a phrase which seemed to include discussion of her – presumably literary – ideas. Virginia modified that view a little later:

> Madge is … like a clever and loveable child, but not in the least mature. She and Will as I see more every day, are perfectly happy. She says herself that no life could suit her better … She … refers to him in everything: and there is a great deal that is charming and clever about him besides all his solid good qualities … I can't imagine what she would do without him to decide things for her.

Madge was still writing whenever she had a spare moment, but Virginia noted that Will expected school duties, such as visiting a sick gardener, to take precedence. Will also had firm ideas about his children's upbringing. Virginia

> was amused … when in answer to Janets [sic] demands I described the appearance and habits of the dragon – whose picture I wear in my watch chain. I had to make him as horrid as possible; and suddenly I found that Wills [sic] paternal eye was on me disapprovingly; he didn't like his children to be told fables, especially on Sunday. They have their Sunday books – but I must say, they don't seem to suffer in spirit … he is a most devoted Father, and husband …[24]

When she returned to Giggleswick in April 1906, Virginia still found Madge immature but charming, and Janet 'growing into a very handsome and intelligent woman'. After a visit to the zoo in Manchester, 'They were all shouting about beasts when I left them, and Madge was screaming with laughter … Madge is really at her best as the mother of children.'[25] The six-year-old Janet, tutored by Mrs Dixon ('Dicky'), the children's first governess, by now knew enough of her alphabet to try to teach it to Virginia. At that time Janet's brother Halford was four and her sister Barbara three. Her brother David was born around a month later, in July 1906. It is clear from this and other sources that her childhood was a happy one, with loving parents who both appreciated the beauty of the natural world, and shared strong Christian principles.

***

With David's birth, the family was complete. There are few accounts of Janet at Giggleswick, but in photographs she is a pretty child, with dark curly hair and a serious expression. According to her cousin Kitty Leaf, she retained the forcefulness which Madge had described in her as an almost two-year-old: 'I had always been impressed by Janet's glowing fires since the first time I remember seeing her, a beautiful, dark child sitting on a stool by her mother's knee, embroidering a bold design of flowers and fruit on a piece of coarse linen.'[26] A story preserved in the family of one of Janet's occasional playmates in these years likewise rings true. It relates how she was once with someone who accidentally chopped off the tip of a finger when closing an iron gate. Janet immediately seized the tip and pressed it back onto the finger, so that a doctor was able to sew it back: early evidence of her characteristic decisiveness and presence of mind, as well as her interest in things medical.[27]

In 1908 Virginia gave judicious praise to a new preface Madge had written for a reissue of *Days Spent on a Doge's Farm*.[28] But the family were placed under great strain in 1909, when the six-year-old Barbara (whom Virginia had described on her 1906 visit as strong-willed and affectionate, with a huge sense of humour) became very ill. Early in the year, Madge spent long periods in London with her, while she had treatment including an operation on a tubercular gland in her neck. In April her sister Katharine was dreading that Madge might break down – and her behaviour during one of Virginia's visits certainly supports that fear.[29] Katharine went to stay at Giggleswick in May after Barbara's return.[30] By August, she was thought to be on the mend, and Will and Madge had a few days away while Madge's Symonds aunt, Charlotte Green (always 'Aunt Char' in the family) came from Oxford to fill their place.[31]

From September, however, Barbara was back in London under treatment. Madge stayed with her from November to January, while Will had Christmas with the other children in Giggleswick. Barbara died on 6 January 1910, about three weeks before her seventh birthday, and was buried in Highgate cemetery, her grave not far from those of Julia and Stella Stephen.[32] Janet and Halford, aged ten and eight, would have been deeply affected by their sister's death, but their parents always spoke warmly and openly of Barbara afterwards. In November 1911, Madge told Halford that she had just planted snowdrops and crocuses on the grave in Highgate, and then 'quantities of Giggleswick saxifrages to make a carpet all over it'.[33] This was Janet's second experience of the death of a loved one, and a further layer of scar tissue must have formed.

A move to Berkshire

Will was shortly afterwards offered a more prestigious headship: that of Wellington College. It was an offer he could hardly refuse, and the family moved south to the sandy, pine-covered plains of Berkshire at Easter in 1910. He may have hoped that a move at this time would help Madge as well as himself to recover from Barbara's loss. The effect was two-edged, however, taking Madge away from a landscape she loved and friends who esteemed and loved her. All the family, including Will, looked back on Yorkshire as a place touched with magic.[34]

Wellington College had been conceived by the Prince Consort in the 1850s as a military academy, intended for the orphan sons of army officers; but financial constraints, and changed leadership following the Prince's death, meant that it was in practice run on similar lines to other public schools. It retained a strong military connection, however, as well as close links to the royal family. The architecture was massive and dominating and, given the use of the local bright red brick in combination with Portland stone, must have appeared strange indeed to anyone accustomed to the restrained grey of Clifton or Giggleswick.[35] Madge's sisters and their families were now within easy reach by car: the Leafs, whose daughter Kitty was around the same age as Janet; and, at Camberley, the widowed Katharine Furse and her two small sons. London was also much closer, and Will's higher salary meant more money for shopping and travel. But the Master's Lodge at Wellington, with its gothic windows, gloomy panelled rooms and large staff including butler (rapidly nicknamed the Fusser) was not to her taste.

From the autumn of 1910 Halford, aged eight, was away in term time at a prep school in Warwickshire. He, Janet and their parents corresponded on a weekly basis from then on, and many of the letters survive in the Rugby School archive. Their contents reveal not only much of the texture of the family's life but also something of the personalities of the writers – including David, once he in turn went away to school in 1914. Both the boys were mainly drawn to the natural world and country pursuits. Janet shared their love of plants and wildlife, but she had a restless energy and wide-ranging interests which were all her own.

Her life was relatively isolated, being educated at home and with few playmates, who were mostly the children of teachers and occasionally her cousins. In both cases, visits had to be arranged rather than happening spontaneously or regularly. She was naturally aware of and often involved in the organisational needs of running the school, from entertaining new boys to annual speech days and garden parties, as well as the planning of dinner parties and chapel services. And she had a wide range of formal and informal activities open to her: dancing and piano lessons (not a success – music was a blind spot); golf, bowls, tennis in the garden and horse riding (again, like most sports, not a success, though she persevered over several years); keeping pets (everything from kittens to butterflies was attempted at one time or another); skating in winter and swimming in summer at one of the local ponds; and climbing trees and playing at 'Indians' under the influence of James Fenimore Cooper's *The Last of the Mohicans*.

Inevitably, however, she spent much of her time with adults and especially her parents. She would recall that the move to Wellington, whilst a great promotion for Will, was unwelcome to Madge:

> She did not like red brick or conifers or the more pompous way of life involving butlers and footmen and a chauffeur driven car … By this time I was possibly aware of conflict between my mother and father bringing … them unhappiness. They were both radicals [politically, with] … many of the same values, but my father had a deep distrust of women getting involved with school-boys, so my mother felt that … there was so little she could do … She read a few papers to the Literary society … visited them when they were sick in the san …

entertained them in a formal way at home, and … watched cricket and football matches … She made a splendid garden … painted a little … tried to write; but compared to the world she had known with J.A.S. it was very grey.[36]

Will was not unfeeling. He took Madge on what he must have hoped would be a healing visit to Switzerland for nearly three weeks in the late summer of 1910. In October, however, she was ill, presumably with depression. Rest was prescribed, a nurse employed, and she went to Brighton in November, and then to her mother at Lyme Regis until Christmas.[37] The children, meanwhile, enjoyed the beach on the Kent coast with the family's Swiss maids Zela (who seems also to have acted as governess) and Deta, as they did every year and often as late as November, to benefit from the sea air if recovering from infections.[38]

Madge went again with Will to Italy and Switzerland in summer 1911, and in the following September to Italy for a month with the Leafs. Janet wanted to support her mother's wish to write. Late in 1911 she suggested to Halford that they club together to buy Madge an 'electric lantern' for Christmas, to use after an evening spent writing in the stables, when she had to lock the door as she emerged into the dark. 'The nicest one' cost three shillings and threepence (then no mean sum). Presumably they did this, and her mother was still going to the stables to write in 1916.[39]

Will, meanwhile, was more absorbed than ever by his work. He was the first non-clergyman to be Master of Wellington, where he was at first regarded as a rough-hewn outsider from the Welsh hinterland – an outsider who had rapidly to learn the punctilious etiquette to be observed when royalty came to visit for speech day and other occasions. He also saw much that demanded reform: over-burdened, underpaid masters, over-powerful prefects, unhygienic dormitories, inadequate food and no richness of cultural life, as well as a curriculum in need of broadening. With the backing of the governing body, he oversaw rapid and effective change in all these areas, but pressures outside his control continued throughout his time at Wellington.

Janet was conscious of the difference in her parents' characters. She remembered her mother's brilliant talk, of books, pictures, history and flowers. Her father was

very different. He never talked except about external affairs. He
was large in every way physically and mentally. I can remember his
enormous concern … to introduce science into the … curriculum …
to give boys a proper evening meal … his excitement at Wellington
about building proper changing rooms. He knew every boy … his
name and something about him. He went every day to the san and
saw all who were sick. He really cared about the young and their
problems and they knew it …[40]

Will's innate unease with the artistic and bohemian, and worries
that such influences encouraged 'morbidness' in Madge, was
reinforced by his consciousness of his own position and the need
to set an example of propriety. He disapproved of the Stephen
sisters' way of life after their move to Bloomsbury in 1904, and they
of course perceived this. Vanessa replied jokingly to a letter from
Madge imagining one of her sons married to a daughter of Vanessa
that this was rash. Such a daughter would have 'an odd bringing-
up probably, & perhaps will be a violent Suffragist or something
else that Will would think too dreadful'.[41] Will was horrified in
February 1910 by the famous Dreadnought Hoax: five young men
and Virginia Stephen had dressed up as Abyssinian princes, an
interpreter and Foreign Office representative and been received
officially – and unsuspectingly – by the officers and crew of *HMS
Dreadnought*. Janet recalled that Madge was secretly delighted,
and stuck the corresponding picture, cut out of *The Times*, in her
scrapbook.[42]

Leonard Woolf wrote a telling account of a visit to Wellington
with Virginia after their engagement in 1911, when Horatio
Brown, Addington Symonds's friend and biographer, and Janet's
grandmother Catherine were also present:

The atmosphere … was … compounded of two … antipathetic …
elements. Will was the public school Headmaster in excelsis …
his feet planted with no nonsense on the solid earth … a liberal of
course, but accepted as invincibly safe by the most conservative
of conservatives. He was charming to me, treating me at once as a
favourite prefect. Madge too was charming … But she, her mother,
and Horatio Brown oozed the precious … Italianate culture of …
the eighties and nineties … Madge … was rather intense, and the
atmosphere of the Doge's farm and Venetian lagoons would not mix

with that of Wellington and Will ... I find few things more distressing than the note of matrimonial exasperation in one's host or hostess when they speak to each other.[43]

A further vignette of Will is given by Janet's cousin Kitty Leaf:

My uncle Will Vaughan ... did ... dominate the scene whenever he emerged from his study ... He was a big, burly man, with massive shoulders, a broken nose, and a powerful voice that was at once rough and caressing ... Later, as an adolescent, I was frightened by his propensity for leg-pulling and prolonged sarcastic jokes ... But as a child, his humour seemed ... entirely jolly and benevolent.[44]

According to her mother the young Janet could be an irrepressible talker. When she was 15, Madge wrote that, since Janet had a friend coming to lunch, she and David would have to sit silent.[45] Yet Janet herself would recall that she had had the advantage of the 'seen and not heard' upbringing of Edwardian children, so had heard the conversation of a lot of important people who visited her parents' house. Both may of course be true; but they have a bearing on how others perceived her in her late teens and adulthood. At college one friend noted that she had a strong streak of shyness beneath her apparently outgoing nature.[46] In adulthood, many said that she had no small talk, but spoke rather of 'subjects', from jam-making to scientific research. In this trait she seems to have resembled her own description of her father. But memories within the Fisher family seem to point to something deeper.

Mary Fisher – later Bennett – remembered that her parents Lettice and Herbert, who were extremely fond of Madge, were surprised to find that Janet as a teenager was very reserved, especially by comparison with her mother.[47] It is not hard to imagine how Janet might have reacted to her father's irritation with her mother's style of talking, with its stress on emotion rather than reason. She would have tried to repress any such tendency in herself, so as to avoid aggravating the situation. She may also have accentuated what seems to have been her own natural disposition to look for the positive in life, so as to avoid, and at times alleviate the effects of, her mother's melancholic temperament. Beyond all this, her rather solitary upbringing, and her father's example, would have encouraged her to 'consume her own smoke': to repress hurts, sadness and negative feelings and take refuge in work and activity of all kinds.

Education

Neither Will nor Madge seems to have considered sending Janet away to school, although by this time a number of boarding schools for girls, such as Cheltenham Ladies' College and Roedean, were available. There was no suitable day school, such as those run by the Church Schools Company or the Girls' Public Day School Company, within easy reach of Wellington. Instead, like most other girls of her class and time, she was taught by governesses at home.[48] Writing to Halford in the autumn of 1910, she described a typical day:

> I do my lessons up till dinner time, stay out longer in the morning and lie down in the nursery after dinner, except Thursdays when I lie down before dinner because of my dancing which is at two ... Do you like French verbs, French grammar, French exercise, French translation? I just hate them. I also hate parsing, in English grammar. Next time I begin to do a map ... putting in the counties and things, Zela is going to do one with me, which will be great fun.[49]

At the beginning of 1912 a new governess – Miss Birch, or 'Pax' as she was known – proved very popular. (She was also teaching the six-year-old David, who would be going to prep school in two years' time.) Besides inventing games like jumping ditches and stalking through the heather, she introduced what Janet called 'thrilling' experiments, growing beans in different kinds of soil and seeing where they grew best.[50] Twelve-year-old Janet's examinations that summer were in arithmetic, grammar, French dictation, history and geography, with history at that time being her favourite. But there was as yet no other language than French, and no science – apart from those intriguing experiments with beans.

Janet absorbed her mother's love of wildlife and flowers, and also a lively sense of drama and poetry. Her father reported in May 1912 that 'Janet and Mother are in the drawing room both crying over a Poem of Tennysons [sic] which Mother is reading aloud.'[51] Her love of history may have arisen in part from Madge's reading of Scott's Waverley novels to the children.[52] The Bible was not neglected, and of course Janet attended the school's chapel every Sunday, where her father usually gave the sermon. Madge wrote to Halford in May 1913 that she and Janet had moved on from Isaiah to reading the 'Book of Revelations', and found it very beautiful.[53]

As to drama, the Vaughan children, and those of assistant masters, sometimes acted in plays at Christmas, when cousin Kitty especially admired Janet in the part of Countess Gruffanuff. At the Leaf home, the cousins acted impromptu shows ending with charades – unscripted and unrehearsed, but certain scenes were so popular and easily adapted to any syllable that they were repeated year after year. She and Janet would perform a duologue between mistress and cook which always brought the house down:

> … Janet was … overwhelmed by schemes for parties, and by conflicting duties. She would tell me, the reluctant cook, that eighty people, arriving unexpectedly for a ball, must be fed like lords. To which I listened with an air of sullen dullness, answering that I supposed a rice pudding would do very well. Janet, throwing herself into her part … would become increasingly excited as the human dramas piled up around her. Until finally, while I squeaked away at my slate, she would clasp her hands, throw back her head and cry: 'Tomorrow is the funeral of my son, and Wednesday is the marriage of my daughter.' The audience 'cried with laughter'.[54]

Madge also provided a privileged introduction to the visual arts, taking Janet to Roger Fry's first Post-Impressionist Exhibition around Christmas of 1910, when they were shown round by Roger himself.[55] In 1913 came purchases from Roger's Omega shop, which drew on the work of Bloomsbury and other artists: 'an enormous garden seat painted red like sealing wax! And also a very funny brilliant coloured lamp shade to frighten the ladies of Crowthorne!!' as Madge put it.[56] In July 1914, when Janet's close friend Ursula Bradshaw, daughter of the headmaster of Halford and David's prep school near Warwick, was staying, Madge took them both to visit the widow of the Victorian painter George Frederick Watts, in their house near Guildford in Surrey. Janet thought some of the pictures very beautiful, and was impressed by the 'huge cast' of a man riding a plunging horse.[57]

It is clear, however, that Janet's nature owed more to her father than her mother. Directness and decision characterise her letters. In July 1911, she visited her cousin Kitty and saw her eight guinea pigs. 'She wants me to have some but I won't. We had them out and they were awful to look after … We also swang [sic] and painted and drew and some tiresome people came and had to be taken over the house and garden.'[58] And in May 1912:

> Felicite [sic] and Maurice gave me some silkworm eggs yesterday, which I have put in your caterpillar cage. I hope you don't mind? You know that spider egg in it don't you? Well just a few of the eggs have hatched out and there were millions of spiders, so I upset them into the garden, as they were no good.[59]

Vanity was foreign to her (her family nickname in her teens and twenties, with which she sometimes signed her letters, was 'the Elephant' in honour of her long nose), and she related her own failures with relish, as in January 1911:

> I went for a lovely ride yesterday morning … I of course came in last although I started first.' [Tea with a friend yesterday] '…we both made some Irish Stew and I made a wonderful sort of apple arrangement, it tasted horrible …[60]

She gave strong practical support to both her parents, and became accustomed to dealing with eminent people from all walks of life. At speech day in the record-breaking heat of the 1911 summer, she presented buttonholes to some of the governors, shook hands and curtsied twice to the Duke of Connaught, and then had to run ahead to warn the servants that the Duke was unexpectedly staying for tea.[61] She helped Madge to entertain parties of new boys every year to tea and games in the house and garden; and each summer from 1911 she assisted at 'Walworth Day', when a large group from the school's Walworth Mission in London came for an elaborate garden party. She also contributed to Madge's remodelling of the garden in 1911 and 1912, zestfully digging up gorse bushes and helping to level the lawn for a new tennis court.[62]

Her mother taught her to sew, and passed on a love of dressing up for grand occasions. When their parents held dinner parties for guests such as the headmaster of Eton, Janet and David were allowed to look over the banisters at the ladies' dresses. On one occasion Will wrote to Halford that 'Janet and David peeped as usual and settled who had the best dresses, personally I thought

Mammah's was the best … as it was simple and in good taste.'[63] Will's pride in and affection for Madge continued alongside his occasional bouts of irritation. Handwritten dedications on offprints of two of his public speeches during the war years read: 'Margaret Vaughan from W W'; and 'for Mother from "The President"'.[64]

War and school, 1914–18
In summer 1914 Madge hired a rectory in Wiltshire for the family holiday; but for Will the break was cut short. Halford later remembered him sending Janet to get a paper to see if war had been declared, as it was on 4 August.[65] Will immediately returned to Wellington and wrote to Lord Derby as chair of governors seeking authority to waive all notice in the case of boys who wished and were able to enter the army at once; and give every facility to masters wishing to volunteer for service. He also sought an early start to term on 2 September – ostensibly to start on intensive work for extra army exams and enable the Officers Training Corps to start special training, but also to lessen the chances of Wellington being requisitioned by the Government for any purpose. Derby gratefully agreed to all this.

Wellington was a very different place that September. All games were cancelled, afternoons were spent on Corps training, older boys had left and retired staff came back to replace those volunteering for military service. There were guard duties day and night to watch for spies who might poison the nearby reservoir or raid the armoury. Term ended with a Memorial Service for the Old Wellingtonian dead. Will was working harder than ever, and coping with staff changes and shortages which would continue throughout the war.

As news from the front worsened, and British casualties mounted, Madge and Janet were busy making warm woollen mufflers, sweaters, socks and bandages for the troops. They were urged on by Aunt Katharine Furse, who had joined the Voluntary Aid Detachment (VAD: in effect, volunteer partially trained nurses, to provide support particularly for the armed forces) in 1912 and moved to London the same year. She was now in her element. She led the first official VAD group to be sent to France in September, and by the end of the year had been recalled to London to become Commander in Chief of the combined Red Cross and St John's VAD under the auspices of the War Office. She built the organisation up over time into an enormous service, supporting hospitals at home and abroad. In 1917 Furse was made a Dame for her VAD work, and towards the end of that year moved on to become founding head of the new Women's Royal Naval Service (WRNS), with the rank of Rear Admiral.

Life for Janet was even more solitary after David started at prep school in 1914, and she was at last being prepared for school. Having started Latin, she began to learn German during that autumn. She may also have begun by this time to harbour ambitions for higher education. Someone of her challenging nature, endowed with so much restless energy, could hardly fail to question the different attitude taken to her education as compared to that of her brothers. There were, too, a number of effective and highly educated professional women in the family circle. The most notable was perhaps Lettice Ilbert, who married Janet's godfather Herbert Fisher in 1899, had a first in modern history from Somerville College Oxford and was a tutor at St Hugh's College from 1902 to 1913, besides teaching economics for the Association for the Higher Education of Women in Oxford. Lettice was also active in social work and women's suffrage, and was one of the university women whom Millicent Fawcett co-opted onto the national executive of the National Union of Women's Suffrage Societies. She chaired the executive in 1916–18. During the war, she also did welfare work among women munition workers in Sheffield, where Herbert was university Vice-Chancellor. She loved little girls, and her daughter realised many years later what a special person she had been for Janet.[66]

Others included Roger Fry's sister Margery, who had studied maths at Somerville as a contemporary of Lettice Ilbert, and served as librarian there before moving to Birmingham to head a women's hall of residence. The Frys were Quakers, and she spent much of the First World War in France, helping to organise the Friends' War Victims Relief work there. Aunt Katharine Furse, now so eminent in the VAD, had at one time wanted to go to Newnham College in Cambridge to read for medicine, but failed on account of her poor maths skills.[67] And (Great) Aunt Char, Addington Symonds's sister, had trained as a nurse after her husband died in 1882, and had been on the governing Council of Somerville College since 1884.

In early June 1914 Janet had an operation on a tubercular gland in her neck – the same operation as Barbara had had in 1909, but this time with complete success. The bandage came off about two weeks later, leaving only a small scar.[68] Perhaps her parents waited to ensure her health was restored before agreeing to her starting in January 1915 as a boarder at North Foreland Lodge School at Broadstairs, on the Kent coast. Her cousin Kitty had been a pupil there since at least autumn 1913. In that same January, however, the school was relocated to Great Malvern in Worcestershire for the duration of the war.

***

Janet would say in later life that the headmistress of her school had once told her father that she was too stupid to be worth educating, and should be encouraged to take up social work in London's East End. After due allowance for embellishment, there was probably some truth in this. The school was not suited to someone destined for a career in medicine and scientific research, and her start there was inauspicious. Like her mother, Janet had fire, enthusiasm and imagination. But though her determination and practicality were also apparent, those qualities had not yet produced any impressive academic results. Her main interest was in history. Kitty Leaf remembered that she and Janet as early teenagers 'gushed together over historical novels' when alone, discussion somewhat hindered by the fact that Janet at that point read the novels only of Bulwer Lytton, and Kitty, Harrison Ainsworth.[69]

Miss Mary Wolseley-Lewis had opened North Foreland Lodge school in 1909, aiming to provide a comparable education to that of the girls' public schools, strongly based on religion, so as to prepare 'the daughters of the leisured class' to be good citizens, daughters, wives and mothers.[70] The school taught no science apart from botany. Janet thought Miss Lewis a remarkable character, who read the girls a great deal of poetry, especially Browning; and she herself was encouraged in her habit of writing large quantities of – by her own, truthful, account – bad verse. Her Christian beliefs were reinforced, and she chose to be confirmed in the Church of

England while at the school. She stayed in touch with Miss Lewis long after the headmistress had retired.[71]

It was in the last week of January 1915 that Madge took Janet to Great Malvern, where the school occupied two large Victorian houses high up in the town, overlooking the old Abbey church. She reported that Janet was not enamoured with school life, finding the weather extremely cold and everyone upset by bad news of the war. Janet soon confirmed that she was doing badly academically, and wished she was at home:

> I sleep in a huge room with 4 other girls ... We don't have breakfast till 8, which is very lazy, but we work from 9 to 1.30 with only 10 minutes break – and from 5.10 to 7.10 in the evening ... [On the plus side, there were 'glorious hills' to climb. Undaunted by her poor performance, she soon wrote] I am feeling rather violent today. There is one very proper and rather silly girl in my room whom I shock greatly ... She thinks me quite mad ... my work is so bad ... Miss Lewis thinks I shall have to go down into a lower division for Arithmetic. Woe is me.[72]

Shortly afterwards, influenza hit the school, in Janet's case turning into pneumonia. When she was allowed to write again, she passed judgement on her medical care: '... the Dr is Scotch and very amusing ... he says very little, but what he does say, is to the point'.[73] High praise, from a girl who could quickly see through and dismiss pretension. She was sent home to convalesce, but Madge, convinced she now had whooping cough, sent her with a tutor to Margate until the end of the summer term. Janet was delighted, enjoying both the swimming and watching naval activity in the bay. At the beginning of June, a letter of hers describing a Zeppelin raid in graphic terms was passed round the family.[74]

Home again by the beginning of July, she was frustrated by the daily round:

> Of all the cruel fates! I have spent agonizing morning directing letters for the Bishop of London, and you know my spelling is so excellent ... [Rain came through in Chapel this morning.] ... and then that fool Mr Wright sent up a prayer for rain ... The Bishop preached a splendid sermon, but though he is nice he tells rather too many pointless stories. Last night ... some boys came to dinner and

> afterwards we all roled [*sic*] and tore bandages, except the Bishop, which was select of him …[75]

Not surprisingly, her progress at school was slow. From the autumn of 1915, however, while still threatened with demotion for maths, she was enjoying lacrosse, gymnastics and long walks on the hills as well as the history and science clubs and some home-concocted dramatics. There was a setback in March 1916, when she had chickenpox, and it may have been at this time that Miss Lewis gave the damning verdict on her academic potential; but there was about to be a dramatic turnaround.

In June, Janet announced that she was borrowing Kitty's microscope in the holidays so that she could cut sections of plants or water animals for the science club.

> The other day to my intense joy I cut a beautiful section of bracken underground stem … Miss Meade says that the tissues are so clean … it is worth keeping forever, so we are going to set it in the proper stuff … I should like to cut and draw sections, all day and all night.[76]

A school friend of Halford's was later 'almost stunned with surprise when I told him how much work you do in the holidays of your own accord'.[77] At last she was fully engaged, initially by an activity that demanded close observation, accuracy and hard grind; but which yielded interesting and beautiful results.

When she returned from a week's stay with Ursula Bradshaw after the end of the summer term, Will wrote: 'Janet has just arrived looking very well very hot not very clean and a good deal thinner.' To which Madge added: 'You should … read her report – 'Good', 'very good' very very good – one long clamour! I am completely <u>dazzled</u>!'[78] A year later, in July 1917, she was secretary of the science club, preparing a paper for the next term and looking for a good monthly science paper to order as well as books for the science library she was starting.[79] The 'glowing fires' noted by her cousin Kitty had found a worthy object at last, as had the steely determination and devotion to hard work inherited from her father.

***

The war was a grim backdrop to these school years. The first battle of Ypres in autumn 1914 had resulted in huge casualties for no gain. April 1915 saw the first use of poison gas on the Western Front. The disaster of Gallipoli was to follow. Conscription was introduced early in 1916. By the end of that year, more than a million men were dead, wounded, missing or captured on the Western Front, and a further 120,000 in other areas. Asquith resigned as prime minister in December, to be replaced by Lloyd George. Will and Madge were naturally appalled by the toll on young lives. Although Will was not a pacifist, he did maintain independence of mind: his presidential address to the Modern Language Association in February 1915 was an appeal to remember good Germans and their history, culture and friendship. Madge in letters described the war as wrong and pointless. And Will's close friend Herbert Fisher was one of those who urged Lloyd George to make peace at the end of 1916, when he joined the government as education minister.

Janet's letters reveal little of her attitude, beyond a gung-ho taste for excitement and adventure; but she tended always to stress the positive, and of course not all her letters survived. Two older cousins and one of Herbert Fisher's brothers died, and friends at school must have been experiencing similar or worse losses. Janet's likely reactions, and her sympathy and support for her parents, are shown by her words to Halford after the sudden death of one of the most able masters left at Wellington, in January 1915:

> ... very bad news ... Mr Pearson died ... last night while he was having tea. For him it was happy that there was no illness, but for others it is a terrible blow. Poor little Nancy was there. I only wish I could do something for her. How Daddy will manage I can't think.[80]

The war may well have influenced her decision to study medicine. Faced with a growing shortage of doctors to cope with unprecedented numbers of casualties, the War Office in 1916 invited women doctors to serve with the armed forces. Oxford and Cambridge universities opened their medical degrees to women the following year, as did the main London medical schools. (The London Medical School for Women had opened in 1874, but could only offer comparatively few places.)[81] Janet's aunt Katharine, at the head of the VAD and having previously wished to study medicine herself, would certainly have offered encouragement if asked. And there was a prevalence of doctors in the Symonds and Vaughan family trees, which were preserved by Madge as unofficial family historian.

Janet herself wrote that her reading of history and interest in current affairs had made her concerned about poverty and social injustice. She believed that medicine would give her the experience and status to be able to speak with authority on these issues. Crucially, she thought it would in itself be interesting.[82] The school science club had given her a taste for the study of living things. She was to say later in life that her father opposed her choice, while her mother believed she should do as she pleased.[83] One can only assume that Will's attitude to this, as to the rest of Janet's education, arose from his experience of his own very unassertive mother and sisters. His opposition made her all the more determined to succeed. And he did of course fund her Oxford studies.

Following the dramatic improvement in her school performance in 1916, Janet started to learn Greek so as to prepare for Oxford entrance examinations. These were in two parts. The test for entry to Somerville College was not too demanding, but the University required a pass in 'Responsions'. Subjects for these included maths, Latin and Greek grammar, Latin prose composition and unseen translation from both languages. This was taxing for girls without the male public school training, and many had to make two or three attempts. In December 1917, Janet wrote that it was 'really perfect madness on Miss Lewis's part to think I can do Responsions in March … but still it will be a great rag my going up to stay in Oxford for them'.[84] Why Oxford and why Somerville? Janet was following family tradition, in that generations of male Vaughans had studied at Oxford's New College; and links with Somerville were close, with Aunt Char and Lettice Fisher both on the college's governing Council at this time.

In March 1918, Will, giving way at last to the strain and overwork of the previous three and a half years, had some kind of nervous collapse following a bad bout of influenza. He was ordered to bed for a complete rest. Janet went to Wellington soon after taking her examinations at Oxford, much to Madge's relief: 'Dear Janet turned up radiant … She has been the <u>greatest</u> comfort to me, and I have been able to <u>laugh</u> once again [after being] somewhat gloomy all alone with Daddy upstairs under the … control of a … hospital nurse.'[85] As expected, however, Janet had failed Responsions. She spent the summer term at a crammer in Malvern, staying as a paying guest with a local family; and went back to them that autumn after failing again (in Latin, Greek and algebra) in the summer. She was anxious to go up in the 1918–19 academic year, so wished to try again in December.[86]

In November Wellington was hit by the second, and most virulent, wave of the influenza pandemic which had such a devastating effect in Britain between early summer 1918 and May 1919.[87] Will became very ill, and Janet was summoned home as her father was not expected to live. (Madge thought, with some shrewdness, that he had not been as seriously ill as the doctors made out; but rather that he 'rushes and tears, and then collapses', his illness partly caused by nerves.[88]) Once at the school, Janet found 'chaos, a few hospital nurses, many mothers and sisters of boys helping … a beloved housemaid dead … I turned my hand to the endless problems … in a … school of over 600 boys hit by epidemic influenza of the virulence seen in the 1918 winter.'[89] She also drank the remains of champagne in bottles prescribed for patients: in the days before antibiotics, much reliance was placed on this for those who could afford it, and it must at least have brought some comfort to many. Nursing care was a key factor in recovery, and Janet, like most young women of her time, had a good knowledge of what was needed. Her own experience would have included numerous school epidemics of childhood illnesses as well as those which affected herself, her family and friends. She continued all her life to give champagne to friends who were seriously ill, knowing its power to raise their spirits and those of their visitors.

This crisis over, Madge took Janet to Oxford for her third try at Responsions, staying at the Mitre, where Madge 'firmly ordered a bottle of claret every evening'.[90] They learnt just before Christmas that this time she had passed. She would start at Somerville in January, one term into the 1918–19 academic year. Her scholarly credentials were weak, and she knew little or no science. But she had proved that hard grind paid off, and her self-belief was strong. More than that, her upbringing had given her, directly and indirectly, the guiding principles for her life: people came first. She could promote their welfare through medicine; and would do so on the same terms as men.

Endnotes

[1] VW Diary, 9.2.1924.

[2] VW Diary, 13.5.1926.

[3] John Addington Symonds (1840–1893). Poet and writer, son of a successful doctor. First diagnosed with tuberculosis in 1866, he finally moved with his family from Bristol to Davos in 1880.

[4] Leslie Stephen (1832–1904), critic and man of letters, first editor of the *Dictionary of National Biography*.

[5] Margaret Symonds, *Days Spent on a Doge's Farm* (London, John Murray, 1893). This quote would be used again by both Madge and Janet in later years.

[6] Clifton Hill House was let out at that time, and sold in 1905 to Bristol University. Albert Road has been re-named, as Percival Road.

[7] UOBLSC, Katharine Furse papers, DM 1279, Katharine Symonds to Lotta Leaf, 29.7.1899.

[8] Margaret Symonds (Mrs W W Vaughan), *Out of the Past* (London, John Murray, 1925), 165. In Cannes, at the age of two, Janet Symonds had captivated Edward Lear, who gave her copies of illustrated rhymes, including the original versions of 'The Owl and the Pussy Cat' and 'The Duck and the Kangaroo', according to Katharine Furse's 1940 autobiography. Their sister Janet had died aged 22, of tuberculosis.

[9] KCC, CHA 1/59/9, VBMV 1 and 2, Vanessa Stephen to Madge Vaughan, 6.3. and 20.3.1900.

[10] UOBLSC, DM 1279, J C Symonds to Madge Vaughan, 23.2.1900. Charles Furse (1868–1904), painter.

[11] VW Letters, Virginia Stephen to Emma Vaughan, 23.10.1900 and 23.4.1901.

[12] RSA&SC, WWV/1/A/91–B/1, Madge Vaughan to J C Symonds, 25.9.1901.

[13] UOBLSC, DM 1279, J C Symonds to Madge Vaughan, 1.1.1903 and 20.1.1903.

[14] JA, 9; and Katharine Furse, *Hearts and Pomegranates*, (London, Peter Davies, 1940), 42.

[15] Photographs in possession of Susan Aglionby, Janet Vaughan's niece; and Vaughan family visitor books in that of her nephew, John Vaughan.

[16] RSA&SC, WWV 2/B, Giggleswick. Will Vaughan's 12.12.1903 application for the Giggleswick headship setting out his career to date; and the character references for that application. H A L Fisher (1865–1940) was also a reforming education minister in Lloyd George's government of 1916–22.

[17] UOBLSC, DM 1279, J C Symonds to Madge Vaughan, 21.7.1900 and 13.3.1903.

[18] Background in R C K Ensor, *England 1870–1914* (Oxford: Clarendon Press, 1966).

[19] RSA&SC WWV/1/A/91, Madge to friend Sarah Bailey, 8.11.04.

[20] JA, 9–10.

[21] These details, and terms of the headmaster's appointment, are given in Edward Allen Bell, *A History of Giggleswick School. From its Foundation, Vol 3* (Leeds, Richard Jackson, 1912), in the Brayshaw Library at Giggleswick School. Republished as a paperback in 2017.

[22] Background in Ensor, *England 1870–1914*. B Seebohm Rowntree, *Poverty: A Study of Town Life* (London, Macmillan, 1901).

[23] JPP, H A L Fisher: unpublished lecture on Dr W W Vaughan, delivered at Princes Risborough on 21.10.1938.

[24] VW Letters, Virginia Stephen to Violet Dickinson, 21.11. and 26.11.1904.

[25] VW Letters, Virginia Stephen to Emma Vaughan, 21.4.1906.

[26] Katharine West, *Inner and Outer Circles* (London, Cohen and West, 1958), 81. Kitty was the daughter of Madge's sister Lotta and the banker Walter Leaf.

[27] Email to author from (old Somervillian) Cindy Gallop, 31.10.2007.

[28] VW Letters, Virginia Stephen to Madge Vaughan, 19.11.1908.

[29] VW Letters, Virginia Stephen to Vanessa Bell, 18.5.1909: 'She was in a wild state … seemed to think that Barbara was dying, and that it was the doctors [*sic*] fault, or hers for having a new nurse … mixed up with rhapsodies about fate, and God, and religion …'

[30] UOBLSC, DM 1227, Katharine Furse to Madge Vaughan, April 1909 and 30.5.1909.

[31] UOBLSC, DM 1279, J C Symonds to Madge Vaughan, 15.8.1909. Charlotte was one of John Addington Symonds's three sisters. She married the Oxford philosopher T H Green, and became a significant figure in Oxford herself after his early death. A second sister married Sir Edward Strachey, and their son John St Loe Strachey was owner and editor of the influential *Spectator* magazine from 1887 to 1925.

[32] Julia was Leslie's second wife, mother of Virginia, Vanessa, Thoby and Adrian; and Stella, a close friend of Madge, was his daughter by his first marriage.

[33] RSA&SC, WWV/1/C/201–80, Madge to Halford, 18.11.1911.

[34] Madge was still remembered fondly at Giggleswick in 1928, when a sundial and surrounding small garden were installed in her memory following her death three years before. All the family at various times went back there to visit the school, see friends or (in Janet's case) stay at an inn to do holiday reading as a student; and Will's letters to Halford refer at least twice to his happy memories of the place.

[35] The background and main events of Will Vaughan's time at Wellington are described in David Newsome, *A History of Wellington College 1859–1959* (London, John Murray, 1959), particularly Chapter VIII.

[36] JA, 10–11. Madge experienced another loss in 1913 when her mother, who had only recently moved permanently to Oxford to be near her sister-in-law Charlotte Green and some Symonds cousins, fell ill and died. Catherine, who suffered from periodic depression herself, had always offered sanctuary and comfort when Madge was depressed.

[37] UOBLSC, DM 1279, J C Symonds to Madge Vaughan, 7.11.1910.

[38] RSA&SC, WWV/1/A/91 to 1/B/50–130, Correspondence between parents and children, 27.8.1910 to September 1910.

[39] RSA&SC, WWV/1/C/121-200. Janet to Halford, undated, late 1911. And KCC, CHA 1/642. Madge to Vanessa Bell, 11.3.1916.

[40] JA, 11–12.

[41] KCC, CHA 1/59/9. VBMV 15, Vanessa Bell to Madge Vaughan, 5.6.1910.

[42] Janet Vaughan, Some Bloomsbury memories, in *Charleston Newsletter* (September 1985), 12, 20–22. Accessed in the Charleston Trust Archive, Lewes, East Sussex.

[43] See Leonard Woolf, *Beginning Again: An Autobiography of the Years 1911 to 1918* (London, Hogarth Press, 1964), 70–73 for account of the visit.

[44] West, *Inner and Outer Circles*, 81–82.

[45] RSA&SC, WWV/1/C/431–510, Madge to Halford, 28.3.1915.

[46] Evelyn Irons, The undergraduate, in Pauline Adams (Ed), *Janet Maria Vaughan 1899–1993: A Memorial Tribute* (Oxford, Somerville College, 1993).

[47] JPP, notes of interview with Mary Bennett, 1994.

[48] The background is in Carol Dyhouse, *Girls Growing up in Late Victorian and Edwardian England* (London, Routledge & Kegan Paul, 1981).

[49] RSA&SC, WWV/1/C/51–120, Janet to Halford, 24.11.1910.

[50] RSA&SC, WWV/1/C/201–80, Janet to Halford, 12.2.1912.

[51] RSA&SC, WWV/1/C/201–80, Will Vaughan to Halford, 12.5.1912.

[52] JA, 9.

[53] RSA&SC, WWV/1/C/341–430, Madge to Halford, 19.5.1913.

[54] West, *Inner and Outer Circles*, 82–83.

[55] JPP, Draft piece by Janet Vaughan on her Bloomsbury friends, perhaps for a talk. Roger Fry had been a pupil at Clifton College, and his family were friends of both the Vaughans and the Stephens.

[56] RSA&SC, WWV/1/C/341–430, Madge to Halford, 25.10.1913. Crowthorne is a village near Wellington College.

[57] RSA&SC, WWV/1/C/431–510, Janet to Halford, 29.7.1914. Watts had been part of London's Little Holland House circle, where Will's father, Halford Vaughan, had met his future wife, Adeline Jackson. A copy of the statue, called 'Physical Energy', is in Kensington Gardens in London.

[58] RSA&SC, WWV/1/C/121–200, Janet to Halford, 23.7.1911.

[59] RSA&SC, WWV/1/C/201–80, Janet to Halford, 19.5.1912.

[60] RSA&SC, WWV/1/C/51–120, Janet to Halford, 28.1.1911.

[61] RSA&SC, WWV/1/C/51–120, Janet to Halford, 18.6.1911, and Madge to Halford, 19.6.1911.

[62] RSA&SC, WWV/1/C/121–200. First mention of helping with Walworth group by Zela (governess) to Halford, 26.7.1911; and of work in garden by Janet to Halford, 1.10.1911.

[63] RSA&SC, WWV/1/C/431–510, Will Vaughan to Halford, 3.6.1914.

[64] JPP, presidential address to the Modern Language Association, February 1915, and address as president of the Headmasters' Association, 5.1.1916.

[65] JPP, interview with Halford's wife Dorothy, 1994.

[66] Mary Bennett interview, 7.2.2000. After Lettice's death in 1956, Janet asked to spend some time in what had been her room.

[67] Furse, *Hearts and Pomegranates*, 124 ff.

[68] RSA&SC, WWV/1/C/431–510, Madge to Halford, 13.6.1914.

[69] There is also a story in the family that Janet, like her own daughter Mary, suffered from dyslexia and was coached, in part by Madge, to overcome it. Certainly her spelling was poor throughout her life (a not uncommon failing in those days); and her well-attested nervousness before occasions when she had to read a speech or paper in public was attributed to a fear that she might, embarrassingly, mispronounce a word or words. The dyslexia in her case must have been less serious than it was for Mary, however, given her ability from an early age both to read widely and to express herself clearly on paper.

[70] North Foreland Lodge, *The Times* (12.5.1930), 18, report of Miss Lewis's speech on school's twenty-first birthday.

[71] HCRO, 112A03/J2/1. Lewis notebook records lunch with Gourlays, 12.5.1935.

[72] RSA&SC, WWV/1/C/511–630, Madge to Halford, 30.1.1915; Janet to Halford, 31.1.1915; and Janet to Halford, 'February' 1915.

[73] RSA&SC, WWV/1/C/511–630, Janet to Halford, 21.2.1915.

[74] RSA&SC, WWV/1/C/511–630, Madge to Halford, 2.6.1915, the enclosed letter from Janet has not survived.

[75] RSA&SC, WWV/1/C/511–630, Janet to Halford, 27.6.1915.

[76] RSA&SC, WWV/1/C/631–710, Janet to Halford, 23.6.1916.

[77] RSA&SC, WWV/1/C/711–810, Halford to Janet, 25.10.1916.

[78] RSA&SC, WWV/1/C/711–810, Will to Halford, 27.7.1916, and Madge to Halford, 28.7.1916.

[79] RSA&SC, WWV/1/C/711–810, Janet to Halford, 28.7.1917.

[80] RSA&SC, WWV/1/C/511–630, Janet to Halford, 24.1.1915.

[81] This school soon became associated with the Royal Free Hospital, and in 1898 the name was changed to the London (Royal Free Hospital) School of Medicine for Women.

[82] JA, 14.

[83] John Pemble, Department of History, University of Bristol, notes of conversation with Janet Vaughan, 22.6.1988, shown to the author on 29.4.2008. Janet did not enlarge on her father's reasons for opposing her wish to be a doctor.

[84] RSA&SC, WWV/1/C/811–880, Janet to Halford, 2.12.1917.

[85] RSA&SC, WWV/1/C/811–880, Madge to Halford, 22.3.1918.

[86] JA, 15.

[87] The pandemic caused most deaths among young adults aged 20 to 40, and especially those aged 25 to 35. But other age groups were also badly affected, as happened at Wellington. (Christopher Langford, The age pattern of mortality in the 1918–19 influenza pandemic: an attempted explanation based on data for England and Wales, in *Medical History* (2002), 46(1), 1–20.)

[88] Peace brought no relief to Will. In 1919 he was organising temporary then permanent replacements for four dormitories destroyed by fire in March, as well as introducing revised fees and a new salary scale and setting up pension arrangements for staff.

[89] JA, 15.

[90] Ibid.

CHAPTER 2
Seizing opportunities
1919–25

A student at Somerville

Vaughan[1] started her higher education at an auspicious time for young women. Although Oxford and Cambridge were still the only British universities which denied degrees (though not courses and examinations) to women, there was now a radical change of opinion in Oxford, where nearly one third of the women tutors served as stand-in university lecturers during or immediately after the war. In May 1920 women were officially admitted to the university's degrees. Momentous change was happening at national level, too. The pre-war campaign for women's suffrage appeared to have achieved at least partial success when the Representation of the People Act of 1918 enfranchised women over the age of 30 who met a property qualification. Women could also become MPs, and on 1 December 1919 Lady Astor became the first woman MP to take up her seat in Parliament. Soon after, the Sex Disqualification (Removal) Act of 1919 began the long process of cultural change needed to enable women to secure access to all kinds of employment and the professions. Vaughan and her friends, unaware of how long and gruelling the struggle for equal opportunities would be in practice, must have felt they were riding a wave of emancipation, despite the pettifogging restrictions which still governed their Oxford lives.

For Vaughan, however, Oxford was the second step – boarding school had been the first – in liberating her from the isolation and constraints of home. She started with many useful contacts. Charlotte Green and Lettice Fisher were still closely involved with Somerville, and there were Symonds cousins in town. Aunt Char's presence was not an unmixed blessing. Vaughan was expected to spend Sunday with her, but much preferred the more cheerful household of her elderly cousin Annie Symonds, sister of a well-known Oxford surgeon. 'Annie enjoyed the good things of this world. Aunt Char clearly disapproved.'[2] A contemporary later recalled being with her when Aunt Char said gloomily 'Janet will fail' – a view which no doubt spurred Vaughan into proving her wrong.[3]

She revelled in the opportunity she now had to make friends with like-minded people and pursue the subjects and activities she enjoyed. Somerville, whose own buildings had been requisitioned as a hospital during the war, was still mainly housed in part of Oriel College. Vaughan spent her first two terms in lodgings, with a small group which included Margaret Huxley, studying history. Huxley introduced her to her brother Julian, then a fellow of New College, and his wife Juliette; and through them she met Jack ('JBS') Haldane – also a fellow of New College – and his family. Haldane was teaching physiology and giving the first lectures on the new field of genetics, but would also recite vast quantities of Shelley, Milton and other poets over tea at the Huxleys' house. Tall, heavily built, with a booming voice, he was unconventional and uninhibited. He was also an atheist and on the left in politics, joining the Labour Party in the early 1920s.[4]

Demobilisation was still under way in 1919, and from then until 1922 the numbers of returning ex-servicemen studying at Oxford placed huge pressure on all the university's teaching and other resources. Maurice Bowra, the future Master of Wadham College, was one of these students, and remarked in his memoir on the levelling effect of army experience. Naturally the Russian Revolution of 1917 was a major topic of discussion, and he recalled that few thought Bolshevism was dangerous, with most favouring social reform. He was friendly with Enid Starkie, two years ahead of Vaughan at Somerville but within her circle of friends. She also saw something of her cousin John Strachey, son of St Loe Strachey, who arrived in Oxford in 1920 and became a friend of Bowra.[5]

Her brother Halford arrived at New College in that same year, helping to widen the circle of his sister's contacts among male students.[6] One in particular would loom large in her later life. She probably knew Will Goodenough already: he was at Wellington in the war years, and head boy before he took up a commission in the army at the start of 1918. He and Halford became friends through a shared interest in beagling, and Vaughan was soon included in the friendship.[7] Goodenough's father was chairman of Barclays Bank from 1917, and Will became local director in Oxford in 1923.

Vaughan's admiration for the 'modern' poets led to a friendship with Robert and Nancy Graves. She often stayed at their cottage in Islip, talking of books and poetry and admiring the way Robert coped with the children while continuing his writing; and kept in touch when they moved away. Her sense of drama is evident in her memory of having supper with them in London '… when Laura Riding came in. She had just arrived in England and sat down to supper with us. I felt disaster had come in … A strange sense of brooding malevolence … cast shadows over a supper party that ceased to be gay … Laura took over.' Vaughan never saw Nancy again, though she continued to see Robert and Laura at their Chiswick home, and said she helped on the occasion when Laura hurt her back by jumping out of a window.[8]

She soon made friends with other intending medical students, notably Cicely Williams and Mathilde (Thilo) Bugnion, both two years ahead of her at Somerville; and through them with Sybil Eastwood, a mature student at the Society of Home Students (later St Anne's College). Cicely was 24 at this time, a tall redhead who had grown up in Jamaica but was educated in England. She later recalled her time at Oxford as 'three and a half years of human and social pleasure, marred only by the abysmal bore of science'.[9] Disliking theory and exams, she was later to win renown through her clinical work and practical research. Thilo, then 21, was dark, lively and Swiss. Her outspoken French-accented horror at the standard of food and cooking in college delighted her contemporaries.[10]

In her own year, besides Margaret Huxley, Vaughan was friendly with Evelyn Irons, reading English, who remembered her taking time out from her medical studies to attend a popular series of lectures given by the professor of English literature, Sir Walter Raleigh.[11] Irons became the first woman journalist on Fleet Street, the first female winner of the French Croix de Guerre, and a distinguished American correspondent of *The Sunday Times*. She recalled:

> All the petty restrictions endured by Oxford women in those days seemed pretty silly to a free soul like Janet. She couldn't join the Union, or OUDS [Oxford University Dramatic Society] … she couldn't go to tea in a man's college rooms without a chaperone. She

had to laugh at these and other absurdities, but they exasperated her too. Politically she was a leftist, and burned to reform everything … [Although a dedicated scientist, she] wrote poetry – lots of it … one evening when I was working late … a rap on my door. It was Janet, waving sheets of newly-composed verse which she proceeded to read to me at top speed. She always spoke fast, as if she could scarcely keep up with the torrent of her thoughts.[12]

Vaughan also played her part in college dramatic productions. In the going-down play of 1921, *Bolshevism in Baghdad*, she doubled as the minister of finance and (with Margaret Huxley) one half of a camel.[13]

Irons remembered a strong streak of shyness underlying Vaughan's outgoing manner, tempered by 'a passionate interest in other people's troubles. Like the rest of her Oxford friends, I found her full of sympathy and concern for anything that bothered me, and equally shrewd about finding a way out … she was boundlessly generous and kind.'[14] There was a striking example of this towards the end of 1919. Winifred Holtby, a good friend of Cicely Williams and later to become a journalist and novelist, had returned in the summer term from VAD service. She was open-hearted, energetic and popular, and was elected secretary of the newly formed debating society alongside Vaughan as treasurer. Vera Brittain, who would make her name through her memoir of the First World War, returned a term later, also from VAD service. At 26, Brittain was socially more mature than her fellow students, and still mourning those she had lost. Others interpreted her reserve as arrogance, and, hoping to puncture this, invited her to speak for the motion 'That four years' travel are a better education than four years at University.' Holtby, opposing her, was uncharacteristically drawn into making wounding personal attacks. Afterwards Vaughan tried to make peace by encouraging Brittain to seek a formal meeting with Holtby as secretary of the society. As a result, Holtby apologised handsomely and she and Brittain became close friends.[15]

During that same autumn, with Somerville back in its own premises, Brasenose College debating society were guests when the proposer of the motion 'That this House views with apprehension the use of the strike as a political weapon' was 'severely handled by his opposers Miss Vaughan and Mr Hall. The debate never flagged … until the local early closing laws enforced a decision at 10.30.'[16] There were joint debates with other men's colleges, and the quality of Vaughan's contributions may have impressed those who in 1919 elected her as the only female member of the Mazzini Society in New College. With a female don as chaperone, she attended meetings to discuss papers given by members on contemporary political affairs. She was elected president of the Somerville debating society in 1920.[17]

Vaughan was also president of the college Student Christian Movement branch that year, her leftist views compatible with a fervent Christianity and a desire to convert others.[18] But there was a lighter side to her social life. Her friend Maisie Somerville arrived in 1921, aged 24.[19] Vaughan recalled her as a 'femme fatale', who became devoted to Madge and eventually married Halford's friend Pete Brown whom she met while staying at Rugby. At Oxford, Vaughan 'walked … up and down St Giles in the dark listening to the young men [Somerville] had half promised to marry and couldn't quite send away … She was amazingly good company if only one had time.' Maisie for her part said it was no good inviting Vaughan to tea parties, because she always wore tweeds.[20]

Preclinical studies

Vaughan's chief priority was clear. Alongside her enthusiastic pleasure in drama, debate, poetry and the company of friends, she had little concern for her own appearance and no interest in men as potential partners. The fire of her nature was being channelled into intellectual inquiry. A would-be doctor coming to Oxford in 1919 faced a long haul. After preliminary examinations in natural sciences (chemistry, physics, botany and zoology), the honours degree course in animal physiology, which included biochemistry, provided intellectual discipline and training in research methods. Most took four years to achieve this first degree, after which a minority spent a fifth year in Oxford studying pharmacology and pathology ('drugs and bugs') at the Radcliffe Infirmary, followed by at least two years of clinical study in London. They could qualify as doctors by being licensed to practise by the Royal Colleges of Physicians and Surgeons. The more academically inclined (including

Vaughan) took the Oxford medical degrees (Bachelor of Medicine, Bachelor of Surgery) after on average eight years' study and practice; although women generally took six or seven years.[21]

Madge's support for Vaughan's ambitions was by no means unwavering. Writing to Vanessa Bell in January 1919, she had 'a strong feeling that she has mistaken her career. She is struggling with Science, & her whole nature is ... non scientific ... She is so good & so beautiful. The life of a Medical student was never intended for her: but she insists on it.' Madge would have preferred to have her daughter's help at home.[22] Vaughan, however, willingly embraced the struggle with science, passing in three of the four subjects after two terms and successfully retaking physics a term later. By then she had embarked on physiology, having read an E H Starling textbook on the subject over the summer vacation (prudently staying in an inn in Yorkshire to do so, away from her family). She found it a revelation, discovering 'the excitement of learning how biological mechanics explained biological observations'.[23]

Professor Charles Sherrington had made the Oxford department of physiology a world centre for research in neurophysiology. He was President of the Royal Society from 1920–25, and a joint Nobel Prize winner in 1932. He was also noted for his humility, friendliness and generosity: a good role model.[24] The most popular lecturer was Alice Chance (Carleton from 1923) in the separate subject of anatomy. Vaughan found this, in which the whole body was dissected in great detail, especially taxing, recalling that for years afterwards she would be greeted as 'the dunce of Alice Carleton's anatomy class'; but she passed.[25]

In summer 1920 her friends Cicely Williams and Thilo Bugnion graduated, with a third- and second-class degree respectively. They both planned to go to the London Hospital for their clinical training, but all the London medical schools, which had opened their doors to female students during the war, were now under pressure to admit returning war veterans. The London Hospital stopped taking women from 1921, and for 1920–21 took only those with written offers of places. Bugnion got in, but by some oversight Williams's name was not recorded. She managed to get into King's College Hospital instead.[26] Sybil Eastwood, with a first-class degree, went to University College Hospital (UCH), which was then the most academic of the London schools. Significantly, UCH continued to take 12 women a year after the war.

Vaughan, having started at Oxford part-way through the 1918–19 academic year, could have taken her physiology degree in the summer of 1921, the end of her third year. Leaving aside any wish to do well rather than adequately, however, her friends' experience would have given her pause. She too wished at first to go to the London Hospital, but that was now impossible. At some point she decided on UCH, and was undeterred by her father's eminent friend the paediatrician Sir Thomas Barlow, who advised that she go to the all-female medical school of the Royal Free Hospital.[27] She may well have decided on the basis of advice from JBS, as well as Eastwood. JBS's relative, Lord Haldane, had led the commission which recommended in 1913 that the teaching of clinical medicine be professionalised through the establishment of clinical units with modern laboratories and full-time academic leadership, as opposed to the part-time teaching previously supplied by practising consultants. And JBS would have been in touch with post-war developments by which, after the government decided to fund such units at UCH, St Bartholomew's and St Thomas's Hospitals in London, the Rockefeller Foundation was sufficiently impressed by UCH to provide lavish funding for an exemplary unit there.

Whatever the reason, Vaughan opted for another year's study before taking her degree. When her tutor in physiology left Oxford in summer 1921, Haldane sent a message through Margaret Huxley that he was prepared to tutor her: a considerable compliment. According to Vaughan this led to 'a battle royal' with Miss Kirkaldy, the formidable Somerville science don, who already disapproved of her wide reading, and thought Haldane would distract her still further from the syllabus. She stood firm, however, and went 'solemnly with a chaperon [*sic*] to New College once a week to read my essay to JBS'.[28]

She found him the best of tutors: '… he prowled round to cheer us on in the terrible six-hour biochemical final examination, he talked … of the exciting things … happening in physiological investigation. I remember still the drosophyla fruit fly he … showed me down a microscope … talking of chromosomes and genes.' Haldane encouraged her to read widely and write critical essays. His interest in psychological developments in neurology led him to introduce her to the papers of Henry Head and W H R Rivers, on which she wrote a long essay in the final exams.[29] At the end of June 1922, when she was 22, she was informed by telegram of her first-class degree.

Vaughan implied in her memoir that she owed this result mainly to her good fortune in having Haldane as a tutor. Some years later, however, Professor Sherrington attested that she '… had a remarkable undergraduate career, and impressed all her teachers … as of particular promise for distinction … Thorough, capable, earnest, and level-headed, she did her work … with uniform success at high standard.'[30] UCH recognised her quality by awarding her a Goldsmid Entrance Scholarship worth 112 guineas a year.[31] Her right to study medicine was unassailable.

She stayed in Oxford for two more terms doing pathology and pharmacology. This included spending time at the Radcliffe Infirmary doing post mortems, working in casualty and learning the elements of history-taking and medical examination in outpatient clinics. She also did some coaching in physiology and went on Sunday morning ward rounds with the Regius professor of medicine. As a graduate, she was now largely removed from the social life of college, and Halford reported that she did 'the work of two or three ordinary people'.[32]

One person at least who knew Vaughan well in later life thought her many activities were the result of impulse: she saw that something had to be done, so she did it.[33] There was nonetheless an underlying consistency of motive and priorities throughout, springing from convictions arrived at in her formative years. A notebook of hers with occasional handwritten entries reveals something of the progress of her thought. The earliest dated 'musings', as she called them, were written in September 1920 – just before the start of her third academic year at Somerville.[34] She lists books read, ranging from novels by Tolstoy, Hardy and Conrad among others to a commentary on the Book of Job, followed by undated direct thoughts. She had known God once but now all was chaos: 'what have I – a passionate belief in personality in ideals in truth a great sorrow at all the pain of the world & a great why … there must be some answer some meaning to life'.

She was trying to reconcile her Christian beliefs with her scientific studies. At one time she favoured Henri Bergson's *Creative Evolution* as welding together science and philosophy 'to give a scheme and the meaning of life'. More tellingly in someone so practical, she quoted Bertrand Russell's *Mysticism and Logic*: 'The good which it concerns us to remember is the good which it lies in our power to create – the good is in our own lives & in our attitude towards the world.'

In January 1923, when she fell ill for some days, despair crept in.[35]

> What is the good of Beauty in truth … when all one sees is ugliness & pain … knowledge is in vain – faith is in vain because in what can one have faith … I just go on living – doing the work – often enjoying books & people but … there is no purpose … except existence.

Her active, decisive nature, however, did not allow her to give in to such moods for long. She would always keep despair at bay when it threatened – by work above all, supported by relationships and her belief in the imperative of using one's talents to do good.

Family matters

Madge and Will faced mixed fortunes during Vaughan's Oxford years. Madge's friendship with the Stephen sisters was effectively ended in March 1920, over an aborted plan for the Vaughans to rent the Bells' house at Charleston in Sussex for a family holiday while Vanessa and her family were away. Will disapproved of the way Vanessa was openly living with Duncan Grant while still legally married to Clive Bell, especially after the birth of her daughter Angelica. Madge sent two letters on the same day, first seeking to settle dates, and then – clearly following a conversation with Will – wanting to 'talk things out', in particular regarding Vanessa's current way of life, before confirming the rental. Vanessa and Virginia were both furious about this, and although an apology was made and accepted, there was no real forgiveness on their side.[36]

Later that same year, however, Madge's only published novel, *A Child of the Alps*, was issued. Vaughan's copy is inscribed: 'To my dear friend and daughter Janet, whose unfailing encouragement has helped me in the publication of this book, as in so many other things! June 14th 1920.'[37] The novel is sentimental and unconvincing, with a plot turning on the heroine's decision (having grown up in the Swiss Alps) to marry the wrong man, a highly conventional Englishman devoted to what he sees as 'duty' above all else. It is doubtful that Will ever read it. Its reception was kind enough to please Madge, however, and her resolution for 1921 was to be 'more generally genial & to <u>conceal</u> my terrible depressions when they come … <u>But not to inflict them on Will</u>.'[38]

In June 1921, Will became headmaster of Rugby, his old school. Once again, there was much in need of reform. Rugby as a place, however, situated in the red brick flatlands of east Warwickshire, had little to recommend it to Madge. In August, she and her daughter went abroad together to old Symonds haunts for the first time. They took the train to Lugano, and stayed first in a hotel on Monte Generoso in Ticino, the Italian-speaking part of Switzerland. Vaughan at first was not euphoric:

> Fog descended and for six days we lived in a thick mist. My mother was happy; I was desperate … I read War and Peace, but why read … when one might be exploring the world of the Renaissance? Finally … Milan … and there began my … love of Italian painting.[39]

Meanwhile a further problem loomed for Will. In October 1920, Horatio Brown had told Madge that, as Addington Symonds's literary executor and biographer, he proposed to publish a selection of her father's letters. Given the improved status of psychoanalysis after the war, and an associated tendency, in some circles at least, to regard homosexuality as a pathological condition rather than a sin, Brown thought he might be more relaxed in what he chose to publish than had been the case in the biography he had written. Will and his brother-in-law Walter Leaf, however, feared the damage this might cause to their own reputations. After a long and acrimonious correspondence between Madge and Brown over this issue, Leaf finally used his influence with the publisher to ensure that the letters published in 1923 made no mention of homosexuality.[40]

Madge seems to have decided to publish her own memoir of her father in part to safeguard the respectability of his reputation. She was fighting a painful illness, loosely described as 'rheumatism', in these years, but the memoir *Out of the Past*, which painted a generally innocent and rosy picture of Symonds, was published in March 1925.[41] This time it was dedicated 'To my daughter Janet, whose unfailing help and sympathy have enabled me to write this book.'[42]

Medical School 1923–25
Vaughan, meanwhile, was living in London as a medical student. From the autumn of 1923 until summer 1925 she was training at UCH, living in Chelsea with her aunt Katharine Furse at first, and then with old friends of her parents. Areas to be covered, using the terminology of the time, included medicine, surgery, midwifery and diseases of women, forensic medicine, hygiene, fevers and insanity (the last two of which involved short spells working in specialist hospitals).[43] UCH Medical School had separated from University College London in 1907, but retained the academic tradition established when it was part of the college. Ten of the staff in post at the end of the First World War were or became Fellows of the Royal Society (FRS). They included Will Vaughan's friend, the paediatrician Sir Thomas Barlow, the professor of the medical unit, T R Elliott, the cardiologist Sir Thomas Lewis, who was director of the Medical Research Council Research Unit at UCH, and A E Boycott, the future professor of pathology. The new medical and surgical units opened in January 1920, but the new obstetrics unit only in 1926, with wards and laboratories funded by the Rockefeller Foundation.

In 1923, medical students were still taught and trained in ways that caused Vaughan dismay at times. She remembered no introductory courses. The student started at once as a clerk on a medical consultant's team, or a dresser on a surgical team. Vaughan was on a surgical team, and one night found herself alone on 'Casualty' when two women came in who had been fighting, one of them with a badly cut cheek and mouth. She had no idea what to do, and called the house surgeon for advice. 'All he said … was "sew it up" and walked away. What sort of needle? Cat gut? Silk? Thread? Sister was tactful and handed me the right tools and I sewed away.' The consulting surgeon, Bill (Gwynne) Williams, on the other hand, expected all his dressings to be done by his dressers and came in on Sundays to check that they were at work.

'He threw scalpels at us in the operating theatre if patients were not properly prepared, but he taught us well. When it came to the war, I, a pathologist, found myself dealing with air-raid casualties. I knew, to some extent instinctively, what to do.'[44]

She did her medical clerking to F J Poynton, a children's physician who always wore a swallow-tail black coat and striped trousers, never a white coat. He taught her to put on leeches and was known to hate professors and clinical science. But Vaughan believed he also taught her 'how to care for … sick people, especially children … sometimes six or seven children at a time propped up in bed with rheumatic hearts'.[45] She would also have met the professor of medicine, T R (Tom) Elliott, who would be an important figure in her early career.[46]

In the 1920s UCH's main building was a cruciform block completed in 1906 on a site bounded by Gower Street, Grafton Way, Huntley Street and University Street. Like other 'public' hospitals, it cared for those who could not afford to be treated privately. Vaughan did her midwifery practice in the hospital's North West District. This large area behind Euston Station, stretching northwards as far as Chalk Farm to the west and the Nag's Head to the east, was characterised by bad housing and overcrowding. One lecture constituted the only preliminary teaching on labour. A 'List' of five students was made for each month, and each new List-member would go with someone from the previous month's List to see a birth, before taking on the next case notified. Vaughan was unimpressed:

> I never saw a delivery properly carried out … [or] … forceps put on. I sewed up bad tears by the light of a tiny pocket torch held by the old woman who came in to help … The slums … were grim: bugs climbing up the walls, nothing on the bed but newspapers, sometimes older children in the room during the delivery. At night we rode bicycles, and sometimes if we asked a policeman the way he would say: 'Oh don't go there Miss, its [sic] pretty rough', but go we did … One night I climbed a dark rickety stair to be greeted by a very belligerent husband: 'Ain't there any men doctors in …'. However we all parted good friends. The old half tipsy attendant promised to come and rub my back when my turn came …[47]

Long a prey to religious doubt, Vaughan said her experience as a medical student destroyed her remaining belief in God. In practice her stance shifted over time, and what she always seems to have loathed is the conscious or unconscious hypocrisy to which organised religion is prone: outward show unsupported by genuine understanding and commitment. Politically, she moved to the left. Later she said it was hard to understand how anyone could do medicine in those days and not become socialist. 'What I hated most was people's acceptance: "Yes, I have had seven children and buried six, it was God's will." I hated God's will ... I knew it was only our unjust society, that accepted poverty as inevitable, that was responsible for these endless burials.'[48] Many other medical students reached the same conclusion.[49] She achieved the Oxford degree qualifying her in medicine in the summer of 1925. In the following months, however, both her career and her personal life would develop in unexpected ways.

Endnotes

[1] Since Janet has effectively entered adulthood, I call her 'Vaughan' from now on.

[2] JA, 6.

[3] Aunt Char remark reported by contemporary Jane Harvey (Somerville, 1918–21) to her daughter Julian Harvey (née McMaster), also a Somervillian (1947–50). Julian refers to this among her reminiscences recorded for the Association of Senior Members, of which there is a copy in Somerville College Library.

[4] Descriptions of Haldane at this time are in Julian Huxley, *Memories I* (London, George Allen & Unwin, 1970); and Juliette Huxley, *Leaves of the Tulip Tree* (London, John Murray, 1986).

[5] See Maurice Bowra, *Memories: 1898–1939* (London, Weidenfeld & Nicolson, 1966). St Loe Strachey was an eminent journalist. His mother was Mary Isabella Symonds, and his son John became a writer and politician.

[6] Halford was reading agriculture, after a major row with his father when he decided he wished to be a farmer rather than following the family tradition by reading classics. (RSA&SC, WWV/1/C/881–1010, Halford to Madge, 26.6.1919 and 6.7.1919.)

[7] RSA&SC, WWV/1/C/1011–1114, Halford to brother David, 2.2.1923. Vaughan and he were visiting Filkins, the Goodenough home near Oxford.

[8] JA, 30. This was an occasion when the melodramatic Laura made a gesture that misfired. There is no mention of Vaughan in other accounts of the incident, so she may have helped as a haematologist when Laura was being treated in hospital.

[9] Sally Craddock, *Retired Except on Demand: The Life of Dr Cicely Williams* (Oxford, Green College, 1983), 32. Reproduced with the permission of the Principal and Fellows of Green Templeton College University of Oxford. Cicely had originally intended to read history.

[10] Pauline Adams, *Somerville for Women* (London, Oxford University Press, 1996), 95.

[11] SCA, Evelyn Irons: Somerville 1918–21, in Somerville Association of Senior Members (ASM) Report 1993.

[12] Evelyn Irons, The undergraduate, 11–13.

[13] Winifred Holtby, Alice Holtby and Jean McWilliam, *Letters to a Friend* (London, Collins, 1937), letter dated 20.2.1921.

[14] Evelyn Irons, The undergraduate, 11–13.

[15] JA, 21.

[16] SCA, Log Book Vol 2, report of debate.

[17] SCA, Log Book, Michaelmas Term 1920.

[18] Ibid.

[19] Somerville would join John Reith's British Broadcasting Company in 1925 and rise rapidly in the successor corporation to be head of education broadcasting.

[20] JA, 23 and 20.

[21] Charles Webster, Medicine, in Brian Harrison (Ed), *History of the University of Oxford: Vol VIII: The Twentieth Century*, (Oxford, Clarendon Press, 1994), 317–43. One assumes that the shorter average time taken by women is owing to their being more highly motivated, and perhaps also to less generous funding by their families.

[22] KCC, CHA 1/642 MVVB 13, Madge Vaughan to Vanessa Bell 22.1.1919.

[23] JA, 17, E H Starling (1866–1927), professor of physiology at UCL from 1899–1923. As a researcher, he made many important discoveries, including the role of a hormone (a word he introduced to the language) in pancreatic secretion.

[24] Sir Charles Sherrington, Biographical. NobelPrize.org. Nobel Prize Outreach AB 2023: https://www.nobelprize.org/prizes/medicine/1932/sherrington/biographical/ accessed 22.6.2023.

[25] JA, 17.

[26] The story is told in Anne Dally, *Cicely: The Story of a Doctor* (London, Victor Gollancz, 1968).

[27] JA, 25.

[28] Ibid., 18–19 for references to JBS (Haldane) as tutor. Miss Kirkaldy was actually a member of St Hugh's, and honorary fellow of Somerville.

[29] Henry Head (1861–1940), neurologist, and W H R Rivers (1864–1922), psychologist, both pioneers in their fields who also collaborated in important research. Rivers was particularly known for his work with British officers suffering shell shock during the First World War.

[30] TNA, FD 1/2650, Vaughan's application for a Rockefeller Medical Fellowship for 1929–30 includes Sherrington letter dated 5.6.1929.

[31] The award was a joint one. The Cambridge graduate Phillip d'Arcy Hart (or more simply, Hart) was the other holder. Their paths were frequently to cross thereafter.

[32] RSA&SC, WWV/1/C/1011–1114, Halford to Madge, 26.11.1922.

[33] Interview with Mary Bennett, 7.2.2000.

[34] JPP, Vaughan's personal notebook.

[35] RSA&SC, WWV/1/C/1011–1114, Halford to Will Vaughan, 25.1 and 31.1.1923 for Vaughan's overwork and illness.

[36] KCC, CHA MVVB 18 and 33, Madge Vaughan to Vanessa Bell, 7.3.1920; and V-4 and V-5 (Vanessa Bell to Madge Vaughan, 10.3 and 16.3.1920).

[37] Margaret Symonds, *A Child of the Alps* (London, John Murray, 1920). Vaughan's copy was given to the author by Mary Park.

[38] JPP, dated entry in small leather-bound notebook in which Madge wrote occasionally from 1905 onwards.

[39] JA, 23. Vaughan recalls this first visit as taking place in the summer of 1922, but correspondence held at Rugby School shows they first went in 1921. She could have gone again in 1922, and/or in the early summer of 1923 or 1924, given her mother's reference in the (September 1924) introduction to *Out of the Past* to having finished the book in Italy when accompanied by 'one of its old home's latest descendants'. (Madge also reported 'finishing' the book in 1923.)

[40] The full story is given in John Pemble, *Venice Rediscovered* (Oxford, Clarendon Press, 1994), Chapter 3: Strange Secrets and Broken Fortunes. Symonds's homosexuality was one important factor – besides his chronic tuberculosis – in the decision to live in Switzerland rather than England.

[41] KCC, CHA 23, Madge Vaughan to Vanessa Bell, 29.10.1924, mentions the illness.

[42] Symonds, *Out of the Past*.

[43] For training in this period, see W R Merrington, *University College Hospital and its Medical School: A History* (London, Heinemann, 1976).

[44] JA, 25–26.

[45] Ibid., 26.

[46] T R Elliott FRS (1877–1961). Brilliant early research led to his FRS in 1913. After that he concentrated rather on the administration of research, as professor in the medical unit until retirement in 1939, and as adviser to successive secretaries of the MRC.

[47] JA, 27.

[48] Ibid., 26.

[49] The Socialist Medical Association was formed in 1931, and many of its members were Vaughan's contemporaries.

SCALING THE HEIGHTS 1925–39

CHAPTER 3
All about choice
1925–30

Family, duty, friendships and pathology

In 1925, Madge's health deteriorated badly. She was only 55, but after the publication of *Out of the Past* in March that year, she went for treatment to the spa town of San Pellegrino in Italy, as well as visiting Florence and other old haunts. Vaughan, now an adult professional woman, spent the greater part of the months of July and August with her. They had three quiet weeks together in the small settlement of Macugnaga in the mountains of North Piedmont, before joining her father and the Fishers in Maloja, in Switzerland's Italian-speaking mountain and lake country. She was shocked by the change in Madge, and especially her lack of energy. Vaughan had been used to her mother

> walking with that springing eager step … darting here & there to pick some flower or look at some queer stone … a sense of life & interest in every movement. Now she sat still … looking very small & fragile & strangely young, until you saw her eyes, with shining black hair combed back off her forehead …[1]

Madge must have recovered a little at Maloja, where the 13-year-old Mary Fisher was amused by the way she was taken in by Herbert's tall stories about fellow-guests, and the holiday group was a happy one.[2] The Fishers had brought their friend Hilda Matheson, who had been taught by Lettice at Oxford and briefly acted as Herbert's part-time secretary. Although she was eleven years older than Vaughan, they rapidly became friends during long walks in the mountains around Maloja.[3] It is easy to see why. Matheson had an energy that matched her own. Recruited into MI5 during the First World War, she had risen to a key position in devising and maintaining record systems.[4] She was currently working as Lady Astor's political secretary, and could access a wide network of people with influence in the political, cultural and social fields.

Back in England at the end of the summer, Vaughan faced a critical choice. She had until this time intended to be a consultant physician, or, failing that, a general practitioner (GP).[5] For this she needed to complete resident hospital appointments in at least one medical and one surgical specialty, usually lasting six months at a time. Ideally, they should be at UCH where she had trained, and which allocated them on the basis of competitive examinations. It was extremely hard for women to obtain these or any other jobs in medicine, and she needed to apply as soon as possible.

Instead, she stayed at home. She seems not to have hesitated. She and her mother had always been close, and she had sensed in Italy that Madge was mortally ill. On her return to Rugby in September, Madge said that for the first time in her life she was glad to get home; and Vaughan noticed that she often seemed to think that her life was over. Through September and much of October, she was content to be choosing new curtains and ordering bulbs and a flowering cherry tree for the garden. Vaughan went once a week to London to do a clinical assistant job at a hospital for sick children in Chelsea ('I look back in horror to the tonsils I used to take out with a guillotine and wonder how the unfortunate children have since fared').[6] Then one day Madge retreated to bed, where she was ill for three weeks with a severe sore throat, and having to be propped up to help her breathe. 'The last day, a cold frosty Tuesday, she … talked in a short disjointed way of the people & the places she had loved – above all the Yorkshire moors & the country round Brecon ...' It is fitting that the main memorial to Madge is at Giggleswick School: a sundial with an Italian inscription, reflecting that mentioned in *A Child of the Alps*.[7]

On the evening of that day, Madge fell asleep holding her daughter's hands, and never woke again. The next morning, Vaughan picked armfuls of Red hot pokers from the garden and stood them round her bed. 'The Autumn sunshine streamed in … lying there in a blaze of colour & light … she just stopped breathing.' After watching her mother's pain and distress in those last weeks, she had a sense of happiness and of 'the peace which passeth understanding which had come into her room with the coming of the day'. Madge's belief in heaven was unquestioning, and Vaughan too could still draw comfort from Christian teaching.

Katharine Furse had visited Madge on that last Tuesday, and now wrote: 'You are splendid – and I am so delighted for your sake that you have been at home this Autumn. Your mother appreciated it immensely – she knew the cost.'[8] Clearly the family had understood her dilemma, and she had made her choice for the sake of her own peace of mind. Although she felt it right, however, she must still have felt some regret. The interest she always took in individual patients, and her enjoyment of doing hands-on medicine during the Second World War, show some of the longing she must have felt for the road not travelled. In later life she did on occasion steer young women into thinking hard before sacrificing their own hopes and wishes to the needs of older relations.

Madge was buried on 7 November at Highgate Cemetery, in the same grave as her daughter Barbara. Faced with grief and loss, Vaughan and her father both instinctively took refuge in practical activity. As he said in reply to a letter from Vanessa Bell: 'sometimes I feel more like a stone than a living being but … work is a help'.[9] Vaughan must also have felt considerable relief from pressure and anxiety, and her new friend Hilda Matheson immediately offered support. She was an experienced mountain walker and climber, and after Madge's funeral she swept Vaughan off to Val d'Isère in the French Alps for a few days.[10]

They shared a love of mountains, and for Vaughan a new kind of companionship. Matheson was used to camping, or staying in remote hostelries rather than fine hotels, enjoying a true freedom to roam. More than this, as an older, independent woman, she would be a useful listener as Vaughan thought through what to do next. She must have begun to do so before her mother's death, and her options were not finally closed down for some time afterwards. Looking back many years later, she said it was 'obvious' that she must be able to come home at least for weekends and if necessary one or more nights in the week, to look after Will and act as his hostess at Rugby.[11] This made it impossible to do the resident jobs necessary to become a consultant physician or surgeon, and led her to choose a career in pathology, which would leave her free at night and at weekends.

The choice, however, was not necessarily so clear-cut at the time. She may have accepted the then-conventional view of a daughter's obligation to put her father's needs first in these circumstances. Neither of her brothers was yet married, so there was no sister-in-law to help out. Halford, after gaining his degree in agriculture, had started work on an estate in Hampshire; and David, at 19, was still working at a junior level in the London Midland and Scottish Railway Company. It was hardly Vaughan's style to accept meekly the dictates of convention; but even if she had completed two resident posts, women's normal difficulties in obtaining work were still compounded by the post-war 'bulge' of men returning from the conflict to take up or resume careers; and only the South London Hospital for Women (SLHW, opened in 1912) and the Elizabeth Garrett Anderson Hospital were staffed almost entirely by women. Her friend Cicely Williams obtained two resident posts from 1923 to 1925 at the SLHW, and in 1926–27 was house physician at the Queen's Hospital for Children. There Williams met the paediatrician Helen Mackay, conceived her vocation of working with mothers and children, but then failed to get a permanent job, even in general practice. She finally took a diploma in tropical medicine and, after a battle to overcome entrenched opposition to the employment of women, was appointed to the colonial medical service and departed for the Gold Coast in 1929.[12]

Vaughan did manage one six-month resident post, as house physician to Sybil Eastwood at the SLHW, from November 1926 to May 1927.[13] Presumably one of Will's sisters covered for her at Rugby, and a similar arrangement could have been made twice. Crucial time had been lost in autumn 1925, however, and Vaughan may well have considered the possibility of a career in pathology earlier that year, when she spent three months (presumably from May to July, after her final degree examinations in Oxford) acting as a voluntary assistant to H M (Hubert) Turnbull at the Bernhard Baron Institute of Pathology at the London Hospital. Turnbull, a Fellow of the Royal Society (FRS), was one of the leading pathologists of the day, an expert on bone and especially the bone marrow. Postgraduates from Britain and abroad came as voluntary assistants

> to learn the organisational and practical work … and attend lectures and demonstrations. Almost all were training to be or were already pathologists. They took a share in the work of the Pathology

Assistants [with] the same facilities for preparing microscopical sections.[14]

Vaughan seems also to have worked as a voluntary assistant in the UCH pathology department from 1925 onwards, perhaps as a trial period on both sides.[15] Her memoir indicates that, apart from the six-month spell at the SLHW, she did 'odd jobs' between September 1925 and July 1927. These must have included the unpaid work at UCH as well as the children's hospital in Chelsea. For the rest, she only mentions some part-time work in a birth control clinic in North Kensington, where she must occasionally have stood in for one of the regular doctors for one or more sessions of an hour and a half. However brief, this experience would have been formative.

During the 1920s, the scale of maternal mortality and morbidity in England and Wales prompted a campaign to set up government-funded clinics to offer contraceptive information to married women; while a growing number of voluntary clinics gave advice and information for a small fee. The North Kensington Women's Welfare Centre, in what was then the very poor area of Ladbroke Grove, was the second of its kind to open in London, in November 1924. Vaughan's friends Lettice Fisher and Julian Huxley both gave talks at fund-raising events for it. The aim was to enable women to 'space' their babies in the interest of their own and the children's health; and to limit their families to a number they could afford to bring up 'decently'. It also served women who had been advised on medical grounds to have no more children.

Examples of the 'worst cases' dealt with by the Centre in 1927 included 'Mrs W', aged 38, her husband a railway worker who gave her £2 6s. a week (worth £142 in 2021).[16] After 15 pregnancies, four children had died in infancy and the youngest of the others had rickets. Another was 'Mrs G', aged 35, her husband a labourer on pay of £1 17s. 6d. a week. After 12 pregnancies, two children had died from measles, three were stillborn and seven ended in miscarriage (this word was very often a euphemism for abortion, illegal at that time and so self-induced or bought from a back-street abortionist). As a replacement doctor, Vaughan would have examined such women and advised them on the most appropriate form of contraception. Even after her student experience of the slums north of Euston, she must have been moved by these insights into the world of women living in comparative poverty. She was committed to the Centre's work: having in 1924 been one of its original subscribers, she continued her subscription until 1963.[17]

Bloomsbury and David Gourlay

For her various jobs, she needed a base in London; and at 26 she could at last live independently. Bloomsbury, within walking distance of UCH and neither fashionable nor expensive, was a practical option, made even more attractive by the presence of the Woolfs and the Bells. Virginia had sent a touching note after Madge's death, saying how much she would like to see her.[18] Will disapproved of the area for precisely that reason, but Vaughan was undeterred. Matheson directed her to the communal house in Bloomsbury where her own brother had rented a room in 1924, and Vaughan moved in early in 1926.[19]

Number 19 Taviton Street was a town house built in the early nineteenth century, part of a terrace in the short street leading from Endsleigh Gardens, behind Friends House, the Quaker headquarters in Euston Road, into Gordon Square.[20] In 1920 it was taken on by four people who had worked for the Friends' War Victims Relief Committee (FWVRC) in France during and after the First World War. All were pacifists, and the men had been conscientious objectors. They included Francis (Frankie) Birrell, who with his friend David Garnett ran a bookshop on the ground floor of the house from 1920 to 1922, when it moved to Soho. Another was David Gourlay, a junior civil servant in the Post Office. He was in France with the FWVRC in 1919–20, and became friendly with Birrell and with Geoffrey Franklin, eldest son of the banker Ernest Franklin and his wife Netta.[21] Franklin and Gourlay founded the Wayfarers Travel Agency, which succeeded the bookshop on the ground floor of Taviton Street until 1923, when it moved to 33 Gordon Square.[22] The agency had a mission to promote international understanding as a way of preventing war.[23]

Gourlay was still living at number 19 when Vaughan arrived. Up to ten people lived there at any one time. Most were young people starting out on careers in medicine, academia or the arts. A couple living in the basement provided breakfast and an evening meal on a round table in a common dining room, did the minimum of cleaning, and ruled us all with a rod of iron ... though we were none of us well off ... we were interested in the same sort of things – books, music, pictures, the theatre and good talk.[24]

Vaughan had found her milieu, and had time to enjoy it while seeking a full-time job. She took up Virginia's invitation, and saw a good deal of the Woolfs and their circle. At first, like many others, she was overawed by Virginia's penetrating gaze and questions. Faced with the question, 'Now Janet, you are a young medical student. What do you think about [some contemporary issue]?' her mind went completely blank.[25] Her confidence grew over time, but this story is a reminder of the streak of shyness that Evelyn Irons remembered, and perhaps accounts for Virginia's early reaction to her as 'good, dull Janet Vaughan'.[26]

Frances Marshall (later Partridge) worked in the Birrell and Garnett bookshop, and saw the Bloomsbury group as:

... a number of very different individuals, who shared certain attitudes ... quite uninterested in conventions, but passionately in ideas. Generally ... left-wing, atheists, pacifists in the First War ... lovers of the arts and travel, avid readers, Francophiles ... what they enjoyed most was talk ... from the most abstract to the most hilariously ribald and profane ... I had never ... come across people who set so high a value on rationalism ... integrity and originality ... Comfort didn't rank high ... (though beauty did), but there would be good French cooking, and wine at most meals ... homemade bread and jams ...[27]

Many of Vaughan's own attitudes and her preferred lifestyle, then and later, match that description.

She now plunged happily into a new bout of network-building. Thanks to her position as hostess at Rugby, she could and did invite old and new friends to stay there for weekends. Of the new, Matheson remained close. Later in 1926 John Reith offered her a senior position in the British Broadcasting Company, where she became the first director of talks, and established the first news section when the BBC became a corporation in 1927. Reith had also recruited Maisie Somerville, in 1925, to work in schools broadcasting. She lived at 19 Taviton Street in 1926–27, and

Vaughan naturally heard a great deal about the workings of the BBC from both of them.[28]

Her left-wing sympathies led to a small but energetic role in efforts to achieve a peaceful resolution of the General Strike in 1926. Lady Astor opposed government policy in this instance, and Matheson on her behalf organised concerts for strikers and the unemployed in empty churches and other halls, so as to provide entertainment and keep tempers in check. Vaughan rode her bicycle around London to help serve tea and sandwiches at these events, keeping it at the Woolfs' house because there was no room for it at Taviton Street. This meant more questions from Virginia over cocoa in the evenings. 'Virginia was fascinated to know what London was like on a bicycle. "Did you go down Piccadilly? Were there hills? Did people shout at you?"'[29]

When it was clear that the strike would fail, the academic R H Tawney told Leonard Woolf he wanted well-known people to sign an appeal to the government to see that there was no victimisation when the strike was over.[30] Woolf contacted prominent writers and artists, and recruited young people to cycle round London collecting signatures. Only Sir John Galsworthy refused to sign. 'The young woman who bicycled up to Hampstead and received a pretty curt refusal' was Vaughan.[31] Then came a last-ditch effort: at 11pm on 11 May,

> Janet Vaughan appears, who says that Lord Haldane and a friend of hers are bringing out an emergency paper and [she] will give them our letter and list of names to be printed at once … and though she has just bicycled from Wandsworth where she has been acting to strikers, she will bicycle with it to Fleet Street …

But it was too late. The settlement of the strike was announced on the radio as Virginia wrote this letter.[32]

***

Vaughan also indulged the strain of bohemianism inherited from her mother at the many parties she threw in 'the big front room' at Taviton Street. 'They were sometimes very wild. I … remember to my horror meeting the Professor of Surgery – a rather solemn gentleman – in hospital one morning. He accosted me, saying: "I was staying opposite your house … last night and I gather you had a good party!'"[33] That was the night when a young biologist, later Professor Sir Alan Parkes, had thrown most of the glasses out of the windows, and the artist Nina Hamnett had in the small hours been escorted home, clothed only in an old mackintosh, by Halford's friend Pete Brown.[34] Vaughan also knew well Elsa Lanchester's Cave of Harmony nightclub, popular with artists and intellectuals including H G Wells and Aldous Huxley. Lanchester, known for her socialism and bawdy music hall songs as well as for acting in plays by Pirandello and Chekhov, had a reputation for loose morals. Vaughan remembered something quieter: a 'rather shabby bohemian night club where one met one's friends over beer and sandwiches, fried eggs and bacon usually in the small hours of the morning'.[35]

A young sculptor then living in Paris became a close friend. They met when Gourlay asked her one night to put up a Russian girl whom he had found stranded at Victoria Station. Dora Gordine had brought a Wayfarers party of school children from Paris but could not get back there that day. Vaughan found her 'an exciting person, full of courage and laughter'. After that Gordine often accompanied such school parties to London, and stayed with Vaughan in Taviton Street and sometimes at Rugby.[36] Vaughan also spent a week in Paris, where Dora made a portrait bust of her head. She remembered (with typical dramatic licence) 'frenzied Russian lovers rushing into my room, waving pistols [and] threatening to shoot me or Dora or themselves or Dora's prospective husbands'.[37] When Dora in 1928 asked Vaughan and Gourlay to arrange for her to exhibit her work at London's Leicester Galleries, they enlisted the help of his colleague Geoffrey Franklin's banker father to do so. One of the pieces most praised was the portrait bust of Vaughan. She also treasured all her life the little laughing figurine of a naked woman which Dora gave her and David in thanks.[38]

Vaughan learned the true nature of her grandfather, John Addington Symonds, from her Bloomsbury friends, for whom it was an open secret.[39] Like them, and again rejecting her father's attitude, she 'accepted that the loves of men and women were their own affair, and that as long as harm was not done to others moral problems did not arise'.[40] She could not, however, tolerate any breach of what she saw as intellectual probity. Edmund Gosse, an old friend of both Symonds and Madge, was now a grand old man of the English literary scene.[41] She occasionally went to Sunday tea with him and his wife in their house overlooking Regent's Park. 'Then one day Gosse called me over to the sofa: "I must tell you, my dear Janet, what I have just done"', he said in a conspiratorial whisper.'[42]

Horatio Brown, her grandfather's literary executor, had died in Venice in August 1926, leaving all his papers, including those of Symonds, to Gosse. And Gosse was sure Vaughan would be glad that he and Charles Hagberg Wright, then librarian at the London Library, had acted to preserve her grandfather's good name. A few nights previously they had burnt all his papers except his autobiography, which would be embargoed in that library for 50 years.

> It was not safe to let myself speak as I thought of those two old men destroying … all the case histories and basic studies of sexual inversion [homosexuality] that JAS is known to have made, together … with other letters and papers that would have thrown … light on JAS's work and friendships. Gosse's smug gloating delight as he told me … was nauseating. There was nothing to be said. I walked out and never went back.[43]

A number of her women friends were lesbian, including Matheson, who in December 1928 began an affair with Vita Sackville West, telling her soon afterwards that Vaughan was

> nice and terribly intelligent both with her mind and her imagination … I gather from her that not only is Bloomsbury talking about you and me … but also the BBC … Janet talked to me for hours about homosexuality, of which she approves … and told me … Katharine Furse has been side-tracked because the powers-that-be have dubbed her homosexual … I left Janet in the dark about us by the way …[44]

Virginia Woolf was also a lover of Vita, and in summer 1929 Vaughan unwittingly stirred her jealousy by implying that a trip to France by Hilda and Vita had been long planned. Vita denied this, and Vaughan was invited to spend a weekend with the Woolfs at Monk's House in part at least so that Virginia could reassure herself – which she did, saying afterwards that if she had to choose between Vaughan and Matheson to love, she would choose Vaughan.[45]

***

There had never as yet been a whisper of love interest, with either sex, in Vaughan's own life. Her strong character, that streak of shyness, and her determination to succeed as a doctor and maintain her independence all militated against it. She was certainly attractive; but work was her priority, and she could never have met the conventional expectations of most potential husbands. These years, however, were for her a time of comparative relaxation and expanding social horizons; and it seems likely, in the year or so after her mother's death, that she would have been more open to the possibility of forming an emotional attachment. In any event, her personal life now found a new focus. Two entries in her personal notebook, dated 29 May 1927, signal how exciting she found it to be alive:

> From the vastness of astronomy to the infinitely small of physics … evolution … Einstein & relativity … experiments and advance in social work. Communism & Soviet Russia … men of science are finding laws … which can only be the result of a mind transcending anything that we can imagine … the man with no religion is a pessimist …

The second entry describes how impressed she had been by the belief in God and goodness of a young man she had met, and then, working in the slum, she found the good in people outweighing the bad:

> … always I found good – even in the people the world is so apt to condemn as sinners … Then I fell in love … & that taught me never to judge again – I was caught up in … some power [showing me] what a weak creature I was … that mind I was once so proud of could not at all control my emotions … God is no adequate explanation but here the world is … I find unending joy in my fellow men & women.[46]

She had fallen in love with David Gourlay – according to family tradition, over the early breakfasts they both favoured in the Taviton Street house.[47] This seems likely, since she was always an early riser, and he was doing two jobs – running the travel agency in London while Franklin did the foreign travel required, and still working for the Post Office. The match was not an obvious one. Gourlay was tall but not good looking, 10 years older than she and the son of a Scottish carpenter and a gardener's daughter (albeit both his father and maternal grandfather rose to responsible positions). His secondary education had been at a grammar school in Stockton and, though a linguist and an avid reader who had done well in passing the civil service examinations for his entry and grade, he had not been to university.[48]

Gourlay, however, was a soulmate, whose qualities both matched and complemented hers. He had shown strength and independence of mind by embracing the hard lot of the conscientious objector (CO) in the First World War. In 1916 he told the local Military Service Tribunal that he 'conscientiously believed in the sanctity of human life, the brotherhood of man and international solidarity, and could never consent under any circumstances to become part of the military machine'.[49] He refused non-combatant status and underwent court martial and imprisonment before accepting 'work of national importance' in, among other places, Wakefield Prison.

Gourlay's 'university' was in fact the socialist circles he moved in and the associated study; the Wakefield Work Centre, as it then was, and other places where he must have been imprisoned during the war; and finally the relief work and his fellow-workers in France in 1919–20. At Wakefield in November 1917 he was giving a German class each Tuesday. Other classes on offer at the centre included trade unionism, philosophy, Greek, popular science, Esperanto, French (elementary and advanced), popular astronomy, economic history, composition, maths, history, music, logic and philosophy, geography and shorthand (elementary and advanced).[50] COs were drawn from many branches of thought and religion, and many occupations and professions; with a propensity for sharing and discussing their beliefs. His year in France enabled him to meet a different mix of people who were again mostly well educated and included Quakers from the United States.

The task of establishing the Wayfarers Travel Agency was formidable. There were already several well-established rival agencies, and the founders' aims were idealistic rather than commercial. Their guiding principles included 'To study the taste of each individual, with a view to offering disinterested advice as regards hotels, routes, places of interest, etc.' Gourlay enjoyed this work, and won a wide circle of clients who were loyal to him as well as the agency. Pioneering offers also included all-inclusive holidays and organising school exchange trips. In 1921 their first job was arranging travel for delegates to a conference at Salzburg of the Women's International League for Peace and Freedom. In the process they learnt the need to 'secure agencies of as many railways, steamship, and airline companies as possible [and] establish friendly relationships with the passport and other offices ... '.[51] Thereafter Franklin travelled to establish contacts and win representation rights, while Gourlay did most of the London-based work. He must also have supplied linguistic expertise, as Franklin, whose French remained always rudimentary, had no talent for languages.

The Friends and other major organisations used the Wayfarers, and it was soon the travel agency of choice for Bloomsbury, with a reputation for enterprise. 1925 saw special tours to Rome for Catholic pilgrims, and a planned three-week 'Land Cruise' by special train across Europe for over 200 people.[52] They also tried to give groups of workers inexpensive holidays abroad, including an Industrial Welfare Tour in America. In 1927, the 37-year-old Gourlay was no woolly idealist, but a shrewd and tolerant businessman with a dry sense of humour and a love of life, travel, books and French culture in particular; strong enough to win and keep Vaughan's respect, with a work ethic to match her own.

A career for life

Vaughan was also ready to decide on her career. It was almost certainly in that momentous month of May 1927 that she obtained the post of assistant to the clinical pathologist at UCH, from July 1927 until October 1928 (in practice renewed for a further year).[53] Also in May, she paid a 'clubs union' subscription for the following three months to the London Hospital's Institute of Pathology. No activity is listed, so she may have been a part-time voluntary assistant, or just have attended lectures or post mortems.[54] Either way, she was again learning what she could from the great Turnbull. Pathology as practised in most hospitals still had inferior status within the medical profession, but Vaughan had seen Turnbull's contribution to cutting edge research, and knew how satisfying and rewarding that research could be. She was also shrewd enough to see that this less highly regarded specialism would offer more opportunities for a woman to advance.

Events within her own family were positive too. Her brother David married the sister of a school friend in September 1928, and at last settled on a career. He would join Barclays Bank early in 1930.[55] More importantly for her, her father became engaged in January 1929 to Elizabeth (Betty) Geldart, an old friend from Giggleswick days. A delighted Vaughan told Halford: 'Daddy is marvellous – his happiness is incredible … It is so good to feel that marriage is going to mean not only companionship but the much rarer thing of real love.'[56] Will and Betty were married in April 1929.

***

Vaughan was starting her career as a pathologist at a time of optimism and rapid progress. The importance of the laboratory-based sciences of physiology, pathology and pharmacology in diagnosing and treating disease was by this time well recognised; and while Britain lagged behind the United States in the funding and organisation of medical research, important work was being done in the main teaching hospitals with medical units attached. In haematology (the study of the blood), the development of microscopy in the second half of the nineteenth century had enabled the discovery of haemoglobin, blood platelets and the formation of red and white blood cells; that the bone marrow was the main source of blood cells in humans, and that white blood cells led resistance to disease.

Microbiological research promoted by Pasteur was followed by the rise of immunology as a scientific study from the 1880s, with vaccines being developed from the treated organisms of plague and cholera. Around the same time, the ideas of dietary balance as a means of normal development and health, and of deficiency disease, caused by the lack of chemical components essential to a healthy diet, gained ground. The term 'enzyme' came into use to describe organic substances that activate chemical changes in the body; as did 'essential food factors', or vitamins, to describe the components of a healthy diet.

The major deficiency diseases were starting to be recognised. Pellagra, for example, caused high mortality among many of the world's poor. The deficiency concerned was proved by the 1930s to be of nicotinic acid (niacin, later called vitamin B3), caused by dependence on maize not treated by lime. Beriberi, usually affecting the poor in Asia who depended on rice, was linked to thiamine, another vitamin B deficiency, caused by eating rice without husks. Cicely Williams, working as a colonial medical officer in West Africa, would identify and name the disease of kwashiorkor, caused by weaning from the breast to a cereal pap containing little or none of the whole protein needed for growth and development. It was momentous for doctors to be able to diagnose and prescribe with confidence for diseases which had hitherto been untreatable, because their causes were unknown. For Vaughan, pathology also offered a chance to work for real social change by highlighting the health inequalities that arose from and confirmed economic inequalities.

The UCH department of pathology was headed by A E Boycott who, like Turnbull, believed in advancing pathology as a science.[57] Vaughan became a family friend, and stayed in touch with Boycott's sons in later years – one a farmer, the other a pathologist. Her immediate superior was the clinical pathologist G W 'Bunny' Goodhart, who taught her that 'it was no good looking at specimens in the laboratory unless one knew the patient they came from in the ward or the outpatient clinic'.[58] In 1927, the UCH clinical pathology lab did all the routine bacteriology, biochemistry and haematology tests (including blood counts, urines and blood chemistry) required by the clinicians, so Vaughan gained a broad range of experience. And she was soon engaged on scientific investigations. Her rigorous Oxford training under Sherrington was enriched by her experience with Turnbull, and she had as a student encountered Sir Thomas Lewis, a cardiologist who was then the most influential figure in British clinical research.[59]

Another mentor was Cecil Price-Jones, who worked with Boycott.[60] His 1917 book *Blood Pictures* gave a brief and clearly written introduction to clinical haematology and included his analyses of the distribution of different red-cell diameters in the blood of healthy people and in the main types of disorder then known. Vaughan discussed with him the results of routine tests, learning a lot of haematology and 'the essential importance of a proper mathematical analysis of biological data. He used to despair of my arithmetic, but I learnt the essential principles and have always insisted that anyone who worked with me should submit their results to rigid statistical analysis.'[61] Haematology was developing, through these methods, from being a study of appearance of blood cells to one of quantitative analysis of cell production and the ways in which blood diseases developed.[62] By early 1928, she was working on a DM (Doctor of Medicine) thesis under Goodhart. Revealingly, he was to say in 1931 that research was for Vaughan 'an essential need'.[63]

She also became involved in a study led by Lewis, from summer 1928, of the effects of cold on the skin. Vaughan supplied one of the three study cases when Lewis learnt on the hospital grapevine that she had, inadvertently, produced hives in a patient by putting him in a cold bath.[64] A series of experiments with the three chosen cases yielded results which supported Lewis's hypothesis. As with Gosse, however, Vaughan dug in her heels over a matter of principle. True to her Oxford training, unauthorised by Lewis, she 'insisted on repeating some of the observations on other patients. The results were not the same … I said that all the results should be published, and Sir Thomas walked out of the room slamming the door … saying: "It's all a question of conscience."'[65] The final article, published in 1930, nonetheless included an additional case with a discordant test result.[66] Vaughan had won her point, and the negative result was available to inform other researchers.

Few were prepared to stand up to Lewis in this way. Another young doctor who worked with him found that Lewis counted an observation as established if they obtained three consistent positive results. Once, when things were going well, this doctor remarked that the only thing that could now upset them was a single negative observation. Lewis curtly replied no, and he knew that if this happened Lewis might, as he had seen him do, consign the paper with the unwanted observation on it to the waste paper basket.[67]

Vaughan did learn from Lewis the importance of starting to write up results before finishing the experiments, 'because it was only in this way that you often were able to formulate the further experiments … needed … the further questions that had to be asked'.[68] Despite the row, Lewis later asked her to give a paper on her thesis work to UCH Medical Research Society: a rare honour for a woman.[69]

Pernicious anaemia

She had meanwhile become interested in a new treatment for pernicious anaemia, hitherto a fatal disease caused by the failure of red blood cell production within the bone marrow. In the early 1920s George Whipple and his colleagues at the University of Rochester in New York showed that the iron content of certain foods, including liver, could cure anaemia in dogs. In 1926, George Minot and William Murphy in Boston found that feeding pernicious anaemia patients with up to half a pound a day of raw or lightly cooked liver 'cured' the disease by enabling the bone marrow to function normally again. Edwin Cohn, the professor of physical chemistry at Harvard Medical School, then managed to produce a fraction of whole liver which retained the factor effective in treating pernicious anaemia. After publishing his first 'recipe' for this in 1927, he and others refined the process over the next few years, producing smaller and smaller potent fractions, but could not identify the active factor itself. The extracts, however, administered first orally, then intravenously, spared patients the rather impractical liver diet. In 1930 another colleague of Minot, William (Bill) Castle, deduced that since people in normal health had no need of such intervention, there must be an 'intrinsic factor' in the stomach or the gut which enabled them to absorb the crucial factor in liver.

This research stimulated great interest in studying further the conditions under which liver feeding would work; in what other forms of anaemia it might help; and, most fundamentally, why it worked: what were the causes of the disease? That question was not finally answered until 1948, when vitamin B12 was identified; but research meanwhile proceeded apace. On her own initiative, Vaughan entered the fray in 1927. With the connivance of a house physician and a ward sister, she arranged to feed liver to pernicious anaemia patients at UCH. In her words, she 'did the blood counts, the house physician kept a straight face ... when the Senior Physician ... demonstrated to the students the magnificent effects of his ... treatment with arsenic, and the patients got well.'[70]

Tom Elliott as professor of medicine then agreed that she could make some liver extract according to Cohn's published recipe, and she obtained good results.

In later years, with her usual relish for a story, she liked to tell how she borrowed equipment for making the extract, such as mincing machines and pails, from friends including Virginia Woolf; that when it was tried on a dog, it made the animal sick; whereupon she resolved to try some herself. Her UCH colleagues greeted her with relief when she appeared the next day in good health, and then allowed her to try some on a patient, who survived and got better. Virginia Woolf was fascinated by her account of this work, and used it in *A Room of One's Own* in the story of Chloe and Olivia, who shared a laboratory and investigated the use of liver in cases of pernicious anaemia. 'Chloe watched Olivia put a jar on a shelf and say how it was time to go home to her children. That is a sight that has never been seen since the world began, I exclaimed.'[71] The sight in question was that of two young women focused on paid professional work alongside their domestic responsibilities.

When Elliott among others was asked by the Medical Research Council (MRC) to test commercially produced liver extracts, Vaughan took the lead at UCH and the results of these and other tests provided the material for her DM thesis, completed in 1929 and dedicated to Bunny Goodhart.[72] Some of its content was published in *The Lancet* in spring 1928, and she submitted the essence of the thesis as a 'critical review of the anaemias' to the *Quarterly Journal of Medicine* in September 1929.[73] She wrote in a lucid style and demonstrated keen analytical and critical skills. Faced with conflicting theories, she focused on the evidence in arguing for a particular conclusion, and pinpointed the questions still to be asked about the action of liver. Her cogent summary of the then-known position concluded that pernicious anaemia must be recognised as a deficiency disease. In the absence of some principle (or substance) present in liver, and also in kidney and some other foods, the bone marrow could not produce its normal quota of red cells.

Boycott at this time praised her hard work and scholarship, saying that she stood out in her capacity for active independent thought and ability to tackle a problem for herself. She also had 'a first rate personality'.[74] That emphasis on how welcome a colleague she was recurs in other references. Her upbringing in successive public schools, and with two younger brothers, had prepared her well for fitting into a predominantly male environment.

New horizons: the USA

Vaughan emerges as a different being in Virginia Woolf's observations in the late 1920s. At a dinner party, she 'seemed rapid, decided & lustrous, all in gold ... with Madge's gold necklace, & something very like Madge now & then; but tempered with the Vaughan decision. She is an attractive woman; competent; disinterested, taking blood tests all day to solve some abstract problem.'[75] The emotion shown by Vaughan in her private writing had to be suppressed in her work; but the other qualities she inherited from her mother were critical to success in medicine and science, where imagination and intuition inform creative questioning and the finding of solutions to technical as well as theoretical problems.

Her father's remarriage early in 1929 set her free – a year earlier than if she had waited for his retirement – of the obligations that tied her to Rugby. She and Gourlay had by then decided to marry, but first she wanted if possible to work with Minot in Boston so as to learn all she could about American work on the identification and treatment of anaemia. The only way to do this was through a Rockefeller travelling fellowship. These usually lasted a year, enabling promising young researchers to work with eminent people abroad and, ideally, build a network of contacts for the future. The aim was to bind the scientific community more closely together as well as advance individual careers. The Rockefeller Foundation delegated to the MRC the choice of British fellows – usually six or seven a year, including at most one or two women.

Tom Elliott was secretary of the MRC, and he and Vaughan wrote early in 1929 asking Minot if he would accept her in his lab for a year. At first he refused, because she was a woman; but the chance intervention of the Bostonian Lady Osler, a family friend of the Vaughans who had known her at Oxford, prompted him to read her published papers, and he was sufficiently impressed to change his mind. Vaughan was one of only three women researchers admitted to the Thorndike Laboratory under Minot's direction, between 1928 and 1948.[76] She spent the next few months completing her DM thesis as well as planning the future with Gourlay. Talk with Bloomsbury friends, and her experience of the family planning clinic, may have prompted one rather unusual step. Halford later told his wife, with great amusement, that he had been asked to chaperone his sister and Gourlay on a holiday in 'France or Italy', so that they could try out their physical relationship. If it hadn't worked, they would have called off the engagement. Fortunately it did, and he found himself superfluous.[77]

Another practical move on Vaughan's part was to agree with Gourlay that she would keep her maiden name for work purposes, since she had already used it in published papers.[78] The close affection they now had for each other is shown by the inscription in a book of Donne's poems which she gave him as a parting gift. It reads: 'To David, from the doormouse [sic].' She must already have developed her lifelong habit of falling asleep on the sofa following a bout of overwork.[79]

***

Whatever Vaughan's feelings at parting, she would have rejoiced in the voyage on the Cunard liner *Samaria*, begun on 28 September 1929, and even more in the sight of New York's Manhattan seven days later. After three days spent meeting staff at the Rockefeller Institute, she went on to Boston, new colleagues and a fresh set of research problems.[80] The Thorndike Memorial Laboratory (TML) was opened in 1923 as part of the Harvard University medical unit. It provided care to hospital and clinic patients and offered research opportunities to students and academic staff. An imposing neoclassical building within the Boston City Hospital complex, it had relatively restricted bench space, corridors crowded with equipment, and one ward for studying the effects of particular diets on patients. The upper floors housed labs, animal quarters and offices for a small full-time staff.

The TML director, George Minot, was a Bostonian from a distinguished medical family, imbued with the Calvinist tradition of hard work, integrity and an abhorrence of the pursuit of money for its own sake. In 1922, aged 37, his own life had been saved by the newly discovered treatment of diabetes with insulin. After that he worked with renewed dedication to contribute to other life-saving research.[81] The man who became his deputy and then successor, Bill Castle, was made in the same mould. Modest but authoritative, with a well-developed sense of humour and an overwhelming curiosity about 'how things work', he became a great researcher and teacher.[82] He had spent a weekend at Rugby with Vaughan the summer before, when he was visiting England.[83] Both men and their wives became her good friends.

She soon settled in. There were staff conferences every Wednesday, when a researcher would report on their work so that others could learn, ask questions and make suggestions; and plenty of less formal discussion, as indicated by a note from Minot's secretary a few years later, saying how much everyone missed Vaughan, 'especially I at T time!'[84] Her main research project was linked to her wish to find out whether the effectiveness of Cohn's liver fractions could be tested on non-human subjects: if it could, the whole testing process, for producing the fractions for treatment, might be speeded up.[85] With the help of Gulli Lindh Muller, an assistant physician on the laboratory's staff, she led a study to see whether pigeons' bone marrow would, like that of human beings, respond to injections of liver extract.[86]

Soon a third person joined the team: Louis Zetzel, a young student just starting at medical school, but forced by illness to take the year out. At first he found Vaughan intimidating. When he arrived, she invited him to hang up his jacket and put on a lab coat, saying that a new shipment of 40 pigeons must be weighed. Zetzel, not daring to confess his total ignorance of handling pigeons, went reluctantly to the animal room on the top floor of the building. Only when the 40 pigeons had been reduced to 36 (3 escaped, one dead) did he decide to admit defeat: 'I walked down the five flights of stairs ... and took off my ... lab coat before telling Dr Vaughan what had happened.' He expected to be dismissed, but instead she apologised for having assumed an experience he didn't have, took him back to the top floor and showed him herself how to deal with the pigeons.[87]

The study showed that while pigeons' bone marrow did respond in the same way as that of humans, further work was needed to confirm a direct and exclusive link between the factors effective in pernicious anaemia and the effect noted in the (apparently healthy) pigeons.[88] Unfortunately there was no follow-up to these experiments, and hence no animal alternative to human subjects for testing liver extracts; but in 1985, Bill Castle, by then professor emeritus at Harvard, published an article proving that the experiment with pigeons had been the first successful animal test for the anti-pernicious anaemia principle of liver, finally identified in 1948 as crystalline vitamin B12. This was the substance lacking in the diet of grain-fed pigeons.[89]

Vaughan revelled in the work, and often visited Cohn at the Harvard Medical School, half an hour's walk away, to discuss the chemistry of liver and its extracts. The Rockefeller Foundation administrator noted in mid-February 1930 that she had been working every day including Sundays since the previous November, and that Cohn and Minot thought she had 'very exceptional ability & has a great future. Dr Minot would like to have her as a permanent member of staff.'[90] By March, Minot had arranged for her to present her research results to the prestigious American Society of Clinical Investigation at its meeting in May at Atlantic City. This was a great honour, especially for a woman, and 'much deliberation' preceded the decision.[91]

Vaughan thought Minot a great teacher. He was ruthless in teaching the young how to prepare papers for delivery to a learned society. Besides checking on style and clarity of expression, he insisted on high quality slides. Two days before the Atlantic City meeting, she delivered her paper to a laboratory seminar. Minot 'picked up all my lantern slides and threw them on the floor; they were not good enough'. She was given a student to make a fresh set, with firm instructions on how to do so. As usual, she was unfazed by a dictatorial male, and was instead deeply grateful for his guidance, which she passed on to all the young people who worked with her thereafter.[92]

The society meeting was followed by a three-week tour of other institutions and labs for Vaughan as a travelling fellow. They included the United States Public Health Service in Washington and the Johns Hopkins Medical School in Baltimore, as well as the medical schools of the Universities of Pennsylvania, Chicago, Wisconsin, Michigan and Rochester (New York), the Mayo Clinic at Rochester, Minnesota and the Children's Hospital in Detroit.[93] Both the knowledge gained and contacts made were invaluable. A particular highlight was meeting the Detroit paediatrician T B Cooley, whose papers on what was then known as 'Cooley's Anemia' (later called sickle cell disease, and now beta thalassaemia major) she had read. Being able to see some of his patients, and study the X-ray material, enabled her to diagnose with some confidence a case at the London Hospital a few years later. There was at least one setback: people knew she had worked with Sir Thomas Lewis, 'the great cardiologist, and never shall I forget my horror on arriving at Johns Hopkins … to find all the most obscure cardiac cases lined up for my diagnosis and advice … it was difficult to explain that I was really only a pathologist.'[94]

***

Vaughan returned to Boston at the end of May 1930. Her evenings at least seem to have allowed for some socialising during her stay there, and once again her pedigree and upbringing gave her distinct advantages. Going out to dinner on her first night in the city, she met an elderly gentleman on the doorstep. She introduced herself, only to hear 'Oh yes, the granddaughter of John Addington Symonds.'[95] He turned out to be the philosopher A N Whitehead. Boston society was very hierarchical, but Vaughan came armed with useful letters of introduction as well as years of experience of dealing with distinguished guests at Wellington and Rugby. She was welcomed especially by one elderly lady whose house on Beacon Hill was full of impressionist pictures and other treasures. Mrs Putnam, sister of the then President of Harvard, belonged to Boston's aristocracy and wanted Vaughan to live with her. But she preferred her independence, taking a small one-room flat in a less distinguished part of Beacon Hill.[96]

Mrs Putnam epitomised social exclusivity. Either during her May tour or afterwards, Vaughan spent some time in Chicago at the art galleries. She wrote about the 'superb' pictures there, but Putnam responded that she did not know they had any pictures in Chicago. After following up an introduction to a collector, given her by the William Blake expert Geoffrey Keynes, Vaughan was very excited to have seen his picture, 'The Gates of Heaven'. Mrs Putnam, after consulting the book on the table beside her sofa, ended the conversation with: 'She is not in the Social Register.' The owner of the Blake picture was consigned to outer darkness. Social snob she might be, but Mrs Putnam had a large heart. Vaughan was always grateful for her parting gift: a generous cheque given on condition that the money be used only to buy flowers – as it was, 'every week for many years'.[97]

Boston's Museum of Fine Art, and the Isabella Stewart Gardner Museum, were not far from Harvard Medical School, while Harvard's art museums were easily accessible across the river from Beacon Hill. Vaughan may well have managed visits to galleries elsewhere during her travels, in Washington and New York especially. All these riches must have expanded her knowledge of European art of every era, illuminating Virginia Woolf's remark a few years later that Vaughan knew more than she did about art as well as science.[98] Her love of visual art also helps explain her skill in reading microscope slides, and the beauty she often perceived in them.

Not without regret, she refused Minot's offer of a further year at the Thorndike, and returned to England on the liner *Mauretania*, arriving on 19 August 1930. The Rockefeller Foundation administrator reported to the MRC that she had 'done outstanding work and is one of the best of the Foundation's fellows in this country. Dr Minot has given her very unusual opportunities and is most enthusiastic about her work …'[99]

Marriage and another career choice

Vaughan was keen to start on further research in her new job as assistant pathologist at the Royal Northern Hospital; but first she and Gourlay must start their new life together. *The Times* of 13 August announced their engagement and they were married a month later, in St Pancras Registry Office. The witnesses were Frankie Birrell as best man, and brother Halford. The choice of a quiet ceremony probably arose from a wish to avoid the fuss and expense of a traditional church wedding. Even Will was not told the date, although he did present the couple with a car afterwards, in what Halford thought a very forgiving gesture.[100]

Gourlay had met Will Vaughan several times, having stayed at Rugby in February 1929, and again in February and June 1930; but there is no record of Will's reaction to him. Gourlay cannot have fitted any image he had formed of a future son-in-law; but he would have recognised the need to accept with grace the choice made by his decisive daughter. Vaughan was now 30, financially independent, and marrying a man of 40 whom she had known for nearly five years. The relationship had also survived the test of a long parting. They chose Wales for their honeymoon, and may well have gone walking in the Black Mountains around Llantony Abbey, where Will and Madge had enjoyed staying. They reported to friends, however, that the weather was disappointing and the accommodation uncomfortable.[101]

Back in Bloomsbury their welcome was secure. Virginia Woolf had written in August:

> My dear Janet, I hastily send this off, on seeing in the Daily Telegraph about Mr Gourlay … we want to aim our love & congratulations at your head … I hope [he] was the young man who once charmed me behind a counter. And I hope you'll come & see us … I send, dear Janet, what is really a token of deep affection, remembering Madge, & feeling … some … maternal affection … in her place for you.[102]

They spent their first months in a shared terrace house in Albany Street, looking over Regent's Park from the rear windows, before moving in mid-1931 to a flat above the Wayfarers at 33 Gordon Square.[103] They occasionally went to Bloomsbury parties, and one or both of them would at more relaxed times sit in the square in the evening, talking with whoever was there – most often Roger Fry, Clive Bell, Leonard and Virginia Woolf and Julian Bell.[104]

The travel agency had secured a major coup in 1930: by moving early to win the co-operation of smaller agents, it sent over 2,000 people to see the Oberammergau Passion Play. The volume of its business had increased immensely. Sadly, however, it was not long after this that Franklin became seriously ill. He died on 11 September 1930, two days before the Gourlays' wedding. His death was a severe blow for Gourlay, in personal as well as professional terms. The generosity and idealism of his character were attested by all who knew him.

Franklin's parents, however, were good friends to both Gourlays. In 1931, David Gourlay with their support became managing director of the Wayfarers, now a limited company, with Geoffrey Franklin's younger brother Michael as his assistant. He resigned his civil service post, and was soon undertaking a busy travel schedule, including spending nearly six weeks in the United States in January and February 1932.[105] The Gourlays themselves made good use of the agency throughout the 1930s, usually for walking in September in the Swiss or Italian Alps, but also visiting the Bavarian Highlands in 1933 and possibly (or Vaughan may have gone with a separate medical party) Russia in 1934. Vaughan had inherited her mother's love for travel.

Her first job in a non-teaching hospital, however, begun after the honeymoon in September 1930, was a great disappointment. It was potentially lucrative because of the fees she could earn, and she had done well to get it. Crucially, however,

> Research was an unknown word, the work was routine ... and the object of my colleagues was to make money in private practice. I used to do locums for them when they went on leave and they would grumble if I had not extracted the last penny from some poor patient ... I was not allowed to take interesting ... pathological material for a second ... opinion. I must confess that I often crept back into the laboratory at night to collect some precious specimen which I thought needed further investigation.

Her interests included monitoring the blood of bone marrow disease patients.[106]

She and Gourlay decided they would rather be poor than have her stay in this uncongenial post. She was still close to her college friend Thilo Bugnion, whose husband, Donald Hunter, was a consultant physician at the London Hospital and was working with the great pathologist H M Turnbull on bone disease.[107] Both men were interested by Vaughan's observations on the blood picture in such cases and agreed that, provided she could get funding, she should resign her post at the Royal Northern and join their research at the London Hospital's Bernhard Baron Research Institute. One of the few possible funding sources available for a woman was a Beit fellowship. In 1931 junior fellows, on £400 a year for three years, could apply for fourth year funding of £500; and after that for a three-year senior fellowship of £700 a year. They could then, if not before, expect appointment to senior academic and research posts.

Minot, Goodhart and Boycott supplied Vaughan's three references.[108] Minot praised her scholarliness, originality and charming personality, saying she had received invitations to continue working in America. Goodhart stressed her originality and 'ever-inquiring mind', while Boycott said simply that she was one of the ablest women he had met. Already an expert in the field of study, she would 'combine the laboratory work and post mortem room in a way which is not common'. As to her financial position – always a crucial factor for Beit Trustees, especially in considering married women – 'She is married, no children, and though it is I believe not absolutely necessary ... it is desirable that she should earn something.' She became the twenty-fifth woman out of a total of 144 Beit memorial fellows as of that date. Unsurprisingly, given the barriers faced by the relatively few women doctors and researchers in those years, very few of her female predecessors had been married. And it was usually assumed in such cases that they had no need of financial help, but were supported by their husbands.

Endnotes

[1] JPP, Vaughan's account of her mother's last months is in a small home-made handwritten book. The cover quotes Tennyson, as her mother had done in dedicating *Days Spent on a Doge's Farm* to her own father: 'Oh Love we two shall go no longer / To lands of summer across the sea'.

[2] Interview with Mary Bennett, 7.2.2000.

[3] JA, 29.

[4] See Michael Carney, *Stoker. The Life of Hilda Matheson OBE 1888–1940* (Llangynog, Wales, self-published, 1999). Re-published 1923, co-authored with Kate Murphy as *Hilda Matheson: A Life of Secrets and Broadcasts* (London, Handheld Press, 1923).

[5] JA, 31.

[6] Ibid. This was the Victoria Hospital for Children, in Tite Street.

[7] *Segno le ore si. Ma non piu quelle* (translated by Madge as 'I mark the hours thus, but those ones nevermore'). In talking of the country around Brecon, Madge would be thinking of Llantony Abbey (now called Llantony Priory) in the Black Mountains, where the family letters show that she and Will had often stayed.

[8] UOBLSC, DM 1227, Katharine Furse to Vaughan, 9.11.1925.

[9] JPP, Will Vaughan to Vanessa Bell, 25.11.1925.

[10] UOBLSC, DM 1227, Katharine Furse to Vaughan, 9.11.1925.

[11] JA, 31.

[12] Helen Mackay (1891–1965) was a paediatrician, trained at the London School of Medicine for Women. She was the first woman physician at the Queen's Hospital for Children, Hackney; and, in 1934, the first woman FRCP (Fellow of the Royal College of Physicians).

[13] TNA, FD 1/2650, Vaughan's application for a Rockefeller Medical Fellowship. Eastwood had started at this hospital in 1926 as assistant physician.

[14] RLHA, PP/TUR, H Turnbull: autobiographical notes for Royal Society. Turnbull lists Vaughan among the voluntary assistants who came in 1925.

[15] TNA, FD 1/2650, Vaughan's application for a Rockefeller Medical Fellowship shows her to have been 'Clinical Assistant' (presumably part time and unpaid) in the UCH Clinical Pathology Department from January 1925 until November 1926, when she took up the resident post at the South London Hospital for Women.

[16] www.measuringworth.com, using purchasing power calculator, accessed 21.11.2023.

[17] Wellcome Collection, North Kensington Women's Welfare Centre Annual Reports 1924–28 (NK 206/1–3). The annual reports include a list of subscribers except during the Second World War. In 1927, there was a vacancy from the end of May for one of the two female doctor posts, and 'several doctors' had taken sessions until the post was filled.

[18] VW Letters, Virginia Woolf to Vaughan, 15?.11.1925. Vanessa was married to the writer and art critic Clive Bell.

[19] JA, 37. Also LMA, London Electoral Register 1924 shows MacLeod Matheson as a resident. Vaughan gave this address when advertising for a parlour maid for her father at Rugby, in *The Times* (28.4.1926), 3.

[20] The house is now gone, but most of the terrace remains.

[21] Henrietta (Netta) Franklin, 1866–1964, educationist and suffragist. Pacifist in the First World War.

[22] LMA, London Telephone Directory 1923.

[23] David Gourlay, The Wayfarers Travel Agency, in Franklin, *Geoffrey Franklin 1890–1930* (London, Chiswick Press, printed for private circulation, 1933), 103. Copy of book given to the author by Mary Park.

[24] JA, 38.

[25] Interview with Diana Reynell, 12.2.2008.

[26] VW Diary, 13 May 1926.

[27] Frances Partridge, *Memories* (London, Victor Gollancz Ltd, 1981), 76–77.

[28] In July 1928 Somerville married Halford's old school friend Pete Brown, now working as a journalist, whom she had met while staying with Vaughan at Rugby.

[29] Janet Vaughan, Some Bloomsbury memories, 20–22.

[30] R H Tawney (1880–1962), historian and political thinker, on the staff of London School of Economics from 1920.

[31] Leonard Woolf, *Downhill All the Way 1919–1939* (London, Hogarth Press, 1967), 217.

[32] VW Letters, Virginia Woolf to Vanessa Bell, 12.5.1926.

[33] JA, 39.

[34] Alan Parkes (1900–1990), went to UCL as a research scholar in 1923. Nina Hamnett (1890–1956) was an artist whose 1926 exhibition in London was reviewed by Roger Fry.

[35] JA, 50. The nightclub was in Gower Street, Bloomsbury from 1924–28.

[36] Ibid., 38. Dora Gordine (1895–1991), a successful sculptor from the 1930s to the 1950s. She generally claimed to be Russian, but was born in Latvia and later moved with her family to Estonia. This first encounter was probably in 1927, since Gordine stayed at Rugby three times in 1928, as shown by the visitor book in John Vaughan's keeping.

[37] JA, 39.

[38] *The Sunday Times* (7.10.1928), 7; and *Daily Telegraph* (6.10.1928), 15. Also JA, 38. The figurine is on the mantelpiece, above the picture of Madge, in the portrait of Vaughan by Victoria Crowe, now in the National Portrait Gallery.

[39] John Pemble, notes of conversation with Janet Vaughan, 22.6.1988; shown to the author on 29.4.2008.

[40] JA, 41.

[41] Edmund Gosse (1849–1928), critic and writer.

[42] JA, 40.

[43] Letter from Vaughan to the editors of Addington Symonds's letters, 23.9.1967. Quoted in Ann Thwaite, *Edmond Gosse. A Literary Landscape 1849–1928* (London, Secker & Warburg, 1984), 540 (note to p. 321).

[44] Vita Sackville-West Papers, General Collection, Beinecke Rare Book and Manuscript Library, Yale University, Hilda Matheson to Vita Sackville-West, 3.1.29. Long afterwards, Vaughan confirmed that her aunt's lesbianism had ensured that she was not given another public sector job after the First World War, but that it had also given her 'extraordinary qualities' (John Pemble: notes of conversation with Janet Vaughan).

[45] VW Letters, Virginia Woolf to Vita Sackville-West, 27.8.1929.

[46] JPP, Vaughan personal notebook.

[47] JPP, interview with Joan Gourlay, 1994.

[48] Family background from UK census records. Also JPP, interview with Joan Gourlay, and author's interview with Colin Gourlay, 2006.

[49] Surbiton: War Service Exemptions: Persuasion Not Force, *Surrey Comet* (4.3.1916), p. 5. Gourlay's appeal against the requirement of non-combatant service failed on 18.3.1916, County Appeal Tribunal: Conscientious Objectors Dealt With: Impressed by Jaures [*sic*], *Surrey Comet*, 22.3.1916, p. 2.

[50] Library of the Society of Friends, Temp MSS 585, Terence Lane. Programme dated 19.11.1917, for recital of popular violin music at New Theatre, Works Centre, Wakefield at 7.15pm. Timetable of classes on back of sheet, headed Education Committee.

[51] Franklin, *Geoffrey Franklin* (London, printed for private circulation at the Chiswick Press, 1933), 104, 106. Copy given to author by Mary Park.

[52] The General Strike in 1926 caused the cancellation of the planned 'cruise', and a considerable loss, so there were no more; but the idea was taken up by the Great Western and other railway companies on more modest lines, with success.

[53] UCLSC, Medical School Resigned Staff, 1927, MS/A7/8. The annual salary was £250, very acceptable for a first post at the time.

[54] RLHA, MC/S/1/32, Register of part-time medical students at London Hospital Medical College T–Z.

[55] JPP, Will to Vaughan, 28.10.1929.

[56] RSA&SC, WWV/1/C/1011–1114, Vaughan to Halford, 19.1.1929.

[57] Arthur Edwin Boycott (1877–1938).

[58] JA, 32.

[59] Sir Thomas Lewis (1881–1945). Arthur Hollman, *Sir Thomas Lewis* (London, Springer, 1997).

[60] Janet M Vaughan, Cecil Price-Jones (1863–1943). *The Lancet* (18.9.1943), 2(6264), 369, obituary written by Vaughan.

[61] JA, 32–33.

[62] A Victor Hoffbrand and Bernardino Fantini, Achievements in haematology in the twentieth century: an introduction, in *Seminars in Haematology* (October, 1999), 36(4), Suppl 7, 1–4.

[63] Wellcome Collection, Beit fellow file for Vaughan, SA/BMF/A2/142. Vaughan's application for Beit Memorial Medical Research Fellowship, 25.3.1931.

[64] JA, 35. Lewis was to add that he was fortunate in having Vaughan's help in studying haemolysis (red cell destruction), 'of which she had special experience' – presumably a reference to her work with Price-Jones and Goodhart. Lewis, *Clinical Science Illustrated*, 90–91.

[65] JA, 35–36.

[66] Kenneth E Harris, Thomas Lewis, and Janet M Vaughan, Haemoglobinuria and urticaria from cold occurring singly or in combination; observations referring especially to the mechanism of urticaria with some remarks upon Raynaud's Disease, in *Heart* (1929), XIV, 305–37.

[67] Lewis, *Clinical Science Illustrated*, 209.

[68] JA, 35.

[69] Wellcome Collection, Vaughan interview with Dr Arthur Hollman, 1986 (1717 A/1).

[70] JA, 33.

[71] Virginia Woolf, *A Room of One's Own* (London, Hogarth Press, 1929), 83–84.

[72] RSL, Oxford, MS.D.M.d.24.

[73] Janet Vaughan, Twenty-five cases treated at University College Hospital, London, in *The Lancet* (28.4.1928), 1(5461), 875; and Janet Vaughan, Investigation of a series of cases of secondary anaemia treated with liver or liver extract in *The Lancet* (26.5.1928), 1(5465), 1063–66. Janet M Vaughan, Critical review: the liver treatment of anaemias, *Quarterly Journal of Medicine* (1930), 23, 213–32.

[74] TNA, FD 1/2650, Rockefeller Medical Fellowships 1929–30. Successful applications.

[75] VW Diary, 8.11.1928.

[76] See F M Rackemann, *The Inquisitive Physician* (Cambridge, MA, Harvard University Press, 1956).

[77] JPP, interview with Dorothy Vaughan, 1994. James Park also found a book of Vaughan's dated 1930, titled *The Sexual Side of Marriage*. The story is supported by the fact that Vaughan told a Rockefeller Foundation administrator that she would be away from England in the early part of September, with some doubt about a forwarding address. (TNA, FD 1/2650, Rockefeller Medical Fellowships 1929–30, letter dated 28.8.1929.)

[78] JA, 48.

[79] Book in possession of Mary Park.

[80] RAC, R.G.10 (Fellowships), Fellowship Recorder Cards, British Medical Research Council Program.

[81] W B Castle for the National Academy of Sciences, George R Minot 1885–1950, *Biographical Memoirs*, (1974), 45, 337–83.

[82] James H Jandl for the National Academy of Sciences, William B Castle 1897–1990, *Biographical Memoirs* (1995), 67, 15–40.

[83] W W Vaughan visitors book, 1–2.7.1929. In the possession of John Vaughan.

[84] HMLC, Minot. Minot to Vaughan, 9.7.1931.

[85] See Rackemann, *The Inquisitive Physician*.

[86] Muller had been working with pigeons since 1926, and observed that the bone marrow of a healthy grain-fed pigeon had a similar predominance of immature blood cells to that found in human beings with pernicious and other anaemias.

[87] Louis Zetzel, *Memoirs* (private publication, December 1990), 26–29. There was a turnover of about 12 young doctors a year at the TML.

[88] Janet M Vaughan, Gulli Lindh Muller, and Louis Zetzel (1930), The response of grain-fed pigeons to substances effective in pernicious anaemia, in *Br J Exp Pathol* (1930), 11(6), 456–68. Vaughan and Muller went on to confirm, through a series of experiments with rats, that the effects on the blood of pigeons were dependent on the characteristic bone marrow of the birds. The rats' bone marrow did not respond in the same way (Janet M Vaughan and Gulli Lindh Muller, The effect of liver and commercial liver extract on the body weight, red blood cells and reticulocytes of normal rats, in *The Journal of Clinical Investigation* (1932), 11(1), 129–32).

[89] W B Castle, Grain-fed pigeons revisited: a pioneer test for vitamin B12, in *Br J Exp Pathol* (1985), 66(4), 503–10.

[90] RAC, R.G.10, WSC (administrator) diary entry 14.2.1930.

[91] RAC, R.G.10, Minot to WSC, 17.3.1930. Also JA, 47.

[92] JA, 47.

[93] RAC, R.G.10.

[94] JA, 47–48.

[95] JA, 41.

[96] JPP, letter from Will Vaughan addressed to 90 Myrtle Street, 28.10.1929.

[97] JA, 45.

[98] Hermione Lee, *Virginia Woolf* (London, Vintage, 1997), 274.

[99] TNA, FD 1/2651, Rockefeller Medical Fellowships 1929–30, typed note handed to Sir Walter Fletcher, Secretary of MRC, stamped MRC 12.6.1930.

[100] JPP, interview with Dorothy Vaughan, 1994.

[101] Interview with Mary Bennett, 7.2.2000. Bennett recalled that her father, H A L Fisher, was 'rather despondent' about David after the newly-weds had visited him at New College in Oxford.

[102] VW Letters, L2220a, 17 August 1930 (late entry, in Vol 6).

[103] Number 49 Albany Street is now gone, but has with its neighbours been replaced – appropriately – by the current home of the Royal College of Physicians. Vaughan's Beit fellowship application in May 1931 gave the Albany Street address.

[104] JA, 56–57. Julian Bell lived at 23 Taviton Street from 1934–35 (LMA, Electoral Register).

[105] TNA, Board of Trade and successors: Outwards Passenger Lists and Inwards Passenger Lists show Gourlay departing for United States on 9.1.1932 and returning on 26.2.1932.

[106] JA, 50. Also HMLC Minot, Minot to Vaughan, 18.11.1930.
[107] Interview with Dr Elizabeth McLean, 18.1.2007. In 1926 Vaughan had found and furnished a flat for the Hunters on their return from the USA, where Donald Hunter had been a Rockefeller Travelling Fellow for a year.
[108] Wellcome Collection, SA/BMF/A2/142.

CHAPTER 4
Forging a career
1930–39

The London Hospital: barriers, blood and bones

Vaughan started work at the Bernhard Baron Institute of the London Hospital in mid-1931, joining the neuropathologist Dorothy Russell as the second woman among the 19 staff.[1] Her colleagues Donald Hunter and H M Turnbull welcomed her, but the London Hospital itself did not. Russell had entered the medical college there during the brief period when, to meet wartime needs, it was open to women. It closed its doors to them again in 1921, and no women were appointed to the hospital's medical staff until after the Second World War. Russell's research was funded initially by a junior Beit fellowship, then, after a Rockefeller travelling fellowship, by the MRC. Vaughan found that she was ignored except by Russell and her collaborator, the Australian neurosurgeon Hugh Cairns.[2] The two women sat with the secretaries and Professor Cairns's medical artists, a table of females, to have lunch in the hospital canteen. Vaughan recalled: 'If a physician or surgeon wanted my advice about a patient they sent me a formal note and I sent a formal reply, but there could be no bedside consultation. Dorothy and I were never invited to any hospital festivity, no one spoke to us if they met us in the passage.'[3] Nonetheless, as her reputation grew, consultants at this and other hospitals increasingly sought her opinion on unusual cases.[4]

In line with her experience at UCH, Vaughan insisted on having her own outpatient clinic (a subset of Hunter's clinic) for patients with anaemia. The catchment area for the London Hospital was in large part the poor areas of London's East End, including Whitechapel and the docks. The international financial crash of 1931 triggered a crisis in the economy, ushering in the National Government, which split the Labour Party and decimated its support among voters. It also exacerbated the effects of already high levels of unemployment and low wages, especially in the older industrial areas. Public Assistance and unemployment benefits, like wage levels, tended to be insufficient to cover the needs of whole families, and Vaughan saw some of the results in her outpatient clinics.[5]

The immediate cause of anaemia is a reduction in the amount of the oxygen-carrying pigment haemoglobin in the blood. The main symptoms are excessive tiredness, breathlessness on exertion, pallor, and poor resistance to infection. Most of Vaughan's outpatients were at best living miserable lives, without the energy to deal adequately with their own and their families' needs. At worst, they might at any time succumb to illness or, if women, complications of pregnancy and childbirth, because they lacked the strength to fight the one or survive the other.

As a result of her experience with Minot in Boston, Vaughan was convinced that anaemia was most commonly caused by an inadequate diet, and especially lack of iron; but this was not yet generally accepted by her contemporaries. It was impossible to prescribe eggs, red meat and green vegetables, but she could and did order patients extra milk through the public assistance board as well as giving them large doses of iron on prescription.[6] It was deeply frustrating, however, to know that so long as their poverty continued the condition would inevitably return. There were also less common but more acute types of anaemia, accompanying major illness of some kind. For the patients concerned, severe pain in the abdomen or joints, osteoporosis, leg ulcers and in extreme cases vomiting and diarrhoea might accompany the other symptoms. Distinguishing the type of anaemia involved, and working out the most appropriate treatment, was critical. Understandably, Vaughan saw her work as life-saving.[7]

***

Not just in the London Hospital, but more generally, women doctors were at that time denied access to traditional medical clubs and societies, and so to important networks of colleagues. Instead, Vaughan networked less formally, through socialising and correspondence, and still remained on excellent terms with her old colleagues at UCH as well as at the Thorndike Laboratory. Early in 1931 she had the rare honour, especially for a woman, of lecturing to the UCH Medical School, on the pathology and treatment of pernicious anaemia.[8] In March that year, she read a paper on treatment with liver at the Royal Society of Medicine, revealing her instinct to teach and to popularise. After a brief, clear summary of her own and others' research outcomes, she focused on the most important conditions for effective therapy: a correct diagnosis (liver was not effective for all types of anaemia, or in all circumstances), and insistence on adequate dosage (considerable amounts were needed on a continuing basis, whether as whole liver or extract). Vaughan was driven, not just by her wish to teach and enable other researchers to advance knowledge in the field, but by the urgent need to inform medical practitioners everywhere of best practice, so as to save lives.[9]

Given such recognition of her expertise, reinforced by the warm plaudits her work had received from Minot and others in the United States, she expected to succeed Goodhart when he retired as clinical pathologist at UCH. Letters from Minot, however, tell the story of her disappointment. In November 1931, he reported having heard that she had been turned down for a post because she was a woman. On reading her reply, he sympathised: 'I appreciate all you have to say. I do so wish that you could have had the post. Even so, disappointments often stimulate one to do even more ... I am convinced ... that you will accomplish much good and it will be done splendidly.'[10] It is hard to imagine a better mentor.

Vaughan might have had a better chance of getting the job had she not been married and of child-bearing age; but her appointment would even so have been unprecedented. It seems unsurprising, given the prevailing prejudices, that her ex-colleagues preferred to appoint a man, Montague Maizels, who also had good credentials as a dedicated research worker: he was particularly interested in the chemical aspects of pathology and haematology. Vaughan could have no quarrel with such a man and she did indeed, as Minot advised, swallow her disappointment and seek to develop her strengths. She had been wise to start her research in the still-new field of haematology, not yet recognised as a discipline in its own right. It was in such pioneering (and less well-paid) work that women could most easily gain entry and win a reputation. Contemporaries such as Helen Mackay and Lucy Wills dealing with nutritional anaemias, Russell in the new field of neuropathology, Kathleen Lonsdale and Dorothy Hodgkin in crystallography, and the biologist Honor Fell in organ culture technique, bear witness to this. It is notable that all of the latter four depended on research grants rather than salaried posts in these pre-war years.[11]

At the Institute, Vaughan now learnt 'more than I can ... put into words from H M Turnbull about both the normal and pathological structure of bone and bone marrow'.[12] She did a lot of post mortems with him, recalling that 'Turnbull's and my great day was when we removed an entire femur through an appendix incision!'[13] This buccaneering spirit extended outside the laboratory, at a time when pathologists were permitted greater licence than could now be imagined. Patients were referred to consultants at the London teaching hospitals from a wide geographical area, and in turn Vaughan travelled far to carry out post mortems on corpses of interest to herself, Turnbull or Hunter. If possible she brought back bones for further study, having first replaced them within the body with broomsticks. An old porter in the post mortem room would tell inquirers: 'She's gone off on one of them filletin' expeditions.'[14]

For such work, a strong physique and good health were essential. Once, on a hot day in 1932, she went to an obscure bone case at a private house in the country. She was pregnant, and found that, having extracted a large part of the skeleton, 'I just couldn't face ... the skull. I came back ... without the pituitary!'[15] There were various investigations of the role of this small gland at the base of the brain in the 1930s, and Turnbull always liked to retrieve it. According to Vaughan he 'for weeks ... went wailing round the hospital: "Janet Vaughan never brought me back that pituitary"'.[16] Her reputation grew as she continued to summarise and publicise the latest advances, hoping their benefits could reach patients wherever they lived, and whatever their income. It helped that she was by 1932 writing book reviews and editorials, including occasional leading articles, on the anaemias for *The Lancet*.[17] She was recruited by the assistant editor Dr Marguerite Kettle, who preferred editorials to convey 'inside information' and authoritative judgements. Kettle sought out experts, and her wide acquaintance included many pathologists, since her husband was professor of pathology at St Bartholomew's (Bart's) Medical School.[18] Regular contributors to *The Lancet* were not then identified by name, but it is unlikely that many were women.

She might be excluded from most formal medical networks, but this and other connections enabled Vaughan to stay at the cutting edge of new developments, at home and abroad. She was a faithful correspondent, and fortunately kept most of the letters she received from Minot. Their correspondence covered current issues in the whole field of blood diseases, together with gossip about colleagues, family and world affairs. They exchanged offprints of interesting papers, and news of other publications and the travels of people it would be useful to meet. Vaughan wrote supporting the applications of at least four colleagues to work in Boston, with Rockefeller or other funding. She could anticipate Minot's questions about potential research workers in a way he warmly appreciated.[19]

**

She was soon to challenge another major barrier to women's advancement, since she and Gourlay wished to start a family. When she applied in early October 1932 to the Beit Memorial Trust for maternity leave, to start in November, she must have known that she was both setting a precedent and giving them very little time to make a decision. She wrote that, when applying for the fellowship, she had been told she was 'extremely unlikely' to become pregnant. She hoped she would not be accused of a breach of contract.[20] This has to be disingenuous on her part. At 32, she was already relatively old to have a first baby. There would never be a 'convenient' time to get pregnant, and it was rare at that time for women to combine full-time work with having children. Indeed many organisations, including the civil service, and local government notably in relation to teachers and public health staff, operated a marriage bar. She must have felt sure of her ground to act in this way, and it may have helped that her old colleague from UCH days, Tom Elliott, was honorary secretary of the trust.[21] He granted the leave on his own responsibility, since Vaughan was so soon to give birth; and then consulted the MRC, a selected trustee, and Sir Alfred Beit as chairman, as to whether the leave might be paid. This focus on the issue of pay looks like a neat diversion of attention from the main request.

The MRC reply was both grudging and revealing. Only one of the two known cases involving their funding had been granted paid leave, for a period which included normal holiday. The more difficult question was 'whether ... having a young child as a primary interest is compatible with doing research work of an original kind!' The Beit trustee, a consultant at the London Hospital Medical College, said Turnbull and Hunter praised Vaughan's 'diligence and success in unqualified terms. She has been early to work and late to leave every day.' He personally would support granting leave without pay. Elliott's letter to Sir Alfred Beit opened with: 'Miss Vaughan is the daughter of Dr Vaughan, recently Headmaster of Rugby; she was educated at Oxford and is a lady of high ability.' He suggested that if Beit agreed with the trustee, they should grant leave without pay and let discussion of the precedent await the July 1933 trustees meeting. Beit agreed. Vaughan told Elliott she had never expected the leave to be paid. She must have been relieved to have achieved this much, and once again her pedigree had perhaps told in her favour. Maternity leave, even for professional women, was still quite rare, although female hospital consultants and researchers, including Kathleen Lonsdale, had continued to work after having children; and Vaughan's friend Maisie Somerville had three years previously been granted paid maternity leave by the BBC.[22]

Vaughan certainly seems not to have reduced her workload because of pregnancy. In late November 1932, just before the birth of her daughter Mary, she submitted a comprehensive essay on the anaemias, which would in October 1933 win the Triennial Liddle Prize of the London Hospital.[23] She added one month from her holiday allowance to the four months' unpaid leave granted for Mary's birth (in total, from 3 November 1932 to 3 April 1933). By her own account she breast-fed both her babies (Cilla, her second daughter, was born in 1935) for the first few months of life, and was no doubt following the paediatrician Mackay's published advice in doing so. In general, however, she sought no other concessions to motherhood, and went back to work full time in April. Like other women of her class and profession, she could afford servants to run her household and provide basic childcare.[24]

During this first 'leave', besides completing the essay and continuing her *Lancet* contributions, she gained membership of the Royal College of Physicians in April 1933 on the basis of her published work, becoming one of fewer than 70 women among a total membership of 1,324.[25] She also started to develop the Liddle Prize essay into her book *The Anaemias*, which was accepted for publication in September 1933 and published in the summer of 1934. In a radical break with previous practice, Vaughan chose to classify blood disorders by cause and symptoms rather than by the blood picture.[26] This links directly to her insistence on seeing, in outpatients and wards, the patients whose blood and marrow samples she was studying in the lab: unusual practice at a time when clinical pathologists were widely regarded as a medical underclass who spent all their time at the laboratory bench.[27] Her motivation in writing the book is indicated by a review she wrote for *The Lancet* in January 1933 of the second edition of *Diseases of the Blood* by a London pathologist called Piney.[28] After pointing out the many ways in which his book failed to take account of the work of contemporaries, including Mackay, she finished by commenting on the inclusion of portraits of 'men who have contributed … to modern understanding of blood diseases. We hoped to find their teaching on the printed page but were disappointed.' Piney's letter of complaint (which assumed the reviewer was male) and her robust and dismissive response were published two weeks later. She clearly saw the need for something better.

Vaughan's preface to her own book modestly acknowledged its provisional nature and the hope that it would stimulate further investigation. It was nonetheless masterly in its careful analysis of published and unpublished evidence concerning different types of anaemia, and their categorisation and occasional re-categorisation in accordance with that evidence. Both this and the expanded second edition of 1936 show how her work was often life-saving, or at least life-improving. Anaemia is always a symptom of a more fundamental medical condition, and she and other pioneering colleagues were trying to differentiate between those fundamental causes so as to enable more accurate diagnosis and, if possible, appropriate treatment. In many cases, this made the difference between life and death.

She believed her greatest achievement in writing the book was to persuade the normally reticent (in print) Turnbull to contribute a long opening section on normal and pathological blood production.

Conversely, of course, his willingness to do this shows how much he respected her as a colleague. Turnbull was internationally renowned during his lifetime for his expertise on the bone and bone marrow, based by 1934 on 20 years of accurate and meticulous observation. Writing in the 1970s, Vaughan said that, while her part of the book was out of date, Turnbull's section had become a classic.[29] He also contributed observations on particular types of anaemia drawn from his long experience of post mortem work, and his comments on the state of the bone marrow throughout the body in each case show very clearly the importance of Vaughan's 'filletin'' expeditions. Attentive reading of the two editions also reveals how her own work, whether for research or routine analysis, corrected misdiagnoses and benefited patients. She mentioned three cases she had seen diagnosed as anaemia related to malaria, which she had identified as in fact belonging to a group of hereditary anaemias then known as 'acholuric jaundice', which could only be treated at that time by removing the spleen. She also described two other cases, one of which had been diagnosed as acute food poisoning, the other 'acute haemolytic (meaning 'blood destroying') anaemia'.

As in the case of some of her *Lancet* articles, Vaughan did not pull her punches if the evidence cast doubt on claims made in the medical literature. In 1934 she questioned the separate existence of the group categorised as 'Acute Haemolytic Anaemia', intensifying the pressure in 1936 by highlighting the lack of evidence for their identification separately from other conditions. She also cast doubt on methods of diagnosis of a group called in both editions 'The Unclassified Anaemias'; and here Turnbull too demonstrated a lordly way with muddled thinking, typified by his opening sentence on the condition dubbed 'Splenic Anaemia': 'Until splenic anaemia is defined more precisely than an anaemia in a patient with a large spleen a discussion of the pathology can be of little profit.'[30]

The impact of gathering together such a wide range of work, hitherto only available in separate articles in various journals, of presenting it in clear and accessible prose, and of organising it into rational categories based on the available evidence, as analysed by someone of Vaughan's acumen and wide experience, was incalculable. The advice the book gave on how to differentiate between conditions so as to arrive at a correct diagnosis and most appropriate treatment must in itself have saved many lives. The 1934 book was quickly recognised as the leading British textbook of its time on the subject, described by the *British Medical Journal* (*BMJ*) reviewer as 'a compact, critical, and up-to-date survey ... a monograph for the research worker, the pathologist, and the consultant physician, who will find in it a mine of carefully documented information ... presented clearly and interestingly, and which cannot fail to stimulate haematological research.'[31] Speaking in 1985, the haematologist Sir John Dacie would call the 1936 second edition simply 'a classic of its time'.[32]

Personal research and medical networking

Vaughan's grant-funded work with Hunter and Turnbull centred first on what was then called idiopathic (meaning 'of unknown cause') steatorrhoea: a debilitating condition characterised by fatty stools and, often, bone deformities. In 1932, they published the first detailed survey of the disease written in English, covering symptoms, how to distinguish it from superficially similar conditions, and effective treatments. The anaemias involved responded, depending on type, either to iron or Marmite, and other symptoms could be mitigated by various means. They suggested that it resulted from disturbance of the gastro-intestinal function resulting in deficient production, absorption or utilisation of one or more essential factors. (The condition, apart from a still-remaining idiopathic form, is now known to have various causes, but predominantly – as coeliac disease or sprue, which is genetic in origin – an intolerance of gluten.) The researchers' testing of Marmite resulted from Lucy Wills' observation that this was as effective as liver extract in treating anaemia of pregnancy – a condition which, like pernicious anaemia, featured the production of abnormally large red cells.[33] Vaughan and Hunter's finding that Marmite was equally effective in one group of their study patients meant that a large group of anaemias could now be told apart from pernicious anaemia by the fact that they responded to Marmite (as pernicious anaemia did not), as well as other factors.[34]

'Acholuric jaundice' was another special interest. Characterised mainly by increased fragility of the red cells and enlargement of the spleen, opinion was divided on its likely cause. Some thought it was due to malfunctioning of the spleen, others to malformation of cells by the bone marrow, and hence their destruction by the spleen. The 1936 edition of *The Anaemias* anticipated Vaughan's published paper of 1937, which concluded (correctly) that the condition was due to an abnormality of blood formation.[35]

Like her UCH mentor Price-Jones, Vaughan recognised the need to identify the 'normal' standard of the healthy person in terms of the various blood measurements available, so as to be more confident of what was 'abnormal'.[36] By 1933, she was collaborating with him in a long-term study of the blood of healthy people in Britain, making some use in the process of improved methods and equipment devised by the American haematologist Max Wintrobe.[37] The outcome was a major article in 1935. Significantly, the name of the graduate chemist assisting with the project, Helen Goddard, was included as a joint author. This was not normal practice at that time, despite the substantial contribution of graduate chemists, who were often women, to research work.[38]

Her fourth major field of investigation, which she first mentioned to Minot in late 1931, was to be of the most long-term interest to her. She initially called it 'osteosclerotic anaemia', meaning anaemia thought to be caused by overgrowth of bone encroaching on the marrow cavity.[39] When Max Wintrobe visited England in 1933, Vaughan was one of those he was determined to meet. He found her slicing long bones lengthwise to learn how far displacement of blood-forming bone marrow was a factor in the occurrence of this form of anaemia.[40] She and Turnbull had by then agreed on the term 'leuco-erythroblastic anaemia' – a condition characterised by an excess of immature red cells and early white cells in the bloodstream – as best describing the characteristic features of the blood when associated with a number of different bone conditions. She had decided by 1934 that this anaemia did not result from, for example, the overgrowth of bone, or the spread of malignant tumours in the bone marrow, but was rather due to a single fundamental and as yet unknown cause.[41]

Her articles on this, in 1936 and 1939, were arguably her most significant contribution to developing knowledge in the period. The first, whose conclusions are incorporated in the 1936 book, including several sections jointly with, or provided by, Turnbull, looked at 13 known cases (some cancer-related, others not), alongside a similar group of patients who might have been expected on theoretical grounds to have the condition. She noted that it had not been seen unassociated with bone changes, and suggested that it was caused by a deficiency of a factor or factors necessary for normal blood formation. The associated abnormalities in bone might be due to an associated deficiency. The 1939 paper (again with contributions from Turnbull) was more definitive. Drawing attention to the wide range of names applied to similar conditions, she suggested that all might be due to the same underlying cause; that there was abnormal development of bony as well as blood-forming tissue; and that both processes occurred simultaneously in response to a single, as yet unidentified, stimulus. All the blood cell types involved were known to be derived from the same primitive cell.[42]

For the patients involved, this new categorisation was very important for their prognosis: they tended to live longer than in typical leukaemia, with which their symptoms had often been confused. Developments many years later were to bear out Vaughan's conclusions.[43] Her work on a variety of other conditions, from the role of infection in inhibiting the process of blood production to the anaemia following gastric operations, informed her periodic surveys of work across the field, including *The Anaemias*. Her wide-ranging interests, and ability to make connections across different fields of research, and analyse and synthesise the results, are reflected in these surveys, and in her publications after the Second World War, when she returned to research focused on blood and bone.

***

Vaughan also increased her standing, as well as advancing the causes which interested her, by making good use of those medical networks which did admit women. She attended and contributed to most meetings of the two national pathologist associations.[44]

In June 1933, for example, she read a paper on the treatment of anaemias to the Association of Clinical Pathologists' summer meeting in Manchester. The meeting passed a resolution urging the establishment under the National Health Insurance Acts of recognised, strategically located centres to enable the initial diagnosis and ongoing differential treatment of anaemias: this would save lives and money by ensuring that treatment was appropriate and properly controlled across the country, rather than in a few places only. They urged too that commercially produced liver and other extracts should be properly tested to ensure consistent potency, which in turn should be accurately described on the packaging. All of this is in line with Vaughan's desire for a countrywide service of a good quality, and her habits of careful recording and standardisation. She wrote a leader in the edition of *The Lancet* reporting the discussion, suggesting that a body like the MRC should oversee the standardisation process.[45]

In November 1934, she was one of two people invited to present papers at a discussion on nutritional anaemias at the Royal Society of Medicine.[46] Despite being widely recognised as a leading authority in her field, however, she had that summer been refused a fourth year's Beit funding to continue her research. Only four women had previously gained such funding, and only one, the (unmarried) biologist Honor Fell who became director of the Strangeways Laboratory in Cambridge in 1929, gained a senior fellowship. Between 1932 and 1939, no women were granted a fourth year. Vaughan must have realised that being married and having a child would have told against her, but that would have enhanced her sense of injustice; indeed, she told Virginia Woolf that she had been refused fourth year funding because of prejudice against women. According to Woolf, 'This led to a fruitful discussion … of the jealousy of the medical male: vested interests; … partly that they dislike competition; partly that they cling to the status quo.'[47]

Desperate to gain alternative funding, Vaughan sought Minot's support, and he replied from his holiday home in Maine enclosing a note for her use

> I should consider it a real catastrophe to modern medicine to have [Vaughan] obliged to stop her useful progressive studies … Her

publications have been [praised] by numerous clinicians in this country. I feel sure her work … will … add new knowledge. She … has an inquisitive mind, an investigative imagination … & very helpful to younger individuals wishing to study disease … in a serious way.[48]

Later in life, Vaughan would name Minot and Turnbull as the only two of her idols who did not turn out to have feet of clay, saying that Turnbull 'had the same scientific integrity and curiosity as George Minot'.[49] (She does not say who the fallen idols were.) Fortunately, the RCP came to her rescue with a Leverhulme Scholarship of £500 for 1934–35. Vaughan did admire and like Lord Dawson of Penn, then president of the RCP and a consultant at the London Hospital, who chaired the RCP Science Committee which decided the scholarships. Other members included, besides Elliott and Hunter, the secretary of the MRC Sir Edward Mellanby, the eminent specialist in tropical medicine N H Fairley, and the director of the National Institute for Medical Research Sir Henry Dale.[50]

The news broke in October 1934 that Minot had, with Whipple and Murphy, been awarded the Nobel Prize for his work on pernicious anaemia. When he and his family came to London for eight days, en route for Stockholm, Vaughan at his request hosted the visit and organised a range of activities. She introduced a discussion at the Royal Society of Medicine, and no doubt influenced his decision to publish his Nobel lecture in *The Lancet* early in 1935. One story she liked to tell was of driving him to the door of the London Hospital to have lunch with the professors and physicians. Far from inviting her in, they merely told her what time to pick him up.[51] Soon, however, both daily social snubs and the uncertainties of living on grants would be over. Her working life would change in ways she could hardly have envisaged.

Recognition and success: Hammersmith 1935–39

Advocates of improved medical education in Britain had long argued the need for a dedicated postgraduate teaching centre in London, to serve hospital medicine as the London School of Hygiene and Tropical Medicine served public health. After much discussion and negotiation, but against a backdrop of public sector austerity in the early 1930s, the London County Council and central government shared the cost of building 'a token school, an outpatient department and a new surgical block', at Hammersmith Hospital in West London.[52] The British Postgraduate Medical School opened in May 1935 as an independent school of the University of London, with Francis Fraser as professor of medicine and E H ('Tom') Kettle professor of pathology. Both were from Bart's Hospital Medical School. They were joined by two more professors, of surgery and of obstetrics and gynaecology. Vaughan recalled being phoned by Kettle about the post of assistant (lecturer equivalent) in clinical pathology at the new School.[53] She said yes, provided she could have a bandsaw for sawing up bones – not standard pathology equipment in those days, since only Turnbull, and now Vaughan, used one. Minot provided a reference in January 1935, asking at the same time if she could take over from him the task of updating the chapters on anaemia in a leading academic publication: the 'Nelson Loose Leaf system'.[54] However busy she was, she would have jumped at such an opportunity.

Vaughan's appointment owed much to the fact that this was a new institution, with no hidebound traditions and with progressive people in charge. Kettle had ensured that, very unusually, pathology was a separate department, of equal status with those of the other professors; but Vaughan's title and salary on her appointment in April 1935 reflected the still-inferior status of clinical pathology. Whereas she was an assistant on a salary of £500, her colleagues in the other sub-departments – Earl King, Ashley Miles and John Gray – were readers in pathological chemistry, bacteriology and morbid anatomy respectively, on a salary of £800 rising by yearly increments to £1,000; and, as readers, were members of the School's governing body.[55] Gray was less eminent than the others, and Kettle had wanted a woman for that post also: B D ('David', short for Davidine) Pullinger, who was working with Professor Howard Florey at Sheffield and was known as an excellent experimental pathologist; but apparently the appointment board preferred someone with more experience of post mortems. Kettle was furious about this.[56] For a woman, Vaughan was nonetheless doing extremely well. A survey of women's careers published in 1935 found that, whilst men and women received equal pay in medicine, there was still a near-invincible prejudice against granting women hospital appointments; and, if appointed, they tended not to advance to more senior grades. Medicine was therefore included in the general statement that 'exceptions apart, the general run of women's earnings is low, and £250 a year is quite an achievement, even for a highly qualified woman with years of experience'.[57]

In practice, she acted as if she too were a reader, co-operating very closely with King and Miles especially. By her own account, she had 'a bit of a battle with dear Fraser' in order to get her own outpatient clinic. But she had it next to his, and also went on staff rounds with him.[58] Another colleague from those days said that Vaughan 'couldn't be kept out of the wards even if anyone had wanted to keep her out'.[59] The workload was heavy. Her department not only dealt with all blood and bodily fluids tests, but was responsible for related supplies to the hospital. She taught postgraduate students on refresher or Diploma in Clinical Pathology courses, supervised research students, and continued with her own research and publications.

She and her colleagues were horrified when they first arrived and saw the bare rooms at the new School. There was almost no lab furniture and it was hard to see where benches and shelves could be fitted in. A surplus of lavatories was quickly converted into laboratories, and Vaughan learnt from Miles the importance of writing convincing memorandums – usually in this case to the London County Council – to winning practical improvements. The whole project was exciting, however, and for her this was a brave new world indeed. As a woman, she was simply one of the staff, 'but it took some time to get used to the fact that I could have lunch with the Professor of Medicine in the canteen and that the Professor of Surgery … talked to me about his patients.' When she and a young female obstetrician colleague were invited to the Christmas dinner, Vaughan, always aware of the need to impress, bought 'a most gorgeous new evening dress' for the occasion.[60]

Further recognition came when in March 1936 she was elected as one of the first female members of Thomas Lewis's prestigious Medical Research Society, with a network including establishment names such as Kettle, Fraser, Elliott, Dale and Mellanby, as well as some of the most promising younger researchers. She had first been invited to give a paper to the Society when it met at the London Hospital in 1933, and would later introduce younger colleagues herself to give and hear papers at meetings.[61]

It was fortunate that, thanks to the teething problems of the new School as well as the need to build up slowly, student numbers were limited in the summer and autumn terms of 1935. Cilla, Vaughan's second baby, was born on 17 August that year. By her own account, Vaughan worked until the last minute, then took six months' leave to nurse the baby at home.[62] Five months (August to December), as in Mary's case, is more likely than six. Vaughan also told the story of returning to the hospital two weeks after the birth and being asked if she had enjoyed her holiday, only to be greeted with disbelief when she said she had had a baby.[63] There is no surviving record of her maternity leave. It seems likely that she visited frequently to give a lead on the work, and spent at least part of her time at home completing the second edition of *The Anaemias*, which came out in 1936, as well as writing up her research. In September, Minot told her he and Castle thought it extraordinary that she had found time to complete the Nelson manuscript and send it off.[64]

The pace at Hammersmith quickened in 1936, with the daily average number of students in the pathology department rising to above eight in March and May (from 0.2 in October 1935), and more than nine in November.[65] From 1937, it was arranged that two students could come on much-sought-after paid six-month appointments, while varying numbers of voluntary assistants came to learn and to do research. At the same time the routine work of the hospital greatly increased, partly reflecting an increase of about 50% in bed numbers. The Diploma in Clinical Pathology course was temporarily suspended for lack of space, but the weekly interdepartmental 'conference day', which was an important feature of the school, continued. It featured pathology staff giving lectures to students attending the clinical departments; as did outside experts such as Fell of the Strangeways Laboratory and Alan Parkes, Vaughan's friend of Taviton Street days who was now an eminent reproductive biologist working at the National Institute for Medical Research, and FRS since 1933.[66]

By 1938, the original refectory and reading room had been converted to laboratories for the revamped diploma course, and other rooms adapted for more lab accommodation. There was, however, a surge in student numbers, so that still more lab space was needed. But staff numbers were still small enough for all to know each other, and any 'event' would be celebrated in the only possible space – the Pathology Museum. One colleague remembered 'very good parties amid all the bottled specimens'.[67] Kettle and Fraser fully supported Miles, King and Vaughan in their battles with the London County Council (for whom Kettle's favourite oath, in public at any rate, was 'God rot 'em for a set of ruddy stoats'); and, despite the rather cramped and primitive facilities, they thrived.[68] Vaughan remarked that the relentless increase in workload was largely down to their own enthusiasm – for instance, for trying out new tests they had read about in the literature. 'Grey Turner [the professor of surgery] used to be awfully patient with us. We would … tell him he couldn't possibly operate on some patient because their Vitamin K level was all wrong, or something. He said bitterly "you young creatures up on that floor run this hospital".'[69]

From February 1936 Tom Kettle was on sick leave, with Ashley Miles acting in his place. In October, Miles (speaking for Kettle, who retained a controlling interest during his illness) urged the Governing Body to promote Vaughan to senior assistant (senior lecturer equivalent), on a salary of £600 rising by annual increments to £750, with a paid assistant to help with the workload. He said the pressure of routine work was delaying publication of her research, and threatening the quality of her teaching.[70] Her expertise and international reputation also merited a salary rise: her monograph on anaemia was the standard work of reference, and overseas students were coming to work under her direction. If she left, it would be very hard to replace her for haematology, and impossible at her current salary. The appointment was agreed, and R G [Gwyn] Macfarlane came as junior assistant in clinical pathology in January 1937.[71]

The pathologists were deeply grieved when Kettle died in December 1936. What was thought at first to be a gastric ulcer had turned out to be slow-burning cancer of the stomach. A shrewd and critical thinker and teacher, he had a warm heart and was greatly loved as well as respected. Miles, King and Vaughan thought the obituary in *The Times* a little cold, and a few days later the paper published their own jointly drafted tribute.[72] In it they stressed Kettle's wish to appoint staff who were pioneers in their fields, his 'power of creating affectionate confidence', which promoted unity, and his sheer enjoyment of life, people and work.[73]

Kettle's successor, the professor of pathology at the University of Liverpool, Henry Dible, did not take up post until the 1937–38 academic year. In the meantime Miles, King and Vaughan continued to manage the pathology department more or less as a triumvirate.[74] Despite the pressures, Vaughan averaged three solo publications a year from 1935 to 1939, including in 1935–36 the second edition of her book. She was devising and modifying courses including the revised diploma, to which graduates came from all over the world; and facilitating Macfarlane's early work on haemophilia, the field in which he would become pre-eminent.

Kettle was behind Macfarlane's transfer from Bart's, with the instruction 'Break him down, Janet, and then build him up'; although she said there was no need to do either.[75] As Macfarlane's biographer put it, however, 'haematology had not been very advanced at Bart's at the time Gwyn was there, and so it was a revelation for him to learn from Janet Vaughan of the importance of distinguishing the various types of anaemia, precision and standardisation of methods, as well as the proper control of experiments'.[76]

The young John Dacie, when he gained a one-year postgraduate studentship from the Medical Research Council, chose to work with Vaughan in the first instance, because he had read the second edition of her book.[77] He spent six months at Hammersmith, in the second half of 1937, recalling that Vaughan fulfilled her wide remit 'with apparently tireless enthusiasm and a rigorous insistence on high standards'.[78] She insisted, for instance, that all blood films be kept as part of each patient's laboratory record. He too noted her stress on standardisation and proper controls. His research undertaken with Vaughan, on acholuric jaundice, marked the beginning of his outstanding work on such inherited haemolytic anaemias.

Vaughan was still writing for *The Lancet*, and her hand is detectable in an editorial of February 1936, supporting the efforts of the British Standards Institution to introduce standardised laboratory equipment.[79] Many clinicians sought her advice on patients with obscure blood diseases: 'The back of my car was always full of interesting specimens which I had collected ... for diagnosis or research purposes, from all over London. I learnt a great deal from many different experts.'[80] Max Wintrobe, who added statistical analysis to the list of her 'must-dos', believed that Vaughan's department was unique in the UK in that, whilst part of the department of pathology, it was devoted almost entirely to the laboratory aspects of haematology.

In June 1938, Vaughan took on a new graduate chemist, Olive Booth, funded by the Rockefeller Foundation, for a planned survey of acholuric jaundice in collaboration with Dr G L (George) Taylor of the department of eugenics at the Galton Laboratory of University College London. Vaughan would investigate the clinical and haematological aspects, while Taylor would collect details of relationships, blood group and other possible genetic factors, and make a statistical study of the data.[81] In November, Vaughan reported that Booth's work was extremely satisfactory, meriting a pay rise; and that most other expenses arose from travel: visiting patients all over the country and arranging for them to come to London. The outbreak of war in September 1939 brought the study to an abrupt halt, but this interest in genetics continued. She would engineer a crucial Nuffield Foundation grant for the subject more than 20 years later, in 1963.

Vaughan's status and achievements were recognised by her peers when, on 11 May 1939, she was admitted as the seventh female fellow of the RCP, at the relatively young age of 39.[82] Fellows were nominated by the Council, or governing body of the college, and elected by the membership. Only fellows could be nominated as members of Council. Needless to say, there were relatively few pathologists among them, and a number supported her with citations such as:

> Author of classical work *The Anaemias* ... the chief authority in this country on the anaemias and leukaemias ... Has established a series of normal values, particularly for red cell characteristics and serum

bilirubin, devising specialised techniques for this purpose ... of international repute and a worker of extraordinary energy.[83]

Vaughan was now one of the few women in Britain to have achieved wide recognition and status in the field of scientific research relevant to medicine. Others among her contemporaries were Honor Fell, Helen Mackay, Dorothy Needham, the physician and researcher Dorothy Hare, Dorothy Russell, the geneticist Julia Bell, Lucy Wills and her old friend Cicely Williams, through her work on kwashiorkor. It is noticeable that only Dorothy Needham on this list was married, and that she was childless. It is hard not to conclude, on the basis of the quality of her research record and the respect in which she was held, that Vaughan would have been nominated Fellow of the Royal Society if at that time the Society had chosen to admit women.[84] Her ability to win liking as well as respect among a wide circle of male colleagues was no small part of her success. All her references over these years mention her energy and enthusiasm, and Dible added to his for the RCP fellowship that she was 'a woman of great culture'. In other words, she contributed good conversation as well as scientific acuity. Dacie would recall that she was 'tall and distinguished looking and at first acquaintance a rather imperious personage who would clearly stand no nonsense; yet deep down she was warm and generous.'[85] This view was echoed by others throughout her career.

Endnotes

[1] RLHA. This is the number of staff in two photographs taken in successive years, undated but including Russell and Vaughan.

[2] Dorothy Russell (1895–1983). After a secondment to Oxford to work with Cairns during the Second World War, she succeeded Turnbull as professor in 1946. Hugh Cairns (1896–1952) was a pioneering neurosurgeon then building an international reputation.

[3] JA, 51.

[4] AICL (BPMS), transcript of D K Hill conversation with Dame Janet Vaughan, 10.11.1980.

[5] Pat Thane, *Foundations of the Welfare State* (2nd edition) (London, Pearson Education, 1996), 162–71. The position was shifting and complex, but the general outcome hard on the unemployed and even the employed poor.

[6] JA, 52–53.

[7] JPP, interview with Dorothy Vaughan.

[8] Printed in *UCH Magazine*, April and May 1931. She later said that this was at Sir Thomas Lewis's request.

[9] J Vaughan, The value of liver in treatment, in *Proc R Soc Med* (May 1931), 24(7), 929–35.

[10] HMLC Minot, Minot to Vaughan, 17.11 and 11.12.1931. The post went to Montague Maizels (1899–1976), ex-clinical pathologist at the Infants' Hospital Westminster. He was a future colleague of Vaughan in the wartime blood transfusion service, and dedicated his life to research and teaching, being elected FRS in 1961.

[11] Helen Mackay (1891–1965). Paediatrician at the Queen's Hospital for Children, London, who specialised in the dietetic deficiencies of infants and young children. Lucy Wills (1888–1964). Pathologist at the Royal Free Hospital, researcher in nutritional macrocytic anaemia, including 'anaemia of pregnancy'. Identified the efficacy of Marmite (folic acid) as a treatment. Kathleen Lonsdale (1903–1971), crystallographer at the Royal Institution (with Bragg), FRS 1945. Honor Fell (1900–1986), Director of the Strangeways Research Laboratory 1929–70, FRS 1952.

[12] JA, 52.

[13] AICL (BPMS), transcript of D K Hill conversation with Dame Janet Vaughan, 10.11.1980.

[14] Ibid.

[15] Ibid., the expected baby was Mary, born in November 1932.

[16] JA, 52.

[17] *The Lancet* leaders, or leading articles, followed the pattern of those in the daily press (most famously *The Times*), pronouncing on issues of importance in columns used for that purpose. Other editorial material, often relating to articles in that issue, followed in a different typeface, and a separate section headed Annotations contained miscellaneous news items, including, for example, news from medical conferences or meetings and appeals relating to Spanish Medical Aid or the Campaign against Malnutrition. Vaughan's hand is detectable in all at various times.

[18] Obituary of Marguerite Kettle, *The Lancet* (13.5.1939), 1128–31. Vaughan says Kettle recruited her to *The Lancet* (JA, 56).

[19] HMLC Minot, Minot letters in 1931–32, 1933, 1935 and 1939; and in particular Minot to Vaughan, 11.8.1932.

[20] Wellcome Collection, SA/BMF/A1/142, Vaughan letter, 4.10.1932. She may have meant to imply that she and her husband were using contraception. The letters referred to in the following paragraph are also on this file, dated 7, 13, 16 and 17.10.1932.

[21] Professor T R (Tom) Elliott, head of the medical unit at University College Hospital Medical School. He and Vaughan did not always see eye to eye, as was clear when they served together on the Goodenough Committee in 1944–46; but he respected both her and her work.

[22] In Maisie Somerville's case, the BBC allowed paid maternity leave on a discretionary basis in 1929 (Kate Murphy, *Behind the Wireless: A History of Early Women at the BBC* (London, Palgrave Macmillan, 2016), 89–91).

[23] JA, 55–56. She revised the proof of an article for *The Lancet* on the same afternoon. When asking the formal permission of the Beit Trustees to accept the Liddle Prize, Vaughan stated (apparently tongue-in-cheek) that she had produced the essay during her unpaid leave of absence, so that it had not interfered with her work under the Beit fellowship (Wellcome Collection, SA/BMF/A2/142, letter 17.10.1933).

[24] Hostility among contemporaries at the London Hospital increased, however, and even Donald Hunter seems to have disapproved, especially when Vaughan conceived a second child and continued to work full time. Her close friendship with Thilo continued, but they did not usually meet in Thilo's home after this time (interviews with Dr Elizabeth McLean, 18.1.2007; and Joan Crouch, 27.10.2006).

[25] RCPL, Annals 1909–10 to 1933–34.

[26] Janet M Vaughan, *The Anaemias* (Oxford, Oxford University Press, 1934; and 2nd edition, 1936), 25–27. She had mentioned this decision to Minot early in 1933 (Minot letter of 7.4.1933), and he had agreed with her.

[27] In 1942, the Goodenough Committee on Medical Schools was told that there were no separate professorships or lectureships in clinical pathology in Scotland, nor were they regarded as necessary (TNA, MH 71/71, written evidence 1942–44).

[28] Reviews and notices of books, *The Lancet* (7.1.1933), 1(5706), 26–27.

[29] JA, 52.

[30] Vaughan, *The Anaemias* (1936), 265.

[31] Reviews – the anaemias surveyed, *BMJ* (2.6.1934), 1(3830), 987.

[32] Sir John Dacie, Dame Janet Maria Vaughan, b.18 October 1899 d.9 January 1993, *Munk's Roll: The Lives of the Fellows of the Royal College of Physicians* (London, Royal College of Physicians, 1993), IX, 542. Sir John Vivian Dacie (1912–2005) worked with Vaughan as a postgraduate student in 1937, and became a leading haematologist. Quote from his 1985 speech honouring her at the fiftieth anniversary of the opening of the British Postgraduate Medical School (copy among JPP).

[33] Lucy Wills, Treatment of 'Pernicious Anaemia of Pregnancy' and 'Tropical Anaemia' with special reference to yeast extract as a curative agent, in *BMJ* (20.6.1931), 1(3676), 1059–64. Wills went to Bombay in 1928 to study 'pernicious anaemia of pregnancy', and found that the 'Wills

factor' in yeast extract was an effective cure. This paved the way for her own and others' later work on folic acid.

[34] It is now known that yeast extract contains folic acid – a B vitamin whose role in blood formation can be affected by a deficiency of vitamin B12.

[35] The term 'acholuric jaundice' covered several conditions now known to be of genetic origin.

[36] Cecil Price-Jones (1863–1943). He pioneered the application of statistical methods in haematology, and demonstrated the unique distribution curve of the red cell diameters in Addisonian anaemia. He wrote *Red Blood Cell Diameters* (London, H Milford, Oxford University Press, 1933).

[37] Wintrobe in 1928 devised an improved haematocrit for calculating the volume of red cells in the blood. He expanded its use to, for example, white cells and platelets; and also pioneered the direct calculation of the mean size and haemoglobin content of the red cells and the expression of these values in understandable terms.

[38] C. Price-Jones, Janet M Vaughan, and Helen M Goddard, Haematological standards of healthy persons, in *J Pathol Bacteriol* (1935), 40(3), 503–19. Goddard's name had also been included in the case of a 1934 article.

[39] HMLC Minot, Minot to Vaughan, 11.12.1931.

[40] Wintrobe's two major works are M M Wintrobe, *Hematology, the Blossoming of a Science – A Story of Inspiration and Effort* (Philadelphia, Lea & Febiger 1985) and M M Wintrobe (Ed), *Blood, Pure and Eloquent: A Story of Discovery, of People, and of Ideas* (New York, McGraw-Hill, 1980).

[41] Vaughan, *The Anaemias* (1934), 121–24.

[42] Janet Vaughan (1936), Leuco-erythroblastic anaemia, in *J Pathol Bacteriol*, (1936), 42(3), 541–64; and J M Vaughan, and C V Harrison, Leucoerythroblastic anaemia and myelosclerosis, in *J Pathol Bacteriol* (March, 1939), 48, 339–52.

[43] Vaughan herself returned to the subject in papers written in 1981 and 1982 (see chapter 14 below), exploring the possible role of failure in the development and/or functioning of one or more stem cells in causing abnormalities of both blood and bone. Eleven disorders are now associated with a 'leukoerythroblastic reaction', ranging from primary myelofibrosis and acute and chronic myeloid leukaemia, to osteopetrosis. A Victor Hoffbrand and David P Steensma, *Hoffbrand's Essential Haematology* (Hoboken, NJ, Wiley-Blackwell, 2020), 356–57.

[44] The Pathological Society of Great Britain and Ireland focused on the science of pathology. The Association of Clinical Pathologists was closely linked to the British Medical Association, and concerned more with working conditions, standards and fee rates.

[45] The treatment of anaemias, *The Lancet*, (8.7.1933), 2(5732), 83–85. (HMLC Minot, Minot to Vaughan 9.8.1933 congratulating her on the leader.) A national network of public health laboratories was finally established during the Second World War.

[46] Janet Vaughan, Anaemias due to a deficiency of the principle in liver which is effective in the treatment of Addisonian pernicious anaemia, *Proc R Soc Med* (1934), 28(5), 15–18.

[47] VW Diary, 1.3.1935.

[48] HMLC Minot, note by Minot headed 'At Blue Hill Maine Aug 7 1934. To whom it may concern.'

[49] JA, 46 and 52.

[50] The following year, Dawson was prompted by Tom Kettle to seek additional Leverhulme funding of £150 to support Vaughan's ongoing research. (RCPL, MS 4960, Science Committee Minutes, 26.5.1935.)

[51] JA, 51.

[52] Charles Newman, A brief history of the Postgraduate Medical School, in *Postgraduate Medical Journal* (1966), 42(494), 738.

[53] AICL, transcript of Vaughan conversation with D K Hill, 10.11.1980. She gave the credit for this to her friendship with Kettle's wife. Naturally, her academic credentials would have been the main factor.

[54] HMLC Minot, Minot letters of 24.1.1935 and 29.1.1935.

[55] AICL (BPMS), figures provided by archivist Jessica Silver. E J King (1901–1962) was by the 1950s professor at the postgraduate medical school and dominant in his field, nationally and internationally. A A Miles (1904–1988) was professor of bacteriology at UCH from 1937, wartime director of the MRC wound infection unit at Birmingham, later deputy director of the National Institute for Medical Research, and from 1952 director of the Lister Institute of Preventive Medicine.

[56] AICL (BPMS), transcript of conversation between Ashley and Lady Miles and D K Hill, 10.12.1980. Pullinger was offered a senior assistantship at Hammersmith in 1936, but chose to go to South Africa instead. Howard Florey (1898–1968) moved to Oxford and, with a colleague there, would later win the Nobel Prize for his work on the development of penicillin.

[57] Ray Strachey, *Career Openings for Women: A Survey of Women's Employment and a Guide for Those Seeking Work* (London, Faber & Faber Ltd, 1935), 70.

[58] AICL (BPMS), transcript of Vaughan interview with D K Hill.

[59] AICL (BPMS), transcript of J G Scadding interview with D W Moss and D K Hill, 23.11.1978.

[60] JA, 60–61. This must have been Christmas 1936. Dr Maeve Kenny joined as first assistant in obstetrics and gynaecology in October that year. (AICL (BPMS), Governing Body Minutes 2.10.1936.)

[61] Wellcome Collection, PP/LEW/D.8/2, MRS. These papers give Vaughan as one of the first two female members. There is no mention of Dorothy Russell, but her *Munk's Roll* entry states that she was the first female member, in 1933: this is certainly credible. L J Rubenstein, Dorothy Stuart Russell, b.27 June 1895 d.19 October 1983, *Munk's Roll: The Lives of the Fellows of the Royal College of Physicians* (London, Royal College of Physicians, 1983), VII, 510.

[62] JA, 56.

[63] JPP, interview with Dorothy Vaughan.

[64] HMLC Minot, Minot letter of 12.9.1935.

[65] AICL (BPMS), BPMS Annual Report 1935–36.

[66] AICL (BPMS), Annual Report 1937–38. Parkes, when not yet so eminent, had attended one of Vaughan's rowdier parties in Taviton Street in the second half of the 1920s.

[67] AICL (BPMS), transcript of J G Scadding interview with D W Moss and D K Hill.

[68] AICL (BPMS), transcript of Miles interview with D K Hill.

[69] AICL (BPMS), transcript of Vaughan interview with D K Hill.

[70] AICL (BPMS), minutes of BPMS Governing Body meeting on 2.10.1936.

[71] R G Macfarlane (1907–1987). Clinical pathologist at the Radcliffe Infirmary, Oxford from 1940. He became a leading haematologist specialising in the management of haemophilia.

[72] AICL (BPMS), transcript of Miles interview with D K Hill.

[73] Professor Kettle: a rare personality, *The Times* (4.12.1936), 21.

[74] AICL (BPMS), transcript of Miles interview with D K Hill.

[75] JA, 61.

[76] Alastair Robb-Smith, *Life and Achievements of Professor Robert Gwyn Macfarlane FRS* (Royal Society of Medicine Services Ltd, 1993), 10.

[77] RCPL and Oxford Brookes University, Wellcome Medical Sciences Video Archive, Sir John Dacie FRS. Interview with Sir Christopher Booth, 7.3.1991.

[78] Sir John Dacie, Dame Janet Vaughan DBE, FRS, DM, FRCP, *BMJ* (30.1.1993), 306(6873), 326; and Dacie, *Munk's Roll* (1993), IX, 541.

[79] Standard blood counting apparatus (editorial), *The Lancet* (1936), 1(5867), 323.

[80] JA, 61.

[81] RAC, P.G.1.1 401A BMRC – Janet Vaughan (Heredity, Neurology) 1938–39 Box 6, folder 74. Also TNA, FD1/3194, correspondence from 22.10.1937 to 30.12.1939.

[82] RCPL, MS 4198–4205, College annals 1938–53. Mackay had been the first, in 1934.

[83] RCPL, MS 4683–4685, with Council Minutes of 12.10.1939, nominations from early 1939 by Drs P H Manson-Bahr (clinical tropical medicine, research including sprue); J G Greenfield (1884–1958, neuropathologist, President of Association of Clinical Pathologists 1934–37, pathologist to the National Hospital, Queen Square); N H Fairley (specialist in tropical medicine, FRS 1942); J H Dible; S C Dyke (1886–1975, director of pathology, Royal Hospital Wolverhampton, founder of Association of Clinical Pathologists, 1927, president 1937–43); E N Allott (1889–1980, biochemist, director of Group Laboratory, Lewisham Hospital); R J V Pulvertaft (director of Clinical Laboratories at Westminster Hospital, president of Association of Clinical Pathologists, 1953).

[84] The first part of the citation supporting Vaughan's election to the Royal Society in 1979 reads: 'One of the first laboratory-based haematologists, she was for 15 years a pioneer in integrating clinical and pathological observations with blood pictures and measurements of blood cells and author of *The Anaemias* – 2 editions, one of the first specialised books on blood diseases in the English language.'

[85] Dacie, *Munk's Roll* (1993), IX, 541.

CHAPTER 5

Private life and public concerns
1930–39

Life in Gordon Square

Vaughan tried always to look to the future rather than the past, but in old age the thought of her life in the 1930s gave her pleasure. Her memoir speaks of the joy of her marriage, of four happy years of investigation in the Bernhard Baron Institute, the rich life she and Gourlay had with friends and on holidays, further enriched by the birth of Mary and then Cilla.[1] She also spoke in later years of how interesting and enjoyable her work at the London Hospital was, what a happy five years she had at Hammersmith, and what enormous fun (a favourite word) she had there.[2] Her career progressed in ways she could not have predicted; and her personal life, in the flat on two floors above the Wayfarers Travel Agency in Gordon Square, was happy and fulfilling.

Friends and family agreed that she and Gourlay made an odd but well-matched and very happy couple. Relations spoke of David as being large and untidy, with egg stains on his tie and cigarette ash on his clothes, often slouching in a chair and looking indolent; but thought this gave a misleading impression. Vaughan's sister-in-law Dorothy, who married her brother Halford in July 1933, said that she usually led except where travel was concerned. Gourlay, however, 'had a wonderful way of keeping his end up very quietly'. In Dorothy's view, there was no question of Vaughan dominating: the marriage was a partnership. And she liked being simply 'Mrs Gourlay' on their annual holidays, which they 'so enjoyed', usually walking in the Swiss and Italian mountains.[3]

Each worked as hard as the other, sharing a sense of dedication to their chosen pursuits. At the travel agency, Gourlay specialised in advising clients, including schools, on holidays tailored to meet their needs. Vaughan often quoted him in her memoir, and one of her 'he always saids' was that they 'knew at any time where any of the intellectuals and academics might be in Europe and who they were with'. He travelled frequently to agree and renew contracts and negotiate fares and accommodation prices. In summer, the busiest time, he often worked until late at night alongside his staff; and those same staff were regarded as 'family', coming every year to a Christmas party given by the Gourlays.[4] Frankie Birrell and his partner Raymond Mortimer were fast friends, and Birrell was a director of the Wayfarers from its inception as a company in 1931.

In the early years of the decade especially, there was still some time to relax. The Gordon Square garden featured in Vaughan's memory as a place where babies were left in prams under cat nets, and, when older, played on the grass and expected ice cream when the Wall's van bell rang out. In the evenings she remembered talking with small groups, typically including Roger Fry, Clive Bell, Leonard and Virginia Woolf and Julian Bell. She liked to relate how, the first time she pushed Mary in her pram in Gordon Square, the psychoanalysts James Strachey and Adrian Stephen gave her separate and contradictory advice about whether the baby should have a rattle. Understandably, she decided to use her own common sense for this momentous decision. Gourlay chaired the garden committee for some years: 'a difficult body', like all such committees, in her experience.[5]

Vaughan and Gourlay both enjoyed entertaining, and seeing friends old and new, who provided a wide range of experience and news. Vaughan's cousin Kitty was now married to the journalist and publisher Douglas West; while Maisie Somerville, having married the journalist Pete Brown in July 1928, and had a son in 1929, was still increasing her responsibilities in schools broadcasting in the BBC. Although valued enough to be granted generous paid maternity leave, she had nonetheless to fight every step of the way to win a salary comparable to that of male colleagues.[6]

Vaughan's friendship with Thilo Bugnion, now married to Donald Hunter, had of course contributed to her gaining the position at the Bernhard Baron Institute, researching with Hunter and Turnbull. An old school friend, Molly Hoyle, was head of a school in Exeter from 1930, while Mary Glover, a classicist friend from Somerville days, was a don at St Hugh's College in Oxford. Cicely Williams was home from the Gold Coast in the early 1930s, writing her DM thesis on her identification of kwashiorkor as a protein deficiency disease and winning entry to the RCP on the basis of her published work. Meanwhile Vaughan's childhood friend Ursula Bradshaw had married the artist Gilbert Spencer (brother of Stanley) in December 1930, and she became godmother to their daughter in 1936.

Dora Gordine went to Singapore in 1930 with a commission for a number of sculptures. She came back to London on leave in 1932–33, when she was captured in a family photograph holding baby Mary. She returned finally in 1935 with Richard Hare, an ex-Rugby School pupil whom she had met through Vaughan.[7] The two were married in 1936, and the Gourlays became regular visitors at their house in Kingston-upon-Thames, purpose-built as both home and sculptor's studio. Another close friend from the 1920s was Daryll Forde, by then professor of geography and anthropology at Aberystwyth, with tales of field trips in Mexico, Arizona and Nigeria.[8] The flat in Gordon Square rang with loud talk and laughter when friends came to visit, and Vaughan, with her endless curiosity, was fascinated by their varied experiences and knowledge.[9]

Family ties remained strong. Will Vaughan retired in 1931, and from 1932 he and his wife Betty lived at the Manor House, Princes Risborough, as tenants of the National Trust. Will served on a number of educational bodies including, through Somerville's influence, the Central Council for School Broadcasting. Halford's health was an ongoing worry. He had his second breakdown around 1931, before getting engaged to Dorothy, and a third, very bad one in 1941. Fortunately, Dorothy was resilient as well as loyal, and Vaughan recognised these qualities with gratitude, doing what she could to help her in times of crisis.[10] Her brother David and wife Norah had two sons in the early 1930s, when they were living in Hertfordshire. There were visits to and from both brothers, and Vaughan and her children enjoyed shared holidays with Dorothy and her two elder daughters, including a beach holiday at Bexhill-on-Sea in 1938.

For the Gourlays, the birth of their children – Mary in November 1932 and Cilla in August 1935 – brought joy. They employed a cook/housekeeper to prepare meals and look after the flat, while a nursery maid, who was, in true Bloomsbury style, a girl from the country rather than a trained nanny, looked after the children.[11] Vaughan's letters to Minot, who had a young son of his own in these years, detailed Mary and Cilla's progress, and the family enjoyed their time together on weekends and annual holidays. Childhood illnesses could be a worry. It was probably in the early summer of 1934, when Mary was about 18 months old and Vaughan was applying for the Leverhulme Scholarship, that she became very anxious about Mary and sent her to stay with Halford and Dorothy for a few weeks. 'She was very intent. And I think at that time she was bidding ... And she was having a terrific battle ... as a woman. I think all her energies were focused on that.'[12] Again in May 1936, when Mary had an ear infection, baby Cilla was sent to stay with Gourlay's mother and sister for a week or two, out of harm's way.[13]

There was one great sadness in these years. Gourlay's friend Frankie Birrell was noted for his sparkling intelligence and immense sense of humour, combined with a wide knowledge of European history and literature; but it was his innocence that made Frankie's friends love him.[14] No entrepreneur, he regarded selling books at a higher price than he had bought them for as cheating. Frances Partridge found him one of the sweetest natured men she had ever met: 'a very "unsoigné" dresser, usually wearing a good suit well-covered in spots and drips, and a very wide black hat with the bow worn in front ... underneath which was a wide, irrepressible grin'.[15]

Birrell developed a brain tumour in the second half of 1933. An operation in September that year left him semi-paralysed, and when the tumour returned the following year, nothing more could be done. He died in January 1935. Vaughan and Gourlay had both loved him. Their second daughter was named Frances in memory of him, although always known by the shortening (Cilla) of her second name, Priscilla. Birrell's partner, the journalist Raymond Mortimer, succeeded him as a director of the Wayfarers, and as such was a loyal supporter of Gourlay, and later Vaughan, until the late 1960s.

The values in their home were those of respect for people as individuals, unselfishness, duty, and the life of the mind rather than the pursuit of material things. Each Christmas, once they were old enough, Mary and Cilla were allowed to choose one present from all those they had been given. The rest they took to Hammersmith

Hospital, to give to the sick children there. At that time, these children would necessarily come from poorer families, known by medical workers as 'the hospital class'. Mary only remembered resenting this once, when they had to keep a large slide they had been given, rather than the 'beautiful green velvet ball' which she dearly wanted. The message was that it was wrong to keep hold of more money and possessions than they actually needed. 'People come first', their mother would say. If one of the children should ever grumble about the want of something, their father would tell them to look at what they had already. Vaughan would urge them just to want knowledge.[16]

By 1937, when Mary was four and Cilla two, Gourlay was 47. He was not the kind of father who would play boisterous games with small children; but he was consistently calm, loving and comforting, especially when Vaughan lost her temper over some breakage or other mishap.[17] While the values of the home might be in some ways austere, the atmosphere was not. Both parents loved good food and wine, beautiful objects and pictures, gardens and the countryside. The children remembered them constantly discussing the books they were reading, and holidays, as well as talking of the Wayfarers staff and other friends.

Vaughan had plenty of energy and could be an enchanting parent. Each evening, she would run up the stairs, 'terribly excited', shouting 'Cooee' to the children. When she came back from work on Saturday lunchtimes, they would eat together and then she would take them to choose a cake each at a shop nearby. She played imaginative games (and later charades) with them, and when she read poetry 'her eyes would flash and she would be the person'. On holiday, she loved swimming, making sand castles and climbing trees, shouting 'Sixpence if you can climb higher!'[18]

The Gourlay side of the family was not neglected, but Vaughan had no rapport with her mother-in-law, 'Granny Gourlay'. After Mary was born, Granny Gourlay came up to London to see her; but when she went to pick the baby up, Vaughan deeply offended her by saying it was 'not the right time'.[19] Gourlay's mother, a strong woman herself, did not forget such things. David usually visited her on his own, but the children spent two weeks with her and his elder sister Nellie each summer as soon as they were old

109

enough. His younger brother Bertie, with his wife Joan and their two young sons, would come to lunch in Gordon Square at the weekend from time to time, and all would walk in Regent's Park with the prams afterwards. Joan remembered that Vaughan had no concern for appearances on such occasions. She was liable to wear a jumper turned inside out, and would simply 'plonk' a hat on her head before setting off.

In Bloomsbury, the Gourlays were part of the intellectual left-wing world. One group of relations who were also part of that world were Vaughan's cousins, Amabel and John Strachey. The St Loe Strachey family had long lived at Newlands Corner, near Guildford in Surrey, and the Gourlays often spent weekends with St Loe's widow Amy (known as Gigi) at her thatched house there, meeting many interesting people among Gigi's huge circle of friends, and those of her children. Vaughan had first got to know John at Oxford, and admired his eloquence on political subjects. Having initially been a friend and ally of Oswald Mosley, by the mid-1930s he was on the extreme left of the Labour Party, publishing Marxist books for Gollancz; and Jennie Lee and Aneurin (Nye) Bevan were among the friends who came with him to Newlands Corner.

Gourlay described Amy as 'one of the last of the great Victorian ladies', and 'the only person who really knew how to make and pour out afternoon tea'. Vaughan called her a great listener, and 'propper-upper' of those in difficulty. The actors Charles Laughton and Elsa Lanchester were friends of Amabel and her architect husband Clough Williams-Ellis, and from about 1930 took over their country house on the downs near Amy. Towards the end of 1933, they also moved into the upper floors of 34 Gordon Square, next door to the Gourlays. The last play in a season Charles was doing at the Old Vic was *Macbeth*, and he was very anxious about the part. But 'Amy ... took us all to supper at Etoile in Charlotte Street, after the first performance and propped up Charles'.[20]

It was at a party early in 1935 that Vaughan told Virginia Woolf the story of the ending of her Beit funding the previous summer, and the difficulties she faced as a woman trying to do research work. Woolf found their discussion fruitful for the book she was working on, the feminist tract *Three Guineas*, published in 1938. Vaughan's correspondence, and conversations like this, reveal the

110

resentment she felt, but had to repress in her professional life, about the barriers she encountered as a woman. She was a doer rather than a theorist, but a doer who owned first editions of all Woolf's books, including *Three Guineas*. Many of the ideas there expressed were embodied in her own life, including the importance of women earning their own living so as to be independent; scepticism about patriarchy, and the conventions and status symbols that signify the dominance of one group over another; rejection of the idea of earning more money than one actually needs; and the importance of helping other women to employment suited to their talents.

The Socialist Medical Association and the Committee against Malnutrition

During these years Vaughan was increasingly drawn into public causes. The Wall Street crash happened while she was in the United States, in October 1929. Few believed this was anything worse than a cyclical economic downturn until well into the following year, when the financial system again collapsed, triggering the Great Depression. In August 1931 the Labour government fell, the party split, and the National Government took over in Britain, instituting an austerity programme. The general election that year resulted in a sweeping win for the coalition, which was dominated by the Conservatives and faced by a residue of only 46 Labour Party members in Parliament. Unemployment reached a peak in late 1932, with a slow and incomplete recovery in the following years.

Vaughan's outpatient clinics, first at the London Hospital and then at Hammersmith, were very busy with mostly poor patients. She prescribed iron and extra milk to women (the majority were female) suffering from anaemia, but knew that these were mere temporary sticking plasters in the absence of proper financial support. All too often, they would ask her not to prescribe any more of the medicine she had given them, because it made them hungry for food they could not afford to buy.[21]

She made no secret of her left-wing views, but was never a party-political activist. This may have been partly self-protection: it did not do for a woman in particular to be too closely aligned with a political party, or to be an overt feminist, if she wished to succeed in the still overwhelmingly male, conservative world of medicine. Vaughan seems not to have referred publicly to her membership of the Socialist Medical Association, founded in September 1930; but she was certainly a member by 1947, and always sympathised with its aims.[22] A number of her friends and colleagues, including her former fellow-student Philip Hart, now an assistant to the medical unit in UCH, were active within it. The Association's programme included a socialised medical service both preventive and curative, free and open to all. It was affiliated to the Labour Party from 1931.

Vaughan also became an associate of the Committee against Malnutrition, founded in 1934 by a group of scientists and doctors. In response to growing evidence of undernourishment among the families of unemployed and low paid workers, they aimed to publicise the facts about proper nutritional standards, and make them available to anyone, of whatever political persuasion, who wanted change. As Vaughan said, 'between us we produced a cyclostyled bulletin for general circulation called "The Bulletin against Malnutrition"'.[23] They also held meetings throughout the country, and supported direct campaigns to raise food standards – for instance, for free school meals for the children of unemployed workers, free milk at clinics, and adequate public assistance. Importantly, they publicised the paediatrician Helen Mackay's work on the anaemias of infancy, which she had shown to be largely owing to a lack of iron.

Vaughan wrote on the anaemias and their links to nutrition in the Committee's publications, and lectured at public meetings. She also helped to publicise the Committee's message in *The Lancet*: the editorial in November 1934, on the occasion of Minot and his colleagues' Nobel prize, stressed their contribution to 'knowledge of the extreme importance of an adequate and varied diet in maintaining the general health of the community', concluding that it remained for the 'statesmen of the world to apply such information to the organisation of society'.[24] Other editorials and leaders pursued the same theme.[25]

The 1936 edition of *The Anaemias* quoted Mackay's work with pregnant and nursing mothers, their babies and young children; and also the results of population surveys in English industrial areas and of the unemployed in Scotland, published in 1933 and 1935. These made clear the link between iron-deficient anaemia in all these groups, as well as generally in women aged 15 to 44, and the poverty which was the primary cause of their iron-deficient diet. Vaughan stated simply that the prevention and treatment of such conditions were 'largely economic problems'.[26] If people could afford to eat a diet which would maintain health and fitness, there would be no need for iron supplements.

The Committee's work supported lobbying and campaign groups such as the Children's Minimum Committee, chaired by the independent MP Eleanor Rathbone. More ammunition came in March 1936 from John Boyd Orr's *Food, Health and Income*, which used statistical methods to show that nearly half the population earned too little to afford an optimum diet.[27] Public pressure on local authorities led to increased provision of free milk and meals, and that on central government led to some expansion of relevant local authority powers, and a small improvement in assistance scales for children of the unemployed. Ultimately the exigencies of wartime enabled the Committee's ideas to win through, in the form of a national food policy based on established nutritional needs. That policy, however, was easier to implement because, after so much public discussion and reporting, many among the general public were used to the idea of calories, essential vitamins and protein requirements.

Not surprisingly, there was cross-membership between the Committee against Malnutrition and the Socialist Medical Association. The London County Council Senior Medical Officer Dr Stella Churchill, the secretary of the London Branch of the Socialist Medical Association Dr Samuel Leff, Professor Marrack of the London Hospital and Frederick Le Gros Clark, a blind writer and left-wing activist, were key members of both. The two organisations co-operated on distribution of publications, and co-ordinated other activities so as to complement each other's work.[28] Vaughan was part of a network of left-wing doctors which, unlike more traditional medical networks, was open to and included many women.[29]

Spanish Medical Aid, 1936–39

Far different in kind and scale was her work for Spanish Medical Aid. This huge mass movement was linked closely to a growing abhorrence of fascism, particularly at first on the left of British politics. Like all in her close social circle, Vaughan was appalled by events in Germany after Hitler came to power in 1933. She was well-informed. Her cousin Amabel Williams-Ellis went as a representative of the PEN Club to witness the trial in September 1933 of those accused of starting the Reichstag fire. Vaughan herself met many of the refugee German doctors and scientists who came to London; and Ernest and Netta Franklin were prominent in the Jewish-led organisations who were helping Jewish refugees.[30] Gourlay's contacts in and journeys to Germany and Italy would have given him additional insights into what was happening there.

The international situation grew threatening as Hitler's policies drove German rearmament, and in this and other ways broke the terms of the Versailles Treaty which had ended the First World War. Italy, under the fascist dictator Mussolini, invaded Abyssinia in 1935, and had taken it over by May 1936. Both events demonstrated the ineffectiveness of the League of Nations, and the lack of will and/or ability on the part of France and Great Britain to enforce the rule of international law.

By 1936, the mood on the liberal and socialist left was one of near-despair about the apparently unstoppable rise of fascism. Labour's support for pacifism and the League of Nations was shared by many of all political persuasions; but its well-founded fears of the Soviet Communist version of totalitarianism prevented it from forming the kind of 'popular front' alliance with those on its left which some advocated. Meanwhile the Communist Party had made gains among the young and the left wing, in terms of sympathy as well as actual membership, by appearing to offer a more radical and determined opposition to fascism. The Socialist Medical Association changed its constitution in 1936 to allow full membership to Communist Party members within the medical or allied professions (rather than, as before, only doctors who accepted the rules of the Labour Party).

This was the background when the Spanish Civil War broke out in July 1936, precipitated by an army-led rebellion against the Popular Front government elected in Spain the previous February. The fascist governments in Italy and Germany were soon covertly supporting the rebels. Soviet Russia, also covertly, gave help – albeit less effectual – to the government, or Republican side. British government observance, supported by the Labour Party, of the policy of non-intervention which others were flouting caused further dismay on the political left. As Vaughan said, the Spanish Civil War 'became for many of us the great opportunity to take a stand against Fascism'.[31]

The first, national, Spanish Medical Aid Committee was set up in August 1936, under the auspices of the Socialist Medical Association. Most of its members were non-Communists, but Isabel Brown, who had inspired its formation and ensured her own membership, was a leading Party activist.[32] She and her Communist allies, who soon included Frederick Le Gros Clark (also secretary to the Committee against Malnutrition), tended to be the most committed and efficient members and fundraisers.[33] Initially, the aid was to be given to the wounded of both sides in the civil war, but sympathy and aid increasingly focused on the Republicans as the legitimate government and the side most in need of help.

In September 1936, Vaughan and others set up the Holborn and West London Committee for Spanish Medical Aid. Despite having two small children and her demanding job at Hammersmith, she became chair of one of the most effective of the many local committees across London and throughout the country. It included representatives of political parties, the Holborn Peace Council and trades unions as well as scientists, doctors, artists and professional workers. The publisher and typographer Francis Meynell was one, and the committee soon took on most of the publishing work for Spanish Medical Aid, producing pamphlets and Christmas cards, and, from May 1938, the monthly bulletin of the central Committee. The pamphlet 'Spain and Us', published in November 1936, couched its appeal in vivid terms: 'Give – give till it hurts. It will not hurt so much as a bullet in the belly.'[34]

Fund-raising methods included house to house canvasses, exhibitions of Spanish art and culture and written appeals to individuals. Artists including Vanessa Bell and Duncan Grant, and Claude Rogers, who would later paint Vaughan's portrait for Somerville College, gave pictures to be auctioned. In October 1936, Vanessa was working on posters for a fund-raising meeting: 'Janet Vaughan asked me and Duncan to do some – and Q[uentin] and A[ngelica] have done one each too'. By November, Vaughan was seeking her help with a show of Spanish art.[35] In less than four months, by Christmas 1936, the Holborn committee raised more than £684, the equivalent of £49,440 in 2021.[36] In early summer 1937, when a typhoid epidemic threatened in Spain, it enabled the national committee to send laboratory equipment costing over £300, and five borrowed microscopes obtained by Vaughan. A colleague at the Postgraduate School, Dr Maeve Kenny, went to Spain to help set up the equipment.[37]

In May 1937, the Holborn committee published *Spain: The Child and the War*, with a preface by Leah Manning, the ex-teacher and ex-Labour MP who at this time brought 4,000 Basque refugee children to England. The pamphlet emphasised the privations child refugees would face in the coming winter. The Committee against Malnutrition's pamphlet, *Children in Spain Today*, also warned of possible famine among over one million refugees in the Republican-held area. The Holborn committee's next campaign culminated in a 'Spain Week' in January 1938, when public speakers included Clough Williams-Ellis on Spanish Architecture, and Vaughan on the work of the British medical unit in Spain. The £750 raised paid for three ambulances for Barcelona.[38]

The death of Julian Bell in Spain, in July 1937, touched Vaughan personally. He had lived at 23 Taviton Street in 1934–35 before his departure for a university post in China, and became very friendly with the Gourlays. In spring 1937, his decision to volunteer as an ambulance driver for Spanish Medical Aid, rather than as a soldier, was intended to allay his mother Vanessa's anxiety. After his death, Vaughan gave what practical help she could. She gave Philip Hart's contact details to Leonard Woolf, saying that Hart had seen Julian in hospital, and could speak of the high regard felt for him by all who had met and worked with him.[39] A Holborn committee member arranged for two of the doctors who had treated Julian to meet Vanessa. Vaughan showed empathy, too, in suggesting that Vanessa design a Christmas card that year to be sold in aid of Spanish Medical Aid. This seems to have been therapeutic, since Vanessa offered to manage the reproduction process after completing the design.[40]

Alongside all this, while work at the postgraduate school was increasing, Vaughan was a member of the national Spanish Medical

Aid Committee from spring 1937. The Committee chair was Dr Hyacinth Morgan, prominent in the Socialist Medical Association and Medical Adviser to the TUC. He had to fight hard to ensure that the committee was controlled by its more moderate members, as opposed to the Communists and fellow-travellers. During 1937 there were not only tensions between these groups, but personal antagonisms, particularly between Leah Manning as honorary secretary and George Jeger as organising secretary, which threatened the effectiveness of the aid work. Morgan's solution that autumn was to appoint a sub-committee, chaired by Vaughan, to review the administrative arrangements. Their report enabled him to steer decisions on action to improve efficiency. Vaughan was appointed to the reconstituted organisation sub-committee, and also vetted volunteer medical staff.[41]

Her own stress must have been mounting, however. There can have been few evenings, from late 1936 to spring 1938, when she was not working on Spanish Medical Aid business: the central committee and its sub-committees met weekly, and the Holborn committee had office hours in the evening as well as the day. She had effective members to whom she could delegate, but eventually she overtaxed herself. Her resignation letter to Morgan in April 1938 blamed a septic throat, and doctor's orders that she do no work apart from the day job for three months. She had already resigned as chair of the Holborn committee.

Dr Morgan sent a personal as well as an official reply, saying how sorry he was that she of all people should resign. 'You are one … I can confidently consult in difficult matters arising in the Committee's work, & I shall deeply regret … your departure. Had you stated any other reason except health, I would have asked you strongly to reconsider.' Vaughan's reply concluded: 'I hope I have learned something from you in the last year of the value of a conciliatory chairman.'[42] She did indeed learn much from her experience with Spanish Medical Aid, about organisation, fund-raising, publicity and the management of volunteers, as well as the handling of committees: knowledge soon to be used in meeting British wartime needs.

An unexpected personal blow in February 1938 must have helped precipitate these resignations. Her father and his wife Betty had gone to India with delegates to the Indian Science Congress late the previous year. In December, while visiting the Taj Mahal by moonlight, he slipped and broke his thigh. His next few weeks in hospital were a time of continuous worry for the family at home in England. Finally gangrene developed, his leg had to be amputated, and he died on 4 February of shock and pneumonia. He was buried at Agra.

Vaughan organised the memorial service held at St Martin-in-the-Fields two weeks later, dealing with all the arrangements from the music to readings and hymns and, of course, the guest list. This was a big occasion. The composer Ralph Vaughan Williams, married to Will Vaughan's cousin Adeline Fisher, played the organ; and, thanks to Will's chairmanship of the Central Council for School Broadcasting, the BBC Singers sang. As her sister-in-law Dorothy said, it was accepted in the family that Vaughan would take the lead in such things.[43]

She had always loved and respected her father despite his domineering ways, but in the summer of 1938, when she sorted through her mother's papers, her attitude changed. Returning some of Vanessa's letters, including one sealed packet, she wrote:

> She left so much that was tragic – I only hope this is nothing to distress you. I burnt all her unhappiness yesterday ... I should never be able to publish it while there are so many people living who knew W.W.V. & ... there is so much stirring in the world today that perhaps we had all best to try & go forward instead of grieving over the past. She ... would have been so excited & alive to this rising up ... against all the things she hated most – snobs & shams & war ... I often think of you because I hear people back from Spain talking of Julian always with the same admiring affection.[44]

Vanessa's reply shocked her, and she responded after returning from her holiday with Dorothy and her family:

> I have been looking after a houseful of babies at the seaside & somehow consecutive thought is then impossible. I never knew you had quarrelled with mother ... I always understood that ... she never saw you & Virginia in later years ... because of the absurd attitude of my father. He destroyed ... all her friendships in some subtle way – cut her off from all the people she had loved ... It has always seemed so tragic that she died just at the time when I was old enough to have

> … escaped from the domination of W.W.V. & could … have given her back her old freedom.

She felt that Madge's love for Vanessa was expressed in 'the sense of magic she was able to weave about you for us children'. One of her most vivid memories was of Madge taking her to see Vanessa in Gordon Square 'her excitement & my own picture of you & your house & the view out of the long windows on to … the square'.[45] Always after this time, Vaughan's love for her father was mixed with anger and bitterness because she blamed him for the depression and misery her mother had expressed in her writing.

This letter to Vanessa also revealed how much her social life was constrained by her many commitments, as well as referring back to the difficulties she had discussed with Virginia at the party three years before:

> The last 5 years with work & babies I have seen no-one – even now professional women seem to have to do twice as much work as the average man to be recognized as worthy of existence … The barrier you have felt is I am sure partly my utter inaccessibility except to the people who just walk in – as Julian sometimes used to do – but you will always … be one of the real people in my life.

After the spring of 1938, she limited her Spanish Medical Aid activities, as a 'Vice-President', to speaking at meetings, signing public appeals and joining deputations. Her concern for individuals shines through in the help she gave in summer 1938 to a sick nurse, Penny Phelps, just back from Spain and being treated in Hammersmith Hospital. Having come across her by chance, Vaughan made sure she had a change of nightgown, a dressing gown and toiletries before reporting her plight and medical prognosis to Hyacinth Morgan and the national committee.[46]

Barcelona fell to the Nationalists on 12 February 1939, marking the effective end of the Republic. In London the central committee had decided on 1 February to form a new medical unit to establish emergency dressing stations and relief posts in Spain, but changed their minds a week later because of the deteriorating situation. It appears, however, that Vaughan meant to go with that unit. She remembered dealing with passport and visa formalities: 'I felt it my duty to go to Spain … I'm always one who likes to do things rather than to theorise ... and sitting in a committee trying to run affairs from afar wasn't the sort of thing I cared for doing really.'[47] An ironic statement in light of Vaughan's then-current and later career, but it is borne out by her declared favourite activities, namely research and setting up from scratch a new regional hospital board after the war.

It was this sense of frustration, as well as respect for the quality and determination of her Communist colleagues, that led her to join the Communist Party in 1938. Those colleagues included her deputy on the Holborn committee, Eva Reckitt, as well as Isabel Brown on the national committee. Vaughan was never active in the Party, and let her membership lapse a few years later – she thought in 1941.[48] But the publicity she attracted as a left-wing activist probably explains her inclusion on the Nazi 'black list' of 2,820 British subjects and European exiles who were to be arrested in the event of a successful invasion of Britain.[49]

In later years, she spoke of walking in poster processions, speaking on soap boxes at street corners and in public meetings, and selling 'many treasured possessions' in aid of the Basque children. Also of committee meetings 'night after night in a small attic room up many dark stairs'. Her sacrifice was shared by her family. Gourlay supported her fully, though he did grumble about those late-night committee meetings. And he shared Vaughan's ruthless attitude to personal possessions. The children were less able to understand. Mary, aged four and a half in May 1937, remembers standing alongside her mother's soap boxes on Saturday afternoons. She also has a vivid memory of returning one day to find the flat dark and empty, the car and much of the furniture sold. And of her mother's 'absolute delight' because of the amount of money she had raised.[50]

Another organisation with members in common with the Socialist Medical Association was the Medical Peace Campaign, set up in 1936 by a small group of doctors led by the pacifist and politically left-wing John Ryle, then Regius professor of physic at the University of Cambridge. This group emphasised the moral duty of doctors to preserve life, and focused on strengthening the League of Nations as a means of preventing war.[51] Vaughan soon joined its 'Advisory Council'.[52] She never mentioned having been a pacifist, but would have supported these general aims at least. The Campaign's first public meeting, in November 1936, discussed aerial warfare and the inadequacy of current and known possible defences against bombing, and against poison gas such as Italy had used in Abyssinia.[53] Efforts to persuade the BMA to set up a scientific inquiry into such defences failed. In February 1939, Ryle said the Medical Peace Campaign was now making plans for dealing with mass casualties and feeding large numbers of refugees. Vaughan spoke on this last point, citing the Committee against Malnutrition's publication on the food situation in Spain.[54] When war came, Ryle and most of his allies renounced pacifism in order to fight fascism.

Vaughan's habit of packing multiple and usually physically and mentally demanding activities into every day was now well established. She achieved it by ruthlessly compartmentalising her time, delegating where possible, and operating at speed. When impatient and frustrated, she could be quick tempered and sarcastic; but this repressed frustration showed itself most often at home. Usually it was the live-in cook/housekeeper and nurse who provoked her wrath. Her daughter Mary remembered frequent rows and tears, and certainly few of these unfortunates stayed more than a year or two. The longest serving was Ivy Sheales, who arrived as the children's nurse in 1937 and was to be employed as such until the end of 1943.[55]

As the children grew older, they noticed that it was unusual for a mother, as in their family, to drive the car and carve the Sunday joint.[56] Vaughan's impatience was manifest in her driving, and stories about it multiplied over the years. One colleague at Hammersmith usually refused her offers of a lift home. One day, however, she picked him up from the bus stop. All went well until they reached a crossroads on Harley Street. After running into a car and bouncing off, she said: 'He didn't stop so why should I?' Those venturing to be driven by her needed strong nerves.[57] Her saving graces were her sense of humour, her enjoyment of friends and all kinds of visual and literary beauty, her enthusiasm for and belief in the value of all she did, and a fundamental optimism about the trajectory of human affairs. In her research, in the campaigns against poverty and malnutrition, and in the struggle against fascism, she believed that, ultimately, the true, the right and the good would triumph.

Why did she take on so much, when she had, professionally, already achieved so much, and could expect higher honours in return for continued hard work in medical research and teaching alone? The answer has to lie in the Christian ethics absorbed in her childhood, which prioritised selfless service to others over personal ambition for power or wealth. She never forgot her resolve as a teenager to use the experience and status gained through a medical career to try to combat poverty and social injustice. The more she took on, the more her natural leadership qualities were developed and, with them, her confidence in her own ability. One result was that she repeatedly drove herself to her own physical limits. Her occasional breakdowns in health usually happened at times of extreme stress.

Vaughan said in old age that the most important political event of her life had been the Spanish Civil War. This was for her the defining time for her commitment to fighting fascism as well as to socialist solutions to the problems of health and other inequalities. Long after 1939 she continued to donate money for the support of dissidents in Franco's Spain and to the International Brigades Association, and in 1984 bought a pendant made by a member of the Association from a stone picked up on the Jarama battlefield in Spain. By late 1938, a general European war, of non-fascists against fascists, was widely regarded as imminent. Vaughan would soon play a significant part in the medical planning for this.

Endnotes

[1] JA, 50–55.

[2] AICL (BPMS), transcript of D K Hill interview with Dame Janet Vaughan.

[3] JA, 49. Also JPP, interview with Dorothy Vaughan.

[4] JPP, interview with Potter, a retired employee of the Agency, 1994; Also JA, 54.

[5] JA, 54–57.

[6] See Murphy, *Behind the Wireless* for the full story.

[7] The Hon Richard Hare was a younger son of the Earl of Listowel, working in the Diplomatic Service until 1931, when a legacy enabled him to resign. He later became an academic specialising in Russian literature. See also JA, 39.

[8] Daryll Forde (1902–1973). From 1930 to 1945, he was Gregynog professor of geography and anthropology, University of Wales Aberystwyth.

[9] Interview with Mary Park.

[10] JPP, interview with Dorothy Vaughan.

[11] Others with this approach included the Clive Bells and the Keynes family.

[12] JPP, interview with Dorothy Vaughan.

[13] JPP, interview with Joan Gourlay.

[14] David Garnett, *The Flowers of the Forest* (London, Chatto & Windus, 1955), 55.

[15] Frances Partridge, *Memories* (London, Victor Gollancz Ltd, 1981), 75.

[16] Interview with Mary Park, 22.3.2006. The velvet ball was a present at Christmas 1938 from the family of Dr Van de Vries, a Dutch pathologist working in Vaughan's laboratory, whose two daughters were friends of Mary and Cilla. His experience of helping to group potential blood donors in 1939 proved useful when he had to set up the Dutch army's transfusion service that November. The family were Jewish, and Vaughan pleaded with him not to take his wife and daughters back to the Netherlands. He survived the war, but they died in Auschwitz. (JA, 68.)

[17] Interview with Mary Park, 22.3.2006.

[18] Interviews with Mary Bennett and Mary Park. Mary Bennett, whose father H A L Fisher was Vaughan's godfather, used to see Vaughan when she herself was a child, and remembered the imaginative games.

[19] JPP, interview with Joan Gourlay.

[20] JA, 58.

[21] JA, 52.

[22] TNA, MH 90/9, SMA letter of 12.3.1947 to Ministry of Health refers to Vaughan as a member.

[23] JA, 53.

[24] Annotations, The Nobel prizewinners, *The Lancet* (1934), 2(5801), 996–97.

[25] For example, an editorial in February 1935 praised a Committee pamphlet on the optimum diet, aimed at housewives.

[26] Vaughan, *The Anaemias* (1936), 47. See also 48, 61–62, 64–71.

[27] The publishing company which produced the book was that of the left-wing Conservative MP Harold Macmillan.

[28] HHC, DSM2/5, letters between Committee against Malnutrition and Socialist Medical Association staff, 1934–36.

[29] Known women participants included, in the Committee against Malnutrition: Dr Stella Churchill, Dr Helen Jardine, UCH paediatrician Dr Audrey Russell, Miss Marjorie Green (who spoke on 3.3.1938); and in the Socialist Medical Association: Dr Stella Churchill, Miss Esther Rickards FRCS, Dr Caroline Maule, Drs Elizabeth Jacobs (GP, treasurer of Marylebone Spanish Medical Aid Committee and prospective Labour candidate for Marylebone, 1938) and Elizabeth Bunbury (psychologist and honorary joint secretary of the Camberwell Aid Spain (Refugee)

Committee, also propaganda secretary of Socialist Medical Association, 1938); and Dr Joan McMichael (anaesthetist and Communist Party member).

[30] HMLC Minot, Minot letter of 21.10.1933 responds to her information about German refugees in London. See also Monk Gibbon, *Netta* (London, Routledge and Kegan Paul, 1960), 177–80.

[31] JA, 62.

[32] IWMSA 844, interview with Isabel Brown.

[33] For background, see Tom Buchanan, *The Impact of the Spanish Civil War on Britain* (Liverpool, Liverpool University Press, 2007); and *Britain and the Spanish Civil War* (London, Cambridge University Press, 1997).

[34] MML, 'Spain and Us', YC08/SPA.

[35] Tate Archive, TGA 9311/62 and/66, Vanessa Bell to Julian Bell, 4.10.1936 and 1.11.1936.

[36] www.measuringworth.com, using purchasing power calculator, accessed 21.11.2023.

[37] MML, YC08/MED; also MRCUW, TUC Archive, MSS 292/946/32/37, letter 16.10.1939 from Dr Morgan to Vaughan refers to microscopes. OBL, Oxford, MS.Addison.dep.c.207, minutes of central committee meeting, 15.6.1937.

[38] MML, YF 172 (bound pamphlets), 29/B and 29/C/5.

[39] USSCK, Leonard Woolf papers, SxMs13/3/A/1/U/3, Vaughan to Woolf, 25.7. and 2.8.1937.

[40] Tate Archive, TGA 851, letters from Vanessa Bell to Portia Holman, the medical student who was honorary secretary to the Holborn committee.

[41] OBL, MS.Addison.dep.c.207, 341–67.

[42] MRCUW, TUC Archive, MSS 292/946/32/38. The whole exchange is at pp. 72i–73ii.

[43] JPP, interview with Dorothy Vaughan.

[44] KCC, CHA 1/641, VBMV 20. Vaughan to Vanessa Bell, 20.8.1938.

[45] KCC, CHA 1/641, VBMV 21.

[46] MRCUW, TUC Archive, MSS 292/946/32/38, Vaughan letters 14.6.1938 and 24.6.1938.

[47] IWMSA, 13796, interview with Janet Vaughan.

[48] JPP, Scientific Correspondence, letter from solicitors dated 23.2.1973 mentioned Vaughan's memory of having been a CP member roughly from 1938 to 1941.

[49] Walter Schellenberg, *Invasion* (London, St Ermin's Press, 2000). The list is somewhat random. It includes Professor Marrack, Leah Manning, Margery Fry and John Strachey, but not Isabel Brown or Eva Reckitt.

[50] JPP, interview with Mary Park, 1994.

[51] Its initial members included Somerville Hastings (also a member of the Socialist Medical Association and Spanish Medical Aid Committee) and Professor Marrack. Dr Stella Churchill was honorary secretary from April 1937.

[52] HHC, DSM3 14/8.

[53] Preparation for air-raids, *The Lancet* (1936), 2(5910), 1340 and Protection against aerial attack, 1355–57.

[54] Medical Peace Campaign, *The Lancet* (1939), 1(6027), 538.

[55] LMA, Local electoral rolls.

[56] JPP, interview with Cilla, 1994. David Gourlay never learned to drive, and as a pathologist Vaughan was supremely well qualified to carve meat.

[57] JPP, interview with Honor Smith, 1994.

WAR 1939-45

CHAPTER 6
Blood transfusion
1938-45

Planning for war 1938-39

Autumn 1938 brought a turning point in the lives of many, including Vaughan. On 22 September, the British and French governments were on the brink of war with Germany because of Hitler's demands for Czechoslovakian territory. In that event they expected cities to be bombed. Staff at Hammersmith and other London hospitals were told in confidence to prepare for over 50,000 casualties the following weekend. This meant that large quantities of blood had to be obtained and stored. Vaughan quickly reviewed the literature, but none of the published articles, in English, Russian or Spanish, gave precise technical details of the methods used.[1] She acted decisively, and soon went on to play a leading part in the planning and delivery of a new civilian blood transfusion service, which would save many lives during the Second World War, and prove a lasting peacetime legacy.

Before 1938 Vaughan, like most British pathologists, had not been interested in storing blood.[2] She knew about the blood banks and transfusion services set up in Madrid and Barcelona during the Spanish Civil War, but her attention was not caught, even after Dr Reginald Saxton wrote about the Madrid Blood Institute in *The Lancet* of September 1937.[3] Military doctors had learned the value of stored blood during the First World War, but afterwards its use developed only slowly. By 1937, there were a few centres in the United States and Soviet Russia as well as, more recently, Spain. In Britain, however, doctors still relied on schemes such as that run by the Red Cross in London, by which registered volunteers made donations as and when needed.

Vaughan and her staff now decided on methodology, bought apparatus, bled volunteers and stored their blood. Concessions by Britain and France then preserved the peace, but preparations for war accelerated, including health ministry plans for an Emergency

Medical Service (EMS). Vaughan's team went on to test stored blood kept for varying numbers of days and in two types of preservative, and published in detail the methods used and the broadly favourable results.[4] A general upsurge of interest was apparent when, in January 1939, the Spanish Medical Aid Committee and Socialist Medical Association held a reception for medical volunteers recently back from Spain. Saxton was one of those who addressed a large audience, most of whose questions, in a session chaired by Vaughan, were about the blood transfusion service.[5] Duran Jorda, who had headed the Barcelona blood bank, had by the end of March been brought to England to share his expertise with British doctors. Vaughan gave him work in her lab for a time before helping him find a permanent post in Manchester, and learned all she could from him about the Barcelona service.[6]

The Royal College of Surgeons (RCS) and army doctors had been planning a transfusion service for the army since autumn 1938. Meanwhile the health ministry had for EMS purposes divided the country into nine regions plus London, where, because of the city's concentration of medical research and teaching centres, it delegated co-ordination of services to the MRC. As to civilian blood transfusion, by April 1939 they had only reached the 'in principle' position that pathologists would need to group donors and probably store blood.[7]

Vaughan now gave a lead. On 5 April she hosted a meeting at the Gordon Square flat. Those attending included pathologists from London's ten sectors (based on major hospitals), and other interested people including George Taylor of the Galton Laboratory, a leading authority on blood groups.[8] George Wright, professor of pathology at Guy's Hospital, had taken part in the MRC planning meetings and agreed to act as chair.

This group decided that the new service should comprise four blood supply depots on the periphery of London, each serving one or more of the ten sectors, and under the overall control of the MRC. Discussion of staffing and equipment took account of the army's plans as reported by Wright. Vaughan volunteered to head one of the depots. As unofficial secretary to the group, she wrote the paper they discussed at a further meeting on 11 April, and refined it into a memorandum for Professor Topley of the London School of Hygiene and Tropical Medicine, who headed the Emergency Pathology Services. Speaking by phone on 13 April, she promised a rough costing for each depot, and Topley accepted the scheme as outlined, urging rapid implementation.[9] The informal group became an official MRC committee on blood transfusion, meeting on 17 April at the RCS to discuss its proposals with the London sector lead pathologists and with L E H Whitby and a Dr Beattie, representing the army interest. Whitby, a researcher in pathology, bacteriology and haematology at the Bland Sutton Institute in London between the wars, would lead the army blood transfusion service from its Bristol headquarters. The army, like Vaughan, was drawing heavily on Spanish experience.[10]

Dible at Hammersmith only learnt of Vaughan's initiative through the memorandum sent to Topley. 'What right had I, he said, to send out a memorandum of this sort without his knowledge. I said I was very sorry and that was that.'[11] The new committee, usually comprising the four depot officers and Taylor, chaired by Wright, continued to meet largely at her flat. A Professor Beattie of the RCS was officially a member, and showed his worth by securing the intervention of the prime minister to get Treasury approval of funding in May.[12]

Vaughan's decision to become a depot head appears unwise in career terms. It meant that for the six war years she was cut off from her academic base with its facilities for cutting edge research. She went from leadership in her field to also-ran, with no immediate strong claim to an academic chair and fellowship of the Royal Society such as fell to Dorothy Russell after the war. What were her motives? The main one was no doubt her instinct, as a doctor, to give help where it was most needed. Her chosen location at the Slough depot would be within easy reach both of Hammersmith and the safe haven she and Gourlay chose for the children; but also the hint, in her accounts of Dible's displeasure, that she did not respect him as she had respected Kettle, may have influenced her choice of a more autonomous role.

Whatever the reason, the die was cast. Detailed planning and organisation proceeded apace, with Vaughan and Wright liaising with the sector pathologists to keep them on board and agree on the choice of equipment. Their own meetings were held at intervals of between one or two days and three weeks, until the last on 11 July.[13] Vaughan persuaded the Wall's Ice Cream company to lend their refrigerated vans to transport stored blood, and used her contacts in the publicity world to help plan a campaign to register thousands of donors.[14] Through her, the Incorporated Society of Advertising Consultants offered its advice free of charge, and her notes provided the basis for posters ('Where's George? – gone to register …') and briefing to the BBC, where Maisie Somerville was the contact. A news broadcast on 30 June launched an appeal for volunteers to register as potential donors. Vaughan briefed national press editors at two lunches, and wrote an article for the *BMJ* and *The Lancet*.[15] The campaign was a success. By the end of July, 11,000 donors were registered by the Slough depot and comparable numbers by the others, and the process of public education about the use of stored blood had begun.[16] By August, she was drafting MRC guidance on the transfusion equipment, later adapting it for a *BMJ* article in December.[17] An article for the Ministry of Information followed in January 1940, and she continued as prime contact for publicity throughout the war.[18]

Practical matters were time-intensive: it took five weeks to agree on the type of bottle to use, leading to complaints from the children about 'old bottles' littering the flat. Finally a waisted (for ease of handling) milk bottle was chosen, which became standard across the country.[19] By early August Vaughan showed signs of stress, pleading with the MRC for delivery of sufficient bottles, caps and other equipment. She became ill before going on holiday alone to the hotel in Clough Williams-Ellis's architectural fantasy resort of Portmeirion in North Wales; but was soon restored in that 'grand place for a holiday if abroad is verboten'.[20]

Back at Slough on 28 August, she persuaded men of the Royal Army Service Corps (RASC), who were billeted nearby, to help with blackout and other protection measures; then returned on 1 September from settling the children in the country, in time to obey a telegrammed instruction to 'start bleeding'. Next day she sent an elated postcard to the MRC: 'Slough – Hurrah! VADs – RASC all the men in the street mobilized on our behalf, everybody giving a hand – 100 bottles+ waiting in ice chest to go to London this afternoon. Nearly all personel [*sic*] have all apparatus excellent. JV.'

On Sunday, 3 September, they stood in the Slough Social Centre bar to hear the prime minister's announcement that the country was at war, then resumed bleeding volunteers.[21] From a standing start the previous April, all four depots were up and running. This achievement owed much to Vaughan's drive, enthusiasm and organisational flair.

***

During the 18 months leading up to that time, weekend visits to Gigi near Newlands Corner involved watching a new house being built. Will had left each of his children an immediate legacy of £3,000, and the Gourlays decided to spend theirs on a country cottage. When Gigi heard this, she said Clough should build it on her land so that she could still see them at weekends. They called it Plovers Field, after the birds they usually saw there. Reached only by an unmade track and surrounded by greenery, it would become a much-loved place of retreat and relaxation. During the Munich crisis, they planted a sackful of daffodils in front of the house: a symbol of hope at a dark time.[22]

They had of course thought hard about how best to keep the children safe in the event of war. Vaughan wanted to send them to friends in the United States, out of reach of bombing. The 49-year-old David wanted to help the war effort in some capacity, without yet knowing where he would be deployed. He insisted, however, that the little girls, aged seven and four, should stay in England; and they then decided that Plovers Field would be the safest place, tucked away as it was in the Surrey hills. The nursemaid, Ivy Sheales, could look after them, Gigi was nearby, and it was within three quarters of an hour's drive of Slough.

Many things could not be predicted in 1939, including the length of the war, and the fact that Gourlay's job as a temporary civil servant would take him to Glasgow and Northern Ireland, to manage contracts for aircraft manufacture. His annual leave and entitlement to rail travel home was limited to one week a year and two journeys respectively, so he could only manage rare visits. It also turned out that, while Slough was in theory a prime target, in practice more bombs fell around Plovers Field, located as it was en route to London from the continent. Vaughan herself became so busy that, although she visited the cottage for occasional nights, her daughter Mary remembered that she was often too exhausted to do much more than sleep on the sofa once there. Although it seemed the right choice in September 1939, she wished later that she had taken them with her to Slough. Occasional visits from her and Gourlay, and an annual week's holiday, could not compensate for their isolated existence. They had few playmates, and attended an unsatisfactory school run by a local vicar, until she brought them to live with her in a house near Slough at the end of December 1943.[23]

The Phoney War 1939–45
Organisation

Fortunately, there was no bombing campaign in 1939, and the new service had nearly a year to refine its methodology. The four London depots were at Sutton (South West), Slough (North West), Luton (North East) and Maidstone (South East), chosen on the basis that blood supplies should be as far away as practicable from areas likely to be heavily bombed, but within reach of the main hospitals. There should be a good supply of local donors and alternative routes to London in case roads were blocked by bomb damage. They and the ten sector blood supply officers began with standardised equipment and donor record cards. Vaughan insisted on clear and comprehensive records, and soon designed a bottle label to show the origin of each donation and details of its use. The regional service for the rest of the country, under the health ministry, was in place by late autumn 1940, using the same equipment and record systems as London.[24]

The MRC gave depot directors wide discretion to organise and run their local services, within a framework of staffing and salary norms, so allowing each to play to their strengths. Vaughan's activities were eclectic. Dr Brewer at Luton was less interested in research, and not so well placed to recruit donors. At Maidstone, Montague Maizels, the clinical pathologist from UCH, was highly efficient, and focused his research on the technique of preparing liquid serum and plasma, in collaboration with MRC staff at Cambridge. Dr Loutit at Sutton was especially interested in the haemolytic anaemias. Salaries were set at £950, soon raised to £1,000. This was a step up for Vaughan, though a big reduction for someone like Brewer at Luton, used to receiving large fees in a non-teaching hospital.[25]

Her depot soon served an area from Reading in the west to Buckingham in the north. The Slough Trading Estate had its own water supply and power station, and factories employing 23,000 workers. Noel Mobbs, whose company owned the estate, had built a social centre in 1937, run jointly with the local authority. There was a swimming pool, gymnasium and playing fields as well as a canteen and bar; and the depot staff soon had a hockey team, dressed in red and jokily named the Vampires.[26] The depot eventually occupied two large halls in the social centre, used for bleeding sessions, storage and enrolling donors. Small rooms contained stills for distilled water and three large autoclaves for sterilising equipment with high pressure saturated steam; plus a sink for simple bottle washing, a small lab for checking donor blood groups and other tests, and Vaughan's office. Outside was a large ice chamber with shelves and crates for bottled blood, and of course the adapted Wall's Ice Cream vans.

Vaughan soon wished she had more research space, but the location was ideal for recruiting donors and volunteer helpers. She had established friendly relations with most factory owners and public health staff in Slough and also High Wycombe, another area with many factories where she had a sub-depot. Donors were called by post to attend between 8.30am and 11pm each day, so staff worked shifts. On Vaughan's initiative, they had surgical equipment so as to provide first aid if needed. Routine tasks included cleaning apparatus, making up 'taking' and 'giving' sets, filling bottles with preserving fluid and sharpening needles.

By late November about 14,000 donors were registered, encouraged by loudspeaker vans, announcements at local cinemas, leafleting and talks to groups in factories and public halls by Vaughan and her staff. Those staff came mostly from Hammersmith, and included five doctors, who bled donors, gave transfusions and were soon taking part in research. Three female graduate chemists did bacteriology and blood tests, and they and the one senior and four junior technicians contributed to research. One trained and three untrained nurses were soon supported by larger numbers of VADs (in effect, volunteer nursing assistants), who helped supervise the bleeding, care for donors and clean and sterilise equipment. There was one mechanic/driver to maintain and drive the vehicles, and a secretary and housekeeper supporting all. All young male staff were liable to call-up, as were younger women including, later, married women without children. Given also the normal reasons for turnover, there was a constant hunt for staff at all levels throughout the war.

The depot also, and crucially, relied on a large number of mainly female volunteers. 'Factory hands by day would drive in response to emergency calls at night. Housewives acted as relief drivers in times of stress or worked in the technical departments in the evening, or wrote the thousands of cards required for the call up of donors.'[27] At its busiest the depot had about a hundred staff, including about 50–70 volunteers.[28]

Methodology
At that time the four main blood groups of AB, A, B and O were internationally recognised. Transfusing a patient with blood of an incompatible group could cause a fatal reaction, except, generally speaking, in the case of group O. At first they focused on this 'universal donor' blood, which could be used in emergency when there was no time for proper cross-matching. Transfusions of plasma (the protein-rich fluid in which the blood cells are suspended) and serum (similar, but without the substances needed for clotting) could be given to all regardless of blood group. Prepared from the blood of all donors, they were as effective as whole blood for the initial treatment of blood loss and traumatic shock.

The depots soon increased their bleeding programme, issuing group O blood for whole blood transfusion and keeping other groups for plasma or serum. The government feared epidemics, especially among children evacuated from cities, and launched an appeal for group AB blood to make anti-measles serum. In the hard winter of 1939–40 donors responded well, even braving six-foot snow drifts to reach the depot, according to Vaughan.[29] She and her team trained local hospital staff and GPs in transfusion techniques, with dramatic results. One night in October they rushed blood to the maternity hospital for an evacuated mother, and local doctors were thrilled to find that a GP acting alone could handle the transfusion. The simplicity of the standard equipment was paying off.[30]

Doubts remained about stored blood, however, partly because ignorance of good practice led to bad reactions, and even deaths, among recipients. Vaughan believed that 'some of the Sectors think tap water is as good as distilled water, which may [account] for the trouble'.[31] (It must also be borne in mind that the Rhesus factor had still to be discovered.) She arranged for a letter to be published in *The Lancet* and *BMJ* in November, setting out the experience of the four depot directors in safely using stored blood. Reassurance was vital, for volunteer donors as well as hospitals.

That winter, many of the depot staff, including Vaughan, went down with German measles or flu. Blaming the fact that they lived in a permanent blackout because the one-storey hall's skylights had been wired shut and painted, she arranged for remedial work which was completed in May. By then, too, the unsatisfactory Wall's Ice Cream vans, always a temporary expedient, had been replaced with more reliable, purpose-designed vehicles.[32]

Research led to agreement on the optimal preservative, enabling blood to be kept safely for three weeks rather than, as at first, just one. The crucial ingredient was glucose. Doubts about using blood banks were finally removed by a thorough study of the relative merits of stored and fresh blood by all directors, with specially allocated staff, in the first few months of 1940.[33] There were trials with plasma and serum, too, but plasma's tendency to clot caused problems. Dried serum and plasma were far more convenient, and by June 1940 the MRC had established a large-scale drying plant at Cambridge to produce them in bulk.[34]

In the thick of it 1940–45
Dunkirk and the Blitz

War became a reality for Britain in the spring of 1940. Norway fell in April, and the Netherlands and Belgium in May. A publicity campaign, aimed at increasing supplies of A and AB serum, resulted in Slough recruiting 1,000 donors a week in May. Vaughan was sleeping either at her digs there or at the depot, so as to be on hand for any emergency. When the bulk of the British Expeditionary Force was evacuated from France through Dunkirk, the rising demand for blood led to the first real test of liquid plasma: 'We sent all the blood we had … for the first … casualties ... Then came still more ... We could not keep pace … We knew men must die if we didn't transfuse them … so we took a risk ... The plasma, bad as it looked, full of fibrin clots, worked like magic.'[35] After Dunkirk, Britain was braced for attack. Donor panels ranged from 12,500 at Luton to 38,000 at Sutton, with Slough at 30,000. All were recruiting fast. Paris fell on 14 June, but morale at Slough was high: 'I wish you could look in on us – the Eton ladies washing bottles by the thousand, typewriters banging away & blood flowing in every bottle & a general buzz of excitement.'[36] Her first delivery to air raid casualties, at a nearby airfield, was on 3 July. A week's holiday at Plovers Field at the beginning of August would be her last respite for some time.[37]

Although she said the depot was at risk of being bombed, Vaughan never made clear what a prime target the trading estate became. This large manufacturing centre, close to London, was soon devoted almost exclusively to the war effort. Shift working meant that the streets, almost empty of cars because of petrol rationing, were thick with bicycles at all hours. 'The whole place was going … You could always hear … the steady thump of the presses at High Duty Alloys as it turned out armaments.'[38] That plant made castings for Spitfire engines, undercarriages for Halifax bombers, and components for Lancaster aircraft. Another company made parts for the Churchill tank. At nearby Langley, Hawker Aircraft produced the Hurricane fighters which were crucial to the Battle of Britain. In July 1940, a massive explosion at High Duty Alloys, attributed to enemy action, killed at least one person and injured over 40.[39]

Defensive measures included an anti-aircraft battery, camouflage, air raid shelters, barrage balloons and, in time, a decoy: a series of wooden sheds at nearby Datchet forming a mock industrial estate, partially lit up at night. No wonder Vaughan thought her children safer at Plovers Field. But they did benefit from one quirk of government policy: Mars Bars were still produced at Slough for the armed forces, and on her visits she always brought some for the children.[40]

***

London was bombed every night between 7 September and 2 November 1940, and heavy raids continued until the following May. Each sector hospital held only a small stock of blood, so as soon as they were told how many casualties to expect, they rang the depot for supplies. Thanks to the volunteer drivers' knowledge of the terrain under blackout conditions, and willingness to drive when a raid was still in progress, the deliveries always arrived in time.[41] In heavy raids, Slough and one of the other depots would also send mobile transfusion teams.[42] On 21 October, Vaughan reported a very busy weekend, with three teams out giving transfusions '& blood & plasma flying in every direction'.[43] Her hospitals soon learnt that

> Slough could hear and see the bombs falling and would arrive. The police, as we drove into London up Western Avenue or the Great West Road, could … tell us to which hospital the casualties were being taken. We learnt to carry an electric light … to wear on our foreheads, the sort that ear, nose and throat surgeons use, so that if electricity failed or the lights were off because the windows were broken and … blackout curtains … blowing in the wind, we could still see to stick in our needles and hang up our bottles.[44]

In the midst of all this, Vaughan was dealing with refugees from bombed areas who took shelter in the social centre. She pointed out the risk of epidemics and other medical needs to the Slough Council of Social Service, a voluntary body she had joined, and told the MRC in October that she personally was coping with expectant mothers and 'we have entirely unofficially given medical help'.[45] There were emergency calls too. One night she was called to a farmhouse on the far side of Buckingham, more than 40 miles away, where a woman in labour was bleeding heavily. The route was complicated, the blackout complete, but

> I found the whole village out lining the roadside with lighted candles to show me the way. I dashed upstairs to find a woman … cold, sweating and deadly pale … [Unable to see or feel a vein] I just stuck in my needle and hoped. 'Digging for Victory' we called it when no vein could be located. Luck was with me … and the emergency obstetric service arrived from Oxford as the woman's colour began to come back.[46]

***

It must have been her can-do attitude, as well as its good supply of donors and volunteer drivers, that made Slough the first depot for others to turn to in emergency. Between late August 1940 and March 1941, they sent large quantities of plasma to Cardiff, Coventry, Birmingham, Portsmouth and Liverpool after heavy bombing raids. When the Liverpool transfusion centre was wrecked in March, Vaughan sent 500 administering and taking units, having supplemented her own stock with others collected from Sutton and Luton.[47]

Her optimism must at times have been undermined by exhaustion, and she found Minot's letters 'almost life-saving – they brought us a link with a safer outside world … when we sometimes felt very isolated.' His secretary, too, contributed, as in February 1941: 'Dear Dr Vaughan: I think of you with great affection and admiration … My sister and I are glued to the radio … we listen constantly … to the doings in London … thinking hard of better times when we can look you up in London and drink a toast to victory … Love Marjorie Curtis.'[48]

Despite the pressure, the depots found time for trials of plasma, serum and reconstituted red cells, with important and influential results. Liquid plasma, normal concentrated serum and whole blood appeared equally effective in treating shock (the trauma associated with circulatory collapse, lowered body temperature and pallor). For the anaemia often found in air raid casualties, it was best to give both blood and plasma or serum. These last two were definitely more effective in the first 24 hours for patients with burns and haemoconcentration (an increase in the proportion of red blood cells relative to plasma, which could be caused by a severe loss of water from the body); whilst local swelling in the same cases might be reduced by concentrated serum. Finally, concentrated red cells would raise the haemoglobin without greatly increasing blood volume, in cases such as elderly patients before operations, and anaemia of infection.[49]

Somehow Vaughan continued to give regular lectures at Hammersmith, and groups of students from two London medical schools worked at the depot for a week or two to learn about blood transfusion. January 1941 brought a bigger commitment. Blood collected in naval establishments was sent to Slough to have the serum separated, sent to Cambridge to be dried and then returned to the Navy; and Vaughan delayed the call-up of an experienced doctor so that he could take charge of teaching naval transfusion officers.[50] The Navy was grateful, giving her a 'terrific day out' at Chatham in June, where she felt transported to a different world while watching croquet lawns and tennis courts. The training need was nearly over in November, when she asked to keep the extra room involved, saying she currently had only a desk in the main hall: she needed somewhere quiet to conduct interviews, and more space for records.[51] The Royal Naval Blood Transfusion Service was set up in January 1942, but Slough continued to handle the separation work until June. Vaughan represented the blood depots at a meeting to assess military needs in February 1943, and received an OBE at New Year 1944 – the only depot head to be so honoured – as 'Organiser of the Royal Naval Blood Transfusion Centre'.[52]

She was still consulted at times on difficult individual cases, and recalled one in particular. The eminent physician Lord Dawson, with whom she had worked in the 1930s, and greatly admired for his empathy as well as his skill, asked her to see his grandson. The boy was thought to have acute leukaemia, then always fatal. 'It was late at night and I was very tired when I drove out to a country nursing home to do the … tests.' She disagreed with the diagnosis and gave a far more hopeful one, 'and all was well'.[53]

The turning of the tide: 1942–44

The United States entered the war in December 1941, but the next few months were still anxious. Japan took Singapore in February, and invaded Java and Burma. In North Africa, the long hard struggle against Rommel's troops was still to come. The enthusiasm of donors could slacken when air attacks eased off, but they always responded in emergency. Vaughan remarked after the Dieppe debacle in August that 'As soon as it was overheard in the canteen that we were bleeding for Dieppe casualties donors came streaming in unasked … managements rang up to ask what people they could send us – even factories that had always been too busy to help…'.[54]

The trading estate suffered only limited damage during the Blitz period, but its potential danger grew over time. There was a large Canadian camp and repair shop nearby and British Army depots all round Slough, and by the end of 1942 more than 40,000 people worked on the estate. One factory housed 100,000 incendiary bombs in various stages of production. This was the one place in England where a single stick of bombs could do immense damage to both industrial and military sites, and the danger continued until around D-Day in June 1944.[55]

From June 1941, however, Germany's focus switched to the Soviet Union, and the worst of the bombing was over for Britain. Vaughan managed an August seaside holiday with the children, and found time that autumn to oversee the completion of a film about blood transfusion made for the information ministry.[56] Demand for blood and blood products still rose, both to rebuild reserve stocks of plasma and serum and because civilian doctors had learnt their value. In 1942–43 a much larger drying unit opened at Cambridge, and by 1943 the depots had sufficient stocks for all emergencies until the end of the war, with any surplus sent to the armed forces and the colonies.

On the home front, raids and accidents continued. Vaughan's experience with air raid casualties and pilots who survived plane crashes had made her an expert on transfusing patients with shock resulting from wounds and burns. She and others soon found that such casualties did not fit the textbook picture of shock (they had high blood pressure rather than low) and that, especially if burns were severe, it was essential to give large amounts of blood. Vaughan was constantly trying to improve their treatment, and notified the MRC policy head of several problem cases in July 1942. Passing her notes to the MRC Burns Unit in Glasgow, he said of one: 'According to Janet the surgical treatment of this burn was atrocious' and she had the patient moved to a different hospital; but the next case admitted fared much better, thanks to the pains she had taken with the surgeon concerned. The Glasgow unit was much in need of her advice when she visited them in September that year. Apparently they had not been transfusing people with burns, nor giving them glucose.[57]

Problems with provincial hospitals and surgeons continued. In February 1943, pilots whose plane had crashed were sent to a poorly equipped cottage hospital in her area. A doctor from the depot, 'with no assistance except a small boy scout', tried to transfuse an extremely restless patient coming round from anaesthetic, and one of the depot's 'completely untrained' male drivers came to her help. Vaughan herself went the next day, and the men were soon transferred to a well-equipped military hospital nearby, but this was no isolated case.[58] In May that year, she unburdened herself to Minot: 'I only wish I could get some sense into the surgeons … I can deal with [patients'] transfusions and their anaemias but it is very difficult … to get anything done about proper splinting of hands, proper movement, etc.'[59]

That year saw better news from both Russia, with the German surrender at Stalingrad, and North Africa, with British advances. Following the Sicilian landings in July, the Italians were out of the war in September, and by November Berlin was being bombed. In August, Vaughan reported that service provision was now better organised. She was investigating the anaemia associated with trauma, and spent a lot of time travelling to visit patients:

> You have … a nice batch safely established in one hospital and … suddenly find half of them transferred to a head centre … another to an orthopaedic centre, and a few more to a chest centre – so off you go to all the points of the compass! It is very odd to think that this problem connected with everyday accidents has never been tackled before …

She was annoyed, however, by the surgeons' lack of interest in something so important to their patients, and remarked tartly that 'practically all the work on trauma in this country … has come from experimental physicians or pathologists'.[60]

***

In September 1943, the navy asked whether sternal puncture needles (used, in the absence of an accessible vein, to give transfusions straight into the bone marrow in the chest) should be issued for use at sea. Vaughan's affirmative reply reveals how wide an experience she now had of treating casualties. One of the chief difficulties, she said, was to keep the needle or cannula in position once inserted. This increased if patients had to be moved, especially up and down stairs. A needle in the sternum was far more secure than even a cannula tied into a splinted leg. Cutting down to insert it into a leg vein took time and, if a patient was restless, needed a second pair of hands; and a transfusion running into a leg vein needed constant attention, at least for the first half hour. One in the sternum needed less. All of this was relevant to treatment in small boats at sea, and she was on the group which met in January 1944 to prepare guidance.[61]

Early in that year the depot was again busy with casualties. There were a lot of bad burns in January, and February brought the five-night bombing of London known as the 'little blitz'. In April there were

> ... heavy raids and casualties. What a strange experience ... raging heat in burning buildings one moment, soaked to the skin the next ... through the hoses to get blood to the theatres where they are operating behind the flames, and then on again into the pitch blackness ... in areas that have not been bombed to hospitals which have been hit elsewhere. Wards and wards of casualties – a child in one hospital, father in another – cups of hot tea thrust into one's hand by complete strangers ... in the street [or] in ... casualty departments, struggling to get into veins – cutting off clothes – on and on, day merging into night – at the end ... an unforgettable sense of the fortitude of the men and women in the little houses that are now heaps of rubble ...

> [This is when] sternal puncture is so valuable ... these multiple injuries ... legs and arms so bashed that there are no veins and the sternum is the only place. I had a little girl the other night badly burnt whom I left for dead while I got on with some people whose lives I thought I might save. When I got them running I went back to the child ... I put a needle into her sternum, pumped with pressure [three and a half] pints in and she came alive again under my very eyes. It was used ... in the Sicilian and ... Italian campaigns and will I hope be a routine issue to all naval Medical Officers. It is extraordinary ... that you can pump the stuff in with high pressure and not get any fat embolism.[62] We have to take the risk as the people will die if we do not, and so far we have been justified.[63]

In 1954 that little girl's headmistress wrote to Vaughan to tell her she was applying to Somerville. She was accepted, and did well. Nearly 50 years later she wrote that when she was seven and staying with family friends, she was caught in a domestic fire and had to spend the next eight months in hospital. She enjoyed Vaughan's visits. 'She sucked blood out of my undamaged ears

… explained what she was doing and spoke to me as if I was as interested and intelligent as she was. I was very glad when her lost pearl earring was found safely in my bed.'[64]

D-Day and beyond

In spring 1944 the invasion of Europe was imminent. From the end of May, the depots were collecting at least 600 pints a week of group O blood, and the needs of all Allied casualties after the June landings in Normandy were met. Slough raised its bleeding level from between 800 and 1,000 donors a week to over 3,000.[65] At the end of September *The Lancet* reported that during August Vaughan's depot, and the EMS regional centres, provided a large proportion of the blood flown to France, as well as supplying home hospitals receiving wounded from overseas and casualties caused by a frightening new weapon. London had been hit by the German V1s, or flying bombs, since mid-June. They were followed by the even more deadly rockets, the V2s, from 8 September until late March 1945.

The strain at Slough is indicated by a complaint, eventually escalated by a local MP to prime ministerial level, about its use of the local Communist Party to help recruit donors in Aylesbury. Vaughan responded that there was a desperate need for blood for the casualties from London and Normandy, and they could not afford to seek donations anywhere unless they were certain of at least 200 bottles a day. 'The CP in Aylesbury actually volunteered to do a house to house canvass for us … They have in other areas given us remarkable help.'[66]

***

Vaughan had taken a week's holiday with the children during August in every year of the war, going to the seaside in 1941 and 1943, and to rural Gloucestershire in 1942. Mary remembered one of those holidays as a golden time when her mother read *The Cloister and the Hearth* to them, with all her usual dramatic expression. At the end of December 1943, when Ivy Sheales was leaving to marry a Canadian serviceman, she brought them away from Plovers Field to live with her in a cottage near Slough.[67] The following August they spent a week on Exmoor, this time with Halford's wife Dorothy and her family. Dorothy remembered it as a time when Vaughan was completely relaxed, forgetting the war and living in the moment, watching deer and foxes, riding ponies, cooking meals and enjoying everything with the children.[68] With victory in Europe now confidently expected, she could allow herself to make plans for a more peaceful life, with the family living together once more.

Wartime research
MRC-led projects

Nationally-managed medical research and trialling activity had intensified from the summer of 1941, with Vaughan concerned in every major field involving the blood transfusion service. She herself published, usually jointly with one or more colleagues, 13 articles relating to work done in the war years. She also co-ordinated or contributed to two major MRC War Memoranda and the 1945 report on a national nutrition survey. She published two summaries of the state of play on blood transfusion, and supervised the production of nine research publications by junior colleagues whom she had trained, as well as a number of unpublished internal papers produced for MRC committees. In November 1942 Sir Thomas Lewis recruited her to the committee of the Medical Research Society, hoping that she would be more active within it. She gave a paper to the Society, with two Slough colleagues, in December 1943.[69]

Blood transfusion practice was transformed by the discovery in 1940, by United States researchers, of the Rhesus (Rh) blood group factor. This explained haemolytic (that is, red cell destruction) disease of the newborn, and also why some blood transfusions might cause potentially fatal reactions. Put simply, about 15% of those tested were found to be Rh-negative, and therefore liable to develop an immune reaction to later Rh-positive transfusions. Similarly, a Rh-negative mother carrying a Rh-positive baby could develop the same form of immune reaction, possibly leading to haemolytic disease in a later baby at birth.

By 1942 the American work had been confirmed and, in a remarkable advance led by George Taylor at the Galton MRC Serum Unit in Cambridge, a whole series of Rh factors were described and their inter-relationship determined. A doctor and two graduate chemists from the Sutton depot worked with Taylor's team, while Vaughan co-ordinated the drafting of the MRC War Memorandum which gave guidance on blood group determination, taking account of the new findings. She also contributed to health ministry guidance on the risks posed by the Rh factor, and both documents helped ensure that from that time there was a remarkable freedom from incompatible transfusion reactions.[70]

She volunteered her depot to pilot, from October 1942, the supply of Rh-negative blood for transfusion, and determination of the Rh group of samples submitted for test. The issue of special group cards to all expectant mothers found to be Rh negative was important in educating the public and GPs about the importance of these tests; and the information on the incidence of the Rh factor was used for an analysis published by three of Vaughan's medical and technician staff in September 1945.[71]

War Memorandum No 9 was issued in May 1943, after a long process which severely tested Vaughan's committee-management skills. In February she told Alan Drury, the MRC policy head for blood transfusion, that only two major drafting problems remained. One could be dealt with by rewording. The issue was complex, but 'certain individuals wish to over-simplify it. I do not feel that the Medical Research Council should put out a document which sacrifices facts to simplicity.' The second was more difficult:

> I have … written to Whitby (very sweetly) saying how grateful we are … for his help & how interested … in his suggestion & that the Sub-Committee would be most grateful if he would submit a more detailed scheme … I propose … to have all the corrections … circulated before the meeting.' Drury should be able to make a soothing general statement to the main committee, although she was 'supplying sedatives by telephone & letter to an almost hysterical George Taylor. The problems of North Africa & the Solomon Isles are quite clearly of minor significance![72]

A second major project was a nationwide nutrition survey, carried out over six months in 1943. Through rationing, subsidised public restaurants, school meals and other means, the government had tried to ensure that, despite wartime shortages, the whole population had a nourishing diet; and they wanted to check the effectiveness of these measures. Depot staff took blood samples to check the adequacy of food intake, primarily by measuring haemoglobin and serum protein levels. Vaughan and five members of her staff took part, and two papers by those staff appeared in the final report.

The subject was of course close to her heart, with her memories of pre-war malnutrition. In July 1943, a Dr Steven of the Cumberland Pathology Laboratory sent the MRC committee '330 cards. Originally when asked to do it I protested that I was under-staffed & over-worked & could not tackle it ... Janet Vaughan with her characteristic persuasiveness made me alter my opinion & I offered to do 500.'[73] In April 1944 she was hard at work, trying to correlate with previous work the data sent to her by the statisticians.[74] In the event, precise comparisons with more limited pre-war surveys proved impossible; but the survey did show that, after four years of war, the nutritional health of the population was reasonably good, although more could still be done to improve that of young children, pregnant women and poorer people. The national policy was vindicated.

Her last MRC-inspired project concerned the risk of transmitting jaundice, or liver disease (now known as Hepatitis B or C) through transfusion. It had gradually become clear that this danger derived most often from transfusion with filtered, pooled and dried human serum and plasma. In summer 1944, the health ministry urged that pools be restricted to the product of not more than 10 individual donations of blood, rather than the usual 300. The invasion of Europe was under way, however, and the MRC decided this was not practicable if adequate supplies were to be maintained. The key information needed to assess the risk involved was the incidence of the disease among transfused patients. Vaughan said she could get this from the Slough depot records, the most complete available, if she could recruit a social worker for the follow-up work. The study began in October 1944.[75]

Her time over the following two years was very limited. She was out of the country for some weeks at the end of 1944 and in spring 1945, and some months later took up her new peacetime role. The interim report on the study, up to April 1945, supported the implementation from June of advice for the blood transfusion service to use only small pools of plasma or serum. The full results, published in September 1946, showed that on the basis of 1,054 patients studied, the incidence rate of jaundice was 7.3% within five months of transfusion with pooled serum and/or plasma. The incubation period varied from 45 to 150 days, with the majority of cases occurring 60 to 90 days after transfusion. None of 891 patients receiving whole blood alone developed a proved case. Among a control group of 1,284 patients in hospital at the same time, who were not transfused, none developed jaundice within five months of discharge. Since there was no laboratory or animal test able to detect the disease in blood or blood products, it was recommended that human serum for prophylactic purposes should not be pooled; for transfusion purposes, only small pools should be used; and the procedures for notifying jaundice following transfusion should be strengthened, so that the material involved could be withdrawn and further cases prevented.[76]

In wartime conditions, it was remarkable that such a comprehensive piece of analysis could be achieved. It was broadly confirmed and effectively superseded by a study of a larger group published in 1949; but its recommendations were observed in the National Blood Transfusion Service until the 1980s.[77]

Personal research

The hands-on medicine which Vaughan so enjoyed during the war enabled her to study the anaemia associated with infection on which she had published a 1939 paper, and a follow-up article in 1944.[78] In a 1946 article, she focused on the first fortnight after injury, when the degree of anaemia that might develop appeared out of proportion to the amount of blood lost.[79] Apart from burns, few accurate and detailed studies had then been made of the complete blood picture in such patients.

The strands were drawn together in her Bradshaw Lecture to the RCP in November 1947, as the first woman honoured in this way.[80] Her subject was 'two extremely common anaemias the cause of which remains obscure and the treatment unsatisfactory', namely, those found in association with infection and with trauma. The appearance of the blood cells was the same in both and there was no effective treatment beyond supplying already matured red cells through transfusion while waiting for improvement in

146

the underlying infection, or the healing of injured tissues. The available evidence suggested that the cause in both conditions lay in a failure of some kind in the synthesis of haemoglobin. The picture relating to these types of anaemia is now far more closely delineated, and, as Vaughan indicated, very complex.

Many years later, a friend sent her a cutting from *Biomedical News IV* dated March 1973. It was about victims of trauma in the Vietnam War, experiencing a 'condition once known as vanishing blood syndrome'. Patients with tissue trauma lost 20–30% or more of total blood volume and required as many as 12 units of transfused red blood cells to correct the anaemia. A Harvard professor thought many lives might be saved once this 'new knowledge' was applied to civilian accident victims. This anaemia, 'first recognised in 1945 by Dr Janet Vaughan, had been ignored until the Korean War, and then forgotten again until Vietnam'. The lessons of war still tended to be neglected by the peacetime medical profession. But Vaughan's own interest had begun in peacetime.

The role of women in research at Slough
In 1939, 12 of Vaughan's 21 staff were female, including two of the doctors.[81] By December 1943 there were five doctors, including one working half-time; three graduate chemists supported by a former volunteer who was trained and then promoted to do all the grouping work; one senior and seven supporting technicians; between nine and twelve VADs, two secretaries and one driver/telephonist. Of these 31.5 staff, only the senior technician was male.[82]

The picture must have been similar at other depots, but women played a greater part in research at Slough. At least four female doctors were engaged on one or more research projects during their time there, and three of these produced or contributed to nine published and at least one unpublished paper (such papers did not always survive on the files). Three female BScs were named in five published and two unpublished papers. Two of the women trained up as technicians were named in one published paper, and the female social worker employed for the jaundice project in another.

By contrast, at Sutton two female doctors contributed to three published papers, and four BScs, almost certainly all female (one was published with initials of first names only), were named in a total of eight published papers. No female researchers feature in publications from the Maidstone or Luton depots. At the Army Blood Supply Depot in Bristol, women formed more than half the workforce from the start, and in March 1942 it was organised specifically 'to make maximum use of woman-power'. Despite this, only one research paper was published by female army doctors.[83]

It is clear that Vaughan was keen to enable staff at all levels to improve their qualifications and experience, especially by training them in research methods. And she understood the importance of part-time and flexible working for women in particular.

The significance of the wartime blood transfusion service

In June 1943, the health ministry held a conference on post-war blood transfusion services.[84] Both Vaughan and Loutit argued for a centralised state-funded service, using volunteer donors, with the MRC continuing to run at least the research side. Loutit's summing up was trenchant. He said it was generally agreed that the blood transfusion service constituted one of the greatest medical advances resulting from the war. Its success could be attributed first to centralisation, including uniform apparatus, simple in construction and use. This ensured an easily learned technique by which a clinician could give a transfusion anywhere, whatever the circumstances. It had led to a safe product and the new specialty of intravenous therapist. The MRC's role in stimulating and funding research, and disseminating its outcomes, had also been crucial.[85]

By 1945, those achievements were widely recognised. A service begun in simple form, for an emergency situation, had become a sophisticated and still developing system for producing blood products to meet a wide variety of medical needs. Vaughan had played a pivotal role, as initiator, driver, administrator, publicist, teacher, physician and leader in research and trials. The experience would be invaluable in her future roles. Her own overriding memory was of the human goodness the service evoked. The most important lesson for her was 'always to say yes to any call for help'. People could hold on once assured that help was coming, and others would follow the lead once given. 'The people of Slough, the men and women who worked whole time and part time in the blood transfusion service ... the man in the social centre bar, all rose to every demand made on them with joy and pride.'[86]

Endnotes

[1] JA, 64-65.

[2] The Association of Clinical Pathologists discussed stored blood at their summer conference in June 1937, but only one contributor (Dr Norah Schuster) was seriously interested in, and well-informed about, storage methods. Others, including Vaughan, spoke rather of the dangers of incompatible donations, and how they might be mitigated or avoided (Association of Clinical Pathologists, *The Lancet* (26.6.1937), 1(5939), 1523-24).

[3] R S Saxton, The Madrid Blood Transfusion Institute, in *The Lancet* (4.9.1937), 1(5923), 606-607.

[4] G A Elliott, R G Macfarlane and J M Vaughan, The use of stored blood for transfusion, in *The Lancet* (18.2.1939), 233(6025), 384-87.

[5] The War in Spain, *BMJ* (28.1.1939), 1(4073), 168-69.

[6] For Jorda's escape to the UK, see N Coni, *Medicine and Warfare: Spain, 1936-39* (London, Routledge, 2008); and Joseph Trueta, *Trueta: Surgeon in War and Peace* (London, Victor Gollancz, 1980). For connection with Vaughan, see JA, 65.

[7] Wellcome Collection, Vaughan papers, GC 186/1, note of meeting on 5.4.1939.

[8] TNA, FD 1/5894, Galton Lab Serum Unit Report. And FD 1/5845, Taylor to MRC, 28.9.1938. The Galton Laboratory was at UCH, but moved to Cambridge in August 1939. It had at the behest of the MRC been producing sera for the Emergency Medical Service since November 1938.

[9] Wellcome Collection, GC 186/1, note of meeting on 11.4.1939, and note of phone conversation on 13.4.1939.

[10] Whitby was Regius professor of physic at the University of Cambridge from 1945 to 1956. A colleague of his, Dr Beattie 'modified Duran apparatus for withdrawal and administration of blood' according to Wellcome Collection GC 186/1, note of 17 April meeting. See also L Palfreeman and P H Pinkerton, Transfusion in the Spanish Civil War: Supply and demand, the role of the 'blood transfusion officer' and British planning for the outbreak of the Second World War, *Transfusion and Apheresis Science*, (December 2019) 58(6), 102671: https://doi.org/10.1016/j.transci.2019.102671, for a detailed discussion. After this, close liaison with the Army does not appear to have been maintained, and they adopted somewhat different apparatus and practice: TNA, FD 1/5859, Vaughan to MRC, 31.10.1939: 'Major Harewood Little came over to see me yesterday. He far prefers our type of apparatus to the Army type.'

[11] AICL (BPMS), transcript of conversation between D K Hill and Dame Janet Vaughan,. The account in her memoir is stronger, with Dible calling her '"a very very naughty little girl" (his words) …' (JA, 67).

[12] Wellcome Collection, GC 186/1, sub-committee meetings on 4.5 and 12.5.1939.

[13] TNA, FD/1 5846 gives the story.

[14] TNA, FD 1/5859. Vaughan told the MRC on 8.5.1939 that she would see the MD of Wall's Ice Cream about transport next day. Also TNA, FD 1/5883. Vaughan was depot representative on an informal sub-committee on publicity, set up on 19.5.1939.

[15] Janet M Vaughan, Blood transfusion, in *BMJ* (6.5.1939), 1(4087), 933–36.

[16] TNA, FD 1/5883-4 for publicity arrangements.

[17] Janet M Vaughan, The Medical Research Council Blood Transfusion Outfit as provided for the sectors and depots in London and the home counties, in *BMJ* (2.12.1939), 2(4117), 1084–85.

[18] TNA, FD 1/5860, Vaughan to MRC 5.1.1940 and 25.1.1940.

[19] JA, 66.

[20] TNA, FD 1/5859, Vaughan to MRC 20.8.1939.

[21] TNA, FD 1/5859, correspondence with MRC, 13.8.1939 to 2.9.1939. Also JA, 69.

[22] JA, 59.

[23] TNA, FD 1/5907, Vaughan to MRC, 28.12.1943. Characteristically, she was inclined to give priority to staff holidays over her own at Christmas.

[24] TNA, FD 1/5861. Vaughan advised on equipment for the regional service at a meeting on 20.8.1940. Also TNA, FD 1/5917: Regional Blood Transfusion Officers were sought following a meeting at the Ministry of Health on 1.7.1940. On 3.10.1940, the pathologist Howard Florey in Oxford was urging the MRC to 'put a bomb' under the MoH to organise a proper regional BTS. On 24.10.1940 he said it was starting to function, and a conference was planned for early January to secure effective co-ordination. He suggested that Vaughan represent the depots at this, as she did.

[25] TNA, FD 1/5855, Brewer to MRC, 8.11.1939 and 1.7.1940. Also TNA, FD 1/5876. Vaughan wrote in September 1939 that she was the only wage earner for her family. The Wayfarers kept going on a minimal basis during the war, and at that time Gourlay had not yet got a civil service job.

[26] TNA, FD 1/5859, Vaughan to MRC, 31.10.1939: 'The Transfusion Hockey Team … is covering itself with bruises, if not with glory!!'

[27] *Medical Research in War. The Report of the MRC for the Years 1939–1945*, Cmd 7335 (London, HMSO, 1947).

[28] JA, 69.

[29] TNA, FD 1/5885, Vaughan to MRC, 2.2.1940.

[30] TNA, FD 1/5859, Vaughan to MRC, 11.10.1939.

[31] TNA, FD 1/5859, Vaughan to MRC, 13.10.1939.

[32] TNA, FD 1/5859, MRC to Vaughan 12.2.1940. Also TNA, FD 1/5847, meeting on 26.1.1940.

[33] H F Brewer, M Maizels, J O Oliver and J M Vaughan, Transfusion of fresh and stored blood, in *BMJ* (13.7.1940), 2(4149), 48–53. Also TNA, FD 1/5890. Vaughan had drawn up the initial guidance and played a major steering role.

[34] TNA, FD 1/5892, progress report from emergency blood supply depots, 22.11.1940.

[35] JA, 73.

[36] TNA, FD 1/5860, Vaughan to MRC, 14.6.1940.

[37] TNA, FD 1/5861. Vaughan wrote on 31.7.1940: 'I am bad tempered, stale, stupid & intolerable. I therefore propose to go away for a week …'.

[38] Michael Cassell, *Long Lease! The Story of Slough Estates 1920–1991* (London, Pencorp Books, 1991), 84–87.

[39] RAF Campaign Diaries, Saturday, 13 July 1940 (RAF History/Battle of Britain 70th Anniversary/Campaign Diaries, accessed 20.4.2012); and BRO, AC 4/6/1, 133. The factory was on the 'Secrets list', according to the Fire Department report to Slough Borough Council.

[40] Cassell, *Long Lease!*; and information from Mary Park.

[41] *Medical Research in War. The Report of the MRC for the Years 1939–1945*, Cmd 7335 (HMSO, London, 1947).

[42] According to the official history, at least two depots maintained these teams. Slough was one, and the other must have been either Sutton or Maidstone.

[43] TNA, FD 1/5925, Vaughan to MRC, 21.10.1940.

[44] JA, 72.

[45] BRO, AC 2/23/3, 127. The Chief Sanitary Inspector reported to Slough Borough Council on 8 October that more than 1,100 official and unofficial evacuees had been received at the Social Centre the previous month, pending billeting arrangements being made. Also TNA, FD 1/5861, Vaughan memorandum dated 4.10.1940.

[46] JA, 75. Vaughan gives no date for this incident, which could have happened at any time during the war years.

[47] TNA, FD 1/592, Vaughan to MRC, 15.4.1941.

[48] HMLC Minot, Vaughan covering letter of 25.8.1976, when sending the Minot letters for deposit at Harvard; and addition to letter from Minot to Vaughan, 3.2.1941.

[49] Discussion reported in Col L E H Whitby CVO, MC, The therapeutic value of transfusion of derivatives of blood, *Proc RSM* (March, 1941) 34(5), 261–66. Vaughan applied in November for a new lab building, and it was ready in March 1941. Space remained very tight, however. (TNA, FD 1/5861, Vaughan to MRC 15.11.1940 and 3.3.1941.)

[50] According to the official history, nine naval staff 'helped' at Slough, but it is clear that many were taught. In May, there was also an RAF unit attached to the depot, learning the methods while collecting blood for their own use.

[51] TNA, FD 1/5861, Vaughan to MRC, 2.11.1941.

[52] TNA, FD 1/5885, MRC to MoH about a meeting on 23.2.1943. The Home BTS had given much of its day-to-day supply to the army for overseas needs. Also TNA, PREM 2/116.

[53] JA, 61–62.

[54] TNA, FD 1/5862, Vaughan to MRC, 22.8.1942. More than 50% of the British and Canadian troops involved in this disaster were casualties.

[55] Cassell, *Long Lease!*, 89–91.

[56] TNA, FD 1/5861; and FD 1/5885, correspondence 13.3.1941–15.1.1942.

[57] TNA, FD 1/5925, MRC to Glasgow unit, 6.7.1942. And MRC Special Reports: Reports of the Burns Unit, Royal Infirmary, Glasgow 1942–43 Part III: Replacement therapy in burns shock. Gibson and Brown. Also HMLC Minot, Minot to Vaughan, 26.10.1942.

[58] TNA, FD 1/6042, Vaughan to MRC, 15.2.1943.

[59] HMLC, Minot, Vaughan to Minot, 28.5.1943.

[60] HMLC Minot, Vaughan to Minot, 15.12.1943. At this time she was also encountering the conservatism of surgeons through the Goodenough Committee.

[61] TNA, FD 1/5903, notes of 13.9.1943 and 19.1.1944.

[62] Passage of fat tissue into the bloodstream, often associated with trauma.

[63] HMLC Minot, Vaughan to Minot, 6.4.1944. She gave a rather different account of this in her memoir, written over 30 years later, but the basic story is the same (JA, 74–75).

[64] Harriet Proudfoot (Higgens), The doctor, in Adams, *A Memorial Tribute*, 18.

[65] Lieut Col C L Dunn, *The Emergency Medical Services, Vol 1: England and Wales* (London, HMSO, 1952). Chapter 11 The Civilian BTS, 334–55. There was a very large demand from the army for whole blood during the invasion of Europe.

[66] Wellcome Collection, GC/107/1. The matter was smoothed over. One of the few changes made to Vaughan's draft history of the London BTS (dated 1946) was the removal of the Communist Party from the list of voluntary bodies which had helped recruit donors. Final publication came in Dunn, *The Emergency Medical Services*.

[67] TNA, FD 1/5907, Vaughan to MRC, 28.12.1943. She was on leave and unpacking furniture at a cottage in Beaconsfield.

[68] JPP, interview with Dorothy Vaughan.

[69] Wellcome Collection, T Lewis (PP/LEW/D.8/2 and 3). The paper was 'Changes in the circulating blood following blood loss or transfusion of concentrated red cells.'

[70] TNA, FD 1/5957, EMS.I.413, 19.4.1943.

[71] G Plaut MD, M L Barrow and J M Abbott, The results of routine investigation for Rh factor at the NW London Depot, in *BMJ* (1.9.1945), 2(4417), i, 273–81.

[72] TNA, FD 1/5901. Vaughan is referring to two of the long-running campaigns of the time, against the Germans in North Africa and the Japanese in the Pacific, including the Solomon Islands.

[73] TNA, FD 1/5946, Steven to MRC, 27.7.1943.

[74] HMLC Minot, Vaughan to Minot, 6.4.1944.

[75] TNA, FD 1/590, meeting of MRC Transfusion Sub-Committee, 11.7.1944; and JC 32: interim report on study.

[76] Nancy Spurling, John Shone and Janet Vaughan, The incidence, incubation period, and symptomatology of homologous serum jaundice, in *BMJ* (21.9.1946), 2(4472), 409–12.

[77] D Lehane, C M S Kwantes, M G Upwood and D R Thomson (1949), Homologous serum jaundice, in *BMJ* (10.9.1949), 2(4627), 572–74.

[78] Janet M Vaughan and M F Saifi, Haemoglobin metabolism in chronic infections, in *J Pathol Bacteriol* (1939), 49(1), 69–82; and M F Saifi and Janet M Vaughan (1944), The anaemia associated with infection, in *J Pathol Bacteriol*, 56(2), 189–97.

[79] Janet Vaughan, Margot Thomson and Mary Dyson, The blood picture and plasma protein level following injury, in *J Pathol Bacteriol* (1946), 58(4), 749–65.

[80] Janet Vaughan (1948), Anaemia associated with trauma and sepsis, in *BMJ* (10.1.1948), 1(4540), 35–39.

[81] TNA, FD 1/5859, Vaughan to MRC, 2.9.1939. Only the Maidstone depot had a similar gender ratio, presumably because Maizels drew his staff from UCH, which still took a small number of female students each year and appointed them to postgraduate posts. The Postgraduate Medical School, of course, usually took staff on merit and suitability, regardless of gender.

[82] TNA, FD 1/5859, Vaughan to MRC, 2.9.1939, total calculated on basis of correspondence with MRC during 1943.

[83] Faith C Poles, Captain RAMC, and Muriel Boycott, lately Lieutenant RAMC (ABTS), Syncope in Blood Donors, *The Lancet* (7.11.1942), 2(6219), 531. ('Molly' Boycott, a friend of Vaughan's whose first marriage was to Boycott's pathologist son, had returned to her hospital work as a surgeon.)

[84] HMLC Minot, Vaughan to Minot, 28.5.1943.

[85] Wellcome Collection GC 107/3, papers on planning of post-war blood transfusion service, 1943–46.

[86] JA, 75–76.

CHAPTER 7
Medical education and the NHS
1939–45

The Royal College of Physicians (RCP) and social medicine
Alongside her blood transfusion work during the war, Vaughan had an increasing commitment to medical and social reform. Her responsibilities on MRC committees, and liaison with London hospitals, allowed her to take part in other activities in the capital. At last, she and her friends on the medical left wing found themselves aligned with majority opinion. For the first time, the deficiencies of medical provision in the country at large were exposed to practitioners who had spent their working lives in the more advanced teaching hospitals, and they were horrified. Meanwhile the EMS effectively nationalised the hospital service on a regional basis. As in the new public health laboratory and blood transfusion services, hospital staff were salaried, and increasingly allocated according to need. The will and the opportunity for change coincided. Vaughan, with a uniquely high profile as a woman, in both academic and, now, practical medicine, was poised to step onto a more public stage.

She already knew some of the more powerful men who backed reform, starting with Will Goodenough, who was now deputy chair of Barclays Bank, treasurer to the MRC and trusted adviser to Lord Nuffield.[1] As chair of the Nuffield Provincial Hospitals Trust (NPHT), set up in 1939 to promote the co-ordination of hospital and ancillary services outside London, he appointed its members. They included his neighbour and friend, Noel Mobbs of Slough Industrial Estates Limited, and Farquhar Buzzard, Regius professor of medicine at Oxford and advocate of preventive medicine. Buzzard chaired the Trust's Medical Advisory Committee, to which he recruited Wilson Jameson, professor of public health at the London School of Hygiene and Tropical Medicine and, from November 1940, chief medical officer (CMO) at the health ministry. Also John Ryle, Regius professor at Cambridge; and James Spence, a paediatrician who had collaborated with the Newcastle city health department in a 1934 study of the health and nutrition of

155

small children. Vaughan knew Ryle through the Medical Peace Campaign, while Spence and Jameson were familiar to her through her nutrition and public health interests.

Jameson, Spence and Ryle also served on the MRC and its committees, including those on Industrial and Preventive Medicine. In the 1930s and later, the MRC funded research in nutrition, genetics, and maternal and child health. It could influence decisions on university staffing levels, including the establishment of new departments. Its secretary, Sir Edward Mellanby, was another member of the NPHT's Medical Advisory Committee.[2]

Most of these men were active in the RCP, of which Vaughan was now a fellow. The RCP treasurer, Charles Wilson, wanted to raise the status of the profession, and therefore standards in medical education.[3] He steered its decision in October 1939 to designate the Council (the College governing body) as a War Emergency Committee with power to co-opt; and encouraged a group of younger fellows, including Vaughan, to elect two of their number for co-option.[4] She then became active in the Younger Fellows Club (open to all aged under 45, and fellows for five years or less), which met monthly from July 1940. It agreed tactics for debates in Comitia, the college assembly of fellows, and nominations for Council; and discussed the reform of medical education. Vaughan was elected the sole female member of the executive committee in July 1942, for a year. Other club members included her friend Philip Hart, now head of the MRC Pneumoconiosis Research Unit in South Wales, paediatricians Alan Moncrieff and Reginald Lightwood, the academic psychiatrist Aubrey Lewis, public health specialist James Mackintosh, physicians George Pickering from St Mary's Hospital Medical School and Harold Himsworth from UCH, and Vaughan's old colleague from Hammersmith, the bacteriologist Ashley Miles. All wanted radical reform of health services, and state intervention in order to achieve it.[5]

Vaughan first spoke in Comitia in December 1940. The BMA had invited the college to join a projected Medical Planning Commission, to examine the development of the medical profession. Wilson and Ryle wanted a separate college committee, and Vaughan agreed, urging terms of reference in line with the RCP's interest in the whole field of medicine. The vote was won, but she caused a stir by being one of the first younger fellows, and the first woman, to speak in Comitia.[6] She also raised the subject of 'social medicine', arguing that, important as examining, research or consultant practice might be, surely public health and preventive medicine were more so. Wilson was elected RCP president in April 1941, and the new planning committee's remit included reviewing community medical needs and the organisation of medical services and research, with special reference to 'the hospital services … preventive medicine and mental health … and medical education'. Six of the eleven members, including Vaughan, were younger fellows.[7] In July, the committee agreed to appoint a social and preventive medicine sub-committee, asking Ryle and Spence to suggest terms of reference. Ryle asked Vaughan for a paper on the subject.[8]

The term 'social medicine' encompassed, at its broadest, public health and prevention, industrial medicine, epidemiology, and research into the origins of 'positive health' as well as disease and disability. Reform-minded local authority medical officers had long realised the importance to health of factors like housing, nutrition, working conditions, maternal and child welfare, and heredity. They advocated health promotion through education and exercise, and disease prevention through vaccination and immunisation; and also worked with social workers and statisticians on large-scale studies such as those on nutrition and its effects. They were aware of the generally woeful state of hospital provision, and of primary medicine as practised by lone GPs, without specialist training or updating. Vaughan and her allies wanted a post-war national health service to cover all these areas, under the collective banner of 'social medicine'. They were devising a scheme to provide 'adequate hospital and pathological services … Consultants, pathologists and men in municipal medicine … as one group … We often do this to the crash of bombs and the rattle of machine gun bullets …'[9] Her paper for Ryle envisaged the new sub-committee fleshing out such a scheme. In a parallel paper on preclinical medical education for the planning committee, she argued for an academic department of social medicine to give medical students practical insight into the problems of poverty. Silence greeted the social medicine paper, and the younger fellows decided a tighter definition was needed. Vaughan argued that doctors must 'claim the right' to advise government on the minimum conditions for healthy living, which should be recognised as 'the right' of all citizens. Wartime measures to improve nutrition should continue, alongside adequate housing at reasonable rents, and decent specified conditions for work places. Medical students should learn the significance of social background to health, and a central body or bodies should co-ordinate preventive medicine arrangements and liaise with medical schools on research.[10]

In December, Wilson asked her to briefly define social medicine. Her response, dated 3 January 1942, defined it as

> that branch of medicine which concerns itself with the social environment and heredity of man as they affect mental and physical health. Preventive Medicine is the putting into effect of measures … to raise the … level of health in the community and to prevent disease. No rigid distinction is possible between the activities of each.

Associated services, and the implications for medical education, were linked to these definitions in a logical way.[11]

The new committee was appointed in April, with Spence as chair and membership including Vaughan and mostly other younger fellows. Its first report, in October 1943, took forward her stated ideas on medical education.[12] She did more: a report of hers in December 1942 for the Slough Council of Social Service, on the deficiencies of health services in Slough and High Wycombe, informed a paper for the RCP committee arguing that medical training in social medicine would be futile without adequate social services. She recommended cross-service co-ordination of records and personnel, and minimum standards binding on all local authorities.[13]

In 1943 she became the first woman to be elected to the RCP Council, from January 1944 to October 1946. Her ex-boss Dible was among those proposed but not elected. Her nationwide network of contacts expanded, for instance through the prestigious annual dinners at which Wilson, now Lord Moran, gave the annual president's address and senior politicians and health ministry civil servants would attend. In college discussions on medical education and the forthcoming NHS, meanwhile, her views were in line with those of Pickering and Himsworth, two of the younger fellows whose paths would repeatedly cross with hers in years to come.

The Goodenough Committee

The main focus of her activity changed in March 1942, though she remained a member of the RCP committees on medical education and social and preventive medicine. That was when Jameson as CMO set up the Interdepartmental Committee on Medical Schools, soon known as the Goodenough Committee, after its chair. In light of the government's intention to provide a national hospital service after the war, building on the EMS arrangements, it would examine the organisation of medical schools and their facilities for clinical teaching, including postgraduate teaching and research.[14]

Vaughan was in elevated company. She was the pathologist member of the committee, Jameson the public health specialist. Sir John Stopford was Vice-Chancellor of the University of Manchester and specialist in anatomy and physiology. Professor A V Hill, a Nobel prizewinner and MP for the University of Cambridge from 1940–45, specialised in physiology and biophysics. There were two Scottish professors, representing obstetrics and gynaecology, and surgery; a dermatologist from UCH and Tom Elliott as ex-head of the medical unit there; and, as lay member, London businessman Sir Ernest Pooley. The secretary, LSE graduate Leslie Farrer Brown, was also secretary to the NPHT.

Vaughan thought Goodenough a 'magnificent chairman, humorous and hard-working', who insisted that during all-day meetings they must lunch together at a local pub. Meetings were fortnightly, so most got to know each other well. Her fondness for Jameson, a large and genial Scotsman, shows in a story she told about a 1943 meeting north of the border. He was provoked to wrath when a local city councillor 'announced with … pride … that they fed the patients of a large mental hospital for 13/6 a head per week … Jameson … got up rather slowly … and standing upright thumped the table: "but man, you should be ashamed, oh ashamed, to say a thing like that".'[15]

Direct as usual, she told Farrer Brown in October 1942 the 'big principles' she wanted the committee to establish. First was planned teaching by full-time teachers: people whose only private practice was in the hospital compound, so no Harley Street consultants. Second, to make social medicine integral to the practice and teaching of medicine. Third, to make clinical pathology an essential, separate subject: it could not be done by the morbid anatomist, the bacteriologist or the clinical chemist.

> Given these three … principles I will compromise on anything else. I know I have a name for being … a Bolshie & a fighter & for this reason … people are inclined to discountenance what I say. You see I am only learning the art of diplomacy late in life! I don't want … to be regarded as just an argumentative Woman. My belief in the three principles is nothing to do with my belief in State medicine. I have had experience as a teacher in the two types of teaching hospital – one with the Harley Street staff & one with the full time staff – one with an adequate department of Pathology & one without … I base my belief on practice rather than on theory. Because I feel so strongly … I am most anxious to act wisely – & I have seen enough of committees the last three years to know how … intolerable pig headed argumentative individuals can be. (My husband shakes his head at me sadly sometimes & says I am becoming as devoted to compromise as Mr Chamberlain!) I shall trust you therefore to tell me if I am getting troublesome! Please be firm with me![16]

Vaughan was showing considerable self-knowledge in this letter, but had picked the right confidant in Farrer Brown, who understood and worked well with her.

Meanwhile thinking among health ministry civil servants and ministers was also advancing. The biggest stimulus to action came from the Beveridge report on *Social Insurance and Allied Services*, published in November 1942 and soon a bestseller. Reflecting its author's understanding of the tide of opinion, the report stated that 'The primary interest of the Ministry of Social Services is in funding a health service which will diminish disease by prevention and cure …'; and that health service should be comprehensive and free to all. In February 1943 the government announced its acceptance of the principle of a national health service.[17]

In the case of medical education, there was a good deal of agreement among reformers, as papers produced for the RCP planning committee in summer 1941 had revealed.[18] All wanted a slimmed down medical curriculum, with an emphasis on principled reasoning rather than rote learning, and prevention rather than cure. This implied more emphasis on practical pathology and lab work, and more teaching on public health and social services. Practitioners in hospitals, public health and general practice should co-operate, and medical teaching should be planned and organised by full-time salaried staff. As Vaughan's letter to Farrer Brown implied, however, there was considerable opposition from more conservative elements, of whom Elliott was a case in point.

Farrer Brown became an ally. On teaching, the two tried various ways of circumventing or converting Elliott. In December 1942 they asked Francis Fraser, Director General of the EMS since 1941, to produce a note on undergraduate teaching. Vaughan welcomed his insistence that teaching should be under the direction of one person. 'If we carry this the rest follows – the old firm system inevitably goes, planning inevitably comes in …'. They would only get the principle through if they were reasonable about the detail, but Fraser's plan, based as it was on what he had done at Hammersmith, was workable. It was also the practice in some Canadian and American hospitals.[19]

Three months later, however, she had herself to draft something about teachers:

> it is unfortunate that I should appear to sponsor this because the mere fact that it comes from me may raise antagonism – I know Elliott! If you can persuade Elliott to draft a memorandum with you embodying my points so much the better! … On the other hand if we cant [sic] get the committee to accept any radical changes … then I am prepared to stand by what I have written to the bitter end. This question of teachers is one … on which … we can't compromise.[20]

There was strong support for incorporating social medicine in the curriculum, but in March 1943 Farrer Brown confessed that he did not understand the concept. Vaughan sent him a copy of the January 1942 memorandum, saying: 'Though I was responsible for the actual writing … it is a combined effort … Sir W Jameson firmly stated he regarded it as a manifesto!'[21] Two days later she responded to his comments by agreeing that social medicine was really an attitude of mind, unlikely to be needed as a separate subject in the future, 'but first … we have got to train people to think in these terms … I look upon … Departments of Social Medicine … as the initial phase in producing a change of heart.'

Once circulated, Stopford in particular welcomed 'the magnificent memorandum'.[22]

In its support, Vaughan argued that to diagnose and cure the patient was not enough. One must ask why he was ill, and the answer often lay in the environment, starting with patients' diet. As to housing, what was the rent as a proportion of income? Was there overcrowding, poor sanitation, dampness? Adequate cooking facilities and arrangements for food storage? Were working conditions satisfactory, including rehabilitation after injury and suitable work on discharge from care? As to leisure: 'In every big Russian city I visited there was a Park of Culture & Rest ... facilities for the enjoyment of leisure are essential to a healthy community.' When a GP sent a mother of five to hospital, who arranged childcare? The answer was co-ordination of district nurses, health visitors and clinics; of infant welfare, school and industry records; plus trained social workers for all services. These should link with the industrial medical service which had developed during the war. 'We want the health service of which the social workers are an essential part ... to form such a fine net that no individual can fall through it from good health into ill health ... the weaving of this net is the function of social medicine.'[23]

As to clinical pathology, she knew that, in London especially, teaching of all branches of pathology was largely confined to the classroom, unrelated to the patient. In Scotland, separate professorships or lectureships in pathology were thought unnecessary.[24] She drafted her own first note on it for Farrer Brown in unusual circumstances: 'Here is your note ... earlier than I had hoped – but I have been sitting in a remote Buckinghamshire farm house watching my drip transfusion & unexpectedly got the job done.'[25] The scheme was broadly based on Kettle's department at Hammersmith, and predicated on routine collaboration between pathologist and clinician. The pathology unit should offer co-ordinated teaching of theory and methodology as an aid to diagnosis and treatment, and have charge of all pathology investigations. Staff should be full time, and comprise a professor, lecturer and resident in each of morbid anatomy, bacteriology, chemical pathology and clinical pathology. One professor as director, in association with his colleagues, should have financial control and plan both the organisation of teaching and research and provision for hospital patients. Work would be more efficiently organised if many essential but relatively simple lab investigations were carried out by trained technicians, as was commonly done in the United States. Her experience was that a pathology department, apart from research, needed at least 30 technicians.[26]

She asked that Philip Panton, formerly clinical pathologist at the London Hospital, be consulted on the draft.[27] He had been at the health ministry since 1940, developing the regional blood transfusion service and also a countrywide hospital laboratory service, with pathologists of equal status with clinicians. The questions she suggested included one on cost. Adequate teaching could not be done on pre-war figures and

> when Elliott says he ran a department of Medicine on £5,000 the answer is that is why it was so badly done(!!) … Part of the failure of the Postgraduate School is due to the fact that two of the Professors demanded nothing originally in the way of accommodation staff or equipment. We want … Vision & courage for the future. [The pathology department at Hammersmith had in 1939–40 cost more than £16,000, showing that] even a more modest department than I have outlined cannot be run for £5,000 as Elliott suggests. The figure is more like £20,000 & we shall have to face it.[28]

It transpired that she and Panton disagreed on teaching methods, but on that issue she backed down:

> It is clear that … we have to fight to get the mere existence of clinical pathology accepted … Therefore it is no good Pathologists wrangling amongst themselves … Anyhow I have a very great admiration for Panton … He is one of the few men with Wisdom I know & no axe of his own to grind.[29]

A dinner party she arranged in March 1943, inviting Farrer Brown and Stopford to meet 'some of the more go ahead Professors in the Pathological world', may have been timed to counter the conservative influence of the Scottish medical establishment, whom she and others were meeting in April.[30]

In November, Panton found her draft chapter on pathology excellent, saying that schemes like this were known to work in practice. As a result she hoped Farrer Brown would feel that 'the battle is worthwhile. Panton is not given to being polite to me … If he is satisfied … we are all right because he stands for the forward looking people … & I am happy to stand the racket of the others.' Medicine remained a problem, and she suggested he draft the section himself and get it vetted by Pickering: 'I know Pickering very well & we can easily do this in confidence … & then it can go for circulation.' Of all the 'younger school', Pickering was 'likely to be the wisest & also more discreet than any of the others'.[31]

She welcomed the draft report's 'emphasis … on health & the social aspects of medicine' while wanting it made clearer that research was an integral part of teaching, so not confined to a separate chapter. An interesting pet hate emerged, clearly drawn from her youthful experiences of Christian missions of one kind and another:

> no, not mission … it raises all sorts of awful pictures. I would like 'job of work' I know it won't do. 'Function' might pass – we might change perform to carry out & mission to work – even duty ('stern daughter of the voice of God') is better than mission.

The idea of private patient blocks in teaching hospitals struck another nerve. 'We must ensure that the private block is of relative size to the hospital, that it gets no preferential treatment … & that it is used only by hospital [medical] staff.' It would also be polite to say that 'the clinical teachers want time & facilities for research – they don't – that is why they are many of them bad teachers. We have got to choose … teachers who want to research.' Non-teaching clinicians must be banished to other big hospitals.[32]

Vaughan wanted the position of women to be headlined, as it was. She did not, however, have to argue personally for their admission to all the London medical schools. A V Hill, prevented by other commitments from attending meetings, wrote twice to say that it would be hard to justify financial support for medical schools that refused to take *all* tax-payers, or children of tax-payers, on their merits. Stopford and Jameson were also on side, and Jameson very influential with the committee on this.[33] Seeking a lever, the committee suggested to the University Grants Committee (UGC) that it might withhold grant from any school that was not prepared to admit women, and received a positive response. Vaughan did urge careful handling when the all-female Royal Free was at one point threatened with closure, pointing to the loyalty and affection it inspired, and the fact that its recent decision to become co-educational was on the part of the older women very generous; 'if we just abolish them ... it is going to be very bitter'.[34] The committee finally recommended that it become co-educational and paid tribute to its history and achievements.

In February 1944, the health ministry urged the committee to report swiftly, given that the White Paper on the National Health Service was about to be published. Shortly afterwards Vaughan advised that the section on accommodation and equipment must provide facts, not pious aspiration, to satisfy the Treasury. Medicine and surgery departments needed properly equipped small laboratories, as at the 'more progressive' medical schools. Putting them in a central shared block would save on technicians and apparatus. Himsworth or Pickering would advise on what was needed. She was under some strain at this time, with the MRC nutrition survey report to complete as well.[35] In April, however, she urged strengthening the sections on industrial medicine, the direction of teaching and the source of funding (state or local authority) to support medical students from poorer backgrounds. And joked that they would have to wear coats of armour after the report was published. But she was content, telling Farrer Brown:

> I felt halfway through that I should be ... producing a minority report or having a terrible time being made to compromise but I think ... any far seeing man can now build the medical school he wants on the foundation we have given ... your own job has been magnificent.[36]

Vaughan had resigned from the RCP planning committee in March 1944, when it was clear that the college report (published in April) would differ substantively from that of the Goodenough Committee. Pickering and most younger fellows supported Goodenough entirely, but Moran, wishing to keep conservative opinion in both the RCP and RCS on side, held back on certain issues.[37] Published in June 1944, while the invasion of Europe was under way, the Goodenough Report stressed that medical education was an essential part of a comprehensive health service, and the necessary staff, equipment and facilities must be provided for it. Many of its findings were built into the 1946 NHS Act.

In 1961, when postgraduate medical education was under discussion, Pickering wrote to the *BMJ* on the subject:

No one who is closely familiar with ... every aspect of learning in our teaching hospitals, can doubt that an almost miraculous change has been wrought in the last twenty years, and that the greatest single factor has been the report of the [Goodenough Committee on Medical Schools] ... and its implementation.[38]

Medical education and a health service for India

As the war in Europe entered its last stages, Vaughan's expertise brought her some unexpected travel. In 1943, Lord Wavell as Viceroy of India had appointed a committee under Sir Joseph Bhore to plan India's post-war health services.[39] John B Grant of the Rockefeller Foundation, who was then director of the All-India Institute of Hygiene and Public Health, encouraged them to interview British, United States, Australian and USSR experts so as to draw on international experience. Vaughan joined a British party of three, selected by Jameson as CMO to spend six weeks in India during November and December 1944. Ryle led the group, and Weldon Dalrymple-Champneys, Deputy CMO at the ministry, was a distant cousin whom she knew well.[40] He spoke on public health planning for the NHS, and Vaughan on medical education. Dr Mountin of the US Public Health Service, H E Sigerist, professor of the history of medicine at Johns Hopkins University, and Dr Cumpston of the Australian Federal department of health toured Indian health facilities with the British team, and largely shared their policy viewpoint. Sigerist indeed was an enthusiastic supporter of the Soviet health system and of state planning.[41]

Vaughan, with extra clothing coupons to prepare for the Indian climate, sought advice and kept the reply cable from India: 'Black unsuitable. Hats unnecessary light suit heavy overcoat cotton frocks evening dress essential.'[42] The only cotton available was red and blue check gingham, so her day-dresses did little for her morale; but her silver lamé evening dress proved invaluable. It took them six days to reach Delhi, and she enjoyed the journey, despite the discomfort of the converted flying boat which took them to Cairo, and a bad attack of food poisoning between there and Bahrain. In Cairo the men were exhausted (Dalrymple-Champneys was 53, and Ryle, at 55, suffered from angina), so Vaughan went alone by taxi to see the pyramids.[43]

A V Hill had recently spent five months in India, advising on the organisation of scientific research, and his report informed the new group. He found that at every age up to 55, the rate of mortality in India was four or eight times that of the UK. Ill health and malnutrition were widespread, and the country needed to produce at least 50% more food to feed its growing population. It needed at least seven times more doctors, 20 times more midwives, 70 times the number of health visitors and 100 times that of nurses. More of the ablest young people should go abroad for advanced study, work experience and research training; and he quoted the Goodenough Report in key recommendations for Indian medical colleges. Specialist research institutes should be associated with university medical schools, and an All-India Medical Centre should produce teachers and research workers, with scholarships and bursaries to improve access.[44]

Vaughan wrote letters to her children as 'Dear Puskins'.[45] Impressions of New Delhi were mixed:

> You wouldn't know your Mother … in this fantastic world … Ryle & I are staying with Sir Jogendra Singh … He is … wise & kindly & we talk about life & death & … destiny … sitting on the verandah … looking at his garden full of white roses. I have a huge bedroom … dressing room … bathroom & … lavatory all to myself … Last night … a grand party at Viceregal Lodge … We walked up a … wide marble staircase & through marble halls with painted ceilings. The Indian women wore lovely saris and jewels … Behind all the … glitter I couldn't help seeing the black faces of my burnt airmen & my battered air raid casualties. War here seems infinitely remote. I like the men. I like a few of the women but most of them talk Bridge & scandal … & grumble at the heat & I could scream.[46]

The group were shocked by the wealth gap, contrasting this life of luxury with that of the poor living in tiny mud houses, with little furniture and 'no clothes except the rags they wear … no water and no lavatory just an open ditch down the middle of the road'.[47] On 6 November the visits to health centres, hospitals, mother and child welfare centres, VD clinics, nursing schools, factories and anti-malarial works began. At a cotton factory, she entered a long dark room where rows of women were 'spinning … with … their children sitting round them on the floor & even tiny babies … who ought to have been out in the sunshine & there they sit all day for 8 hours.' Elsewhere, children of eight or nine were working all day, illegally.

> It made me cry – I can't bear the children – I find it very difficult to be polite at cocktail parties ... especially as the attitude of so many important men ... is that nothing can be done ... There isn't any money ... for hospitals & schools & drains. Fortunately at least 3 men in the party feel as strongly as I do ... & will not be afraid to say so.[48]

She felt the stress of being sole female and youngest visiting expert, reacting with horror when told she must lecture at Lahore on medical education and research, to academic and city notables and the Governor of the Punjab.[49] Social gaffes were inevitable: 'I ... yesterday dropped a fearful brick as I mistook a high official who is an Englishman for an Indian & asked him if he had ever been to England! One of those difficult moments.' Another hazard was being forgotten. On an official picnic, there was a tent for the men to wash in but none for her. 'I could see the ADCs running round in circles ...' but they finally decided she could wash when all the men had finished.[50]

They went by train to visit Lucknow, Calcutta, Cuttack in Orissa, Madras, Bombay and finally Lahore before returning to Delhi on 3 December. Comforts could prove superficial, as on the first overnight journey to Lucknow, when Vaughan could neither shut the windows nor turn off the electric fan, so '... had to put on my fur tippet in bed to keep my teeth from falling out!'[51] In Madras a British missionary doctor, R G Cochrane, had charge of a leprosy clinic, and also the Christian Medical College at Vellore. After seeing some leprosy patients, they drove about a hundred miles to Vellore, talking about 'India ... Christianity and Communism ... medicine and medical education', arriving about 10pm and swallowing a meal before resuming a discussion of leprosy and looking at slides until midnight. After touring the college and hospital next day, she returned alone to Madras through a sudden deluge of monsoon rain.[52] She stayed in touch with Cochrane in later years, as with many others in India. Her companions appreciated her energy and fitness. Dalrymple-Champneys wrote:

We dashed about in heat or rain / To find the perfect village drain /
You've no idea what came to mean / The sight of a bore-hole latrine
/ A soak pit or a ventilator… / So we went on from place to place /
Our Janet V. setting the pace …[53]

In Bombay, visiting a cotton mill, the group were shown a crèche
and treatment room for injured workers, then ushered off to lunch.
But Vaughan and Dalrymple-Champneys questioned the hours of
work (nine hours a day, six days a week) before, led by Vaughan,
all toured the mill itself: '… rooms packed with machinery no …
ventilation everywhere the frightful [cotton] dust … The workers
… have no restrooms & … eat their food sitting by the machines
… wages are a mere pittance.'[54] In this land of contrasts, the
Governor's launch took them that afternoon to see beautiful carvings
in rock-cut temples on Elephanta Island.[55]

Back in Delhi, Vaughan acted as scribe, drafting the analysis
of needs and suggestions for reforms which they agreed with
the other experts on 3 December, as a basis for their advice.[56]
Besides greatly increased staffing and other resources, they called for
central and provincial planning and co-ordination of services,
both preventive and curative, and radical improvements to
medical education in line with the Goodenough Committee
recommendations. Far more women should be recruited, selection
should be on merit alone, and subsidies should prevent poverty
being a bar to entry. They suggested gradual investment over a
series of five-year plans; and more opportunities for postgraduate
study abroad, with a UK body to arrange the exchange of
postgraduate students throughout the British Commonwealth.

Vaughan's heaviest session with the Bhore Committee was the
next day, when she spent around seven hours answering questions
'so I arrived to dinner [with the Viceroy Lord Wavell] more dead
than alive'. She enjoyed meeting Wavell's private secretary,
however, who couldn't understand 'why anyone as smart as me
in my silver lamé frock could be trailing round India looking
at borehole latrines!'[57] She also spoke to Wavell, but thought he
looked as tired as she felt.

The Bhore Committee Report, published in 1946, recommended
that India should have healthcare which was free to all, paid
for through general and local taxation. Plans should include a

comprehensive programme in the distant future, and a short-term scheme covering two five-year periods. The report is generally agreed to have formed the basis for health policy and healthcare developments in independent India.[58] Thanks in part to Grant and the overseas experts, the then-prevailing view in the developed world was taken on board, and added, after independence in 1947, to the nationalist aspirations of the Indian people and the socialist beliefs of their leadership. India's first five-year plan, from 1951–56, implemented the Bhore Committee's suggested pattern of development.[59]

The group had a weekend sightseeing break during the evidence sessions, including a visit to the Taj Mahal. It was here in 1938 that Vaughan's father had suffered his ultimately fatal fall. On the Saturday afternoon she went alone to visit his grave, finding it 'covered with beautiful Indian shrubs … a good place to rest at the end of his busy life'.[60] Although angry about his treatment of her mother, she still retained much of the love and respect she had felt for him as a child. After the farewell lunches and dinners, the group left on 15 December and were home five days later. The return to drab, bomb-damaged, blacked-out and multiply-rationed England must have increased the dreamlike quality of this Indian adventure.[61]

For Vaughan its effects would be long-lasting; and the group travelling home in December 1944 were full of optimism for a happier future once the war was over. She later compared India to fairyland. There were no bombs, no need to choose a seat at table so as to miss a leg and be able to duck to safety. People constantly asked if she was overworked, but she could only reply that it was lovely not to be in danger and to see so much beauty.[62]

Endnotes

[1] Goodenough was from 1937 head of the finance and general purposes committee of the postgraduate school at Hammersmith, so knew of Vaughan in that context too.

[2] Sir Edward Mellanby (1884–1955), famous for proving in 1918 that rickets is caused by lack of vitamin D. MRC secretary 1933–49, campaigner in the 1930s for improved nutrition, and scientific adviser to the War Cabinet in the 1940s.

[3] Charles Wilson was at that time Dean of St Mary's Hospital Medical School in Paddington. During the war he was physician to Winston Churchill and was raised to the peerage as Lord Moran.

[4] RCP MS4198–4205, College annals, 1938–53, meeting of 'Junior Fellows', 26.10.1939.

[5] RCP MS 94, Formation of Younger Fellows Club 1939–48. James Mackintosh was CMO Scotland from 1937–40, and professor of public health at LSHTM from 1944. See also Wellcome Collection GC 186/3, Vaughan's YFC papers for 1940–43.

[6] JA, 77. Vaughan said she was told that she had been the first younger fellow to speak in Comitia, but the College annals show that Pickering had spoken briefly at the previous meeting. As a man, he would have drawn less attention.

[7] RCP MS 4199, Comitia 7.4.1941.

[8] RCP MS 4900 and 4901, minutes and papers of planning committee, 1941 and 1942, give the story; supplemented by Wellcome Collection, GC 186/3.

[9] HMLC Minot, Vaughan to Minot, 7.3.1941.

[10] Wellcome Collection, P D'Arcy Hart (PP/PDH/K/1) and J M Vaughan (GC 186/4).

[11] Ibid., meeting of YFC sub-committee, 2.12.1941. Also RCP College annals MS 4901, for early 1942. Vaughan's main collaborator was R C Lightwood (1898–1985) paediatrician at St Mary's Hospital Paddington. He seems to have been the main originator of the definitions of social and preventive medicine.

[12] It had also submitted a memorandum on the design of dwellings to a health ministry committee on the subject in January 1943. This paper was highly influential, proposing generous and well thought-through standards.

[13] Copies of her report, titled 'The instruments of social medicine outside the hospital', and of the paper for the social and preventive medicine sub-committee are in the Wellcome Collection, GC 186/3. A file note records her belief that it was after Goodenough had seen a copy of that report that he selected her as a Nuffield Foundation trustee.

[14] The Minister of Health had announced the government's post-war hospital policy on 9 October 1941.

[15] JA, 79–80.

[16] TNA, MH 71/76, Vaughan to Farrer Brown, 3.10.1942. The ending implies that she had seen Gourlay recently – perhaps in Glasgow in September, as well as exchanging letters as they must have done.

[17] Detailed discussion is in Thane, *Foundations of the Welfare State*, 217–19.

[18] RCP MS 4900, College planning committee papers.

[19] TNA, MH 71/65, Vaughan to Farrer Brown, 11.12.1942.

[20] TNA, MH 71/65, Vaughan to FB, 31.3.1943.

[21] TNA, MH 71/65, Vaughan to FB, 4.3.1943.

[22] TNA, MH 71/65, Stopford to FB, 18.3.1943.The NPHT had by this time agreed to fund for ten years an Institute of Social Medicine in Oxford. Ryle was appointed as the first Director from 1943.

[23] Wellcome Collection, GC 186/3, speaking note, which internal evidence suggests Vaughan used at the Goodenough Committee.

[24] TNA, MH 71/71, written evidence 1942-44.

[25] TNA, MH 71/66, Vaughan to Farrer Brown, 12.6.1942.

[26] TNA, MH 71/65, letters of 12.6.1942 and 17.6.1942 (the latter covering financial aspects).

[27] P N (Sir Philip) Panton (1877-1950). Clinical pathologist to the London Hospital 1908-46.

[28] TNA, MH 71/66, Vaughan to FB, 2.8. and 20.8.1942.

[29] TNA, MH 71/65, Vaughan to FB, 8.9.1942.

[30] TNA, MH 71/65, Vaughan to FB, 11.3.1943.

[31] TNA, MH 71/65, Vaughan to FB, 4.11.1943.

[32] TNA, MH 71/76, Vaughan to FB, 11.9.1943.

[33] JA, 80.

[34] TNA, MH 71/65, Vaughan to FB, 10.6.1943.

[35] TNA, MH 71/76, Vaughan to FB, 16 and 21.3.1944.

[36] TNA, MH 71/76, Vaughan to FB, 11.4.1944. She had by now also been working with Farrer Brown as a Nuffield Foundation trustee, for a year.

[37] The main issue was the Goodenough Committee recommendation that all doctors should qualify by gaining a university degree. This threatened the major source of income of the two Royal Colleges, through their Conjoint Board examinations.

[38] G W Pickering, Education facilities for overseas graduates, *BMJ* (8.4.1961), 1(5231), 1034.

[39] Field Marshal Archibald Wavell, first Earl Wavell (1883-1950), Viceroy of India 1943-47. Sir Joseph Bhore (1878-1960), eminent Indian civil servant, brought out of retirement for this purpose.

[40] Sir Weldon Dalrymple-Champneys (1892-1980). Like her, he was a descendant of one of seven Anglo-Indian sisters with the surname Pattle: in his case Sofia, who had married a John Dalrymple in the first half of the nineteenth century. Doctor John Jackson had married Maria, whose daughter Adeline married the academic and lawyer Henry Halford Vaughan. The pioneering photographer Julia Margaret Cameron was another of the sisters.

[41] H E Sigerist, *Socialised Medicine in the Soviet Union* (London, Victor Gollancz Ltd, 1937). Sigerist looked only at the positive aspects of the Soviet system. The USSR expert arrived after the others had left India.

[42] Wellcome Collection, GC 186/6, cable dated 20.9.1944.

[43] Wellcome Collection, GC 186/6, letters of 27.10 to 1.11.1944.

[44] A V Hill, *Report to the Government of India on Scientific Research in India* (London, Royal Society publication, April 1945). Hill also gave Bhore a copy of Vaughan's 1943 paper on preventive and social medicine (TNA, MH 71/65, Vaughan/Farrer Brown/John Stopford/A V Hill correspondence of March 1943); and it was quoted in support of the industrial health section of the Bhore Report.

[45] Vaughan's own mother had used the same word when writing to her children.

[46] Wellcome Collection, Vaughan, Dame Janet, India, 1944–45, GC 186/6, letter to family, 3.11.1944. Sir Jogendra Singh (1877–1946) was eminent as journalist and writer, politician and administrator, and first Sikh member of the Viceroy's Executive Council from 1942, with a portfolio including Health, Lands and Education.

[47] Wellcome Collection, GC 186/6, letter 5.11.1944.

[48] Wellcome Collection, GC 186/6, letter 8.11.1944.

[49] Wellcome Collection, GC 186/6, letter 4.11.1944.

[50] Wellcome Collection, GC 186/6, letter 11.11.1944.

[51] Wellcome Collection, GC 186/6, letter 10.11.1944.

[52] Wellcome Collection, GC 186/6, letter 21.11.1944.

[53] Wellcome Collection, Dalrymple-Champneys, Sir Weldon (1892–1980). GC/139/H.2/2. Dalrymple-Champneys enjoyed writing doggerel verse.

[54] Wellcome Collection, GC 186/6, letter 27.11.1944. Also GC/139/H.2/2.

[55] They also visited the Ajanta caves when en route to Lahore. Vaughan, with her love of visual art, must have revelled in all this.

[56] Wellcome Collection, GC 186/6, letter 27.11.1944.

[56] Wellcome Collection, GC/139/H.2/2.

[57] Wellcome Collection, GC 186/6, letter 5.12.1944.

[58] Shirish N Kavadi, *The Rockefeller Foundation and Public Health in Colonial India 1916–45* (Pune/Mumbai, Foundation for Research in Community Health, 1996).

[59] Rameshwari Pandya (Ed), *Health, Family Planning and Nutrition in India – first five-year plan (1951–56) to eleventh … (2007–12)* (New Delhi, New Century Publications, 2009). If readers are wondering why India still falls so far short of the type of universal health service envisaged by the Bhore Committee, the answer lies in the unbridled expansion of the private sector which took place while the state reforms were being slowly implemented, fed by the increase in trained staff which the state was funding. For this

see Ravi Duggal, Resurrecting Bhore, *MFC Bulletin* (November–December 1992), 188–89, 1–6 (Centre for Enquiry into Health & Allied Themes www. cehat.org/publications/pa05a8 accessed 31.7.2012).

[60] JA, 85.

[61] She brought some of the dream home in presents for Gourlay and the children; and had sent a cable to Mary on her twelfth birthday (30 November), besides leaving presents behind for her.

[62] JA, 83.

CHAPTER 8
An establishment figure
1943–48

The Royal College of Physicians and the coming of the National Health Service

During the war, Vaughan gained considerable national recognition as public spokesperson for the blood transfusion service, contributor to the Goodenough Committee on medical schools as well as MRC research committees, and prominent member of the RCP Council. All of this led to other high-profile roles, consolidating her position on the national stage.

First, she remained an RCP Council member until October 1946, and continued in the post-war period to be a valuable ally of Lord Moran in college affairs. In particular she helped him win a series of compromises to secure College support for the NHS Act that year, and its implementation in 1948. To begin with, when a full-time salaried service was under discussion, many fellows opposed the idea because they feared the loss of consultants' fees, and the absorption of the old voluntary hospitals (which included the London medical school hospitals) into a state system. When the Bill was published in March 1946, the RCP Council suggested approving that absorption provided that the new regional hospital boards were not dominated by local government; but in April a majority in Comitia voted for an alternative, hostile motion. Moran then adjourned discussion to a further meeting in May 'to allow more Fellows to express their views'. This time Vaughan was present, and spoke for the Council resolution. During the war, she said, she had worked in every sort of hospital over a large area, finding it 'a very shattering experience', with some services worthy of the pages of Dickens. The reorganisation proposed under the Bill might not be perfect, but it was comprehensive and workable. Realistically, this Bill would pass (the BMA had dropped its opposition following a plebiscite of its members). Fellows must not fail in their prime duty of caring for sick people, and this was 'the most remarkable attempt … ever … made in any country to provide a complete health service'. Council's motion was passed by a large majority.[1]

175

In the final debate two years later, opposition focused primarily on the idea of a full-time service, with no private practice allowed. At a special meeting of Comitia in March 1948 (after Nye Bevan as health minister had relinquished the full-time requirement), Vaughan supported the Council policy of seeking negotiation on the remaining points in dispute. She believed the proposed alternative motion would mean condemning the whole NHS Act, despite the fact that many doctors supported at least the hospital and specialist sections. Those like her who were Regional Hospital Board members had found those parts of the Act 'eminently reasonable', and the ministry 'often … willing to meet the points raised by the Boards'. It would be 'little short of a tragedy' if Comitia condemned the Act as a whole. The Council's resolutions were carried, and voting on the negative resolution postponed until the outcome was known. In the event, the College negotiated satisfactory terms which proved acceptable to the consultants.[2]

Vaughan was similarly pragmatic in other areas of Council business. Having used her own teaching experience to point out the ineffectiveness of current GP refresher courses, she joined with Pickering and Hunter among others to look into GP training, and their report was approved in January 1946.[3] She was RCP representative on the Advisory Board on Nursing Education of the Royal College of Nursing (RCN) from 1944 until at least the late 1950s.[4] Here she was most active in the early days, when the RCN was trying to raise standards by involving universities; and also on a committee set up in 1946 to consider the training of 'Industrial Nurses'. She played a major role on a new Board of Studies in Industrial Nursing, which ensured by 1949 that this training was linked to the new university departments of Industrial Medicine; and, having brought it within the purview of the RCN Board of Studies for Nurse Education, she served too on that board. Her attendance at RCN meetings after that was intermittent to rare, but she probably exerted influence by networking and correspondence. At the June 1947 Industrial Nursing Board meeting, for example, she reined in an impractical proposal for a degree course for nurses; and in January 1949 commented favourably on a proposed University of Manchester part-time course for industrial nurses. Still by letter, she approved the revised course in February.

Vaughan was the first woman to give an official RCP lecture (the Bradshaw) in 1947. A second woman succeeded her on the RCP Council in 1946, but there was a long gap after that, and it was not until 1989 that the first female President was elected.[5]

The Nuffield Foundation

Vaughan had in the meantime been recruited to a body which would be hugely significant for research and development, nationally and in the British Commonwealth. In 1943 Lord Nuffield made the largest of his bequests: a £10-million endowment of Morris Motors ordinary stock. In the post-war years, while that stock was rising, this was the wealthiest grant-giving foundation in the UK, with aims encompassing

> the advancement of health and the prevention and relief of sickness ... in particular ... by medical research and teaching and by the organisation and development of medical and health services; the advancement of social well-being ... in particular ... by scientific research and by the organisation development and improvement of technical and commercial education including the training of teachers and the provision of scholarships and prizes; the comfort and care of the aged poor ...

The aims also included other charitable purposes as determined by Lord Nuffield or the trustees and projects from the British Empire. They could in consequence hardly have been broader or more elastic.[6] Goodenough was chair, Farrer Brown secretary, and the foundation liaised closely with the NPHT. The six trustees included Stopford and Vaughan from the medical schools committee; Frank Engledow, professor of agriculture at the University of Cambridge; Sir Hector Hetherington, philosopher and Vice-Chancellor of the University of Glasgow; Sir Henry Tizard, then President of Magdalen College Oxford and a leading physicist used to advising government; and Geoffrey Gibbs, a banker who eventually succeeded Goodenough as chair. Vaughan's stature as a medical education and research expert was confirmed by this appointment, and her independent spirit was soon in evidence.

The trustees met at the Café Royal on 1 April 1943 to consider working methods and initial priorities. Soon afterwards, Nuffield produced a long list of 'special items' to which they should give attention. Vaughan was not alone in perceiving a red line, telling Farrer Brown:

> My Plymouth Brethren are all up in arms! Nuffield appointed us as trustees ... responsible for how that money is spent ... if he wanted to arrange what was done ... he should have appointed a lot of clerks ... If the Foundation spends money at the direction of the founder in ways the trustees consider unsuitable I shall feel the only thing to do is to cease to be a trustee.[7]

In practice, it was tactfully established that Nuffield did not intend to pre-empt the trustees, but Vaughan had as so often taken a stand on principle, and acted as spokesperson.

Decisions on methodology were taken after consultation with bodies such as the Rockefeller Foundation as well as the MRC and government departments.[8] First, they decided against proposing ideas themselves, but rather to await those put forward by others, and choose which to support. Next, expecting increasing government involvement in health and research, they positioned the foundation as a risk-taker and a supplementer, funding work which government was unwilling or financially unable to support. Third, they adopted a framework of five-year plans, within which particular areas of research would be emphasised for support. Finally, they decided to employ only a small staff, using outside advisers with relevant expertise to help decide the value and grant-worthiness of proposals.

By December 1943 they agreed the first five-year plan, which Farrer Brown drafted after much discussion with Vaughan and Engledow. It allocated £80,000 each per year for medical and natural sciences and £40,000 for social sciences, plus some specific proposals for the medical programme. This plan 'coloured the Foundation's approach to medicine for more than two decades', and its influence continued beyond that. Medicine, it emphasised, needed to encourage good health as well as fight disease, and the nine specific fields outlined were child health, prevention of premature ageing, eugenics (soon more usually called genetics), nutrition, industrial health, psychological medicine, dental health, social factors affecting health, and devising standards of normal health.[9] The link to social medicine is clear.

They wasted no time. The project resulting in the highly influential Rowntree Report 'Old People', published in January 1947, began in 1943. It led to the establishment of the National Corporation for the Care of Old People, grants for research into the causes and results of ageing, and shorter-term measures to improve relevant provision.[10] Advised by an expert committee also set up in 1943, they agreed in 1945 to improve dental training and research through major grants to four universities, and also scholarships. The RCP's social and preventive medicine committee was considering industrial medicine from summer 1943, and Vaughan drew on their work to advocate academic departments in the subject in industrial areas, saying privately: 'One of their main functions … must be to run proper courses … for … industrial medical officers … these people are [currently] the dregs of the profession with no special knowledge.'[11] She steered informal discussions with the MRC secretary, and arranged a dinner in January 1944 for Farrer Brown and Donald Hunter, long a specialist in industrial medicine, plus Hart from the MRC pneumoconiosis research unit.[12]

By October 1944, departments were agreed for the universities of Durham, Manchester and Glasgow, warmly supported by central government and the MRC. This provision dovetailed with the RCP committee's recommendations in January 1945 that an Industrial Health Service should not only promote health through the working environment and worker education, plus emergency treatment, rehabilitation and resettlement; but also promote research.[13] Meanwhile, her 1942 paper on services in Slough and High Wycombe contributed to a project inspired by Noel Mobbs. His company, with the NPHT, planned a service for all local manufacturers: an industrial health centre, casualty and rehabilitation clinics and a remedial workshop on the estate, plus a recuperative centre nearby.[14] In 1946 the foundation gave a five-year grant towards associated research. By 1963 there were seven such services around the country, mainly for small firms not covered by national provision.

Discussion of possible Dominion fellowships in 1943 led, in consultation with the Colonial Office and others, to schemes covering medicine, science and education: 'it soon became difficult to name any department of science or medicine which was not represented by at least one Nuffield fellow or scholar from overseas'. Vaughan, helping to advise on Indian medical awards from 1945, 'had ... a detailed and inexhaustible fund of knowledge about its medical men' as a result of her 1944 visit, and guided the trustees 'through more than one dangerous minefield'. She also ensured that married fellows were soon accompanied by their wives, and then their young families.[15]

Her personal contacts and knowledge were constantly in use. She encouraged Alan Moncrieff, at the Great Ormond Street Hospital for children, to co-operate with the Postgraduate Medical School and the LCC in seeking 10-year funding of a chair at a proposed new Institute of Child Health in London. Agreed by trustees in March 1944, this helped to fill a gap in paediatrics training identified by the Goodenough Committee, and ensure the full development of resources in London for medical postgraduate education and research.[16] A grant in 1945 to a body titled the Population Investigation Committee contributed to the establishment of a longitudinal survey of the health and development of children born in one week in March 1946, resulting in a study which was one of the first and most influential of its kind in the world. A further grant went to Moncrieff in 1947 for work connected to the study.[17]

The Equal Pay Commission 1944–46

Vaughan's wartime prominence also led to an invitation to join the Royal Commission on Equal Pay, which she accepted in October 1944. Returning from India that December, she was soon 'immersed in blue papers and economic text books on wages etc. It promises to be extraordinarily interesting but also difficult.'[18]

She was of course familiar with the dominant contemporary view of women's role as primarily mothers and home-makers, while men as family breadwinners had first call on available employment. The mass unemployment of the 1920s and 1930s (consistently more than one million for nearly 20 years from 1921) reinforced the weakness of employed women's bargaining power and led to the increasing imposition of a marriage bar, whereby they had to resign on marriage, even from comparatively high-status employment in local government, teaching and the civil service.[19]

Examination of the equal pay issue by four government committees since 1915 had usually resulted in dissension.[20] The least contentious area was public service, where it was clear that, especially in higher administrative grades of central and local government, and in teaching, the work of men and women was interchangeable. The House of Commons passed resolutions in favour of equal pay in the civil service and local government in 1920 and 1936, but governments were too fearful of the cost implications to act. Women in the public sector generally received no more than 80% of the men's rate for the job; and in industrial and commercial sectors, often less than half that rate.[21] Only in some newer professions, such as scientific jobs in industry, or the BBC, film making and advertising, were women graduates starting to get more demanding jobs and be paid on an equal basis with men.

The huge wartime demand for women's labour galvanised campaigners. In October 1940 the National Conference of Labour Women called for a single rate for the job for all work undertaken by women. In 1941 a group of Liberals and Conservatives campaigned to reverse the government policy of paying lower compensation to women than men suffering war injuries. Having won their case in Parliament in 1943, the same core group started an equal pay campaign, supported by public sector unions. The annual women's conferences of the TUC and the Amalgamated Engineering Union passed resolutions calling for equal pay throughout industry, soon supported by women trades unionists generally.

When an amendment to the 1944 Education Bill, requiring equal pay for male and female teachers, was won by a single vote on 28 March, the prime minister had it reversed through a confidence vote. It was now impossible to ignore the equal pay question, but ministers wanted to delay any decision until the country's post-war financial situation became clear. The potential cost was huge: by mid-1945, nearly 50% of government and about 57% of local government employees were women. Concessions to public sector employees would call in question private sector practice, multiplying the cost implications. By 30 April, a Royal Commission had been agreed. Its remit, 'To examine the existing relationship between the remuneration of men and women in the public services, in industry and in other fields of employment: to consider the social, economic and financial implications of the claim of equal pay for equal work: and to report' deliberately precluded making recommendations, so as to spare government the embarrassment of responding to them.[22]

The Commission's remit, chair and membership were settled by 12 October. The prime minister had suggested a small group of both sexes, so far as possible publicly uncommitted on the issue. The chair decided on four men and four women, representing general experience of public work, employers, trade unionists, and economic expertise. Having failed to find a suitable female economist, a doctor was sought since in theory medical women already had equal pay. Vaughan was highly commended by the health ministry as a married professional woman with children, and practical experience of public work.[23]

Her first reaction to her new colleagues was that 'some ... members ... are not the wisest choice and ... lack mental ability'.[24] The chair, Sir Cyril Asquith, was a judge whom ministers thought lazy and rather weak; but they could find no alternative. He was often absent from meetings for whole or half days and relied increasingly on the economist member, making him his official deputy from June 1946. This was Denis Robertson, professor of political economy at Cambridge.[25] He had fallen out with fellow economist Maynard Keynes in the 1930s when Keynes departed from classical economic theory and advocated state spending to stimulate employment, spending and growth. Robertson preferred to cut it so as to pay off debt, avoid inflation and encourage private sector investment. The male trade unionist member, John Brown, showed some predilection for equal pay, but was absent for more than a third of commission meetings.[26]

Charles Robinson, the male employer representative, was open-minded. In July 1945 he challenged private sector employers on the pay disparity, saying his experience as Director-General of the wartime munitions factories was that women produced at least as much as men and even more, in spite of often doing two jobs (by also looking after home and children) and travelling between them.[27] Unfortunately, he could only attend a few meetings after that, since he was on the Control Commission in occupied Germany. Jasper Ridley, a banker, was the male generalist member.[28] In a paper about banking and insurance, he quoted opinion rather than evidence, concluding that men would virtually always be superior to women in higher posts, and equal pay would damage women's promotion chances.[29]

Dame Anne Loughlin, a member of the TUC General Council since 1929, had built up the National Union of Tailors and Garment Workers and supported the principle of equal pay.[30] Lucy Nettlefold, with a Cambridge law degree, had in her youth campaigned for women's admission to the legal profession. Since the First World War, however, she had worked in her father's manufacturing business, and now ran Nettlefold and Sons. Lady Limerick was deputy chair of the joint war organisation of the Red Cross and St John, with experience only of voluntary work.[31] She made no substantial contribution to discussions, and genuinely believed that more than three quarters of industrial work was beyond women's physical capacity: the effect of equal pay would be to price them out of jobs.

Vaughan, at 45 the youngest member, missed the camaraderie of the Goodenough Committee. The equal pay group never lunched together, and never really got to know each other in an informal way.[32] They did, however, agree that equal pay could apply in the non-industrial civil service, local government and teaching; while disagreeing on the private and commercial sectors.[33]

The employers' evidence tried to justify the status quo, arguing that women were physically weaker, and more prone to sickness absence; less adaptable, and less able to cope with routine machine maintenance; of low career value because likely to leave on marriage; and constrained by legal protections such as the prohibition of night work and limitation of working hours in factories.[34] Men's family responsibilities also justified their higher pay. For Vaughan, these arguments were based on 'unexamined beliefs and prejudices'.[35] The great majority of medical experts she consulted found no evidence that physiological differences affected relative efficiency, especially if methods and machinery were adapted to suit women's (and weaker men's) generally inferior strength; and exclusion from certain types of work affected working class rather than professional women, who could afford childcare and other domestic help. High sickness rates were not general: married women were affected more than single ones, and clerical staff much less than factory workers. Overall, about 16% of the female workforce accounted for about two thirds of its sickness absence. Additional work in the home did contribute to fatigue and ill health, but higher pay could only produce benefits.

Her own experience supported these conclusions. During the war, the numbers of women working on the Slough Trading Estate grew, and their work switched almost entirely to producing armaments. Nationally, by mid-1943 women formed over a third of the engineering industry labour force, and Ernest Bevin said in 1945: 'We thought it would need three women for the output of two men, but by the help of our production engineers, new devices and labour aids ... the output is almost equal one for one.'[36]

The conclusions in the final report reflected those of Robertson, its lead author.[37] He held that, given the comparatively low demand nationally for women's labour, it must follow that employers preferred men because they were more efficient. Women's inferior strength and adaptability explained their exclusion from heavy industries and relative inefficiency. Granting equal pay, especially in times of high unemployment, would therefore displace them from 'overlap' areas. The majority of the economists he consulted supported these arguments, apart from one in particular: Joan Robinson, then an internationally respected senior lecturer at Cambridge and a supporter of Keynes. Married, with children, she was also a Fabian socialist who helped to bring about the Labour Party's commitment in 1944 to maintaining full employment.[38]

Robinson argued that women's pay rates were kept low primarily by their poor bargaining power; and that women were probably *more* efficient than men where currently employed on similar work, so granting the rate for the job would not cause their displacement.[39] Robertson rejected her paper out of hand, but Vaughan, Loughlin and Nettlefold refused to let it be dismissed.[40] TUC arguments chimed with it. The British Employers' Confederation said women earned less than men even when, as in parts of the engineering and textiles industries, they were on equal piece rates; but the TUC maintained they were at least as efficient and that in practice men were given higher paying work by one means or another.[41] There was no hard evidence on either side, and in October 1945 the Commission discussed seeking further academic investigation. Vaughan persuaded the majority that this was essential, even though it would delay the finalisation of their report. In the event, the findings of the further investigation supported the TUC argument.[42]

Had Vaughan not been a member, the Commission would have reported at least six months earlier than it did (in spring rather than autumn 1946), and would have been even less favourable to equal pay, with only a generalised note of dissent from Loughlin and Nettlefold.[43] She thought these two were unable to argue their case clearly; whereas she decided there was a sound case for a Memorandum of Dissent from certain sections, and wrote it.[44] Unlike them, of course, she was also used to writing academic articles for publication.

During the drafting process, Vaughan successfully argued for the definition of equal pay to relate (as the TUC proposed) to the 'rate for the job', meaning by 'job' broad categories of work, so avoiding the ambiguity of phrases like 'equal pay for equal work'. She also insisted, despite Robertson's scepticism, on referencing both major political parties' commitment to maintaining full employment, since this would be a game changer: even on higher wages, women were less likely to be displaced if there was high demand for labour. She ensured, too, that the shortcomings of the available information were made clear rather than glossed over.[45]

There were two crunch points, both caused by a conflict of view between Vaughan and Robertson. First was the allegation that women's health could suffer from having to compete with men who were by nature better equipped for a given job. Vaughan and most medical witnesses dismissed this for lack of evidence, but Robertson used it to support the argument that women in general were less efficient. When they submitted alternative drafts, all except Robertson, Ridley and Asquith voted for Vaughan's wording.[46] Next she submitted a note of dissent from two chapters, the first of which argued that women's low pay in the private sector must reflect the low demand for their labour, and so largely accepted the view that women were less efficient. The second concerned the economic and social consequences of equal pay in that sector.

Robertson let members know that, if this note was accepted and the two chapters therefore substantively rejected, they would need a new drafting committee (by implication, he would resign), and a further six months to produce the report.[47] This threat seems to have prevented waverers like Brown and Robinson from backing Vaughan's note. Only Loughlin and Nettlefold voted with her, but she stood her ground, promising a formal Memorandum of Dissent by the third week of September and enlisting Joan Robinson's help in vetting her economic arguments.[48]

Robertson, who had not wanted to serve on this Commission, was losing patience. It was lasting too long, and non-economists were challenging his arguments. When she sent her draft, he was furious because it failed to take account of a revised draft he had sent to Nettlefold when Vaughan was abroad on holiday. She swiftly apologised and amended the memorandum, saying they must negotiate on the kind of point he raised: 'We can disagree on principles but for heavens [sic] sake let us behave in a gentlemanly way about it.'[49]

She argued in the memorandum that the number of women seeking employment before the war was only about one third that of men. To justify the alleged 'low demand' for women, it was necessary to show that there were *more than three times as many jobs* for which men were better suited than women – an impossibility. The importance of physical strength was being eroded by modern techniques and machinery, and in any case less than half the pre-war male labour force were now employed in the 'heavy industries' of mining, steel production and so on. The idea that women were less adaptable seemed linked to wartime experience of them learning completely new jobs from scratch, with little or no training. There was plenty of evidence to the contrary.

If women tended to take less interest in promotion, or had higher absence rates and poorer time keeping than men, this would not justify lower pay for comparable jobs. (The subtext was that poor performers of either sex could be sacked.) The idea that women's lower wages reflected lower efficiency was certainly not true of the public services, and the most relevant alternative data concerned a few occupations with equal piece rates, where women's earnings were generally lower. If other factors were taken into account, however, such as hours worked, type of work allotted and their lower average age and experience, women were not necessarily less productive.

It followed that the main cause of low earnings was women's exclusion from trades in which they could, given training, be efficient; alongside their weak trade union organisation. Equal pay in a full employment context would widen their opportunities and tend to level up their wages in occupations like nursing. In the long run, opening more occupations to women would increase efficiency because the most suitable applicant would be chosen, regardless of sex. Fear of inflation should not be allowed to prevent changes in relative wage rates which were economically desirable.[50]

By the time the report was published, in November 1946, the Labour government elected in 1945 had brought in its austerity programme with the support of trade union leaders. (In 1948 a national pay restraint policy, endorsed by the TUC, effectively precluded pay increases of the size needed to equalise wage rates.)[51] Press reaction was muted, with many finding the report's convoluted style, reflecting vain efforts to keep all members on board, heavy going. The *Financial Times* concluded: 'The best summary is perhaps to be found in the far briefer … Memorandum of Dissent … In its attempt to counter the majority report the minority brings out the salient points.'[52]

The Memorandum was not forgotten. In February 1947, a conference involving the Standing Joint Committee of Working Women's Organisations and the TUC Women's Advisory Committee voted unanimously to agree with the minority note and call upon all interested parties to work for recognition of the principle of the rate for the job in all employment.[53] In June the government accepted the principle of equal pay in the public sector, but deferred acting on it until more favourable economic times. Implementation by a Conservative government, bowing to public opinion, followed in 1954.[54] Sixteen years later came the Equal Pay Act of 1970, then the Sex Discrimination Act in 1975; though this complex battle still goes on.

Vaughan had as always insisted on ascertaining and being guided by the evidence. Despite the physical and emotional pressures she was under in 1945 in particular, she remained calm and courteous under provocation, and took public responsibility for a well-argued case in a field not her own.

Endnotes

[1] RCP MS 4198–4205, College annals, Comitia meeting, 16.5.1946.

[2] RCP MS 4198–4205, Comitia meeting, 22.3.1948.

[3] RCP MS 4683–4685, Council Minutes, 9.1.1946.

[4] For Advisory Board on Nursing Education, see RCN 7/3/6, minutes of meetings 1944–58. The Oxford Institute of Social Medicine was also represented on the Advisory Board, by first Ryle and then (until July 1955) Alice Stewart.

[5] The physician Margaret Turner-Warwick.

[6] The story of the Foundation from 1943 to 1971 is well told in Ronald W Clark's *A Biography of the Nuffield Foundation* (London, Longman, 1972).

[7] Vaughan letter of 26.5.1943, quoted in Clark, *A Biography of the Nuffield Foundation*, 21–22. The reference to Plymouth Brethren was presumably a light-hearted way of indicating the trustees' very firm and united view on this. (Plymouth Brethren are a tightly knit, exclusive Christian sect.)

[8] Doris T Zallen, The Nuffield Foundation and Medical Genetics in the United Kingdom, in William H Schneider (Ed), *Rockefeller Philanthropy and Modern Biomedicine: International Initiatives from World War I to the Cold War* (Bloomington, IN, Indiana University Press, 2002), 224–26.

[9] Clark, *A Biography of the Nuffield Foundation*, 25–26.

[10] Ibid., 41–42 and 49–54.

[11] HMLC Minot, Vaughan to Minot, 14.2.1944.

[12] TNA, MH 71/65, Vaughan to Farrer Brown, 4.1.1944. Hunter was head of an MRC Unit at the London Hospital dealing with industrial medicine, specialising in toxicology.

[13] Royal College of Physicians of London, *Second Interim Report of the Social and Preventive Medicine Committee* (London, January 1945).

[14] NF minutes and papers, F.13/2. Meeting on 14.1.1946.

[15] Clark, *A Biography of the Nuffield Foundation*, 77–78.

[16] Ibid., 37–38. Clark suggests that Vaughan encouraged Moncrieff to be more ambitious in his proposals.

[17] NF minutes, 5.6.1945. This longitudinal survey was in the event extended to cover this cohort throughout life, and provided a basis for study of later cohorts, starting with that of 1958. And NF minutes, 15.10.1947: a proposal by Moncrieff, under the aegis of the Population Investigation Committee. For full account, see M Wadsworth, The origins and innovatory nature of

the 1946 British national birth cohort study, in *Longitudinal and Life Course Studies* (2010), 1(2), 121–36.

[18] HMLC Minot, Vaughan to Minot, 2.1.1945.

[19] The demand for women's labour during and immediately after the war meant that the marriage bar was first suspended and finally removed in virtually all occupations.

[20] The most thorough, though relating only to private sector employment, was the *Report of the War Cabinet Committee on Women in Industry* (the Atkin Committee), which was issued in 1919 (Cmd 135, London, HMSO, 1919). The Minority Report by Mrs Sydney Webb rejected 'male' and 'female' rates of pay, but did not espouse 'equal pay for equal work' because of the difficulty of defining 'equal work'.

[21] H L Smith, The problems of equal pay for equal work in Great Britain during World War Two, in *Journal of Modern History* (1981), 53(4), 652–72. This and following paragraphs draw on that article.

[22] TNA, T 162/874, minute dated 3.6.1944. The intention was later queried twice, by Asquith as chair and then by the Commission members. Each time the Treasury replied that there were to be no recommendations.

[23] TNA, PREM 5/243, letter, 27.7.1944. Also minutes of 18.7, 16.9 and 18.9.1944.

[24] HMLC Minot, Vaughan to Minot, 2.1.1945.

[25] Denis Holme Robertson (1890–1963).

[26] W J Brown (1894–1960), independent MP and parliamentary officer for the Civil Service Clerical Association. Ernest Bevin had ruled out employer or trade union representatives from the engineering industry, already a source of unrest on equal pay. Also TNA, T 189/2, minutes of meetings of the Royal Commission.

[27] MRCUW, MSS 300/B/3/2/C982 Pt 2. Oral hearing of British Employers' Confederation evidence to Commission, 20.7.1945.

[28] Hon Jasper Ridley (1887–1951). Chairman, Coutts & Co and National Provincial Bank.

[29] TNA, T 189/14, paper 316 by J Ridley. Note on the adoption of equal pay in the banking service, 23.5.1946.

[30] Dame Anne Loughlin (1894–1979).

[31] Angela Olivia Perry (née Trotter), Countess of Limerick (1897–1981). Vaughan had briefly known her at school, and liked her, despite their divergent political views.

[32] JA, 132.

[33] *Report of the Royal Commission on Equal Pay*, Cmnd 6937 (London, HMSO, 1946), chapters 10 and 11.

[34] These arguments appear in the 1919 Atkin Report. They are listed at the start of the British Employers' Confederation file relating to the Equal Pay

Commission (MRCUW, MSS 200/B/3/2/C982 Pt 1), and were used in written and oral evidence by the Confederation.

[35] TNA, T 189/2, Vaughan's paper (77) on 'The Physiological and Medical Considerations bearing on the question of Equal Pay' was discussed, and agreed as the basis for a questionnaire, on 12.1.1945.

[36] Smith, The problem of equal pay for equal work, 652–72.

[37] TNA, T 189/2, meeting of 19.10.1945. The drafting committee comprised Asquith, Robertson, Nettlefold and the Commission secretary. Also TNA, T 189/5. Robertson's economic explanation of the [un]equal pay position was first expressed in paper 9, circulated to the Commission on 2.12.1944.

[38] Joan Robinson (1903–1983). See G C Harcourt and Prue Kerr, *Joan Robinson* (London, Palgrave Macmillan, 2009).

[39] *Report of the Royal Commission on Equal Pay*, Appendix IX, 106–108.

[40] TNA, T 189/2, Commission meeting on 21.9.1945.

[41] *Report of the Royal Commission on Equal Pay*, Appendices VI–VIII: written evidence of British Employers' Confederation, Trades Union Congress and Amalgamated Engineering Union.

[42] TNA, T 189/2, Commission meeting on 19.10.1945; and TNA, T 189/13, paper 307, Earnings in the cotton weaving industry.

[43] TNA, T 189/14, paper 318, Loughlin letter of 1.7.1946 expressing general disagreement with the drafting of the chapter on explanations of the prevailing differences between the remuneration of men and women. Nettlefold had indicated agreement with these emerging reservations at a meeting on 11.4.1946 (TNA, T 189/2).

[44] JA, 132.

[45] TNA, T 189/2, Commission meetings from 28.9.1945 onwards.

[46] TNA, T 189/2, meeting of 24.7.1946. As a result, Asquith, Ridley and Robertson signed a note of reservation on this issue: *Report of the Royal Commission on Equal Pay*, 197.

[47] TNA, T 189/16, DC 59 and 60.

[48] TNA, T 189/2, Commission meeting of 24.7.1946; and JA, 132–33.

[49] TNA, T 189/18, Denis Robertson letter, 28.9.1946, and Vaughan response, 30.9.1946.

[50] *Report of the Royal Commission on Equal Pay*, 187–96.

[51] Sheila Lewenhak, *Women and Trade Unions: An Outline History of Women in the British Trade Union Movement* (London, E Benn, 1977), 249.

[52] Trinity College Cambridge Archive, D H Robertson papers, B6/3, newscutting, *Financial Times*, 7.11.1946.

[53] MRCUW MSS 119.1/4, Report of conference at Caxton Hall Westminster on 1.2.1947.

[54] H L Smith, The politics of Conservative reform: the equal pay for equal work issue, 1945–1955, in *The Historical Journal* (1992), 35(2), 401–15.

Plate 1: Madge with baby Janet (JP).

Plate 2: Janet as a small child (JP).

Plate 3: Vaughan family group at Giggleswick, 1906 (JP).

Plate 4: Janet Vaughan as a student (JP).

Plate 5: David Gourlay in the 1940s. © Lettice Ramsey (JP).

Plate 6: Hubert M Turnbull with colleagues at the Bernhard Baron Institute at the London Hospital in 1932 or 1933. © RLHA (RLHPP/RUS/4/1/5).

Plate 7: Janet Vaughan with baby Mary in 1932. © Ramsey and
Muspratt (JP).

Plate 8: David Gourlay with Mary, mid-1930s. © Ramsey and Muspratt (JP).

Plate 9: Wall's Ice Cream vans outside the Slough Social Centre, 1939–40. The National Archives. © TNA, FD 1/5859.

Plate 10: Staff at Slough blood transfusion depot, 1940s (JP).

Plate 11: The new blood transfusion vans at Slough, 1942. Oxford, Bodleian Libraries, MS. 13145.

Plate 12: Enrolling centre, Watford, 1942. Oxford, Bodleian Libraries, MS. 13145.

Plate 13: The Slough depot at work, 1942. Oxford, Bodleian Libraries, MS. 13145.

Plate 14: The Slough depot office at work, 1942. Oxford, Bodleian Libraries, MS. 13145.

Plate 15: Slough staff loading 2,000 bottles of dried serum for North Africa, 1942. Oxford, Bodleian Libraries, MS. 13145.

Plate 16: British, American and Australian experts in India, with Indian colleagues. Wellcome Collection, Sir Weldon Dalrymple-Champneys, Bart, GC/139 H.2/2.

Plate 17: The Gourlays with two friends of their children on holiday in Switzerland, 1946 (JP).

Plate 18: The family at Plovers Field, 1950s (JP).

Plate 19: Mary's wedding, 1955 (JP).

Plate 20: Janet Vaughan in her laboratory, late 1950s (Ray Cripps Witney Press Ltd, Witney, Oxon). Courtesy of the Principal and Fellows of Somerville College Oxford.

Plate 21: Portrait of Dame Janet Vaughan by Claude Rogers, 1957. © Crispin Rogers. Courtesy of the Principal and Fellows of Somerville College Oxford.

Plate 22: Vaughan and Gourlay on holiday, 1950s (JP).

Plate 23: Vaughan chairing a conference session in Italy, March 1970. Courtesy of Mary Sissons-Joshi.

Plate 24: Vaughan (on top step, right) at a conference in York, July 1976. Courtesy of Mary Sissons-Joshi.

Plate 25: Portrait of Janet Vaughan by Godfrey Argent Studio, 1979.
© Godfrey Argent Estate/The Royal Society (IM/GA/JGRS/8149).

Plate 26: Vaughan canvassing as Labour Party candidate for the local council election, 1973 (JP).

Plate 27: Vaughan with family, including three great-grandchildren, in the 1980s (JP).

Plate 28: Vaughan speaking at the unveiling of the memorial to British and Irish volunteers who died in the Spanish Civil War, 1985 (JP).

Plate 29: Portrait of Dame Janet Vaughan, 1986. © Victoria Crowe.
Courtesy of National Portrait Gallery, London.

CHAPTER 9

Belsen 1945:
doing science in hell

The threat of starvation

On 13 March 1945, Vaughan had portrait photographs taken by the long-established firm of photographers Elliott and Fry. Their Baker Street premises were bombed during the war, so the location cannot be certain, nor can the name of the photographer. This is tantalising, since it seems likely that she knew him or her personally. These are among the most informal and relaxed portraits of her to survive, and indicate, more than any others, how attractive she was, and how young she still looked at the age of 45.[1]

Shortly after that day, however, she had a serious car accident – a head-on collision. Her daughter Mary remembers her swathed in bandages around this time, and she told Minot that she had injured her right foot and one arm. He was alarmed to hear she had only taken two days off work, but amused and sympathetic with her 'even lower' opinion of surgeons as a result of the experience. On 10 May, he was still hoping that her recovery was going well. Although she tried to shrug off the incident, she cannot have been in the best physical shape for the ordeal soon to come.[2]

Since early 1944, anxiety had been growing about food shortages in occupied Europe. Thousands of Allied prisoners of war (POWs), in Europe and the Far East, were also expected on their release to be severely malnourished. The MRC, under pressure to advise how best to treat large-scale starvation, set up a committee on protein requirements in April that year.[3] Most of the relevant research had been done with animals. It showed that the digestive system would suffer severe damage through long-term deprivation of food. So long as the process had not gone too far, however, it could revive with careful feeding.[4] In the United States, researchers had recently found that protein hydrolysates, which were effectively pre-digested proteins, could be a successful food substitute for human patients (for instance, after an operation that prevented them from eating for a time), alongside glucose and vitamins. They could be given orally or, where patients could not swallow, by vein or nasal or oral catheter. They were first used to treat starving people during the Bengal Famine in India in 1943. No carefully controlled investigation was possible, but on the basis of clinical observation, it was suggested that intravenous treatment with hydrolysate and glucose, followed by a suitable hospital diet and care, did lower the death rate.[5]

The MRC committee soon commissioned the manufacture and trial of hydrolysates produced to its own specifications. When John Loutit tried out an oral version in November 1944, he doubted it would be palatable to anyone with nausea as a symptom.[6] By February 1945, it had still not been possible to do a proper controlled trial, but the committee had made contingency arrangements for large-scale production. The Netherlands government in exile, hearing of widespread starvation in their country, ordered supplies to treat an estimated 20,000 severe cases. In March, production was accelerated when the estimate rose to 70,000–80,000 people. Hydrolysates for intravenous and oral use, with dried serum and skimmed milk powder as alternative protein sources, plus glucose and vitamins, and the apparatus for administration, were packed in units ready for immediate use. At this stage of the war there were few qualified doctors available, so one hundred senior medical students were trained and placed on alert to go wherever they were needed to administer the treatments. A research team would follow the advancing armies to investigate starvation cases and if necessary adjust the treatment in line with particular circumstances. Loutit joined that team in April 1945.[7]

Meanwhile, the MRC had asked Vaughan to investigate the value of the new treatment for returned British POWs who were in hospital in London. Responding to her letter about this, Minot said her remark that it seemed impertinent to try to get histories from such men told him that 'you are a good doctor, [and] appreciate … the importance of caring for the patient as one would like to be cared for oneself'.[8] On 24 April she was in London, meeting Alan Drury about blood transfusion business, when the Army asked for immediate help in treating returned POWs in Brussels.[9] They decided Vaughan would go straight away with two chemists, to undertake a planned programme of trial, testing and analysis linked to the treatment of starving returned prisoners. She stayed with Drury and his wife at the Lister Institute that night, having got hold of a Red Cross uniform and sewn on a senior officer's pips.[10]

The two chemists were Rosalind Pitt-Rivers, then working at the National Institute for Medical Research; and Charles Dent, who, with a PhD in chemistry, worked in military intelligence for much of the war, but had recently qualified as a doctor.[11] Arriving in Brussels on 25 April, they found very few ex-POWs in the hospital; but when Army medical officers told them about the Belsen camp, which had been handed over to the British on 15 April, the team agreed to go there.[12]

Belsen

The camp, officially 'Bergen-Belsen', but usually referred to simply as Belsen, was located in North Germany between Hanover and Hamburg. It was set up in 1943 as a detention (not an extermination) centre, designed to hold a few thousand people. When the Allied armies closed in from west and east early in 1945, however, Belsen became increasingly overcrowded as the Germans evacuated prisoners to it from other concentration camps. The majority were Jews, mostly from Russia and Poland, but many countries and religions were represented. As numbers grew, administration and feeding arrangements gradually broke down. By the beginning of April, starvation and numerous diseases, including most commonly typhus and tuberculosis, were well established. Fearing that typhus would spread to the surrounding population, the German army decided to hand the camp over to the British, while the war still continued in surrounding areas. There were two main prison areas: Camp 1, soon known as the 'Horror Camp', where the majority of inmates, estimated at around 42,000 on 19 April, were housed; and Camp 2, with around 15,000 more recent arrivals, in somewhat better physical condition and with no typhus.[13] The British gradually converted a neighbouring German army barracks into a hospital of 17,000 beds. Further away was a small, well-equipped German army hospital, still at first housing German wounded.[14]

None of those taking over the camp were at all prepared for what they found. In the huts of Camp 1, the dead and dying lay together in two- and three-tier bunks, and on the floor. Outside, mass graves had been dug, but thousands of bodies lay unburied. Diarrhoea was ubiquitous, so the stench of faeces and of death could be smelt up to three miles away in the surrounding countryside. Since the water supply had broken down some days before the camp was handed over, dehydration was added to starvation.[15] Resources available for the huge task of introducing order, cleanliness and medical treatment were pitifully inadequate. An appeal was sent out, and gradually more help arrived, from Red Cross and Quaker relief teams as well as British and some US Army sources. The turning point in the whole process came at around the end of April, by which time the sick were being evacuated to the makeshift hospital in the former barracks at the rate of 600 or 700 a day. The estimated daily death rate fell from around 1,000 in the first week of the British takeover to around 500 in the second, with a steadier fall from 1 May onwards.[16] Timely help came with the arrival of 97 (of the original 100) medical students from London. They started work on 3 May, under the direction of the United Nations Relief and Rehabilitation Administration (UNRRA) dietician Dr Meiklejohn. Thanks in no small part to their energy, by 19 May the evacuation of the 'Horror Camp' was complete.[17] The final hut was burned on 21 May.

The work of the MRC Team
Vaughan's team travelled to the camp amid the chaos of the closing days of the war in Europe:

> We spent a wild day in captured German military stores collecting … lab. equipment and bedding and primus stoves etc … and set off at crack of dawn next day in a three ton lorry … through Belgium and over the Rhine … on a [pontoon] bridge … The cities are just heaps of rubble …[18]

Next day they joined forces with Pat Mollison, with whom Vaughan had worked on various research projects in the previous few years.[19] Now a Royal Army Medical Corps (RAMC) officer assigned to work on blood vessel injuries, he and his team had an armed guard. The MRC team left Mollison at Celle, from where they continued for a few miles through pine woods to reach the Belsen camp. It was 28 April, eleven days after the first Army medical team had entered the camp, and five days before the medical students started work.[20]

The RAMC men rejoiced on hearing that more doctors had arrived, but their hopes of help were dashed when they learned their purpose. They had to accept the position, however, and gave the team a small room for their patients in one of the barrack blocks that constituted the 'hospital', two of the Hungarian camp guards left behind by the Germans to help, and space for the two chemists in the German army hospital lab. Vaughan always said that the RAMC officers gave her every help possible. Amazingly, she managed after four days to persuade the senior officer to allocate four RAMC nursing orderlies – two by day and two by night – to her 'ward'. It may have helped that there was by this time considerable pressure from the United States to know the results of the hydrolysates testing.[21] Vaughan would have emphasised the temporary nature of the task as well as the need for speed.

The most straightforward account of the team's work is in the full (unpublished) report which Vaughan submitted to the MRC at the beginning of August.[22] In order to determine how effective the hydrolysates might be, they made observations on small groups of patients treated (for three days in each case) with: intravenous hydrolysates; an oral hydrolysate; reconstituted dried serum; and a mixture of glucose and dried separated milk powder; all alongside glucose and essential vitamins. There was no time to seek out exactly similar cases, so the choice was based on three criteria: that the patient, based on a cursory examination, had no complicating disease; was extremely emaciated or had widespread famine oedema (swelling); and was so weak as to be almost, if not completely, unable to move unaided. Thus the remit of treating cases only of severe starvation was so far as possible followed.

The biochemical observations required daily blood tests of various kinds, and measurements of nitrogen intake and excretion in daily samples of urine and faeces. The plasma protein level was the most accessible indicator of the level of body proteins, ideally supplemented by blood volume tests, but these could not be done under the prevailing conditions. A nitrogen balance was more accurate still. The lab left much to be desired. In their appendix to the team's report, Pitt-Rivers and Dent described how they adapted their methods to compensate for, among other things, an unreliable water supply, no gas supply, and a lack of facilities to weigh small amounts of material. The light was often poor and methylated spirit lamps were the only available source of heat.

The language barrier made it hard to get a satisfactory history from most patients, and a complete physical examination was often not possible: for example, there was no X-ray equipment and severely ill patients could not be weighed daily. The makeshift hospital had only wooden beds, blankets and straw palliasses. Nursing and medical support came at first from some of the less ill women from the camp, and internee doctors who were also usually ill. Canteens were staffed by one Red Cross worker assisted by Hungarian soldiers and internee women. The MRC ward had no artificial light during the first week and the water supply often failed for several hours. For the first four days, Vaughan 'stoked stoves, manipulated bed pans, administered intravenous therapy and cooked ... No drinks except a little tea and coffee were available and were prepared in the patients' room on a primus stove.' Conditions gradually improved as more help arrived at the camp. There is a tribute to Vaughan's nursing in an addition to the report suggested by Dent, namely, that clinical observations were subject to an 'unknown correction' because of the better nursing given to the MRC patients. 'They reached us in a state of utter exhaustion after the rigours of the camp and the immediate ordeal of transportation and cleansing. Once in our special ward they had hot water bottles, rest and medical attention. This factor probably played a larger part in the recovery of the first four patients than with the later additions, who had by then already begun to experience more comfortable living conditions.'

With one exception, treatment stopped at the end of the third 24-hour period and the patient was transferred to another ward. Of the 22 patients admitted, three died too soon to form part of the trial. Experience with the remaining 19 was sufficient to show that protein hydrolysates were not a practical form of treatment for this type of patient. The majority found them too unpalatable to take by mouth, and it was not possible to give enough by the intravenous route without dangerously increased fluid intake (a problem with patients suffering starvation). Administration by nasal or oral catheter was not usually practical either in patients who feared both doctors and medical apparatus as a result of their experiences in other camps. By contrast, both the glucose milk mix and concentrated serum given intravenously gave excellent results, and less than 5% of patients were unable to take small oral feeds. Vaughan's handwritten preliminary report on 11 May, for the Army and the MRC, concluded that the skimmed milk mixture appeared at least as effective as hydrolysates, and was by far the easiest treatment to give under these emergency conditions. 'This does not mean the hydrolysates will have no part to play … but at present the nursing hands required for their administration … would be better employed in keeping the patients clean and comfortable.' Two days later, she wrote that the team would be ready to return on 19 May.[23]

Personal viewpoints

Both Vaughan and Dent later gave graphic accounts of the team's experiences. Of 28 April, she wrote:

> We went down to the 'horror' camp that night. We saw the stiff corpses lying under the trees … great heaps of rotting shoes … the one stand pipe that served the whole camp with water … the barrack huts with their three tiers of bunks full still of dead and dying, the urine and the faeces dripping from one bunk to another.

Next day they started work. The army was taking surviving inmates to a former stable block, where they were placed on trestle tables to be cleaned before transfer to the converted barracks. The team chose their patients from these: '… experience in treating air-raid casualties had taught me to choose the young and those whom there was some hope of saving'.[24]

Dent wrote of that first day:

> three British people … dressed in Red Cross uniforms … briefly examining the patients and asking a few questions. After some while the older woman, obviously in charge … spoke rather like this about a wretched scarecrow of a man just washed and dressed and ready to be moved on; 'This one will do, he's survived typhus and looks as if only suffering from simple starvation now, and thank goodness he talks French.' With that … she wrote her initials, J.V., boldly on his forehead with her lipstick … This … was repeated [until four were chosen].[25]

197

At first sight, Vaughan's words and her use of lipstick can sound callous. On reflection, however, they reveal the severe self-control and the practical acumen of the good doctor when faced with a near-impossible situation. The army were using skin pencils to mark inmates' foreheads with, for example, 'T' for typhus, 'E' for knowledge of English and therefore possible value as an interpreter, and 'F' meaning fit for transfer out of the camp. Since the team did not yet have such a pencil, Vaughan used the next best thing that came to hand.[26]

The two Hungarians, with whom Vaughan communicated by signs, carried the patients to the MRC ward. They also chopped up furniture so that she could keep a fire going in 'the very primitive stove which was the only available heating and the only means of getting hot water for sterilising my instruments'.[27] At this stage she herself did the basic nursing, administered the hydrolysates, and collected blood and excreta specimens for the chemists to analyse. On 6 May, she found time to write to her colleagues in Slough:

> My dear B.T., In the midst of desperate chaos – a transfusion with one hand, a bed pan with the other ... and five naked skeletons in the passage screaming for bread in every central European language – it was like a ray of sunshine from a saner world to be brought a bottle of blood with a Slough label and one from Georges – tell the Georges people – I gave the transfusion under conditions you couldn't imagine ... we scrounge – we improvise – we work ... There is a stench in the air of faeces ... and of corpses and burning rags ... Science in hell is hard to do – one wants to get down to just trying to cope with this seething mass of human degradation ... I am triumphant this morning as I have scrounged some onions and ... have ... a strong brew to try and flavour the hydrolysates ... Love to you all ...[28]

She and Pitt-Rivers shared a room at night, and enjoyed one unexpected bonus: 'How I blessed my thick black army rum ration, that I used to find in a cracked white cup on a chair by my bed when I got back to my room about 10pm every night.'[29] The team was working 13- and 14-hour days, and it was not surprising that Vaughan developed an infection in her arm (perhaps the one she had injured in the road accident) and a fever, which put her out of action for three days, from 9–11 May, on a course of penicillin.[30]

On 12 May, she told Minot that they often had no water to cook or wash with.

> Outside the windows … I … watch the human skeletons that can walk turning over … old rags again and again to find something to clothe themselves in … Outside the block each night we stick a board, 11 or 12 or … and the cart comes round and collects the unknown friendless body … often 5,000 in one grave. Yet these bodies when one has time to stop and can speak their language are men and women of … charm and intellect … I have had a boy studying Greek at the university, a doctor, a dentist and a curé … There are children, too, and babies are born daily … What a mass of clinical material – and one has no time to cope except with the most superficial. There is no scurvy and very little anaemia of a severe sort at least among the men … all have diarrhoea, presumably nutritional because it clears up with protein and cultures are negative. Oedema of the feet alone is widespread but the real ones are generalized … Some loss of reflexes, but not constant, and red, purplish, glazed tongues almost the rule, and a pigmentation of the cheeks but no typical pellagra.[31]

> … War and killing is, perhaps, understandable – this place one can never, never understand except as the expression of a most horrible sadism … Not only do we deal with the starved bodies, but the minds are even more desperate. When they come into my … ward which obviously has special apparatus about they scream 'Nicht crematorium, nicht crematorium', obviously expecting to be burnt alive … unable to expect friendliness or kindness. How does one give a stomach tube to a Russian who speaks no language one can speak oneself and regards it only as a new form of torture? Things can be planned in London, but reality is … something which no decent human being could ever have imagined as existing on this earth.'[32]

Her horror, anger and frustration are palpable, but so is her interest in all the patients, her concern for them as individuals, and the scientific curiosity in which she could to some extent take refuge.

Reporting back

The team members returned to London by 19 May, travelling separately. Vaughan herself seems to have got back on the evening of 17 May, since she attended a meeting of the Equal Pay Commission the next day. She travelled in 'various planes', accompanying freight in one, casualties in another. 'We landed at an airdrome in the Cotswolds – it was like getting back to Paradise

– kindliness and happiness and ordered life in the countryside.'[33] Going to London the next day, she first visited the hairdresser to repair the damage done by three weeks' worth of DDT (used liberally at Belsen to kill off typhus-bearing lice), and reported orally on her findings to the MRC as well as going to the Equal Pay Commission meeting. She was asked to visit the Netherlands the following weekend to compare findings from patients there with those at Belsen, but in practice could not go before the beginning of June. On 24 May, she delivered a summary written report to the War Office and the MRC (further tests were being done by Dent and Pitt-Rivers on samples brought back, and other findings carefully checked), and this was the basis of her contribution to a Royal Society of Medicine discussion on Tuesday, 29 May.[34]

On the previous Sunday, while waiting in the House of Lords for another meeting of the Equal Pay Commission, she shared her findings with Minot, saying that she was sure the clinical picture in the Netherlands would be completely different. 'There is no dehydration, no typhus, and no prolonged starvation and the people are clean.'[35] Meantime the MRC accepted her evidence, and by Friday, 31 May she had written a first draft of a directive on the treatment of starvation for the War Office. She seems then to have flown to the Netherlands, where she was allocated a light plane to visit hospitals in the Hague, Amsterdam, Rotterdam and Leyden (Leiden). After a long talk on the night of 2 June with a group of field workers from Britain and the United States, including Loutit, she flew home the next day.[36] Two days later the MRC proteins committee held a conference on hydrolysates, before asking Vaughan and Loutit to embody their conclusions in a revised directive. Broadly, experience in the Netherlands was confirmatory of the Belsen findings, and Loutit's advice covered patients who were generally in a less parlous condition. Vaughan submitted the document to the MRC on 7 June to be forwarded to the War Office. The resulting memorandum was hurriedly finalised following the Japanese surrender on 14 August, and sent to India and South East Asia Command shortly afterwards.[37]

Vaughan and her team had proved beyond doubt that, even when treating patients in the worst possible condition of starvation and dehydration, the most effective approach was the simple and comparatively inexpensive one of small feeds of milk, glucose and vitamins or, in a small minority of cases, intravenous feeding with plasma or serum. Without their contribution, some doubt might have remained about the possible value of hydrolysates in extreme cases. As it was, the final War Office memorandum guided the treatment of the thousands of ex-POWs released in the Far East.

Aftermath – rumour, doubt and accusation

In the nightmare situation at Belsen, it is understandable that the small MRC team might have aroused some hostility. They were using woefully scarce medical resources to treat a comparatively tiny number of patients, even if only for a short time. Resentment and misunderstandings gave rise to some persistent adverse rumours. Some surviving members of the medical students' group, interviewed in the mid-1980s, and later by the Imperial War Museum and the BBC, had a confused recollection of Vaughan as a 'nutritionist', who involved them in trials of 'Bengal Famine mixture' as well as protein hydrolysates. One said he did not think she contributed anything to the patients' well-being, and that students she insisted should help her would have been better employed helping the sick.[38] In January 1993, a former Red Cross worker repeated the allegation about 'Bengal Famine gruel', saying also that Vaughan had only been at the camp for a few days.[39] Ben Shephard, in his generally even-handed treatment of the Belsen story, implied that Vaughan had somehow 'failed' when she found that the hydrolysates did not perform as expected.[40] Vaughan was of course not primarily a nutritionist and not involved at all in testing the Bengal Famine mixture, nor did she make any use of students. She and her team worked in the camp for just under three weeks, and produced solid evidence that hydrolysates had no advantages over more conventional methods. This was a success, ensuring that in future those suffering from starvation received the most effective treatment, while incidentally saving considerable effort and expense.

One cause of confusion seems to have been a continued MRC presence after her departure. The end of the war in Europe on 8 May released Mollison and his RAMC team, who came to Belsen four days later, intending to help Vaughan. Finding that she and her

201

team were soon to leave, he agreed to stay and go on researching the effects of starvation and alternative treatments. With only the comparatively low rank of captain in the RAMC, however, he was unable to resist pressure from Meiklejohn to take part in a scheme of his to test the Bengal Famine mixture alongside hydrolysates, milk and plasma, Mollison's role being to undertake all blood tests. He also agreed (with unsatisfactory results) to use the medical students to make clinical observations. By 8 June he was deeply discouraged and wanted to return to England. Vaughan, when consulted, agreed with the MRC that he was probably achieving more than he realised, and wrote to encourage him. His reply expressed great appreciation:

> On the whole I've made a mess of it but you've almost succeeded in persuading me that there may be something worthwhile … The first and greatest [mistake] was in letting Meiklejohn and others talk me into having more than a handful of patients. I wasted a lot of the first three weeks doing ordinary ward work … I am hoping … that you have the names of your patients because I've made some observations on four or five who claim to have been treated in your 'laboratorium'. You are usually described as the lady with the sweets.

The long letter goes on to discuss all aspects of the work, and say that he will seek her advice on the blood picture when he gets back.[41]

Some who criticised the MRC team's work thought it ethically unacceptable to carry out research at Belsen, rather than simply pitching in and helping a greater number of patients. Vaughan certainly was extremely frustrated by her narrow role, and her patient case notes reveal some of this. Although their treatment stopped after three days, she followed up all those transferred from the ward. In three cases she attributed a failure to maintain their improvement to inadequate nursing and treatment thereafter.[42] Nonetheless, she never doubted the importance of the trial for the thousands being released from concentration and prison camps, as shown in one of her letters:

> … you have to go very slowly with the concentration camp type of patient. How … efficient nursing care is to be provided is the real crux of the problem – and will be in the Far East; thousands of patients all with diarrhoea, all requiring constant small feeds and constant bedpans. If you give them milk you must have something to flavour

[it] – tea or coffee or vanilla, because these people have very nasty mouths and milk alone palls after 12 hours, especially when there are no facilities for frequent mouth washes. This all sounds very obvious but we learned it by bitter experience ...[43]

She has also been charged with failing to obtain patients' consent before, in effect, experimenting on them. The charge applies also to the MRC, which authorised the trial, and other practitioners such as Mollison, Loutit and the United States nutritionists operating in the rest of Europe. The case rests on the fact that informed consent was not sought as a matter of course.[44]

In 1945 there was no written code of medical ethics, and doctors in the UK relied on the 'Hippocratic Oath' to guide their conduct, especially the vow to do good to patients, and never to do harm. The Nazi doctors tried at Nuremburg were accused of breaking their oath, and the Nuremburg Code, for use in legal cases, was produced in 1948 in response to their unethical behaviour. The next major development came in 1964, when the World Medical Association adopted the Declaration of Helsinki, offering non-legal standards for the guidance of doctors. This made a crucial distinction between non-therapeutic research (purely scientific studies without therapeutic value for the subject) and therapeutic research, defined as medical research combined with professional care. The latter did not require informed consent: the physician was free to pursue new measures which he or she judged appropriate, subject to a check on their judgement by an independent review committee.

In 1945 Vaughan and Dent would have used the Hippocratic Oath to guide their conduct, with no formal need to seek consent. Her history, from trials of liver treatments for pernicious anaemia to the treatment of pilots and air raid casualties with severe burns, indicates that she was only ever engaged in 'therapeutic' research on patients, with any novel procedure being one which was either close to established practice or had been tried before with at least no evidence of causing harm. She was also passionate about explaining things to patients, and there is no evidence of her ever acting against a patient's will. Minot's words about her treating patients as she would wish to be treated herself are very telling, as is Mollison's reference to her patients' memory of her. The written reports and case histories support this conclusion. The 19 patients who were treated for three days or more were all described by nationality and in 18 cases by age. Some kind of case history was obtained from 14. The remaining five were too apathetic, or the language problem too great, to give even a minimal history. The only 'novel' treatments being attempted were those with hydrolysates, and had been used before, on patients either starving or unable to eat, without any known harm resulting. Industry was poised to produce them in bulk. Vaughan seems to have tried to use a stomach tube with three patients, of whom only one, a 'Co-operative intelligent young man, reasonably strong' tried the nasal tube, then oral hydrolysates, both of which he disliked very much. The other two were given milk feeds instead.[45] She also mentioned to Minot the difficulty (implied impossibility) of inserting a nasal tube if the nasal tissues were damaged. The fact that 15 patients accepted intravenous treatment with hydrolysates or serum shows her skill and ability to inspire trust. One of those she followed up (the one recorded as shouting 'nicht crematorium' when shown a feeding tube) asked to come back after his discharge to a general ward, and the MRC team did give him additional feeds of milk and coffee.

Aftermath – personal consequences

Vaughan's dedication came at a cost. Her illness at Belsen could have been brought on in part by exhaustion, but she seems to have taken no time off from work before August.[46] Instead, she wrote up the research in various ways, attended meetings, including those of the Equal Pay Commission on 27 May and the Nuffield Foundation on 5 June, made her lightning trip to the Netherlands, and wound up her work for the blood transfusion service at Slough.

A deeply emotional person, she was accustomed as a doctor to avoid open displays of feeling, and to exclude it when reaching professional judgements. Her usual self-help strategies were to focus on the work in hand, to express her feelings in conversation or letters to close confidants, and to look for some good in the situation. All came into play here. The work did help, as did opportunities to discuss it with visiting specialists at Belsen, and, it appears from surviving letters, the assistant director of pathology for the 21st

Army Group. The strategy of emphasising the positive shows itself in her tributes to the Army and others for what they achieved at Belsen; and in her assertion to Minot on 3 June, significantly after her trip to the Netherlands and no-doubt stimulating meeting with experts there, that she had been 'very very lucky' to have had this time in Europe. She also took pride in the fact that her work had and would contribute to the saving of life.

Nor did her achievement go unrecognised. Preserved among her papers is a note from Dr Tom Garland dated 30 May, saying that he had been very impressed by her statement at the Royal Society of Medicine the previous night.

> The film left me curiously unmoved, we seem calloused to horrible pictures, but your words brought the evil and the degradations right home and disturbed my sleep. I also got the impression of no small endurance on your part and it greatly won my admiration. You must I fear feel very exhausted and stressed. Good luck.'[47]

On 27 July, the chair of the proteins committee thanked her for the draft of the final Belsen paper: 'I have no comment ... save to express surprise that you managed to do so much under such adverse circumstances.'[48]

The strain did tell, however. It shows particularly in the way she seems at times to have forgotten her fellow researchers. The interim report was handwritten by her in the camp after three days of fever with a septic arm, and signed by her alone. When on her return she realised it was being circulated, she hastened to have the other two names added.[49] The report to the Royal Society of Medicine on 29 May was presented by her in the names of all three, according to the published accounts. But the summary she sent in October for an RSM memorial publication was again in her name only. When this was queried in June 1946, with a reminder that the paper had been read by her alone and written in the first person singular, she replied that the collaborators' names should appear: 'I know this is a little queer, of course I should have written it all as "we", but I think its [sic] probably impossible to make this alteration now. Their names should be associated with the work, however.'[50]

Such forgetfulness was unique for Vaughan. She seems to have felt isolated at Belsen, however, and not to have bonded with the other two members of the team. They were respectively 8 (Pitt-Rivers) and 12 years younger than she. Pitt-Rivers she must have known – they shared in particular a friendship with John Boycott (son of Vaughan's old boss at UCH in the 1920s) and his first wife. They were never close, however, perhaps because of a combination of very different social backgrounds and dissonant personal chemistry. Dent she probably would not have known previously. It was to him as a qualified doctor that she handed over the clinical side of the investigation for the three days when she was ill.[51] She never refers to this explicitly, however, and said more than 30 years later that

> Charles and Ros devoted themselves to chemistry, and I saw little of them. I tried to interest Charles in what I thought was a beri-beri heart, but at that time he was not interested in clinical medicine, and I don't think he ever came to see any of the patients …

They did grow closer after Dent became an expert on bone diseases, as professor of human metabolism at UCH from 1956. Vaughan told his biographer of his 'utter integrity' as a scientist, saying she felt privileged to have watched the change in him 'from the chemist to the wise physician'.[52]

Her memory of him taking little interest in the Belsen patients is partly contradicted by his own account, telling of spending time with the first four patients, although he found the later groups 'not so interesting humanly, or scientifically, as the first'. He also socialised with the medical students, and in the ambulance drivers' mess where meals were taken.[53] Pitt-Rivers, on the other hand, spoke afterwards of going round the camp in the first day or so with some soldiers, taking tins of food away from the inmates before they could open them and probably kill themselves by eating the contents. She wrote later to thank an RAMC Colonel for his kindness, saying 'The great treat I had was the drive you gave us the evening before I left which was a breath of fresh air.'[54]

The impression is of three people leading quite separate lives in the camp, and finding their own personal ways to cope. Also that Vaughan as leader felt her responsibility for completing the trial most acutely, and pursued that objective almost to the exclusion of all else, partly no doubt as a retreat from emotional pain. Much of the idealism which had in her youth been expressed in Christian belief was now channelled through medicine. She must have found the knowledge that German medical staff had been involved in cruelty and torture almost more horrifying than anything else. The woman who had cried to see the children in factories in India had to repress her feelings now in order to maintain face, before the army and her own team.

One further strategy for coping with Belsen was rage, mostly directed against Germans who, whether Nazi sympathisers or not, tended to be held responsible. This was the most common reaction of the liberating forces, and Vaughan shared it. When she went home her daughter Mary remembered that her eyes no longer sparkled. If the children, now aged 12 and nearly 10, complained about anything, in those first few weeks Vaughan would scream at them in anger, sometimes slapping them, and saying that they had nothing to complain of: they had enough to eat. Gourlay's striped pyjamas were burnt, and he could no longer speak German in her hearing. She told Minot she would never go back to Germany unless for work purposes. 'I am still stunned and bewildered by the mass cruelty … If you see pictures and films realize that they are nothing to the reality … the horror of it all.'[55] In Oxford years later, during a conversation over dinner, someone asked whether anyone who had witnessed something like the scenes at Belsen could ever be the same again. Vaughan simply said no; but was heard to say under her breath: 'After all, I shall never be the same again, and I was only there a short time.'[56]

Endnotes

[1] See cover photograph, one of several taken by Elliott and Fry at this time, and held by the NPG.

[2] HMLC Minot, Minot letters of 2.4.1945 and 24.4.1945 and 10.5.1945. Vaughan was clearly fit and well when the photographs were taken, on 13 March.

[3] TNA, FD 1/6340.

[4] H E Magee in Discussion: the physiology and treatment of starvation, in *Proc RSM* (1945), 38, 388–90.

[5] D P Cuthbertson in Discussion: the physiology and treatment of starvation, *Proc RSM* (1945), 38, 390–93.

[6] TNA, FD 1/6352, Loutit to MRC, 30.11.1944.

[7] TNA FD 1/142, minutes of meeting, 20.4.1945.

[8] HMLC Minot, Minot to Vaughan, 10.5.1945.

[9] A N (Alan) Drury (1889–1980) of the Lister Institute, in charge of MRC policy for the London blood supply depots from May 1941.

[10] TNA FD 1/6995, Drury to passport office, 24.4.1945. Also JA, 88.

[11] Rosalind Pitt-Rivers (1907–1990), FRS 1954. C E Dent (1911–1976), FRS 1962.

[12] HMLC Minot, Vaughan to Minot, 27.5.1945. Vaughan said here, and repeated in other accounts, that she agreed to this although none of the three had been inoculated against typhus. The context is clearly the comparatively low risk involved in travelling across Germany. It is inconceivable that she and her colleagues would have risked going into the camp without these inoculations; nor would the Army have allowed it.

[13] See Ben Shephard, *After Daybreak: The Liberation of Belsen, 1945* (London, Jonathan Cape, 2005), 202.

[14] W R F Collis, Belsen Camp: a preliminary report in *BMJ* (9.6.1945),1(4405), 814–16; and Eryl Hall Williams, *A Page of History in Relief* (York, Sessions Book Trust, 1993).

[15] Shephard, *After Daybreak*, 18.

[16] Ibid., 202–205.

[17] Dr A P Meiklejohn (1899–1970), pre-war lecturer in nutrition at Edinburgh University.

[18] HMLC Minot, Vaughan to Minot, 27.5.1945.

[19] P L (Pat) Mollison (1914–2011), later an eminent haematologist specialising in blood transfusion. Vaughan had introduced him to give a paper at a Medical Research Society meeting in December 1941 (Wellcome Collection, PP/LEW/D.8/2).

[20] Wellcome Collection, Royal Army Medical Corps, 1801 1/1-5.

[21] TNA, FD 1/142, Correspondence on 29.4 and 1.5.1945.

[22] Wellcome Collection, J M Vaughan (GC/186/7). PRC 41 Protein Requirements Committee: Report on the comparative value of hydrolysates, milk and serum in the treatment of starvation, based on observations made at Belsen Camp by C E Dent, Rosalind Pitt-Rivers and Janet Vaughan.

[23] TNA, FD 1/6995, Vaughan to MRC, 11 and 13.5.1945.

[24] JA, 90.

[25] C E Dent, 'Belsen, 1945', in *UCH Magazine* (1966), 49(1), 14–19.

[26] For the use of skin pencils, see Shephard, *After Daybreak*, 57–58.

[27] JA, 90.

[28] Wellcome Collection, GC/186/7, copy of letter dated 6.5.1945. By 'Georges', Vaughan meant St George's Hospital London, also a collecting point for blood.

[29] JA, 92.

[30] TNA, FD 1/6995, Vaughan to MRC, 11.5.1945.

[31] Pellagra is a deficiency disease caused by a lack of nicotinic acid in the diet.

[32] HMLC Minot, Vaughan to Minot, 12.5.1945.

[33] HMLC Minot, Vaughan to Minot, 27.5.1945.

[34] TNA, FD 1/142; HMLC Minot, Vaughan to Minot, 3.6.1945; and *Proc RSM* (1945), 38, 395–97.

[35] HMLC Minot, Vaughan to Minot, 27.5.1945.

[36] Ibid., 3.6.1945. Also JA, 94.

[37] TNA, FD 1/6995, Vaughan to MRC, 7.6.1945; and TNA, FD 1/6346, War Office to MRC, 22.8.1945.

[38] Wellcome Collection, Student Dissertation, 2003. Natalie Paine, The relief mission at Bergen-Belsen concentration camp: the medical students' story (BSc dissertation, University of London, 2003). The Bengal Famine preparation was a mixture of powdered milk, sugar and flour, rejected by most inmates as being too sweet.

[39] Anthony Aspinall, letter: The strange case of 'Bengal Famine gruel', *The Independent* (29.1.1993): https://www.independent.co.uk/voices/letter-the-strange-case-of-bengal-famine-gruel-1481737.html accessed 22.6.2023.

[40] Shephard, *After Daybreak*, 100 and 184.

[41] TNA, FD 1/6995, Mollison to MRC, 8.6.1945; and Mollison to Vaughan, 17.6.1945. In the event, he did not return until late July or early August, by which time Vaughan was winding up her BT work. It was Loutit who gave the necessary advice: P L Mollison, Observations on cases of starvation at Belsen, in *BMJ* (5.1.1946), 1(4435), 4–8.

[42] Wellcome Collection, GC/186/7.

[43] HMLC Minot, Vaughan to Minot, 27.5.1945.

[44] This charge was made most notably in Paul Weindling, Human guinea pigs and the ethics of experimentation: the *BMJ*'s correspondent at the Nuremberg medical trial in *BMJ* (7.12.1996), 313(7070), 1467–70; see also his *Epidemics and Genocide in Eastern Europe* (London, Oxford University Press, 2000).

[45] Dent suggests that there were more, but does so ambiguously. The contemporary case notes seem to provide a more reliable guide.

[46] By contrast, Ros Pitt-Rivers was on her return given a week off by her boss at the National Institute of Medical Research (TNA, FD 1/6995).

[47] Wellcome Collection, GC/186/7. Garland later became head of the Occupational Health Unit at the London Hospital. Contemporary newsreel films, including of Buchenwald Camp, were shown at the meeting.

[48] Wellcome Collection, GC/186/7, MRC (Himsworth) to Vaughan, 26.7.1945.

[49] TNA, FD 1/6995, Vaughan to MRC, 20.5.1945.

[50] Wellcome Collection, GC/186/7, Vaughan to RSM, 12.6.1946.

[51] Ibid. The case notes of three of the patients refer to treatments decided by him.

[52] Albert Neuberger, Charles Enrique Dent, 25 August 1911 – 19 September 1976, *Biographical Memoirs of Fellows of the Royal Society* (1.11.1978), 24, 15–31.

[53] Dent, 'Belsen, 1945', in *UCH Magazine* (1966), 17–18.

[54] Telephone conversation with Anthony Pitt-Rivers, 26 November 2010. The tins were apparently a misguided gift from some of the troops. And Wellcome Collection, RAMC 792/8, Pitt-Rivers to Colonel Lipscombe, 24.5.1945.

[55] HMLC Minot, Vaughan to Minot, 27.5.1945.

[56] JPP, interview with Honor Smith, 1994.

OXFORD 1945–67

CHAPTER 10
Return to Somerville
1945–55

A new beginning

Before she went to Belsen, Vaughan had accepted a new job. The Principal of her old college in Oxford was retiring in summer 1945, and the recruitment process for her successor began the year before. The five women's colleges were not yet fully self-governing, so the Somerville Council had members (including Will Goodenough) from male colleges, and its vice-chair was A T (Sandy) Lindsay, master of Balliol College.[1] Shortlisted candidates were interviewed in late October 1944 by a selection committee comprising female members of council, chaired by Lindsay.

At first, the choice was expected to fall on the tutor in PPE, Lucy Sutherland, a noted scholar and, during the war, highly effective civil servant. A split soon emerged, however, with the crystallographer Dorothy Hodgkin (unusual in being married, with children) foremost in advocating a less conventional appointment. Hodgkin reportedly wanted someone whose career had been outside Oxford, and preferably a scientist.[2] Her view was shared by the classicist Isobel Henderson and the English literature don Mary Lascelles, both very influential in college affairs. Vaughan's near-contemporary the linguist Enid Starkie, and the historian Anne Evans (later de Villiers) have also been mentioned as supporters of the external candidate.[3] Goodenough gave information to the selection committee about her.[4] Lindsay had no formal vote, but may also have favoured her. When she entered his room that October, he said 'I know nothing about you. You are not in *Who's Who*. Women never are.'[5] No doubt there was a twinkle in his eye. Like her, he was politically left wing and knew Goodenough well.

Sutherland told her parents of a strong outside candidate, 'very prominent in public life throughout the war'.[6] Soon only these two remained, and in early December she decided to withdraw. She

211

must have believed that a vote would favour Vaughan, and it was better to have a consensual decision.[7] A unanimous recommendation in December was confirmed by Council the following February.

By spring 1945, when Sutherland accepted the Principalship of Lady Margaret Hall, she was dubious about Vaughan: it might be just 'ill-natured rumours', but she doubted if she would have found it easy to like and respect her as Principal.[8] The rumours are unspecified, but the two women had little in common. Sutherland was calm, measured, unmarried and an efficient administrator, politically right wing. Vaughan's socialism, impatience and passion would have made it hard for them to work closely together.

For the Gourlays the decision to go for the Oxford post was not easy. Their daughter Mary remembered them going for a walk from Plovers Field to discuss it before Vaughan went for interview. Gourlay's work was still in London, and their weekend home in Surrey. On the other hand, the Gordon Square flat had suffered severe damage, and Oxford offered a more attractive home for children than war-battered London. Professionally, Vaughan would be a difficult 'fit' back at Hammersmith, in the cramped department she had criticised on the Goodenough Committee, and subordinate to the man she had beaten onto the RCP Council in 1943. The starting salary at Somerville barely matched her current pay, but for her this was never a critical factor. As a respected academic who was influential on the national stage, she knew her medical and scientific friends in Oxford would welcome her. Crucially, unspecified 'haematological colleagues' offered her research space in two laboratories.[9] As to women's education, she was aware of the inequities they faced within and outside the workplace. Her wartime work had strengthened her wish to encourage more into medicine and science, and indeed any worthwhile careers. Oxford, a short train journey from London, would be a strong base from which to pursue her many interests.

Gourlay must have seen the force of all this, including the advantages for the children. The war had, sadly, accustomed them to separation; but Oxford terms were short, and he would be able to come down at weekends and host social events. They would have Plovers Field in vacations, and Vaughan could stay at the flat when she needed to be in London overnight. Their decision was made. She became the first ever married woman with children to be Principal of a women's college, and, for a number of years, the only scientist to head any Oxford college.[10]

***

Vaughan managed a family holiday at Plovers Field in summer 1945, enrolling the children in the Pony Club with newly acquired ponies and enjoying the countryside. In September they moved into Radcliffe House, the Principal's residence at Somerville, ready for the new academic year starting in early October. Her new job was probably the best antidote she could have found to the psychological shock of Belsen. Oxford was shabby, but still recognisably the place she had known as an undergraduate. Some dons might seem parochial, but their opposition would not have daunted someone used, as she was, to negotiating the entrenched attitudes of conservative men. There were rumours that they initially gave her 'a hard time', for sins unspecified apart from her lack of grounding in Latin and Greek, and tendency to take swift, independent decisions. She had, however, consulted her predecessor Helen Darbishire in January, and must also have talked to Margery Fry, the family friend who was Principal from 1926 to 1930.[11]

Both these women would have warned of the chief pitfalls in college and university politics, and the social reformer Fry was in many ways a kindred spirit, with her impatience of pomposity, priggishness and Oxford 'politicking'. Fry had been popular within the college, and encouraged students to develop interests outside their academic studies. She also favoured Lindsay of Balliol, and had secured the appointment of Isobel Munro (later Henderson) as assistant tutor in ancient history.[12] Where major issues were concerned, especially in wider university affairs, Vaughan felt prepared if necessary to wait until the time was ripe for the changes she wished to see. She had the refuge of her scientific work and also a 'strange new personal resignation' resulting from the experience of Belsen. Family, friends and visual beauty were henceforth the most important things in life, and she could disregard trivia.[13] Events bore this out, with the proviso that 'family and friends' tended for her to include both Somerville and all humankind.

All was not plain sailing. She recalled that W T S Stallybrass 'was the one person in my early days who … treated me as a human being'.[14] Stallybrass, Principal of Brasenose College, would ask her to private dinner parties with 'a sense of warmth and welcome that was very refreshing among all the formalities of Oxford society'. He was her constant adviser, and encouraged her in 1946 to stand for Hebdomadal Council, the governing body of the university, when 'all my fellow women Principals considered it a rash and improper thing for a newcomer to do – although her Somerville fellows gave warm support.[15] His support as university Vice-Chancellor during her first year on Council, until his death in October 1948, was invaluable. She also renewed old friendships, especially with the flamboyant Enid Starkie, renowned for the bright, eccentric clothes which matched her personality, and Maurice Bowra, now Master of Wadham College. Through them the writer Joyce Cary became a close friend, and sometimes stood in for Gourlay at her own formal dinners.[16]

There were other strong links to the past. One of the first visitors at Radcliffe House was her undergraduate friend Cicely Williams, who had been serving in the colonial medical service in Malaya in 1939. She arrived in September after release from a Japanese prisoner-of-war camp in Singapore.[17] The formerly tall, straight-backed redhead was white-haired and thin, her back bent. She had spent months kneeling in a small crowded room after she was accused of spying, and still suffered the after-effects of beri-beri and other ills. A leader in the camp, she had doctored fellow inmates, and was most proud that the 20 babies born there had all survived, because they were breast-fed in accordance with her teaching.[18] After her, Margery Fry, Lettice Fisher and Vera Brittain came often. It was not surprising that Vaughan felt 'at home' in Oxford.

Above all, she cared for the students. She invited them to Radcliffe House at weekends, hosted them at dinner in college and saw them individually at the start and end of each term. The sparkle must have been back in her eyes. And she put the Belsen experience to good use. Once she took an opportunity to describe her work there to the students, and warned of the horrors people were capable of if evil were allowed to develop unchecked. One student who was present later helped raise money for the starving in post-war Germany, and arranged for a German student to come to Somerville for part of 1949. Vaughan was fully supportive.[19]

Her guiding principles were unchanged. The belief that 'people come first' was most obvious in her treatment of anyone who was mentally or physically sick. It also informed the belief in justice and equity which led to her socialism, her drive to ensure that women were on a par with men, and that people around the world had more equal life chances; and her insistence on intellectual rigour in teaching, research and public discourse. One can see these principles playing out in her diverse activities throughout her life, and the years in Oxford were in many ways the crown of that life.

Early challenges
Both college and university faced economic austerity in the immediate post-war years, as the government tried to steer the country out of bankruptcy; also overcrowding as ex-service people swelled the student body; and appalling weather. The winter of 1945–46 was harsh, with fuel and food in short supply. Each Somerville student was allowed hot water for a bath twice a week, but only an inch of it, so its utility was hard to perceive. Those with grates in their rooms could have a fire once a week, when others would join them to work, and anyone with food parcels from abroad was especially popular.

The following winter was worse: in January, on the flat and marshy Port Meadow, there were

> Dons skating placidly round in … circles, children on sledges, people falling … big young men in college scarves playing ice hockey … [A month or so later] Oxford's plumbing seized up for several weeks, and people had to go out at night into gardens or parks … to defecate, digging careful holes in the frozen snow and then covering them, like cats.[20]

The women's colleges were poor compared to most men's colleges, and food was meagre and badly cooked.[21] Fortunately, thanks to the firewood Gourlay brought from Plovers Field, Radcliffe House could be kept relatively warm, and Vaughan made it a haven for those suffering from stress or minor illnesses. She fed them and those in the college sickroom with fresh eggs, at first from Plovers Field and later from hens kept in the Radcliffe House garden.

Vaughan was shocked to learn of Somerville's poverty, but the Goodenough Committee and the Nuffield Foundation had given her some knowledge of financial management. Lindsay suggested making better use of their modest funds through powers under recent legislation to pool trusts; and Goodenough and a colleague then advised on how to use their capital more productively. The financial position steadily improved during the 1950s, through regular fee increases and careful investment.[22] Vaughan often referred to her problems with arithmetic, but she undoubtedly grasped mathematical principles and logic, in finance as well as scientific research. At lunch at Radcliffe House some years later, she asked a young financial journalist what he thought about the stock market. He confidently gave his views, but met with contrary opinions backed by convincing arguments. She said gently that, as chair of the Somerville pension fund, she saw investment advisers every six months; but he wryly felt that she knew more than he.[23] Vaughan understood the need, as college head, to be unbiased politically. But her left-wing views were hardly controversial at a time of strong consensus across society and leading political parties in favour of the NHS, the benefits system, the state education settlement, and nationalised railways and utilities. Most students were left-wing, but Vaughan supported the activities of those of any political persuasion so long as they were committed to democratic values. In her talk to freshers in 1950, she said they were lucky to be at university in England, not the USA where McCarthyism was gathering way, or Czechoslovakia where she had witnessed the Communist takeover in 1948.

Being head of college must have evoked memories, not just of her own student days, but of life at Wellington and Rugby. Like her father, she visited daily anyone who was ill, and took pains to recruit the best possible candidates for teaching posts. Like him she tried to improve the physical comfort of buildings, and the terms and conditions of all staff. The electricity and central heating system in one building collapsed in January 1946 but was mainly renewed in time for the 1946/47 winter.[24] Limited redecoration brightened rooms neglected during the war and the college garden was restocked, including a new rose garden which she donated. In May 1947, responding to a university request, she sought an order of priority for maintenance and building plans over the next five years. This was set (and broadly adhered to) as providing some new undergraduate rooms, a long-planned library extension, additional kitchen facilities and a domestic staff common room.[25]

By November 1947, the college was exploring the possibility of buying Radcliffe House and adjacent properties, and Henderson was deputed to find possible architects for new buildings. Pay increased in line with inflation, and Vaughan informed fellows of potentially untapped sources of grants and scholarships.[26] The Senior Common Room (SCR) and private dining room were redecorated in 1950–51, and when they were again refurbished in 1959 she suggested that the college bear some or all of the cost. On both occasions she contributed personally.[27]

Some contemporary descriptions of Vaughan call her father to mind: the tall, strong physical presence, often combined with untidy hair and clothes, heavy-footed clumsiness (perhaps partly due to the wartime car accident) and a tendency to scatter in all directions the armful or briefcase of papers she was usually carrying. Having grown up with weekly chapel services, she understood the importance of Somerville's non-denominational chapel as a place for quiet reflection. She expressed a wish to give an occasional address and sometimes read the lesson at Sunday services, and fellows who were willing to take regular services then set up a Chapel Committee.[28]

Unlike her father she could not act unilaterally: constitutionally, she was 'first among equals' in relation to the fellows, and must proceed by consensus. Barbara Harvey, the history don who was on the governing body from 1956, thought her 'a natural autocrat who found it hard to school herself to work within the constraints of an Oxford college's way of reaching decisions'.[29] At the end of the 1945–46 academic year, Hodgkin seems to have tackled her on this. 'The trouble with you, Principal, is you take decisions', Vaughan remembered her saying; adding that she took no more quick decisions 'except on most urgent matters affecting individuals'.[30]

Her patience was undoubtedly tried more by the (to her) leisurely pace of decision-making than by the need for consensus. Council met formally to ratify major decisions three times in each eight-week term, and the key subordinate committees, for Education and Finance, also met only in term time. Vaughan acted early to increase the amount of business done, persuading dons to keep more time free for Council meetings. It helped that, under her chairmanship, no meeting lasted a minute longer than necessary.[31]

A wind of change

Somerville was set on an upward trajectory, and fellows could appreciate her part in this. Her status was enhanced through publication of the equal pay report in 1946, election to Hebdomadal Council in 1946–47 as the first Somerville Principal to receive that honour, and appointment to the Oxford Regional Hospital Board in 1947. The fact that she led a research team gave her added authority in academic matters, while the value of her Nuffield trusteeship was shown in a grant gained by Hodgkin, and college participation in a pilot student health service. The woman accustomed since childhood to meeting famous people from every walk of life was also equal to any grand occasion which Oxford presented.

In 1946, Somerville not only had as Principal this very striking married woman with two children, still pursuing her own career in science, but also two fellows, Hodgkin and one of the English dons, were pregnant. To outsiders, the college appeared bold and unusual. Vaughan also understood the importance of appearance. While some students thought her day-to-day tweeds dowdy, others noticed their quality and a sense of style and elegance rare among dons. Notable were her black and gold evening dress, and the deep red and black shot silk dress she wore for a ball given for Princess Margaret in 1950.

Vaughan's character and style were an abrupt change from the quiet predictability of her predecessor. Instead of going to the library each day, she would often don a white coat to go to the Infirmary next door, or a smart suit to catch the London train. The previously austere Principal's room became welcoming, with armchairs and sofa, a good quality carpet, an elegant bureau with bookcase above, a large antique mirror at one end and a portrait of Madge by Charles Furse at the other. Bookcases, and later a sculpted torso of her daughter Mary by Dora Gordine, completed the transformation. Students could call at any time, in college or at Radcliffe House. Other novelties were a direct-line telephone, and sherry and glasses in the bureau.[32] Her wish to treat students like the adults they mostly were was reflected in a May 1946 Council decision to grant late leave until 12.30am for college dances. Such relaxations of the rules were later extended, always in advance of the other women's colleges.

Socially, she brought a sense of warmth and welcome, opening doors to the world outside Oxford. Besides personal friends and family, and Somerville stalwarts like Lettice Fisher, medical friends and colleagues like Dorothy Russell came to stay at Radcliffe House. Vaughan enjoyed parties and in 1947 proposed the first post-war Gaudy (a big summer weekend party for particular year groups of old Somervillians). She used the annual public Bryce lectures to secure eminent speakers, inviting the French writer André Gide, along with his friend and translator Dorothy Bussy, to stay with her when he came in 1947. Later speakers included her American friend Sigerist, from the 1944 Indian trip, the astronomer Bernard Lovell and crystallographer Kathleen Lonsdale. She also seized opportunities to host visiting groups, such as members of the Physiological Congress meeting in Oxford in July 1947, followed in the next two years by Commonwealth conference delegates. Starkie's achievement in gaining the *Légion d'honneur* in summer 1947 was celebrated with a special dinner in Hall, as were those of other eminent Somervillians.[33]

In 1951–52, Vaughan endorsed a more formal way of maintaining links with distinguished old Somervillians, as Guests of High Table. Two were appointed each year for three years, providing a constant total of six, who dined on a particular date and met students and fellows. The first group included Mrs Spedan Lewis, vice-chair of the John Lewis Partnership, and Janet Adam Smith, literary editor of *The New Statesman*, who soon became a close friend. These and other women of note in all walks of life illustrated her message to students that no careers were closed to them.

***

A key milestone was passed when in May 1951, at Lindsay's suggestion, Somerville became the first of the women's colleges to be fully self-governing, through the Principal and Fellows. Vaughan had a wealth of experience of working through committees and managing staff, and it is generally agreed that the governing body was marked during her tenure by its lack of any deep disagreement. The philosophy don, Philippa Foot, found that Vaughan tended to make up her mind on the basis of the papers, and did not argue in the way she, as a philosopher, at first expected. Instead she took the sense of the meeting whilst expressing her own preference in guiding decision-making; and was nearly always right.[34] Others agreed that fellows had to be well organised if presenting ideas, but decisions were consensual.

Some were alarmed by her plethora of activities. Learning in summer 1947 of concern that she was overworking, she said it was part of her job to keep open house for friends of college; it benefited the college and Oxford to have a married woman with a family as Principal; and anyone holding such an administrative job should also be doing academic work. In response the college covered some of the Radcliffe House costs, and improved the staff cover there and in her college room. In 1950 they increased her entertainment allowance and domestic bills subsidy, and by 1960 were paying for all fuel.[35]

Certainly the range of Vaughan's commitments was daunting. She managed them in the way that was by then second nature, by flexible time rationing, effective delegation, swift decision-making, succinct and clear communication, and sheer hard work. Her ability to make connections across subjects, apparent in her scientific work, played out too in other areas. So did her liking for talk, from which she clearly learned as much as she did through assiduous and speedy reading. She rarely missed an important committee or other meeting, but she must have often cut short her time in one to attend another, just as she left Hebdomadal Council at times to check on experimental work at the lab. Relaxation belonged to her time with family, friends and especially Gourlay, but she also found it in bedtime leisure reading.

As Principal, she famously completed routine college business before leaving between 9am and 9.30am, usually for the lab. She normally woke at six, made herself tea using an electric kettle in her room and worked in bed until seven, when she had a bath before having breakfast, settling domestic matters and leaving for college at 8am, to see her secretary and anyone else she needed to talk to.[36] By the sixties, she was dictating answers to letters, and the secretary occasionally found herself typing a dinner menu or shopping list when Vaughan had started speaking to the housekeeper without switching off the machine.[37] Speed was a constant. Her driving was as impatient as ever, and her cars displayed their battle scars. Dining on high table was usually a tense affair for slow eaters and those who were served last, since she would eat quickly before getting up and leading everyone out, regardless of how full their plates still were. Guest nights must have given some welcome relief. She was usually available on the phone during the day, but her telephone manner was abrupt in the extreme, with no social niceties.

Some dons, like Foot who became a fellow in 1950, found her style exhilarating: 'I sometimes felt we were doing something marvellous … like taking the Royal Ballet to the North Pole – getting out to push the sledge when it stuck.'[38] Others, however, preferred a more measured approach, and all objected to her tendency to take unilateral decisions. In October 1947 college archives were established under the control of the history tutor: administrative officers must in future seek her permission before destroying or removing papers. This may have been done in response to a notorious occasion when Vaughan destroyed important records – treating the college papers like her own, of which she periodically made a bonfire.[39]

Her care in recruiting new fellows shows in an exchange about a possible candidate with the biochemist Professor Howard Florey in 1947. She wanted someone 'with some distinction of mind & person, [who might] become a Fellow'. Did she have potential as a researcher, would she be an inspiring teacher and agreeable colleague? Florey replied that the candidate, then on his staff, would be stimulating and 'not a crammer'.[40] Her support for new fellows was recalled by Harvey, to whom she gave the customary present (a cameo, in her case) after the solemn swearing-in ceremony. Harvey knew she had little interest in medieval history, but soon afterwards Vaughan gave her supper at a good country pub, 'solely, it seemed to me from a desire to hear about my research and to administer encouragement'.[41]

Quality was her watchword. When she arrived in 1945, the philosopher Elizabeth Anscombe had a two-year research fellowship.[42] According to Foot, the rest of Oxford thought her unemployable: she wore trousers, smoked cigars, had intransigent Roman Catholic views (and, eventually, seven children) and could be extremely rude, including to Vaughan. Henderson, the distinguished classicist whom Vaughan greatly admired, supported her, and she and Vaughan ensured the renewal of the fellowship and, from 1950, a college lectureship. They later obtained extra Rockefeller Foundation funding so that Anscombe could complete her translation of Wittgenstein.[43] Foot, arriving in 1947, soon took on most of the philosophy tutoring so as to relieve the pressure on her senior. Within a decade Anscombe became a world-renowned asset to the college, attracting increasing numbers of graduate students.

In 1949, the UGC enabled the CUF (Common University Fund) system whereby the cost of lecturers could be shared between college and university, and Vaughan seized the opportunity to recruit more staff. One fellow recalled that, when lecturing at Leeds, she was prompted by Starkie to apply for a university lectureship in Italian; but then heard from Vaughan offering a college lectureship before receiving official notification of the university appointment.[44] By 1950 all Somerville fellows doing college teaching were also university lecturers. College prestige grew: Hodgkin had become the joint fourth woman Fellow of the Royal Society (FRS) in 1947, Henderson led a successful classics school, Starkie chaired her faculty board in 1950, the history don May McKisack was a senior lecturer from 1948, and the economist Margaret Hall, a fellow from 1949, had a high-profile input to government policy work. Jean Banister rose from assistant tutor in 1949 to university demonstrator in physiology from 1952. Fellows were frequently away as visiting professors, on scholarships or sabbaticals to pursue research or writing. Colleagues, including Vaughan, assumed without demur the burden of coping with their normal workload.

The students

As for the students, the vast majority found Vaughan 'accessible and exhilarating'.[45] Her care extended to someone grappling with a call to become a Roman Catholic, and another for whom the rules were stretched so that she could come up a year early and so keep a vital state scholarship. More than one found the college very supportive to those coming from state grammar schools. Students in perplexity or distress benefited from her ability (that of a good diagnostician) to give her complete attention to their problem, before sparing no effort to find and apply the remedy. Her intense eye contact could be disconcerting, however, when she was also driving a car.

Vaughan supported Ryle's 1946 proposal to the Nuffield Foundation for a pilot student health service.[46] With a small five-year grant, it began in 1947 in Somerville and two male colleges, providing a yearly medical examination and advice on any necessary treatment. An accompanying survey of serious illness in 25 colleges in 1947–50 found that TB accounted for nearly a quarter, but mental disorders were more prevalent. A university student health service was recommended in 1951, including basic psychiatric advice; but to Vaughan's surprise the proposal was rejected, and all Somerville fellows voted against. She believed this was partly because they saw no need for psychiatric help, whereas she, already convinced of its value by her RCP colleague Aubrey Lewis, had in her first term seen three students with serious problems. She did all she could for such students, helped by a close relationship with Oxford's psychiatric consultants. She often learned through the twice-termly interviews, or from other students, who was at risk; and there were no suicides during her time at Somerville, although attempts were made.[47]

She did not, as some thought, especially favour those doing scientific subjects. A student wishing in her second year to change from chemistry to PPE found that Vaughan had anticipated this, and agreed immediately. She also went on to placate the irate father who objected to the change.[48] Others took from her the lesson that what mattered in life was not worldly success of any kind, but simply being useful. Or as Foot put it, after relating Vaughan's delight in news of an ex-student's charitable activity, or getting a low-grade job after being down and out, 'Nothing bad … was grist to her mill, but anything good … She had this generosity of heart that … made her delighted by anyone's success.'[49]

Linked to this was the value she put on 'principal's places': that is, her ability as she saw it to ensure a leavening of 'interesting' people in each year, rather than some who had efficiently jumped the academic hurdles but apparently had nothing distinctive to contribute. At first there seem to have been more than ten of these; but they were, naturally, not popular with the dons, and were first reduced in number and then, after Vaughan's time, abolished. She very much regretted the reduction, with feelings summed up in her response to a query about whether some female students were as 'single minded or as highly motivated' as men in relation to academic work: 'I just hate people to be highly motivated.'[50]

Vaughan was particularly sympathetic to students from overseas. Prue Smith (née Pryce) arrived in England from South Africa in 1945. At 21, she was still mourning her dead father, estranged from her mother, and missing her fiancé. Staying in Radcliffe House when unwell one November weekend, she mostly worked by the fire, but met Vaughan's 'two lovely, playful, pig-tailed daughters and a silent though very kind … husband, who brings the firewood and eggs and other goodies … [Janet] is vivacious but untrivial … a powerful presence but simple and friendly.'[51] Thereafter, Prue was often invited socially, and later she and her husband regularly stayed at Plovers Field. The families became lifelong friends.[52]

Another protégé came from Nepal.[53] Learning one day that she was ill, Vaughan visited her lodgings and was appalled by their inadequacy. Wanting to remedy this, and provide opportunities for as many women as possible from developing nations, she conceived the idea of a Somerville graduate house. As an interim measure, the library extension completed in 1956 included some specially designed rooms for overseas graduates, with central heating and space to store trunks over vacations. Little could then be done for graduates living outside college, apart from limited dining rights, and encouraging social contacts through parties and annual 'graduate open nights'.[54]

A scientist with a mission

Oxford in 1945 was dominated by the arts and humanities. The highest-status degree subject was Greats (Ancient History and Philosophy), and any aspiring medical student in a male college would constantly be challenged to justify to others the intellectual content of what he did. A woman doctor was doubly disadvantaged, but Vaughan was well used to being the only woman in a room. Intellectually she could hold her own, and revealed one important defensive strategy to her successor as Principal: 'Always wear pancake makeup: if you're off colour, they can't take advantage of you.'[55] As well as her male allies, she was quick to contact female colleagues who had come to Oxford during the war, including the biochemist Antoinette (Tony) Pirie, paediatrician Dr Victoria Smallpeice (who later helped set up a GP practice which served Somerville), and Honor Smith, who was establishing what became a world famous Tuberculous Meningitis Unit in the neurosurgery department. Smith, an ebullient character whose greatest love outside her work was fox hunting, became like Pirie a close friend of Vaughan. The government wanted to maintain the wartime growth in science and technology specialists, and the founding of the NHS meant a huge new demand for medically trained people. It was a favourable time to try to advance the cause of medicine and science, and of women within them; but the obstacles were still considerable.

One personal crisis arose almost immediately, when the colleagues who had promised lab space for Vaughan's research withdrew their offers. In dismay, she considered resigning from Somerville and returning to London. Research was the most important thing in her working life; but two men came to the rescue. Leslie Witts, a friend in 1930s London and now Nuffield professor of medicine, secured her election as honorary consulting haematologist to the Radcliffe Infirmary, where she worked in his blood diseases outpatient clinic and accompanied him on ward rounds. J W Burn, the professor of pharmacology whom she knew through her blood transfusion work, gave her lab space in his department's basement.

During her tenure the numbers at Somerville studying science and mathematics increased substantially. She encouraged this through the staff she engaged, and, like Hodgkin, by providing postgraduate work in her own lab. Her own and Hodgkin's distinction were in themselves an advertisement for Somerville's medical and scientific credentials. In 1949, Hodgkin wanted to work on vitamin B12 but, with no punched card machine available, was daunted by the level of computing involved.[56] Vaughan suggested applying for Nuffield funding, which was granted almost immediately and continued until 1958, enabling Hodgkin to buy more computing and research assistance. Vaughan also ensured additional teaching assistance to free up research time, and the college granted Hodgkin a sabbatical year for this in 1952–53. Her solution to the structure of vitamin B12 resulted in the award of the Royal Society Gold Medal in 1956 and the Nobel Prize in 1964. She made clear how important the Nuffield Foundation's support had been in encouraging her 'to persist with this research in its more hopeless seeming moments'.[57]

College dining rights enabled Pirie to qualify for an MA in 1947 and in 1949 become a university reader in ophthalmology and honorary research fellow of the college. From 1952 she was a professorial fellow and a valued participant in college governance. Early in 1955 Vaughan, Hodgkin and Banister persuaded the governing body that, given the increasing numbers studying science subjects, they should take on more teachers. In April Anne Cobbe was appointed tutor and fellow in maths and physics, and additional chemistry teaching secured in June.[58] The pool of science teaching candidates was small, and Vaughan encouraged graduate students to help with teaching, partly in the hope of their moving on to become permanent staff.

These efforts benefited from a general growth in female student numbers. Male opposition to such growth waned quickly after the war, and the annual female quota rose from 160 in 1948 to 200 in the mid-fifties before being abolished in 1957. Limits after that were determined by resource constraints. Harvey remembered that at some point (most likely in 1955–56, with the increased intake well established and Cobbe in post), Vaughan used her then-customary right, to determine the final allocation of places by subject after the entrance examination, to make 'quite a major increase' in those for maths and natural sciences, with a corresponding decrease in other subjects. There was no prior discussion, and Harvey thought tutors in other schools might feel the pinch, but 'I doubt whether many of us wished to argue against such a development in principle.'[59] The number of graduate students in all subjects was also rising.

The Nuffield Foundation

Vaughan was respected in the university in part because of her role on the Nuffield Foundation, combined from 1953 with her ten-year membership of the UGC Medical Advisory Committee. The UGC role meant that she took part in two annual 'visitations' to all medical schools in Britain, helping to spread best practice. She carried this overview of the national medical scene to the foundation: 'I could see at first hand where needs for help were greatest, where there were promising men [sic] working on exciting new ventures.'[60]

Useful grants in Oxford went not only to Hodgkin and Witts, but (in 1944) to the Nuffield Institute for Medical Research for developing the technology of radiography.[61] Grants to the Clarendon Laboratory in the 1950s and 1960s for work with archaeologists and art historians helped develop what became the university's department of archaeology and the history of art. Nuffield College was a major beneficiary, and numerous individuals benefited. R G Macfarlane's research unit was funded between 1948 and 1958 (when it was taken over by the MRC), while he and his team found the missing clotting factor in the blood of haemophiliac patients. Others included Florey, and one comment of his is very telling. In 1960, he suggested that someone seeking a grant should approach Vaughan for her private opinion, saying she was 'a straight shooter from way back. I have always admired her; in fact, I think I was her tutor at one point, but I was not quite sure if she was tutoring me or I her!'[62]

Vaughan's wider influence through the foundation was also substantial. In 1952 her own research interest was reflected in an equipment grant to the University of London in the fields of radiography, diagnostic radiology and ultrasonics. Fell's cell biology research at the Strangeways Laboratory benefited, and in 1951 the University of Cambridge mathematical laboratory gained a five-year grant to develop automatic calculating machines, or computers: very significant, not least to Hodgkin. Nuffield support was crucial to developing the moveable radio telescope at Jodrell Bank. First used in 1957, within two months it was tracking Sputnik I, and was at that time the only instrument that could both detect the first Soviet and American satellites and transmit instructions to them. It later acted as a missile warning system, and provided insights into phenomena such as pulsars, quasars, neutron stars and black holes.[63]

The foundation papers, projects and conferences enabled her to keep up to date with what was happening nationally and internationally in subjects ranging from medical and scientific research to sociology, the arts and education. This helped her to give students up-to-date careers advice and useful contacts, whether for research or job opportunities. The comments of those who knew her Nuffield Foundation work throw light, too, on why she was so highly valued on committees. Not only was she knowledgeable, hard-working and enthusiastic, but she often asked 'the potentially disruptive but vitally necessary question'.[64]

Public service

In 1953 Vaughan's public standing led to an invitation to serve on a Treasury-led group examining the economic and financial problems of old age. This had a tightly focused, time-limited remit which she must have felt able to manage alongside other commitments in London. At that time population trends indicated that the number of old people in Britain would grow while the working population remained roughly constant, with worrying implications for government finances and the wider economy. There was also public pressure to raise pension rates in line with the rising cost of living, and the government reluctantly commissioned studies, including this one: to examine sources of income including state benefits and private pensions; and take account of hospital, residential and domiciliary services.

Vaughan was chosen as a not too 'political' woman and doctor, and probably also thanks to her Nuffield Foundation links to experts on old age provision. Fellow members were expert, experienced and hard-working, and discussions were amicable, though bounded by a consciousness of political constraints.[65] Anyone seeking to limit the cost of pensions in the longer term faced two logically inescapable but politically problematic issues. First, the pension age should be the same for men and women: it had for technical reasons been changed to 65 and 60 in 1940.[66] Second, the age for both should be higher. No medical reason for different ages was given in evidence. The health ministry also believed the ages were too low: on average, age-linked disability set in at around 70, becoming severe for both men and women at 75 or more. When the TUC stuck to their policy of pensions for all at 60, Vaughan said tradition seemed to be the main obstacle to change, which might be more acceptable to 'a public better aware of the facts'. (She was delighted, however, by the actuaries' evidence of a spectacular decline in infant mortality since 1947: the effect of improved maternal and child care under the NHS.)[67]

The committee's December 1954 report suggested options for raising pension ages to reduce future costs, but not for equalising them. Vaughan's views were reflected in recommendations that the elderly be encouraged to stay in their own homes, supported by adequate domiciliary care, and closer co-operation between relevant authorities; but both she and the economist Cairncross were frustrated by the inadequacy of the available statistics.[68] Her reservation to the report urged restoration of pension age parity: useful savings would result, and if women expected the same opportunities and working conditions as men, they must contribute equally. Women over 60 were as fit as the men, with longer life expectancy, but there were no comparable figures for morbidity below that age. 'Indeed … a detailed study of … fitness for work in different occupations and at different ages in both sexes is required as a matter of urgency.' Policy should be evidence based.

The government avoided giving a response, partly because higher pensions and benefits were announced at almost the same time as the report's publication. Press and public violently opposed any increase in or parity of pension ages. Only the *News Chronicle* of 4 December broke ranks: 'Which of our … political parties … is going to have the courage … of the lone woman member, Dr Janet Vaughan? Speaking … as one of the few really logical feminists …

229

she says that if women want the same working conditions ... they must wait as long ... for their pensions.' Later, however, *The Times* of 3 March 1955 did favour parity, and acknowledged the strength of Vaughan's argument.[69]

***

International commitments were taxing in different ways. In 1948 Vaughan represented British universities on a new Anglo-Czech Cultural Convention. British members were about to set off for Prague when they heard of the communist coup, on 25 February. They arrived late at night, and two members of the new government briefed them over Slivovitz in the station buffet. Next morning they met Jan Masaryk, still foreign minister and hoping, 'with tears streaming down his face', for continuing mutual friendship. They talked for a few days about cultural exchanges, interrupted at one point by a communist Czech who consulted 'Dr Vaughan' about one of the old government who had just thrown himself out of a window.[70] There were daily marches in the streets, but a quiet and beautiful city in the evening. Vaughan tried on her return to promote ongoing links between Charles University and Oxford, and the Convention met again in London in 1949; but, to her lasting sadness, contacts then petered out.

Also in 1949, she had to refuse to join a commission on university education in India, as it entailed a nine months' absence from Oxford; but she did later manage a trip to Russia, representing Oxford at Moscow University's bicentenary in May 1955. Among academics from around the world she was the only woman and, apart from the representative from Outer Mongolia, the only scientist. She met the President of the Russian Academy of Sciences and visited the Moscow blood diseases centre. Her discussions with the university Rector about student and teacher exchanges contributed to links made afterwards between Moscow University and Oxford.[71] Unfortunately, however, Oxford's administrative officers had overlooked the need for a gift, and Vaughan only learned of this at the formal celebration. In dismay, she abandoned her prepared speech and spoke off the cuff. To her relieved amazement, this evoked tumultuous applause. An American reported that she was 'a great success & made a magnificent speech, emotional ('I bring you no gifts but I bring you my heart ...') and this brought the house down.' On a different occasion, 'The crowds outside the Bolshoi Theatre cheered like mad when they saw her evening gown with hem delicately picked up & held as she walked from saloon to foyer'.[72] The lone woman who also looked beautiful could not but attract attention.

Family and friends

Vaughan's expectations of Radcliffe House as a centre of family life were only partly met. Mary and Cilla were aged nearly 13 and 10 in September 1945. The family did manage proper holidays, such as walking in Switzerland at the beginning of August 1946, but neither this nor the termly breaks at Plovers Field made up for their mother's shortage of time in daily life, when the housekeeper had perforce to fill the gap, and their father's absence in London.[73] Only Saturday afternoons in term time were kept solely for the family. After the lonely war years, they expected to see more of both parents, and made clear their disappointment. Nor did they find it easy at this late stage to adapt to a conventional academic girls' school.[74] Mary was severely dyslexic at a time when the condition was still not widely recognised or understood. She felt humiliated by her backwardness at school, and has a strong memory of being disbelieved when, on Gide's name coming up in class, she said he was staying at her home.[75] Their parents eventually decided that carefully selected boarding schools would serve them better and (reading between the lines) allow them to develop as individuals, away from the shadow of their mother's eminence.

Mary went in 1947, aged nearly 15, to Mayortorne Manor Farm school in Buckinghamshire. Founded by the Quaker Isabel Fry in 1917, it offered a very broad curriculum. Hodgkin's sister had been there, as had one of Amabel Williams-Ellis's daughters. It suited Mary, who made good friends, took up the pottery which would be her life's work, and became head girl.[76] To her great relief she also, finally, learned to read. Cilla, more academic though less stable psychologically, went aged 12 to the unconventional Bedales school, where she too made friends, and went on to gain a degree in political institutions and social studies at the University College of North Staffordshire (later Keele University).[77]

Vaughan wrote twice a week and visited regularly, taking them out for lunch; but they were conscious that her time was rationed. Their mother's perception was different. Despite her absences, she did feel the weight of her children's needs in the war and post-war years. She wrote to Prue Smith in 1948 of having some leisure time to herself after they returned to school:

> not that I don't love them but after 15 years it is fun to have one's life one's own again ... I can start to find myself ... D and I have been hard at the border so ... I hope for flowers & sweet scents ... Stick to the Arts [Prue had a job in Radio 3] ... Think of the joy Venice gives me ... it was a glorious holiday Love J.[77]

The Venice holiday had been a family one, and they went to Florence another year, taking friends of Mary and Cilla with them on both occasions, as they had in 1946. Vaughan's approach to her children's upbringing and education was recognisably similar to that of her own parents, except that she was better able to choose schools suited to their aptitudes and personalities.

Plovers Field was the family's real home, where they usually spent a month in summer. They had a dog and ponies, and the children played on hay bales at the farm where they collected their eggs. The farmer's daughter cleaned at Plovers Field, and kept an eye on it when it was empty. Gourlay usually went down at weekends when not visiting Oxford, gardening and growing vegetables and fruit; and every other summer, they hosted the Wayfarers staff picnic there. One Somervillian came on horseback from Guildford during vacations, to be welcomed without ceremony and join in stimulating conversations over plentiful food and wine. Her parents' marriage was not happy, and she felt the contrast with the Gourlays: she had not realised before that two people 'could be so close while still remaining themselves'.[78]

Vaughan and her brothers, though so different in their interests and political views, kept in close touch. Halford's daughters Jeanetta and Ann came to stay in Oxford several times, and when Ann had surgery to her hip in the late 1940s, Vaughan would bring one of her laboratory rabbits for her to play with in hospital. Whenever Halford suffered one of his periodic breakdowns, she did what she could to support Dorothy. And she intervened decisively when her brother David became extremely ill during a holiday in the north of England in 1948, making sure he was taken to Harefield Hospital as the best place to treat him. He had part of his stomach removed and his health was always at risk thereafter, though he had a successful banking career in South Wales.[79] Vaughan became close to David's younger son John, who joined the family on their holiday in Switzerland and Venice in 1948 before his two years' national service. During his time at Oxford in 1950–54, he and his friends often joined Mary, Cilla and their friends at weekend parties.

***

In 1949 Mary returned to Oxford to train as a potter at art school. At first her schoolfriend Anthea Sieveking, also at the art school, stayed with her at Radcliffe House before getting a job with the photographers Ramsey and Muspratt.[80] Then Mary became friendly with Diana Baldwin (later Reynell), who was studying fine art. Diana rented a bedroom at Radcliffe House in 1951–52. Vaughan was warm and welcoming, and 'Janet' to Diana, which was unusual in those more formal days. She thought Vaughan had a gift for seeing that someone was vulnerable – in her case because her mother had died when she was a child. Vaughan's preference for bright colours and bold designs showed in the dresses she bought for Mary, as did her taste for late Victorian or Edwardian romantic poets in the verse she sometimes read to them at bedtime. She had an eye for beauty in daily life and, advised by an art expert friend, collected Thornton's Temple of Flora prints, of which her favourite was Night Blooming Cereus.[81] Her patrician accent and high-pitched voice assailed the crowds of tourists outside Somerville as, laden with files, she said 'May I pass? May I pass?' They of course gave way, and the phrase became a family joke. If she had to leave these teenagers for any length of time, she would command: 'Don't be bloody to each other until I get back.'[82]

One day Diana saw a man wearing an 'Anthony Eden' hat coming up the path.[83] Vaughan said 'Oh, it's Woosky!' and dashed out to meet Gourlay. They read the same books and discussed them when they met, relaxed and typically sitting on a sofa together with drinks. At Sunday lunches and formal dinners, caterers would bring food, and Diana and Mary helped serve and clear the dishes. She especially remembered the Gilbert Spencers at one charade party, and Vaughan chatting to them about the Italian renaissance artist Filippo Lippi. Diana felt she was 'breathing oxygen' by just being with her. These parties, however, were not universally popular.

Students of both sexes could find the Principal's fierce intellect quite terrifying.

While in Moscow in late May 1955, Vaughan noticed a lump in her breast, and had a mastectomy soon after her return. She told Pirie, and presumably some others; but her note to Somerville's fellows simply requested sick leave for two or three weeks because of an unexpected operation.[84] Another note, on the table at Radcliffe House, said she had gone to have a breast removed and would be back in a few days. Diana and Mary, 'being young and thoughtless', made no fuss since none seemed to be wanted.[85] Gourlay was out of the country and only heard on his return. Mary remembered him arriving at Radcliffe House in a taxi with red roses spilling out as he emerged. After seeing Vaughan, he reported that she had 'got back – so quickly – all [her] old fire – there was no man more relieved and delighted at anything in the whole world.'[86] The Somerville dons sent sympathy and urged her to recuperate for as long as the doctors thought necessary. A vain hope, no doubt. She was back and chairing an informal meeting of the governing body within three weeks.

***

Mary and Gavin Park, a physicist friend of John Vaughan, became close while he was studying for a PhD. They married in September 1955 at St Martha's Church near Plovers Field. When Vaughan told her friend Prue the wedding date, she said she was 'counting the days to being a grandmother'.[87] Only Prue's husband Michael could come, and he was given the task of managing that

> quite incredible collection of people ... Enid Starkie in a pale blue watersilk coat ... The octogenarians who adored my mother, Mrs Krafting a French Tart from the [Wayfarers] Paris Office in furs & high heels ... whose conversation ... brought blushes even to Cilla's cheeks ... Maisie Somerville ... Polly Forde ... The church lovely with ... lilies & pale lemon gladioli & ... Mary's radiant happiness. Cilla started off looking very fine but in true Cilla style got her oleander satin covered with car oil ... David was adorable in his morning coat & a top hat ...[88]

Since then she had been basking in the garden in the sun, while David was wine-tasting in Alsace and Cilla on holiday in Rome, using money earned through a temporary job.

The Somerville lecturer in Italian, Christina Roaf, also married that summer, having been assured by Vaughan that she believed married women made better tutors. The following term, at a party for college heads, Roaf and Mary were summoned to come wearing their wedding dresses. Roaf sat next to Gourlay, who talked amusingly about Italy.[89] It was a happy ending to the first decade at Somerville. The next nine years would bring very mixed fortunes.

Endnotes

[1] The Council comprised the chair, vice-chair, 'Official' (established) fellows of the College, three additional members of the Senior Common Room, the chair of the ASM, plus six representatives of male colleges, an appointee of Hebdomadal Council, which governed the university, and a representative of another female 'society'. The other four were Lady Margaret Hall, St Anne's, St Hilda's and St Hugh's.

[2] Interview with Jean Banister, 13.3.2001. Also Vaughan in her memoir said that some on the governing body 'were anxious to have both a scientist and a married woman', JA, 96.

[3] Banister. Also interview with Jane Hands, 29.4.2001.

[4] SCA, Vaughan personal file, meeting on 18.11.1944.

[5] JA, 96. Her memoir says November, but this is impossible. She left for India on 27 October.

[6] OBL, MS Sutherland Fols 298–403, Sutherland to parents, 16.10.1944.

[7] Barbara Craig was told that Sutherland withdrew after a straw poll showed that she would be defeated. (Interview with Barbara Craig, 18.3.2001.)

[8] OBL, MS Sutherland, Sutherland to parents, 29.4.1945.

[9] JA, 97–98.

[10] Vaughan was not alone at Somerville in keeping her maiden name for professional purposes, or in having a husband who worked in a different city: the philosopher Elizabeth Anscombe did both, and had far more children than Vaughan. The scientist Henry Tizard was President of Magdalen from 1942–46. When the President of the Royal Society visited Oxford, he would stay with Vaughan, JA, 104.

[11] SCA, Vaughan personal file, Vaughan to Darbishire, 20.12.1944. Fry was the art critic Roger Fry's sister, and was by this time chiefly active in the penal reform movement.

[12] Adams, *Somerville for Women*, 173–74.

[13] JA, 105–106.

[14] W T S Stallybrass (1883–1948). A barrister who became Principal of Brasenose in 1936.

[15] JA, 107–108.

[16] Joyce Cary (1888–1957) was a major novelist who lived in Oxford from 1920. He had worked and lived in Nigeria from 1913 to 1920, and wrote several novels based in West Africa, as well as a 1943 pamphlet, *The Case for African Freedom*. Vaughan would have sympathised with this viewpoint.

[17] Radcliffe House visitors' book (in possession of John Vaughan), first page. Also JA, 22 and 97.

[18] Mrs Freddy Bloom, *Dear Philip: A Diary of Captivity, Changi 1942–45* (London, Bodley Head, 1980), gives a good account of Williams in the Singapore prison camp. Williams left the Colonial Medical Service in 1948, and worked briefly with Ryle at the Institute of Social Medicine before joining the newly formed World Health Organization in Geneva as an expert in maternal and child health. After that she filled various academic and consultancy posts in the UK and around the world for the rest of her long working life.

[19] Interview with Lalage Bown, 22.11.2007. Some thought Vaughan had spoken about Belsen after dinner one evening, but Bown thought the talk was in chapel rather than Hall, and not in the first term.

[20] Prue Smith, *The Morning Light* (Cape Town, David Philip, 2000), 229–30.

[21] The food was apparently even worse for students living outside the college. Vaughan seriously considered opening an emergency canteen for them in November 1946, but fortunately the situation eased. (SCA, Council minutes, 27.11.1945.)

[22] Adams, *Somerville for Women*, 262.

[23] Story given by old Somervillian, in conversation on 1.5.2007. (Anon.)

[34] SCA, Council minutes, 19.2.1946; and ASM Report 1945–46.

[25] SCA, Council minutes, 13.5.1947.

[26] SCA, Council minutes, 29.1.1946, first reference to this.

[27] SCA, SCR minutes, 27.11.1950, 15.1.1951 and 23.4.1951; 21.2.1959 and 12.10.59. The Principal did benefit personally. She could only enter the SCR by invitation, but was a frequent visitor there, and used the private dining room for official entertaining, by request.

[28] SCA, Council minutes, informal meeting on 11.10.1945.

[29] Barbara Harvey, written account of Vaughan sent to author on 7.7.2001, with follow-up note giving small amendment on 9.7.2001.

[30] JA, 112–13. It looks as if Hodgkin was deputed to speak to Vaughan, as someone who was both highly respected and appropriately tactful. Vaughan did of course sin again occasionally. Hodgkin's intervention may have been triggered by her announcement, in October 1946, that she had during the long vacation accepted (and chosen a student for) one of

the five medical scholarships recently instituted by Lord Nuffield for the women's colleges. Council learned of this officially around a fortnight later. Some dons must have felt left behind by the speed of events.

[31] In April 1946, fellows agreed to keep two clear hours free for Council meetings so as to be sure of completing the business in hand; and in October to a further two clear hours on a different day to allow for extra informal fellows' meetings if necessary. For chairmanship, see Adams, *A Memorial Tribute*, 4–5.

[32] SCA, unpublished memoir by Hilda Bryant, secretary to Darbishire and Vaughan.

[33] In February 1949, for example, newly appointed Dames Evelyn Sharp and Alix Kilroy came to dinner with Professor Headlam-Morley, elected to the Chair of International Relations (and first woman professor of the university), who was made an honorary fellow of Somerville.

[34] Interview with Philippa Foot, 17.4.2000.

[35] SCA, Vaughan personal file.

[36] Interview with Diana Reynell, 12.2.2008.

[37] SCA, Vaughan personal file, letter from Barbara Craig to University of Liverpool, 15.3.1973, with information for a speech at the presentation to Vaughan of an honorary degree (DSc *honoris causa*).

[38] JPP, Foot to Cilla Vaughan, 14.1.1993.

[39] SCA, Council minutes 9.10.1947. Both Foot and Pauline Adams knew about the destruction of important papers. In 1951, Vaughan apologised to the SCR for selling an item of furniture which was found too late to be theirs. (SCA, Council minutes, 16.1.1951.) The SCR seem to have anticipated (in vain) such an occurrence, when they prepared an inventory of their property in 1949, asserting that '… the claim to SCR's retention & use of its own property was established, as against the claims of … new, projected or hypothetical buildings …'. (SCA, SCR minutes, 22.1.1949.)

[40] RS, HF/1/14/3/62/2, Exchange of letters between Vaughan and Florey, 24.7.1947 and 29.7.1947.

[41] Harvey, written account sent to author.

[42] Anscombe had gained a first in Greats from St Hugh's in 1941, and held a research fellowship at Newnham College Cambridge from 1942–45. She was married to the philosopher Peter Geach, like her a Roman Catholic and devotee of Wittgenstein.

[43] JA, 100.

[44] Conversation with Christina Roaf, 22.5.2007. The CUF system did not, unfortunately, apply to science subjects.

[45] Barbara Harvey, in Adams, *A Memorial Tribute*, 5.

[46] JA, 122. The Goodenough Committee had recommended that such a service be established in all universities; and the third report of the RCP Social and Preventive Medicine committee, in January 1946, recommended that it cover all graduate as well as undergraduate students.

[47] JA, 123.

[48] Interview with Caroline Miles (née Leslie), 20.3.2001.

[49] Foot interview.

[50] OUA, Franks Commission Oral Evidence HC 4/50/27.

[51] Smith, *The Morning Light*, 235.

[52] Prue married her fiancé, the architect Michael Smith, in 1946 whilst still at Somerville. He designed an extension at Plovers Field in 1951, and the new kitchen for Somerville, in use from 1959.

[53] This was Mrs Joshi, who completed a B Litt before reading for the Bar in London. Two years later she told Vaughan that she was Principal of a women's college in Katmandu, and had re-written Nepal's constitution. (JA, 119).

[54] SCA, SCR minutes.

[55] Interview with Phyllis Treitel, 29.4.2001, to whom Craig had told this story.

[56] Punched card machines preceded computers as mechanical aids to number-crunching.

[57] OBL, Dorothy Hodgkin papers, MS Eng. C.5635, file C.98, Hodgkin to Nuffield Foundation, 20.6.1956.

[58] SCA, Council minutes, 16.2.1955, 27.4.1955 and 15.6.1955.

[59] Harvey, written account sent to author.

[60] JA, 137.

[61] NF, Minute Books 1943–44, meeting of 1.6.1944, F.6/1, Interim report of the Radiological Committee.

[62] RS, HF/1/19/1/72 and 73, Florey to Fulton, 12.4.1960. Vaughan must at some stage have sought his advice on issues and/or techniques related to her research.

[63] It is still in use, and the whole of the Jodrell Bank Observatory complex is now a UNESCO World Heritage site.

[64] Clark, *A Biography of the Nuffield Foundation*, 11.

[65] TNA, T 227/264. The chair was a former permanent secretary at the Ministries of Labour and of National Insurance. Others represented employees, employers, nationalised industries and local government. The economist, Alec Cairncross, was professor of applied economics at the University of Glasgow. He was approved as a member by Robert Hall, then working in the Treasury as an economic adviser and married to the Somerville economics tutor Margaret Hall.

[66] This was primarily a concession to married men, who were on average four years older than their wives, and would no longer be able to claim for them as dependants.

[67] The story of the committee can be found in files TNA T 227/264, 265; 230/274; 277/307, 377–81. The report itself is in T 227/416; and follow-up story in T 227/491–92.

[68] Cairncross threatened to resign if the Ministry of Labour prevented the committee from quoting figures taken from a recent cost of living inquiry. In the event they were used in its report.

[69] Years later, Douglas Houghton, then chairman of the Parliamentary Labour Party (from 1967) told Vaughan that he had always thought her reservation the best part of the report, JA, 133.

[70] JA, 138–39. This preceded the death of Masaryk, who fell from the window of the foreign office in Prague on 10 March 1948. Given out to be suicide, most of those who knew him believed it to be murder.

[71] JA, 140–41.

[72] JPP, letter from a friend to Prue Smith and her husband dated 18.5.1955.

[73] One indication of the occasional strain shows in an apology for missing a meeting at the RCN on 10.4.1947, without notice, 'but I had a very sick daughter, which disorganised me'. (RCN 7/10/4, Industrial Nursing Board of Studies 1946–63.) Vaughan's secretary, Hilda Bryant, walked the dog.

[74] Oxford High School for Girls.

[75] In June 1947, when he came to give the Bryce Lecture.

[76] Interview with Mary's schoolfriend Anthea Sieveking, 23.4.2007.

[77] JPP, Vaughan to Prue Smith, undated, September 1948.

[78] Interview with Caroline Miles.

[79] Information from John Vaughan.

[80] Lettice Ramsey (née Baker) was the Gourlays' old friend from Taviton Street days.

[81] This features in the Victoria Crowe portrait now in the National Portrait Gallery.

[82] Interview with Diana Reynell, 12.2.2008.

[83] The hat was a silk-brimmed black homburg, popularised in Britain by the politician Anthony Eden.

[84] SCA, governing body minutes, note read aloud on 25.5.1955.

[85] Interview with Diana Reynell.

[86] JPP, Mildred Hartley to Vaughan, 14.1.1963.

[87] JPP, Vaughan to Prue Smith, undated (February/March 1955). In July 1956 she was making baby clothes for the first of Mary's four children, James, who arrived in August. Vanessa followed in 1958, Henrietta in 1960 and Benjamin in 1961.

[88] JPP, Vaughan to Prue Smith, 26.9.1955.
[89] Interview with Christina Roaf, 22.5.2007. Vaughan had arranged for Roaf's wedding reception to take place in Somerville.

CHAPTER 11
Somerville: inspiration and expansion
1956–67

A focus of respect

In 1956, when Vaughan was 56, the old Somervillians commissioned her portrait from Claude Rogers, whom she had known in the 1930s (see Plate 21). He painted her seated, in academic dress, a definite authority figure. Reactions varied. Some saw suppressed impatience, with fingers about to drum on the chair arm, or a leg to swing to and fro. Others were reminded of the way she would 'jackknife' into a chair, her long legs settling at an angle, before leaning forward, intent and eager, to give her full attention to the person before her. Whilst not overbearing, she conveyed a sense of power, and one student thought her the only woman she had met whose demeanour did not change if ten men entered the room.[1]

Another found her 'tall and wiry, with dark hair tied in a knot at the back of her neck. She walked … at great speed, bending over an armful of books and papers … [and kept] her car warm in winter with an old fur coat thrown over the bonnet …'.[2] A research fellow arriving in 1964 noticed her strong physical presence, and 'striking and elegant' clothes: tweed coats and skirts and silk scarves by day, and stunning but simple evening clothes, such as a brilliant magenta wild silk skirt and jacket, perfect with her black hair which was by then streaked with grey.[3]

Her lack of small talk deterred some. Many found termly interviews difficult, not least because of her schedule-driven tendency to say goodbye (nicely) when they were in mid-sentence. One told anecdotes in short sentences, 'so that she could say "Goodbye" at a full stop, rather than a comma'. The appreciative Vaughan rocked with laughter, and friends waiting outside were 'bewildered to hear what sounded like a cocktail party going on'.[4]

The impact of world politics 1956–57

Autumn 1956 brought the ill-fated Hungarian uprising against Soviet rule, followed by the Suez Crisis. For the first time, Vaughan as Principal was provoked into public activism, but not of a kind

241

to put her own or Somerville's reputation at risk. The Hungarian revolt, which began on 23 October, was brutally quelled after Soviet tanks entered Budapest on 4 November. Vaughan stood up in Hall to make an impassioned plea for help for young Hungarians wanting to escape, and students from across the university met in Radcliffe House to set up the Hungarian Students Scholarship Fund. She made Foot senior treasurer, 'to keep them in order', and five other college heads joined her as sponsors.[5] Thirty-four Hungarians stayed in an Oxford hostel before being dispersed to private houses, including those of Vaughan and Foot, and starting English language classes. Similar action was taken elsewhere and Bill Deakin, Warden of the graduate college St Antony's, chaired the group in London that soon managed a national allocation of places on behalf of the Committee of Vice-Chancellors and Principals. Vaughan and a colleague negotiated with colleges for places in Oxford, and Somerville took a medical student. Much of the office work was done in Somerville, and £13,400 raised, mainly from university alumni.[6] Foot was treasurer until May 1957, while Vaughan was involved, in Oxford and nationally, at least until October 1959.[7]

The other international crisis was shorter lived, but overlapped with the activities in support of Hungarian students. In July 1956, President Nasser of Egypt nationalised the Suez Canal, a vital route for tankers bringing oil to western Europe. On 29 October, Israel, Britain and France launched co-ordinated attacks on Egypt to try to force a volte-face. In authorising this, Prime Minister Eden ignored both government legal advice and United States opposition. Countrywide demonstrations broke out, and on 2 November Vaughan joined four other speakers at a protest meeting in the Oxford Union, where Lord Beveridge struggled to be heard amid loud 'booing and cheering ... the noise ... increased by a large crowd outside trying to break down the doors'.[8] A non-party resolution condemning the violation of UN Charter principles was signed by more than 300 Oxford academics and 10 college heads, including Bowra, Vaughan and those of St Anne's and St Hilda's.[9] Their view predominated, and the United States effectively forced a withdrawal from Egypt. The whole debacle delivered a devastating blow to Britain's prestige.

There was more turbulence in 1957. The British hydrogen bomb was tested in April, and the Campaign for Nuclear Disarmament (CND) founded later that year. Most Somerville undergraduates sympathised, and among the dons Hodgkin, Pirie and Foot at least joined CND. Vaughan may have sympathised to some extent, but did not join.[10] Indeed, many years later she expressed support for the nuclear deterrent. As to peaceful uses, she always believed nuclear power preferable to coal because its extraction caused so many fewer deaths.

College affairs

Matters in Somerville, meanwhile, were proceeding well. More capital funding gradually became available, and the new library building was occupied from autumn 1956. Plans for a domestic staff hall and new kitchen quarters were approved by November, and discussion of new student residential blocks continued in 1957, when the college bought Radcliffe House and other properties.[11] Hodgkin became the first Wolfson professor of the Royal Society in 1960, at last gaining the formal status she deserved at Oxford. Meanwhile, Vaughan became a DBE (Dame of the British Empire) 'for War Service and service to the academic community' in the 1956/57 New Year honours. The dons at least were aware, when she was invited to a prestigious conference in the United States, that her pioneering research into the effects of radiation on bone was internationally respected. Students began to cry ''ware the Dame!' when they saw her rather battered car approach the gate of Somerville.[12]

In 1958 Vaughan and Sutherland proposed to the Vice-Chancellor that the women's societies should become full colleges of the university, and all gained that status in 1960.[13] Their Principals were now eligible to be Vice-Chancellor, and Sutherland, who was part of the inner circle of Hebdomadal Council members managing university finance and administration, was at once appointed Pro[deputy]-Vice-Chancellor, from 1961–69. Despite the potential for a personality clash, the two women generally worked effectively together when necessary, while otherwise pursuing very different interests.[14]

Student well-being remained Vaughan's first concern. In autumn 1957, many succumbed to the Asian flu epidemic. The small sanatorium and temporary extra beds were overwhelmed, and the kitchen so under-staffed that Vaughan did the cooking for the sickrooms. When the college nurse said it was not her job to carry trays, she did that too.[15] Others followed her example, and she arranged for students still on their feet to visit all who were ill and report on their needs.[16] This episode adds to many individual stories of her swift diagnoses of diseases within her own area of expertise, her readiness to offer rest and first aid when needed, and visits to students in the Warneford Hospital.[17] Always first and foremost a doctor, anyone who needed medical care was likely to top her list of priorities.

Her constant message was that, if students worked hard and used their talents, no doors were closed to them. She was teaching by example as well as precept, and they felt empowered by her; but she never claimed it would be easy. One applicant interviewed in 1959 remembered a long discussion about regional inequalities, when Vaughan made clear her passionate belief that Somerville's role was to enable the very bright from all backgrounds to develop their talents so as to change the world for the better.[18] A postgraduate from Ceylon (now Sri Lanka) noted her shock on hearing that women were still barred from the diplomatic service there; and her insistence that the student must work to change this on her return.[19] Esther Rantzen said that most of her school and university teachers had apparently chosen to remain single so as to pursue a career; but Somervillians 'had the example of Dame Janet: wife, mother, internationally renowned scientist and distinguished academic. We often used to discuss her and decided that if Dame J could combine scholarship and having a family of her own, hopefully we could, too.'[20]

For Vaughan, education was as much about character development as degree results, enabling women to shape their own lives and careers. Some students, who were less self-confident or failed for whatever reason to feel her approval, could be hurt by her lack of notice; but most thought her generous and civilised, and Somerville a well-run and happy institution. Vaughan wrote one day warning the students that fresh broken glass (designed to keep out intruders) had been put on the college perimeter wall, implying that they should take extra care if climbing in after the gate was locked for the night. Typically, the tone was that of one adult to another.[21] She preferred to remove the need to climb in, usually by giving students keys to Radcliffe House, or telling them where they might be found. In 1964, Somerville became the first women's college to provide latch keys for students planning to return after midnight, which was then locking up time. A measure which must have eased the pressure on the Principal's house.

These years saw radical changes in social attitudes. Before contraception became widely available in the mid-1960s, instances of students becoming pregnant gradually became more frequent. Decisions about the pregnancy or marriage were primarily for the girl and her family; but the college had to decide whether to allow her to complete her course, based on circumstances and a judgement of her capabilities. Until around 1960, Vaughan and a senior fellow would usually decide this on an informal and confidential basis, in consultation with the girl's subject tutor and her family. They aimed to secure the student's best interests, while also protecting the reputation of the college.[22] In 1958, having found a sympathetic GP, she asked one or two worldly-wise students to discreetly advise the more innocent about contraception and how to obtain it. Although personally in favour, Vaughan could not risk unwelcome publicity by broaching the subject openly.[23] One student was impressed by her freshers talk in 1960, when she said she was always willing to see anyone with 'problems over men and so on'. When her fiancé moved to London in her second year, Vaughan found out how unhappy she was and let him stay in Radcliffe House when spending weekends in Oxford.[24]

By 1960, disciplinary cases relating to rule-breaches were so frequent that seven fellows wrote to Vaughan urging the need to clarify the rules, including on continuing to study after marriage.[25] Soon afterwards revised bye-laws shifted the balance of decision-making to the governing body. Vaughan's notes in the informal record of such decisions show that she tried to keep track of those who were sent down, noting with obvious pleasure the ones who had after all achieved success. It is clear that she particularly admired any who, while remaining single, had kept their babies.[26]

Her care for Somervillians habitually continued after they left the college. One, who went on to teach at Oxford, was rushed to hospital some years later with acute appendicitis. To her great surprise, Vaughan appeared by her bed in a white coat and gave her a bar of expensive soap.[27] Anne Yates, one of the 1945 cohort, visited from South Africa 14 years later, and found that she had called people together to hear about an educational charity Yates had founded to serve black South Africans excluded from that country's universities. Vaughan became a patron, and greatly encouraged those involved at a time when they faced serious harassment.[28] Joan Wicken, a mature student who came up in 1951 and went on to be chief adviser to President Nyerere of Tanzania, was inspired by Vaughan's attitude that 'what mattered … was solid usefulness to <u>people</u> anywhere'.[29]

New buildings and relations with dons
There were some tensions on the governing body, mainly caused by Vaughan's driving through of building plans, including the new wing of the library, before it was clear that money would be available; and also by her efforts to speed up decision-making. In November 1957, she gained agreement at an informal meeting to funding Anscombe as a college lecturer from 1958, while recommending her for a CUF (cost shared between college and university) lectureship. Council could only ratify this the following term, and one fellow asked that in future such matters not be raised at informal Council unless they were on the agenda. More seriously, Vaughan had to agree to her 'Principal's places' right being formalised and minimised in January 1959. The fellows empowered her to fill two to three places after the regular quotas had been filled, from candidates who had reached the required academic standard.

When the quota for women students was abolished in 1957, she was less guarded than usual, commenting that 'In a world which seems to do nothing but erect barriers it is a very great pleasure to see one knocked down.'[30] The change helped stimulate an increase in staff numbers and new building plans. There were new appointments in maths, chemistry and physics in 1957, and in 1959 the first man was appointed, as temporary lecturer in physics.[31]

Capital funds remained low, however. A proposed joint appeal by the women's societies had to be shelved, and discussions with possible donors came to nothing. Nonetheless, in June 1958 Somerville was the first Oxford college to invite architects to produce a site plan for a graduate house, together with an undergraduate block.

In 1961, when £45,000 was still needed for the graduate house by the end of the year, she turned to the Nuffield Foundation for help, urging the importance of women's higher education and their contribution to public services; and also of the rising number of graduates, especially from the Commonwealth. In September she gained Lord Nuffield's and trustees' support for a building to be named after Lady Nuffield as well as Margery Fry, who had died in 1958.[32]

Fellows' nerves were again strained when she pushed through the planning of the undergraduate block, whose need was reinforced by the 1963 Robbins Report's recommendations for the expansion of higher education.[33] Funding negotiations with the Wolfson Foundation were protracted, and in January 1964, with the building already under construction, the college took advantage of a rule change to seek UGC funding. This was agreed by March. Then in June the Wolfson Foundation offered £100,000 for a further hall of residence, and planning began for another new building. At an extraordinary meeting of the governing body, Vaughan read out both the Wolfson letter and one from the university registrar congratulating her on these two crucial grants. Her colleagues could only add warm congratulations. Given that the tender for the Wolfson block was still being negotiated in July 1966, it was remarkable that it was ready for occupation by October 1967.

Discontent among the dons was never serious enough to be divisive. As Harvey later wrote, 'underlying everything Vaughan did as Principal, and the foundation of the huge respect that she enjoyed, was a relentless concern for excellence'. Whilst this extended to all activities, it encompassed 'the constant nudging of tutors about academic standards', the top priority she gave to their research needs, and 'the judgments, based on intuition and arrived at in an instant, yet so rarely anything but splendidly right.

Few [college heads] can have exerted more influence over their societies than she did over hers.'[34]

Marjorie Harding was a tutor in chemistry from 1959, and fellow from 1960 to 1962. She admired the Principal's efficient and effective way of chairing meetings, taking it as a model for her own future behaviour. Vaughan prepared well by gathering relevant information, asking others to do the same. This enabled a sensible discussion leading to decisions, including on what was to be done before the next meeting. (According to Harding, meetings of the university chemistry department were by contrast best described as 'shooting matches.') College organisation was also efficient. She did not remember any personality clashes, and never felt that Vaughan's drive, including on the occasion of gaining Nuffield funding for the graduate house, was viewed as anything other than admirable. She thought Vaughan promoted science but gave due weight to the arts, and presided over the appointment of interesting people with flair as dons.[35]

Not all of those dons were easy to deal with, but Vaughan was both adept and scrupulously fair in dealing with them. The historian Agatha Ramm, who could be prickly and difficult, remembered many interesting conversations, and a private lunch party for the Russian poet Anna Akhmatova, when the conversation 'in which Janet was a vigorous participant' was in French.[36] Her relationship with the outwardly proud but inwardly sensitive and shy Lascelles as Vice-Principal was also generally good. It seems likely, however, that she did not realise how difficult Lascelles found her role at times, especially when she had to deputise at short notice in unfamiliar circumstances. Early in 1956, a diagnosis of glaucoma in her left eye raised the prospect of an operation. At this, Vaughan dropped everything else to go with Lascelles to London, to see a specialist she recommended and attend the Moorfields eye hospital. They also went to see the Rembrandt drawings in the Print Room of the British Museum.[37] This museum visit may well have been Vaughan's idea, and if so it showed empathy with someone in danger of losing her sight. Years later, Lascelles paid her generous tribute, saying she 'always spoke of life in terms of the contribution to be made to it, and … expended herself without stint'.[38]

Vaughan's temper could still flare up, but most people recognised it as transitory and without malice. People like her first secretary, Hilda Bryant, and Jane Hands, who rose from assistant bursar in 1954 to treasurer in 1962, were unaffected by such outbursts; but Foot did suffer hurt feelings. Once she helped a student with symptoms of mental illness, ringing the Principal afterwards to tell her the girl had been admitted to the Warneford. Vaughan, who preferred to see all such cases herself before deciding the action required, reacted furiously. Within hours, she apologised generously and told Foot how grateful the girl was; but the scar remained. It helped that Foot knew the real affection Vaughan had for her, but this would not have applied to everyone.[39] In mitigation, people noted that Vaughan never complained about her own illnesses or people who let her down, or indeed spoke ill of any colleague. Most of her outbursts seem to have resulted from pent-up frustration. As one ex-student said, someone so constantly in advance of others needed far more patience than the average.[40]

University and wider commitments

University

Vaughan's concern for graduates led to membership of a group set up by the university in 1959 to consider their welfare. Numbers had roughly doubled since 1939 as a proportion of the total student body, thanks to more grants, more research degrees in science subjects and a growing intake from other universities. In 1960 the group recommended funding colleges to better provide for single graduates, and building flats for 200 married couples. Vaughan went on to help oversee provision of those flats.[41] She also took a close interest in the establishment of the new graduate colleges of St Cross and Wolfson, in 1965 and 1966 respectively, and in 1981 became an honorary fellow of Wolfson.

She spent an enjoyable week in Karachi in January 1961 as one of three UK delegates to a conference on education, sponsored by the South East Asia Treaty Organization.[42] The event coincided with a visit by the Queen, and Vaughan was struck by the warmth of feeling towards the British; but not, this time, the Americans. As representative of the oldest Commonwealth university, she was asked to give the final vote of thanks, but was pre-empted by a 'rather pompous' American; whereupon 'everyone' got up and made speeches in an effort to restore the balance. She enjoyed the food and the ambience, but was again, as in 1944, shocked by the extreme contrasts of wealth and poverty, and lamented that 'far more than in India the women are still not part of working life'.[43]

The Nuffield Foundation

Nuffield Foundation funds were increasing, as was its influence. Vaughan took a close interest in projects ranging from the National Institute for Social Work Training to the Royal Society's conversion of its London accommodation; from children's theatre to criminology and police training; from libraries to the visual arts; and from environmental conservation to the Institute for Race Relations. She fully supported a massive investment in new mathematics and science curriculums for schools during the 1960s, soon followed by language teaching.[44]

Sir Brian Young, director of the Foundation from 1964 to 1970, found her 'terrifyingly acute and astute' at his interview in January 1964. Once appointed, she invited him to Oxford and introduced him to key people and current research there. At meetings she was brusque and decisive, having made up her mind quite firmly on the basis of the papers; and on medical matters none of the other trustees 'would have dared' to disagree with her. He found her lively, with a good, wry sense of humour, and caring passionately about others: she would treat proposals with impatience if they were not worth much, but never people.[45]

The deputy director from 1960, John McAnuff, recalled that her prejudice in favour of Oxford could lead her astray. Once when she urged funding for a particular academic, saying that Oxford was in danger of losing him to the United States, another trustee reminded her of the need to act as 'disinterested trustees concerned only with excellence, no matter where it is found'. On that occasion she beat a tactical retreat.[46] Happier memories were of social events, including regular dinner parties at Somerville, where Vaughan exercised her great talent for bringing people together and enabling productive conversations. She loved conferences, where the real work was done in the corridors, and constantly brought interesting ideas back for the foundation to consider.

An incisive presence, she could deflate pomposity, ask loaded questions and get to the nub of the matter. Indifferent to then-normal courtesies such as allowing a man to open the door for her, she went further on occasion, notably as a dinner guest at a conference on rheumatism. When, by the usual convention, ladies were invited to withdraw, Vaughan sat tight, saying she could not possibly forego the chance of good talk with these interesting and important people for the sake of an outdated custom.[47]

The Commonwealth Scholarships Commission

It was gratifying when the main Nuffield travelling scholarships were replaced by a government funded scheme in 1960. The Commonwealth Scholarships Commission (CSC) was set up to select and place 1,000 postgraduate scholars and fellows throughout the Commonwealth, mainly for two years of study and research.[48] When Vaughan joined it in May 1964, she was the only woman and only medical representative. There were formal meetings four to six times a year, and various social gatherings. A panel of more than 50 academic advisers helped CSC members with the selection process. By 1966 Sir Douglas Logan, Principal of the University of London and effectively chair of the selection committee, found her 'absolutely essential'.[49] She, Logan and two others were on the busiest committee, responsible for sifting incoming candidates. She had also helped develop a new medical awards scheme, with 150 places specifically for training in medical and allied fields, in order to expand medical education in the overseas Commonwealth. As retirement from Oxford and the Nuffield Foundation drew near, she moved to the centre of a different web of national and international academic contacts.

Vaughan enjoyed this work more than any other job apart from setting up the regional hospital board so many years before. The 'real fun and interest' lay in choosing the candidates, placing them in suitable institutions, and seeing reports on their progress. Meeting scholars and their wives reinforced her optimism about the world's future, and gave her 'a superb bird's eye view … of how different departments in UK Universities are regarded overseas, and how they cope with visiting scholars'.[50] Speaking at the University of London about postgraduate education in 1969,

251

she dwelt on the needs of men and women from abroad. More centres of excellence in specialist fields were needed in universities other than London: it was time for them to step up to the mark.[51]

The UGC and libraries

Vaughan also joined a UGC committee on university libraries which began its work in July 1963. After some Nuffield-funded exploratory work, the UGC had decided on a broad review, backed by the English and Scottish education departments.[52] The context was the need to increase provision in light of the expected post-Robbins expansion of higher education. Vaughan advised on the needs of medical students and postgraduates, and on general legal and funding issues. In July 1965 a librarian member said there should ideally be one national centre, combining the British Museum and other central provision, but thought it impracticable. The tide of opinion was turning, however. With support from the English education department, the group soon swung in favour of a single central provider.[53]

Their 1966 report proposed a national library, to co-ordinate with the national libraries of Scotland and Wales, and the education department then took forward provision of what is now the British Library in London. Vaughan's agreement appears to have been less than whole-hearted. She later noted: 'Librarians I found only too often anxious for most rigid centralisation. I ended up reserving a special circle in hell for those … who wished to behave like dictators.'[54]

Friends and family: joy and sorrow

After 1955 Gavin Park's academic career took him and Mary to Bristol and then London. They soon gave Vaughan her much-wanted grandchildren: James in 1956, Vanessa in 1958, Henrietta in 1960 and finally Benjamin in 1961. Gourlay, too, would 'burst with pride' over these little ones.[55] The family always kept in close touch through visits and shared holidays. Looking after James and Vanessa at Radcliffe House in February 1960, around the time of Henrietta's birth, Vaughan took them round the college and to visit the lab, going with Maureen Owen and her children to tea with the lab secretary, Bunty, and her four cats.[56]

Gourlay was still the rock on which she could lean. Janet Adam Smith often stayed with them, and recalled one Saturday afternoon when he arrived back from Rome. He gave Vaughan an Italian silk scarf, to be greeted with 'Oh, David, you've brought me a fairing, how lovely,' and a warm embrace.[57] With him she could escape into the world of books, ideas and travel, lit by his humane and humorous perspective. In summer 1956 they went to Milan and Florence for three weeks and visited Tuscan hill towns. Unlike Vaughan, he also appreciated music. They spent an especially carefree evening dining with Clive Bell in Milan, while an itinerant fiddler played tunes the two men requested.[58]

Cilla's mental health, however, was now of serious concern. She had at least one breakdown whilst at university, but recovered and started work as a probation officer after graduating in 1958. After another breakdown she was in the Warneford for a time. By summer 1962 she was working again, but later decided to go to New York and make a new start in the United States.[59] Vaughan felt both fear and frustration when faced with mental illness. She had witnessed her mother's debilitating depression, and the way Halford's more serious illness had blighted so much of his life.[60] Her instinct was to give practical and medical help, but in psychiatric cases she had to defer to others.

Other concerns also arose. Around 1960 Granny Betty at Princes Risborough was developing health problems, and a year or so later Vaughan was worried about Gourlay, taking him to consult medical specialists.[61] They planned to retire and live at Plovers Field at the end of the academic year 1963/64, when he would be 74. By the end of 1962, however, she knew he was close to death. She kept this to herself, wishing the whole family to enjoy their last Christmas together. The celebration at Plovers Field was happy, but took place during Britain's coldest winter in more than 200 years. She and David were last to leave and had to wait for a bus to the local station when freezing conditions ruled out going by car or taxi. He was admitted to hospital in London, but Vaughan maintained the fiction that he would soon recover, despite knowing that he had advanced lung and liver cancer. She must have believed that a fresh start in the United States was Cilla's best hope of a stable future, because she kept her too in ignorance, allowing her to leave for New York two days before he died, on 14 January 1963.

After Christmas she shared the position with a few people, but carried on so far as possible with her normal engagements. On 9 January she told Mary 'Daddy is better in himself ... no pain but very drowsy – He loved the children's letters ... I am packing for Cilla tonight.' And on the day after his death she said the flowers Mary sent, and a photograph of the four grandchildren, had been on the bedside table as she sat with him through the night.[62] She asked Janet Adam Smith to do *The Times* obituary, and arranged for his burial on 18 January in the graveyard at St Martha's Church, on a hilltop not far from Plovers Field. The freezing conditions continued, and Prue wrote afterwards: 'if there is any blessing to David's friends it lies in your courage ... and Mary's, whose pain showed in her face but who was so bravely controlled.'[63]

Vaughan's cousin Kitty West recalled her 'putting heart and courage into us – as well as whisky! How Madge and my mother ... would have been moved by that almost alpine funeral!' Adam Smith recalled Rubin Krafting, the head of the Wayfarers Paris office whom she called 'the Toad', sitting by the fire, 'inconsolable', while Vaughan organised lunch. But her sister-in-law Dorothy felt how upset she was, and how her demeanour changed after his death: somehow 'compacted', with a sadness that came into her face when she was off-guard.[64] Once again she used her mother's Tennyson quotation, on service sheet and gravestone: 'My love, we two shall go no longer / To lands of summer across the sea.' Its poignancy was now greater than ever.

Most friends who wrote at this time described his essential goodness and unassuming integrity, and Mary Bennett's 'so absolutely ... authentic and un-second hand. And so kind ...' summed up the qualities Vaughan admired most in others. Her old schoolfriend Molly Hoyle told of her 'admiration of David, whether he was in Mary's early days advising a man friend how to change a baby's nappies or gently suggesting in argument that one of your wilder points might not have the whole of truth behind it'. She would have appreciated Foot's writing of 'the great, great affection & regard ... for you in Somerville. We don't often say this to you, but often to each other.' A letter written following the mathematician Anne Cobbe's death in 1971 may reveal another comforter. Vaughan said that for Cobbe, 'Time was never important where friendship was concerned. She realised the importance of constant unfailing kindliness in healing sorrow.'[65]

As to Wayfarers, a British Railways senior manager called Gourlay the 'Elder Statesman' of the tourist agency world and a true gentleman. Others recalled the early days in Bloomsbury in the twenties and thirties. The photographer Lettice Ramsey, who had lived in Taviton Street before her marriage, described him as a constant figure over 40 years: 'So many wise and human things he stood for … He used to give me dinner from time to time in that splendid old Liberal Club – a fine steak and a bottle of burgundy at "his" corner table near the grill.' Despite the kindness, however, Vaughan was confronting an unfillable gap.

Cilla learned of her father's death when she arrived in New York, saying her mother's account of the service at St Martha's had made her cry: 'it seems so hard to be separated at this time … yet … I know … I had to come away. Nothing is ever simple.'[66] The move seems to have been Cilla's own idea, possibly stimulated by university friends who were already there.[67] This makes the decision to hide the nature of Gourlay's illness from her more understandable. Later letters described her enjoyment of New York, and successful job-hunting. She met 'Esther' whom Gourlay had known in France in 1919, finding her overpowering, and feeling glad that 'Daddy had the good sense not to marry' her. All her letters show courage and a determination to be positive.

***

A relieved Vaughan accepted the fellows' invitation on 21 January to stay on as Principal until 1967. She still had to sort out her financial affairs, including an immediate need to vacate the Russell Square flat. Her friends Polly and Daryll Forde, knowing her need for a London base, gave her the keys of their own home there. In March she told Mary she could afford to keep Plovers Field for the next four years, and then expected a small pension through Somerville and something from Wayfarers, though nothing was yet settled: 'I could have fussed Daddy to make a will in hospital … The doctor did suggest it but David said Oh I will do that when

I am better – & I didn't want him to realise he would never get better. He was peaceful & happy & that is what mattered to me …'[68]

A retired Wayfarers staff member hinted at the difficulty to come, recalling David's 'terrific struggle with the somewhat overpowering Franklin influence … you must have been a tremendous standby.'[69] Raymond Mortimer, still a director, fought her corner, but in December 1963 the company proposed only to divide Gourlay's shares between her and the children. She replied that only a regular pension would enable her to live at Plovers Field as he had wished, and she had already sold her only securities so as to get through the year. Asking that Sidney Franklin, Geoffrey and Michael's brother, be approached, she said he was now sick and old, but 'very devoted to my husband … if he were to die before it was settled … I should be in a … hopeless position.'[70] Fortunately, a settlement was agreed by March 1964. Her solicitor suggested sorting out her own will, but she demurred, saying she had been ill most of the year and must put college and university business first. She was being 'sent away' over Easter and hoped to deal with the will in the summer term.[71]

When the Wayfarers was taken over by another company in 1966 the pension right was honoured, and soon afterwards she exchanged the family shares for more reliable Treasury stock. She resigned as company director in 1968, objecting to the way affairs were being managed.[72] Gourlay's wish that six of the Wayfarers staff should have some shares proved impossible, largely because of tax rules, but one of those affected said the thought itself showed 'a … true and wonderful sincerity … a "Gourlayism". I shall always remain an employee of DG … & work to achieve the things he wanted & through the channels he so rightly believed in.'[73]

***

Two new friends became important around the time of Gourlay's death. Tom Griffiths ('Father Tom') was Vicar of Great Tew, a beautiful village not far from Oxford, and he and his wife Jean shared Vaughan's literary interests. They knew a number of Somerville students, and she first visited them in July 1962. Calmed by the place and their company, she was soon sharing her worries about students' mental health, and before long persuaded them to occasionally host undergraduates who needed a few days' rest.

She and Gourlay went on holiday to Elba that September, and her anxiety about his health perhaps led her to seek spiritual support. After Christmas the couple became close confidants. She told them in early January that David was dying, asking for their prayers and keeping in touch thereafter.[74]

At Easter she said they had 'carried her through' since Christmas. After a happy time with the Parks at Plovers Field, she had taken flowers from the garden to David's grave, 'in one of the loveliest places in the world'.[75] In May she invited Griffiths to preach in the college chapel, going soon after to a conference in Vienna, then the BMA conference in early July: work continued as usual. August was spent at Plovers Field with the family, playing croquet and gardening and also, thanks to Cilla, reading James Baldwin. The Limited Test Ban Treaty signed that month gave her 'bursts of pleasure', as a 'first break for the peace of the world.'[76] In September Granny Betty came to Oxford, needing constant care while having radiotherapy; and two Dutch scientists arrived to work in the lab. Gavin was able to visit Cilla that month, and thought her in fine form, having had a rise in salary. On 11 October, however, around the start of the academic year, Vaughan flew to New York to bring her 'desperately ill' daughter home.[77] Now psychotic and suicidal, she had to be committed to the Warneford; it was 'terrible to hear a human soul in such … distress & … be able to bring no comfort'.[78]

Cilla improved slightly in early November, but her mother suffered a sudden severe haemorrhage, caused it was then thought by a stomach ulcer. The doctors wanted her in hospital as an emergency but she refused, believing it essential to see Cilla every day and hide her own illness from her. Also 'I am half in bed & half about because there are a lot of difficult problems among the young … & I must cope – to say nothing of Robbins.'[79] Shortly afterwards she told Griffiths in confidence about Cilla's history and the way depressive illness dogged some members of the family.[80] A week or so later her spirits were very low:

> Day after day Cilla telling me what a bad mother I have been – going over & over … her father's illness & questioning … whether he is still alive & then her own … sense of guilt & despair & the ward sister merely growls at me if she speaks at all & the doctors never

say anything. I feel I must see her because … in spite of what she says I am the one person who is stable through her life & she is such a sweet beautiful person at times. I think so often of Gt Tew [and] St Martha's but I am too tired & ill to get to either. There seems no escape & little hope …[81]

During this time Vaughan's niece Susan, Halford's third daughter, began to visit. She had thought of becoming a doctor, but on Vaughan's advice that it would suit her better, trained in London as a nurse instead.[82] She had a boyfriend in Oxford, so came up for parties and balls. Vaughan would make her drink cocoa before going out, so as to 'line her stomach'. Susan remembered her reading the Robbins Report in bed, and in a great deal of pain from arthritis as well as suffering loss of blood.

At Christmas Vaughan told Griffiths and Jean that Cilla

remembers nothing of the last two months – the memory is mine … Father Tom reminds her of David. I feel that if anything happened to me she would turn to you. We went … to St Martha's this morning … always beautiful & has the same peace as Great Tew [then] home to our lovely Christmas Tree & … warmth & … books & the place is full of happy ghosts.[83]

The Parks came on Boxing Day, and hopes rose when Cilla started as a probation officer in Essex in February. She continued well until, after a breakdown over Christmas 1964, she was again in the Warneford. Vaughan managed a break at Lake Como the following April, under pressure from the doctor; and in summer 1965 she came from Plovers Field twice a week to visit Cilla in hospital. The doctors now thought the depression was 'bio-chemical – & they don't know the answers yet'.[84] By early October Cilla was home and working in a shop, very quiet and stout because of her medication. Griffiths thought Vaughan more relaxed after her summer with the family at Plovers Field, and she thanked Jean for her birthday presents and for giving her 'a sense of being remembered & thought of which is very precious'.[85]

In spring 1966, she was visiting a very sick Granny Betty at Princes Risborough, as well as supporting Cilla, who was back in hospital by the end of July. Vaughan decided she would have to sell Plovers Field and live in Oxford. 'Not a word to anyone … I don't approve of retiring into where one has worked but I shall need friends at hand & so will she.' Tom and Jean agreed. She had told no one else and, like Cilla, would hate giving up Plovers Field.[86]

Despite all these pressures, Vaughan gallantly volunteered to have all four Park children for a month from mid-August so that Mary could go with Gavin to a conference in Russia. Miss Robey the housekeeper helped, as did Cilla, and they went to the seaside for a week. After that, events moved swiftly. By mid-September, the Wayfarers had been taken over, Plovers Field was due to be auctioned on 1 November and Vaughan had decided to live at Wolvercote in North Oxford, in a house built with the proceeds of the sale. There was some relief when visits to Princes Risborough ended after Granny Betty died on 4 October, and Cilla started to work at the Warneford as a psychology technician, paid from a hospital research fund.[87] By December 1966, the house was under construction and Cilla at home, though Vaughan could not leave her for long, saying she was still very fragile.[88]

Christmas was brighter, producing 'a riot of grandchildren & very sombre Czech research Fellow & Dora Gordine ... who has just lost her husband ... & ... Halford & all his family & beloved Cilla very ill with tonsillitis & doctors running in with syringes of penicillin & JV frantically carrying trays & roasting Turkies [sic]'.[89] Cilla was still working in January, but saying she had contracted out of life ('So one lives with a ghost'). Vaughan longed for Plovers Field, feeling discouraged, disheartened and physically weak.[90]

Testing times: last years at Somerville 1963–67
Vaughan had plunged into work after Gourlay's funeral. Particularly in unguarded moments, however, her face betrayed the devastation she felt.[91] Her resignation from Hebdomadal Council took effect, and she must have missed that central role in university affairs, although she did continue on the Council's medical advisory committee; but otherwise her commitments if anything increased. The college treasurer, Jane Hands, was absent that term because of an emergency operation, and Vaughan and the economics don Hall stepped in to cover finance issues. The fellows were concerned. In March, when she gave notice of a week's absence in June for a conference in Vienna, they urged her to take longer leave if she wished; and on her return they assured

her that leave of six months or more would be granted 'with warm sympathy and encouragement', together with a college grant for any research needs. Vaughan was grateful, but her preference for working on was accentuated by the interest and urgency of her agenda.[92] Her output that year was extraordinary, including as it did the management of the various college building projects, ongoing recruitment issues in part arising from the Robbins Report, commitments in Oxford medical affairs, and the steering of a major new Nuffield Foundation project.

There were some lighter moments. Having taken over responsibility for the chapel in 1960, Vaughan was usually there for morning prayers at around 8am each day and on Sunday evenings, preparing and delivering most of the readings and prayers. On the (still freezing) mornings following Gourlay's death, students noticed her sitting alone on a nearby bench. Not knowing what to say, they asked her to go in with them, and felt that their care gave her some comfort.[93] She then decided to redecorate Radcliffe House, and in February it was 'beginning to look quite lovely ... one didn't realise how shabby it had got until one sees it ... with new paint and some of the Russell Square curtains.'[94]

The Nuffield Foundation and genetics
Vaughan's outstanding single contribution to medical science as a Nuffield Foundation trustee came in this, for her, annus horribilis. Usually trustees awaited proposals, rather than working with researchers to produce them; but she now persuaded them into a more proactive role. Chief protagonist was her friend E B Ford, in Oxford's zoology department, who had created the subject 'ecological genetics' through his studies of butterflies and moths and whose work the foundation had funded since 1951.[95] A colleague, Philip Sheppard, moved from Ford's laboratory to Liverpool in 1956 as senior lecturer in genetics, with his work on butterflies still supported by the foundation.[96] He was already collaborating with Cyril Clarke, a lecturer in clinical medicine there who studied butterflies as a hobby. In 1958, they noticed a similarity between a type of genetic organisation in butterflies and the corresponding rhesus (Rh) gene location in humans. The known problem of potential incompatibility between a Rh-negative

260

woman and a second or later Rh-positive fetus made them investigate further. Eventually they suggested a way of foiling such a mother's immune system by injecting her with antiserum to the critical Rh-complex gene shortly after delivery of a Rh-positive child. If this rapidly destroyed any Rh-positive cells that had crossed the placenta and entered the mother's blood, her immune system would not produce the dangerous antibodies.

In January 1963 they were preparing for human trials of the treatment when Vaughan intervened. She suggested that Ford broaden his research programme to include medical genetics; but immediately accepted his view that this needed a medical lead and only Clarke was suitable, so it must be at Liverpool. Vaughan persuaded the trustees to let Ford explore the idea with Liverpool, then planned a scheme with him in February whose details were worked out with Clarke and Sheppard over the next eight months. Seeing this as 'one of the most promising fields' in medicine, she 'encouraged Ford to think in a big way … it is always easier to prune than to expand'. Having recently, through her UGC work, seen the plans for Liverpool's teaching hospital, she saw the chance to 'insinuate … what we want before it is too late … something … very exciting is going to grow out of all this'.[97] This was visionary boldness. Most of the Liverpool staff were practising clinicians with little experience of research, but Ford saw the importance of their access to patients: 'The fact that neither the Galton Laboratory in London nor the M.R.C. place at Headington have hospital beds attached … is one of the reasons why they have both fallen … behind what is already being done at Liverpool.'[98]

In October the trustees agreed £350,000, one of their largest grants ever, over nine years to establish the Nuffield Unit of Medical Genetics at Liverpool. This funded a building (completed in 1967) to house the research programme and additional staff, fellowships for clinicians to study genetic aspects of disease, and some operating costs. In the next decade or so, the unit housed diverse research activities, and trained scientists and physicians in genetics. Its cross-disciplinary nature chimed closely with Vaughan's vision for scientific research. The new treatment for Rh-negative mothers led to the virtual ending of Rh disease in babies. Researchers also revealed the genetic basis of differential responses to drugs, leading to safer prescribing; and enabled understanding of the genetic details of thalassaemia and other blood disorders. Many unit-trained scientists went on to head other medical genetics centres. David Weatherall, who led research on genetics in certain blood disorders before moving in 1974 to become professor of clinical medicine at Oxford, said of the Nuffield grant: 'Without that building and getting ... the group of people together, [Liverpool medical genetics research] would have died straight after the Rhesus [work].'[99]

The unit enabled medical students to see the importance of genetics for understanding major health problems, rather than just the rarer types of single-gene disorders; understand that susceptibility to a disorder can derive from a particular set of genes which also show predisposition in advance of any symptoms; and recognise that the whole genetic endowment must be considered in devising genetic studies and treatments. It was later taken over piecemeal by other medical units, but 'the legacy of the ... Nuffield butterfly workers and clinicians is still being felt in human and medical genetics'.[100]

The Robbins Report and the Franks Commission
The rest of working life went on as usual. Vaughan's cousin Mary Bennett, Lettice Fisher's daughter, consulted her in 1964 when St Hilda's College approached her about becoming Principal, and came to stay several times. Remarking on how splendid Vaughan looked when dressed for a special event, she was told 'I make rather a point of it.' Bennett believed her 'in a sense – except perhaps for Virginia Woolf – the most beautiful woman any of us have ever seen. It was the animation ... the sense of vim ... that ... made such an impression.'[101] There was much to bring Vaughan satisfaction in these years, not least the changing position of science. With government encouragement, the number of trained scientists produced annually in the UK had risen significantly since the war, but Robbins in 1963 urged a far greater expansion of all higher education, including in science and technology and numbers of women. Oxford knew it had to respond, and in 1964 set up the Franks Commission to advise on how best to do so.

No doubt Robbins was one factor in New College's decision in 1964 to consider admitting women students. This caused consternation in the women's colleges, but Vaughan reacted with characteristic matter-of-fact realism. At a special meeting, she and the Somerville fellows concluded that the New College proposal would be imitated by other men's colleges and, failing a redistribution of endowments, the differences in college incomes would put women's colleges at an impossible disadvantage regarding fellows' pay and certain student charges.[102] They and their sister colleges put their hopes of remedying this in the Franks Commission. Vaughan saw the futility of resistance, saying in written evidence to Franks that the quickest and cheapest way to increase the number of women at Oxford would be for some of the men's colleges to take women and reduce the number of men.

In her oral evidence, Vaughan rather disingenuously denied the existence of sex-linked barriers in Oxford (one Commission member agreed there were no 'formal' barriers); and said she expected more women scientists in future: Nuffield school science would enthuse them, and the university should better publicise the innovative content of its courses. Her science tutors would welcome common entry arrangements for men and women, and an increase in the number of women in higher education would benefit society. When asked if this would be true if the number of men dropped in consequence, she cited two non-feminist colleagues, recently involved in marking both arts and science degree papers, who had been shocked by the poor calibre of many male students (for whom the threshold standard for entry was much lower). Taking five hundred more women and losing five hundred men would *not* be a loss to society.

She agreed that women tutors' workload was excessive. In discussing how more of them might be recruited, she suggested that the university should recognise that many were married, with children. One way of meeting their needs would be to provide crèche facilities such as Somerville shared with St Anne's. She also said that Somerville currently had up to 58 UK and overseas graduates, but would willingly admit around a hundred (then nearly half of their undergraduate total). All the women's colleges urged the need for more teaching staff, and extension of the CUF

263

(Common University Fund, under which college and university shared the cost of lecturers) system to science subjects, so that they could recruit the lecturers they needed rather than being constrained by existing subject staffing profiles.[103]

The 1966 Franks report supported all these points and recommended bringing staff/student ratios in line with the national average, so as to ease the tutorial burden. The proportion of postgraduates should rise, especially in science and social studies, and special steps be taken to increase pre- and postgraduate numbers in applied sciences, including clinical medicine. The proportion of women students should gradually increase, with the same standard of admission as for men. This implied doubling the number of fellows of women's colleges. The university should seek research money from all possible sources and create more professorial posts, especially in science. Provision and practice should be standardised across all colleges, including charges and stipends.[104]

Somerville: succession plan and internal tensions
For all her modesty, Vaughan must have been greatly pleased by the fellows' decision in November 1965 to name the new undergraduate block then under construction the Vaughan Building. It was effectively opened in April 1966 when UGC visitors came for a buffet lunch to meet the women Principals and discuss their problems. When the students asked for a portrait of her, she gave them a copy of the bronze head Gordine had produced in the 1920s, to stand in the hall of the new building.[105] Vaughan was glad when in late January 1966 the classicist Barbara Craig, an old Somervillian, was 'pre-elected' as her successor. She knew her as 'a scholar widely travelled & … I am assured kind'. She was also married, which Vaughan took as an endorsement of her own and Gourlay's contribution.[106]

March 1967, however, brought the shock of Isobel Henderson's death following an operation for throat cancer. Henderson was someone on whom Vaughan had relied, and also admired for her style, wit and gaiety as well as her scholarship. Craig was even more bereft. Henderson, who would have continued as Vice-Principal, was her former tutor and had meant a great deal to her.

Vaughan asked if Foot was willing to fill the gap, if only for a short time, saying that it 'means wisdom & someone to talk to in times of difficulty'.[107] To her relief, Foot agreed. Vaughan's tribute to Henderson reflects her own values. 'She could be ruthless, she could be bored, but she never lacked charity ... above all, what we in Somerville shall remember is her regard for learning & her courage.'[108]

There is a question as to whether Vaughan's physical and emotional stress in these last years led to a more high-handed approach to college business and colleagues. Her advice to Bennett on how to treat fellows was to be 'absolutely ruthless. Otherwise they'll treat you like a kitchen maid'; and Bennett did hear on the grapevine that some at Somerville thought Vaughan dictatorial.[109]

The memories of some newcomers to the college at that time do not fully chime with this, however. Peggy Rimmer came as a research fellow in physics in 1964. After a first degree at Liverpool, then a DPhil at Lady Margaret Hall (LMH), she had little self-confidence. She was one of about four women (to about 80 men) doing maths and physics at Liverpool, and at LMH she and other graduates lived in digs in semi-isolation. At conferences she was one of a tiny female minority. By contrast, at Somerville a sympathetic don from one of the men's colleges was leading on physics, she did some tutoring, and the graduate house common room transformed her social life. She felt part of an impressive female community, where Vaughan set the tone in terms of standards of behaviour and achievement, but in a quiet way. Highly successful but not conceited, she was sociable but kept her personal life very private.

Rimmer was not a fellow, but in more than three years she never heard anyone say anything unkind or unpleasant about Vaughan (as she did about most of the other dons). There was also no snobbery: the daughter of a coal miner, she felt comfortable in Vaughan's company, in a way she had not done at LMH. As to temperament, she thought the Principal was 'programmed' to get through the day. She had to be tough to manage all the college staff, but was 'so very nice', even when occasionally (and informally, over breakfast for example) 'ranting and raving' and saying that she had 'no time for this nonsense', when others complained about

265

something she thought trivial. On any issue, she would simply and unemotionally tell the truth as she saw it.

Generous but discreet, when Rimmer mentioned in passing that three friends from Leicester were coming to a college ball, Vaughan somehow, without telling her, arranged for them to stay in Radcliffe House. No doubt she realised that they would be short of money for hotels. Rimmer spent the rest of her career at CERN (the European Organisation for Nuclear Research) in Switzerland, where only 4–7% of the scientific staff were female. Vaughan and Somerville had convinced her that she could be a woman *and* be extremely successful, so long as she worked hard. A friend who had been a research fellow in law at the same time felt the same fondness and admiration for Vaughan.[110]

When Katherine Duncan-Jones arrived as a new fellow in 1965, she too was impressed by Vaughan's generosity. She met distinguished guests at many private lunch parties at Radcliffe House, and on one occasion was invited to a college ball as one of a party of about 12, mainly fellows and their spouses. The Principal paid for the tickets and cooked dinner. On the other hand, Duncan-Jones was soon a shocked victim of Vaughan's 'right' to determine the allocation of places after the entrance examinations. Informed that her own quota would be reduced by two places, she strongly and successfully resisted. This story supports the view of some others, that Vaughan could only get her way on such things with less assertive colleagues.[111]

Miriam Griffin, a research fellow of St Anne's, was already doing much of Henderson's teaching at the time of her death in March 1967. Soon afterwards Vaughan called at her home unannounced and, unfazed by the 'chaos' caused by two small daughters, discussed Somerville's vacancy for a tutor in ancient history. Griffin somehow found herself agreeing to apply, learning afterwards that Vaughan described her as 'rangée': steady, tidy, well-ordered. The two rarely met thereafter, but 'fellows muttered about how autocratic Janet had been at the end of her reign, before they started muttering about how long meetings took when chaired by the more democratic Barbara Craig'.[112] Given her long tenure, and the personal trials she faced in these last years, Vaughan probably did show scant regard for others' views at times; but she would have loved to stay on for another three years, as was possible under the rules. The fellows, however, understandably saw the need for change after 22 years.

No one doubted Vaughan's achievements. In October 1967, Somerville was numerically second only to St Anne's (365 students to St Anne's 369) among the women's colleges, with two new buildings to accommodate them and one of the first graduate houses in Oxford. It had the highest number of science undergraduates (40% were reading science or maths) and of both arts and science postgraduates. The total number of fellows had doubled since 1945, with science and maths far better represented among them.[113]

Crowned with honours

In June 1967 the university gave Vaughan one of its highest honours, a DCL (Doctorate in Civil Law by Diploma), which gave her great pride.[114] In college, Hodgkin hosted the fellows' buffet supper for Vaughan and Lascelles, who was also retiring. Their thoughtful leaving present was the installation of a garden at the house in Wolvercote. A selection of Somervillians from the years between 1945 and 1967 attended the Gaudy, at which Janet Adam Smith presented a cheque for £1,000 and, at Vaughan's request, a replica of the college Principal's ring. The money she immediately donated to help endow a tutorial fellowship in a science not otherwise represented at Somerville.[115]

In July Vaughan told Griffiths that her final term had been tough, but the Encaenia ceremony in June when she received her DCL 'marvellous', with 'Cilla & Mary & Vanessa in the Sheldonian & … all the last parties have been so full of warmth & friendship'.[116] She and Cilla moved out of Radcliffe House at the end of that month. Her habit was to look to the future; but she always reflected on her time at Somerville with feelings of pride and nostalgia. She had found this 'distinguished group of scholars in many different disciplines … an ideal society in which to live and work'.[117] Although, as an honorary fellow, she could still dine or lunch in college and bring guests, out of consideration for her successor she chose to exercise that right sparingly, and sorely missed the constant talk and stimulation of her ideal society.

There was yet another honour to come from the university, when in November 1970 the Vice-Chancellor in Congregation

267

awarded Vaughan the William Osler Memorial Medal, given five-yearly to the Oxford medical graduate judged to have made the most valuable contribution to the science, art or literature of medicine. The promise she had shown at the time of her graduation in 1923 had been amply fulfilled, and that fulfilment had been shown across a wide field.

Endnotes

[1] Interview with Hilary Spurling, 28.3.2007.

[2] Esther Rantzen, *Esther* (London, BBC Books, 2001), 44.

[3] Interview with Peggy Rimmer, 24.9.2007.

[4] Rantzen, *Esther*, 44.

[5] JA, 114. SCA, Hungarian Students file gives the basic story up to 1959. Some details from interview with Philippa Foot, 17.4.2000.

[6] Interview with Foot. This is equivalent to £356,000 in 2021. (www.measuringworth.com, using purchasing power calculator, accessed 21.11.2023.) In total some 400 students were placed in the UK (JA, 116).

[7] In a dramatic subplot, one student, Judith Cripps, went to Hungary with three male students to deliver medicines for injured students. All four were imprisoned for a short time. Vaughan assured Cripps's mother that she should take as much time off as she needed to recover. In practice she lost a term, then changed her degree subject and was allowed an extra year to complete it. (Interview with Judith Heyer (née Cripps), 10.7.2007.)

[8] Fights at universities during anti-war demonstrations, *Manchester Guardian* (3.11.1956), 3. A counter-demonstration was organised by leaders of the Oxford University Conservative Association.

[9] Nutting resigns on Suez policy, *The Observer* (4.11.1956), 1: the same day as the Soviet tanks entered Budapest.

[10] Vaughan did rejoice when the limited Test Ban Treaty was signed in 1963.

[11] The new kitchen was in use from October 1959.

[12] Interview with Charlotte Graves Taylor, 22.11.2006.

[13] The self-governing status they had achieved in 1950 was an essential prerequisite for this.

[14] OBL, Diaries of Rev Thomas (Tom) Wailes Griffiths, 28.7.1970. Griffiths noted that the two women seemed 'more friendly' than previously; but Vaughan was proud of being the first to be made a dame.

[15] SCA, 1957–58 Oxford Letter, written by the JCR President.

[16] Interview with Joan Townsend, 12.1.2007.

[17] The Warneford Hospital is the main psychiatric hospital for the Oxford area.

[18] Jennifer Bray, email to author dated 30.9.2019.

[19] Manel Abeysekera, statement sent with email dated 18.12.2006. Fortunately the rules were soon changed and she went on to a foreign service career.

[20] Esther Rantzen, email to author, 15.7.2023.

[21] Interview with Hilary Spurling, 28.3.2007.

[22] Interview with Foot.

[23] Susan Segal, emails of 26 and 27.3.2007. She found the level of ignorance among other students 'astounding'.

[24] Interview with Janet Howarth, 12.1.2007.

[25] SCA, minutes of governing body 1960–67, meeting on 17.2.1960. Disciplinary measures included 'rustication' (banning from college for a short time) and 'sending down' (a permanent ban).

[26] SCA, discipline file 1948–66 (Confidential).

[27] Interview with Ann Dummett, 18.3.2001.

[28] JPP, Anne Yates letter to Cilla, 31.1.1993. The charity was SACHED – the South African Committee for Higher Education, set up to counter the exclusion of non-Europeans from South African universities. Another charity, the Joint Action Commission against Racial Intolerance (JACARI), was set up in Oxford in 1955. It sponsored a scholar from South Africa, who stayed at Radcliffe House on his arrival in May 1959 before going on to Wadham College to study history. In the first half of the 1960s the charity supported a SACHED campaign to send books to students in South Africa. (JA, 104.)

[29] Joan E Wicken, in Adams, *A Memorial Tribute*, 3. Vaughan's interest in improving educational standards in African countries had been fired initially by her friend Daryll Forde. She only visited the continent once, in spring 1957, with Gourlay. They visited a new hospital there, but were horrified by a road accident they witnessed, where whites showed callousness towards blacks who were injured. (JPP, Mary Bennett to Vaughan, 13.3.1957; and Prue Smith letter to James Park, 22.10.1993. Also author's interviews with Bennett, 7.2.2000, and with Mary Park, 22.3.2006.)

[30] Oxford ending quota rule on women, *The Times* (30.1.1957), 8.

[31] SCA, Council Report for 1959.

[32] British Motor Industry Heritage Trust, Minutes and Papers 1949–54 (Lord Nuffield's papers). NF meeting, 29.9.1961. Another trustee rightly raised the claims of New Hall at this point: the Cambridge women's college had recently been refused a grant on the ground that the Foundation did not fund student accommodation. That decision was revisited, and New Hall enabled to build a mixed block for graduates and undergraduates.

[33] Report of the Committee on Higher Education (Robbins Report), commissioned by the government and published in 1963.

[34] Harvey and Louise Johnson, Obituary: Dame Janet Vaughan, in *The Independent* (12.1.1993), www.independent.co.uk/news/people/obituary-dame-janet-vaughan-1478124.html accessed 7.4.2014. Also Harvey in Adams, *A Memorial Tribute*, 5.

[35] Telephone conversation with Marjorie Harding (née Aitken), 18.5.2007.

[36] Agatha Ramm, in Adams, *A Memorial Tribute*, 20. Akhmatova (1889–1966) received an honorary degree from Oxford on 7.6.1965. During her visit she edited for publication some of her own texts, which Isaiah Berlin had brought out of Russia for her at the end of the war.

[37] SCA, Mary Lascelles, unpublished memoir.

[38] Mary Lascelles, in Adams, *A Memorial Tribute*, 20.

[39] Interview with Foot.

[40] Interview with Hilary Spurling.

[41] OUA, HC 12/1/1–3.

[42] SCA, governing body minutes 18.1.1961. Grant of leave of absence to Principal for 23.1–2.2.1961 to attend SEATO conference.

[43] JPP, Vaughan to Mary Park undated, written on flight home. Off-duty, she bought a silk 'Jinnah Cap' for Gavin and two lengths of silk for Mary.

[44] Clark, *A Biography of the Nuffield Foundation*, 168–76.

[45] Interview with Sir Brian Young, 28.8.2007.

[46] Interview with John McAnuff, 28.8.2007.

[47] As so often, it seems that she was the only 'professional' woman present.

[48] TNA, DO 35/8208 and 8211; also DO 163/13.

[49] TNA, OD 17/194, 380, 381, internal minutes of 6.1, 26.2 and 2.3.1966.

[50] JA, 142.

[51] Dame Janet Vaughan, The future of postgraduate medical education, in I C Gilliland and J Francis (Eds), *The Scientific Basis of Medicine Annual Reviews 1971* (British Postgraduate Medical Federation. The Athlone Press, University of London), 1–16. First published in *The Lancet* (8.11.1969), 2(7628), 995–99.

[52] TNA, UGC CY 7/594.

[53] TNA, UGC 8/95, minutes of meetings.

[54] JA, 137.

[55] JPP, Vaughan undated [August 1956] to Prue Smith from Plovers Field: 'My grandson is terrific. He weighed 8lbs to start & now … 10lbs after a fortnight here – & M is lovely to see with him & so is my David. He worships & bursts with pride.'

[56] JPP, Maureen Owen to Mary Park, 29.2.1960.

[57] JPP, interview with Janet Adam Smith, 1994. A fairing is a present bought at a fair.

[58] JPP, Vaughan to Prue Smith, August 1956; and JA, 24.

[59] OBL, Griffiths diaries, 9.7.1962 and 8.1.1963. Cilla left on the *Queen Mary* on Saturday 12.1.1963.

[60] Successive bouts of depression had prevented Halford from holding down any job for very long. Relations intervened to help him and his family.

[61] JPP, Vaughan to Mary Park, 29.11.1962, about a 'good report from the specialist about Daddy'. Vaughan had told the MRC in 1961 of her intention to retire in 1964.

[62] JPP, letters dated 9 and 15.1.1963.

[63] JPP, this and other letters quoted written following the funeral in January 1963.

[64] JPP, interview with Dorothy Vaughan.

[65] Obituary for Anne Cobbe, *The Times* (28.12.1971), 8, letter from Vaughan. Foot said that Vaughan regarded Cobbe as a very special person.

[66] JPP, Cilla to Vaughan, 23.1.1963. Other letters quoted in this paragraph sent in February 1963.

[67] JA, 110.

[68] JPP, Vaughan to Mary undated, [March] 1963.

[69] Ibid., letter dated 16.1.1963.

[70] JPP, Vaughan to solicitors, 13.12.1963.

[71] JPP, Vaughan to solicitors, 5.3.1964. Presumably she was 'being sent away' on doctor's orders, probably to Italy as happened a year later.

[72] The company did not thrive and was finally liquidated in 1985.

[73] JPP, undated (1964) letter from Len Cornish.

[74] OBL, Griffiths diaries, 8.1.1963.

[75] JPP, Vaughan to Griffiths, Easter Saturday 1963. Cilla had started working for a children's charity on 4 March.

[76] JPP, Vaughan to Griffiths, 8.8.1963. The Limited Nuclear Test Ban Treaty was signed on 5.8.1963 by the United States, Soviet Union and UK. It limited such testing to underground sites.

[77] OBL, Griffiths diaries, 11.10.1963.

[78] JPP, Vaughan to Prue Smith, 30.10.1963.

[79] JPP, Vaughan to Griffiths, 7.11.1963. The Robbins Report on higher education had recently been published.

[80] OBL, Griffiths diaries, 11.11.1963.

[81] JPP, Vaughan to Jean Griffiths, 18.11.1963.

[82] Interview with Susan Aglionby, 11.6.2000. Susan trained at St George's because Vaughan said it had the best matron. She gave her aunt much pleasure by winning the gold medal for her year, and going on to a distinguished nursing career.

[83] JPP, Vaughan to Griffiths, 25.12.1963.

271

[84] OBL, Griffiths diaries, 3.8.1965.

[85] JPP, Vaughan to Jean Griffiths, 22.10.1965.

[86] JPP, Vaughan to Griffiths, 30.7.1966.

[87] JPP, Vaughan to accountants, 23.5.1969.

[88] JPP, Vaughan to Prue Smith, 28.12.1966.

[89] JPP, Vaughan to Griffiths, 29.12.1966.

[90] JPP, Vaughan to Griffiths, undated, January 1967.

[91] Interview with Janet Howarth.

[92] SCA, Vaughan personal file, notification following meeting of governing body, 19.6.1963; and Vaughan reply, 25.6.1963.

[93] Jennifer Bray, email dated 30.9.2019.

[94] Vaughan to Christian Parham (Somerville, 1950–53), undated, February 1962. (Letter lent by Parham and transcribed.)

[95] Those interested in the detailed story should see Doris T Zallen, From Butterflies to Blood. Human Genetics in the United Kingdom, in Michael Fortun and Everett Mendelsohn (Eds), *The Practices of Human Genetics* (Dordrecht, Kluwer Academic Publishers, 1999), 197–216.

[96] Sheppard became the first professor of genetics at Liverpool, and Clarke was professor of medicine from 1965.

[97] Vaughan to Farrer Brown, 17.2.1963, quoted by Zallen, 209. The UGC meeting at which Vaughan had discussed the Liverpool plans took place on 15 January, the day after Gourlay's death.

[98] Ford to Farrer Brown, 8.4.1963, quoted in Fortun and Mendelsohn, *The Practices of Human Genetics*, 209.

[99] Zallen, The Nuffield Foundation and Medical Genetics, 232. Weatherall (1933–2018) founded the University of Oxford's Institute of Molecular Medicine and served as Regius professor from 1992 to 2000.

[100] Fortun and Mendelsohn, *The Practices of Human Genetics*, 212.

[101] Interview with Mary Bennett.

[102] SCA, Council minutes, 27.5.1964.

[103] OUA, Franks Commission Oral Evidence HC 4/50/27, 58, 73, 88. (Vaughan's evidence regarding the balance of professorial posts in Oxford between the sciences and the humanities is covered in Chapter 12, on Oxford Medicine.)

[104] Lord Franks, *University of Oxford: Report of Commission of Inquiry, Vol 1* (Oxford, Clarendon Press, 1966), Volume 1: Summary of Recommendations.

[105] There was a contretemps with Gordine over this. She suggested an antique pedestal which Vaughan found hideous, and replaced with a plain one commissioned and designed by herself. Vaughan also said she fully accepted that the college might in the future wish, for good reason, to sell both sculpture and pedestal. (SCA, Vaughan undergraduate block file.)

[106] JPP, Vaughan to Griffiths, 1.2.1966.

[107] Copy letters given to the author by Foot: Vaughan to Foot (then in the United States), 3.3.1967 and 11.3.1967. In the event Foot found the post uncongenial, and departed again for the United States in January 1968.

[108] SCA, ASM Report for 1966/67.

[109] Interview with Mary Bennett.

[110] Interview with Peggy Rimmer.

[111] Interview with Katherine Duncan-Jones and others, 22.5.2007.

[112] Griffin letter of 22.7.2007 and interview in August 2007.

[113] Harvey and Johnson, Obituary: Dame Janet Vaughan.

[114] A DCL was usually conferred on visiting heads of state and Oxford Vice-Chancellors in the grand Sheldonian Theatre at Encaenia, the annual celebration in memory of founders and benefactors of the university.

[115] The first such fellow, in molecular biophysics, was appointed in 1968.

[116] JPP, Vaughan to Griffiths, 3.7.1967.

[117] JA, 99.

CHAPTER 12
Oxford medicine
1945–67

The Oxford Regional Hospital Board

During her period as Principal, it is doubtful that anyone in Somerville, with the possible exceptions of her housekeeper and secretary, had a full appreciation of Vaughan's activities outside the college. In Oxford, she mainly focused on the cause of medicine and science, as well as her own research. And in the early years her experience on the Oxford Regional Hospital Board (ORHB) was short but very sweet. She later recalled it as the job she had enjoyed most in her life, because it enabled her to start putting right some of the injustices and inefficiencies of the old system.[1] She must also have enjoyed the comparative freedom it gave her to make swift decisions. Vaughan joined the board in June 1947 as one of the Socialist Medical Association's nominees for appointment to new NHS bodies, on grounds of their 'experience, abilities and interest in the success of the new Service'.[2] The chair, Dr A Q Wells, an experimental pathologist with experience of hospital planning, shared her values and allowed her energies a free rein. She was elected vice chair at the third meeting, in October. Appointments were made and committee structures established at speed. In April 1948 the board moved into permanent premises in Banbury Road, not far from Somerville.

One year on, its annual report listed additional hospital specialists appointed, including in ENT (ear, nose and throat specialism), ophthalmic surgery, radiology and dermatology, accident and orthopaedic surgery, pathology and psychiatry. A regional psychiatric unit was planned, and nursing shortages tackled by appointing part timers and introducing pre-nurse training courses to bridge the three-year gap between the school leaving age of 15, and training proper.[3] A new regional records unit was set up within the Institute of Social Medicine's Nuffield Bureau of Health and Sickness Records. Planned efficiency measures included investment to modify or rebuild premises. Major capital projects were deferred owing to economic austerity, but work begun or

274

awaiting a start date totalled more than £400,000: almost double the financial allocation for the year ahead. They were also spending more than £100,000 on buying properties, including nurses' living accommodation; and, by the end of 1949, discussing the site for a new general hospital in Swindon.[4]

Unsurprisingly, in 1948 the treasurer noted at a meeting with other boards that Oxford was by far the most advanced. Vaughan's interest in improving the spread of consultant services, getting building projects 'spade-ready' and under way, improving psychiatric services and record keeping, and also in nursing and enabling women to work part time, is implicit in all of this. The board located a regional psychiatric unit at Oxford's Warneford Hospital, whose director and medical superintendent were recognised in 1950 as university teachers.[5] It also set up various joint staffing arrangements with the teaching hospital, and went further in January 1949, when facilities were needed for the university's new Nuffield professor of orthopaedic surgery. The board made this a clinical as well as academic post and allocated the necessary beds.[6]

The regional nursing officer recalled Vaughan as 'an experience of electricity that fired many of us … full of dynamism, and fury if needed'.[7] One target of her fury was 'the … mental hospitals, and understaffed asylums where the mentally sick were put away'.[8] Having failed to persuade Jameson, still the health ministry CMO, to allow more funding, she tried a different tactic. When the ministry's permanent secretary came to visit, she took him to the worst mental hospital, to see 'long wards with over 100 beds … with just room … to put … a mattress at night on the floor between them: no lockers, no personal possessions'. He admitted next morning to having slept badly as a result. The board appointed an entirely new management committee, which went on to transform the hospital.[9]

When Wells resigned as chair in 1950, the health minister, Nye Bevan, asked Vaughan to replace him. She regretfully refused, in light of her other commitments. Less than two weeks later, however, Bevan asked her to serve for one year only. Having meanwhile been sought out by the deputy CMO at the ministry, she capitulated: 'if those who can see the whole work of the Hospital

Service feel that my part time is better … than the full time of someone else I [will] … do my best as chairman for one year'.[10] She took over in April, continuing the constant round of meetings in the region and London, and later extended her 'one year' by accepting reappointment the following March.

In November 1950, thanks to having preliminary plans in hand, she landed a one-off health ministry grant of £100,000 to complete the first stage of the new hospital in Swindon in 1951–52. The board also planned developments at two existing hospitals, and she chaired all three project management committees. In April 1951 they took over Stoke Mandeville Hospital, rapidly planning its use as a research, treatment and teaching centre for rheumatic diseases, and a neurological unit linked to provision at the Radcliffe Infirmary. This was followed in July by the Special Injuries Unit, founded in 1944 to treat spinal injuries and already a national centre of excellence.

When the Swindon hospital architect resigned in 1951, Vaughan advised the board to appoint a firm of young architects with considerable experience, though not necessarily of hospital work. The architect Philip Powell, of Powell and Moya, recalled meeting 'a formidable and lovely lady … [who] wanted an architect that she believed in' and liked their previous work, including Skylon, the iconic symbol of the 1951 Festival of Britain. At a lunchtime meeting in August, she 'pumped more drink into us than was reasonable [and] the whole thing turned into a sort of riotous party'. For Powell this was the era of winning work through personal contacts rather than competitions, and of the optimism surrounding the foundation of the NHS.[11]

In practice the board's CMO acted as main client, and involved the architects in consulting doctors and nurses, which Powell thought progressive for the time. They also had to work (very happily) with the Nuffield Provincial Hospital Trust (NPHT) architects, and the first wards at Swindon were based on experimental NPHT prototypes already built in Belfast.[12] Swindon's early start ensured that it was one of the first four new general hospitals to receive funding in 1955, and phased building continued until the 1970s. This was Vaughan's swansong. She resigned before the September 1951 meeting, at which the acting chair said her influence would be felt for many years to come. Others echoed his words, while perhaps feeling as if they had stepped off a roller coaster.

The Oxford Medical School 1947–58
Background and early years

After her election to Hebdomadal Council in 1946–47, backed by Professor Burn and the medical and scientific faculties in particular, Vaughan was for some years the only scientist on it. She also served on all the main university medical committees, plus those dealing with the University Museum's scientific collections. These were important for teaching and research, and the museum was also the centre for administering the university's science area until 1964. Vaughan's authority in Oxford medical circles grew to be almost unparalleled. Her core aims were linked to the key Goodenough recommendations: academic control of medical teaching; incorporation of social medicine into the curriculum; and the promotion of new specialisms including clinical pathology and psychiatry. Memories of Hammersmith, and of wartime provincial hospitals, had seared into her mind the importance of adequate physical facilities and equipment; but she knew the value of biding her time, and being flexible when appropriate.

In 1945, most Oxford preclinical students still gained a scientific education, as she had, through the honours degree in physiology before doing their clinical training in London. Opinion about whether Oxford should have its own clinical school was divided between those arguing that this would supply recruits for the university's research base, and others who believed routine, and costly, clinical instruction was incompatible with advanced medical research. Donations by Lord Nuffield in the 1930s (the Nuffield Benefaction) had established both the Nuffield Institute of Medical Research and the basis for a postgraduate school through five 'Nuffield' professors, in medicine, surgery, obstetrics/gynaecology, anaesthetics and orthopaedics. Some, including the university registrar, or head of administration, Douglas Veale, intended to develop a full clinical school over time.[13] During the war, a small ad hoc group in the medicine faculty had proposed to the Goodenough Committee a clinical school with an annual intake of 25 and teaching with a scientific emphasis, alongside

277

continuing provision for research and advanced postgraduate studies. The University Grants Committee (UGC) agreed funding from 1946–47 to develop such a school.

The Nuffield professorships had meanwhile created discontent among both Radcliffe Infirmary clinical staff and preclinical science professors. The first group felt a loss of status, while the scientists thought they should share the extra money. In particular some able men, including Burn in pharmacology and Florey in pathology, were desperately short of funds to build up their departments.[14]

The 1946 NHS Act created new tensions by requiring the designation of a teaching hospital, which should select patients to serve the needs of clinical teaching. The idea was for this to concentrate on theory and methods, with practice partly to be learnt in a separate, large regional hospital. In 1947, Vaughan and Wells joined representatives of the university, the medical school and Radcliffe Infirmary governors to decide on designation. Oxford, having only one major hospital, did not fit the mould. Since there would be no money for a new hospital for at least 10 years, the Radcliffe Infirmary had to serve both teaching and regional needs. Vaughan and Wells argued that the whole site, plus four specialised hospitals in the area, must therefore be designated a teaching hospital, and this solution was agreed at the end of 1947.[15] Teaching hospital governors, directly responsible to the health ministry, were appointed by the minister, the university, medical staff and the regional board. The university appointed only about one fifth of them.

Tensions between the university and teaching hospital governors
The post-war climate of austerity sharpened discord between departments over funding, and university relations with the governors of United Oxford Hospitals (UOH), as the teaching hospital group was named, were not good. Those (primarily Veale and Witts) who wished to retain and develop a clinical school were disadvantaged by the university's minority position on the UOH board. The clinical curriculum still lacked any social or psychological emphasis, nor was a scientific focus feasible when most training was by Radcliffe Infirmary clinicians who did no research. The reformers wanted more teaching beds, and academic control of

their use; but faced also the fact that the Nuffield departments were not adapted for training clinical students, and laboratory and other facilities were inadequate. The clinical 'school' was held in low regard and admitted only about 20 students a year.

Vaughan could sympathise with all factions. Witts and Burn were old friends, she was on good terms with Florey, and able to appreciate the problems of both service and teaching sides. In summer 1953 she was on a group enigmatically known as the 'Polo Team' (perhaps it had four members), tasked with deciding how to raise the standard of clinical teaching, so as to persuade a doubtful medicine board and Hebdomadal Council that a clinical school would be viable.[16] Her confidential draft report in November presented the options of closing the clinical school; continuing it in hopes of a gradual improvement in facilities; or developing it with an emphasis on teaching clinical science. Essential requirements included enough beds and lab space for research and teaching. Clinical professors should supervise all academic work, and university representatives form a majority on academic appointment committees, so as to maintain standards and also, for example, secure appointments in new specialties not yet recognised for general service purposes. In December 1953 the medicine faculty board voted to adopt Vaughan and Witts' proposal to retain the clinical school, but only just: 12 in favour, 11 abstaining.

Council then decided to submit the university requirements to the health ministry, after seeking comments from UOH governors.[17] In February 1954, Veale sent the Vice-Chancellor letters for governors and ministry, and a paper to Council, all drafted by Vaughan. He thought the letter to UOH good, and 'it would certainly be tactful to adopt it, since we shall depend on her to satisfy [them]'.[18] The university demanded control of academic policy, adequate beds and lab facilities, and a majority voice in appointing teaching hospital consultants. Vaughan stressed the need to be clear that they were motivated by concern for academic standards, and to be as conciliatory as possible.

The UOH chair was David Lindsay Keir, master of Balliol College. He reacted angrily and somewhat disingenuously, objecting that the university had sprung these demands on his board, with their implicit threat to its independence. The board's administrator, on the other hand, said immediately that he thought the document perfectly good and what they were expecting. (It was said that the university's underlying threat to close the clinical school had brought the Infirmary staff round.) Against Keir's advice, governors discussed it at a special meeting on 10 March, when Vaughan said the document was neither hostile nor an ultimatum, but an attempt to put on record the future needs of the medical school. She personally regretted that the university had not communicated with the board earlier, but called for joint consultation on the future of medical education. This was agreed.

Negotiation was not easy, and after the joint group's first meeting she and Witts decided they must first of all secure agreement in principle to the university case. If that proved impossible, they would recommend closure of the clinical school. At the next meeting, Keir was intransigent. Eventually Bowra as Vice-Chancellor said that if the school could not be properly managed and resourced, it would be closed. He then threatened to ask the minister for increased university representation on the board. Vaughan tried to lower the temperature by seeking agreement in principle to the university proposals; but the meeting ended in deadlock. Both sides lobbied the health ministry over the summer, making little apparent progress.

Meanwhile George Pickering, Vaughan's old colleague and friend, had arrived on the scene. He spent a term in Oxford in 1954 through an exchange with Witts, and found that 'everybody seemed to hate everybody else'. Full-time were at odds with part-time staff, UOH governors with university, preclinicians with clinicians, and even the Nuffield professors with one another. He rebuffed three offers to become Regius professor of medicine before finally deciding that it would be a stimulating challenge, 'because Oxford should be so good and was, in fact, so bad'. He accepted on condition of having the same facilities as he was used to at St Mary's Hospital medical school in London in terms of beds, outpatients, staff and laboratories.[19] These requirements were added to the university's proposals to the UOH board.

Pickering (who was due to take up post in 1955) agreed in October to join the talks with the governors, and Vaughan attended a

UOH committee that month which considered the Regius professor requirements. The first issue raised was whether the UOH board accepted that the appointee should be a clinician; but Vaughan 'succeeded in halting the somewhat acrimonious discussion' by stressing that these professors had in the past nearly always been clinicians.[20] Eventually they and Keir agreed to the proposals. This seems to have been Vaughan's last attendance at a UOH meeting, though she only formally resigned in May the following year. No doubt Pickering's arrival changed the dynamics of the negotiations, and in any case the logjam was broken. With full recommendations agreed, he led talks to sort out the financial arrangements. The university and board jointly sought ministerial approval to a solution including a medical school 'of a distinctive kind', but without implying any sharp distinction between the needs of teaching and research and ordinary hospital services. The ministry approved the associated building plans and gave the scheme top priority nationally.[21]

A privately printed history by the then UOH administrator reveals two perceptions of Vaughan: first, as ORHB representative, using her influence to weld more closely the medical school and research interests to the mainly service interest of the regional board; but after 1951 this 'slightly terrifying person, popularly known as the Red Queen to denote her politics and … demeanour' conducts 'a relentless campaign' for university dominance.[22] This may reflect her effectiveness, but ignores others' contributions. Veale in particular was convinced of the need for university control of teaching staff appointments.[23] The writer went on to blame the acrimony of the discussions on a personality clash between Bowra and Keir, and this does seem to accord with the written record. A leading historian of Oxford medicine describes Vaughan as a 'conciliatory influence', and the evidence supports that view.[24]

Social medicine
Given these problems, it is not surprising that Vaughan kept a low profile regarding social medicine. Its survival in Oxford, however, owed much to her tenacious lobbying. She was on the NPHT-appointed governing committee of the Institute of Social Medicine from its inception in 1943. During the war, the staff taught clinical

students social medicine and statistical methods, and helped set up a bureau of health and sickness records.[25] They also began a major survey of the pre-school child, and collaborated with staff at Nuffield's car factories to examine sickness and absenteeism. Nonetheless, by July 1945 the governing committee was restive about poor communication of the Institute's work. When in 1946 Ryle asked for an assistant director, they insisted that the necessary finance and facilities be first assured. Dr Alice Stewart, who had come to Oxford during the war, was appointed in July 1947.[26] There were then 27 staff and a number of projects, including the pilot student health service. Ryle, however, became seriously ill in 1949. He resigned in December and died in February 1950. Stewart was made director of the Institute in 1951.

The university then had to decide whether and how to fund the Institute after NPHT support ended in 1953. There was no backing for a full-time professorship, but Vaughan lobbied Witts and others behind the scenes, and in 1952 argued in Council for its work to continue 'at a lower level'. When her first attempt failed, Himsworth, her colleague from wartime committee days who was now MRC secretary, intervened. Telling Veale that Stewart's work was the best in any British social medicine department, and the MRC was funding several of her studies, he backed Vaughan's proposal that she be supported as a reader attached to the medicine department, with a small staff. Vaughan got the medicine board on side, and in June Council adopted her proposal.[27] Ironically, in 1953 the RCP committee for social medicine, of which Vaughan was still a member, reported that there were social and preventive medicine courses in provincial medical faculties of England and Wales, with chairs in every university apart from Oxford and London. Their second report on student health services showed a similar picture.

Vaughan continued thereafter to watch over the affairs of the Social Medicine Unit (SMU). Stewart, despite her undoubted talent and vision, was apt to lose allies by rushing into too-hasty action. This happened most notably in 1957, when she did not touch base with the MRC working party charged with supervising her leukaemia survey before unilaterally publishing her preliminary findings on the effects of X-rays on the unborn baby.[28] Another instance that year shows one of Vaughan's own occasional lapses of judgement, as well as her loyalty to Stewart. The MRC wished to fund a Human Population Genetics Research Unit at Oxford, headed by a Professor Stevenson, then working in Northern Ireland. Stevenson visited Oxford and suggested to Stewart's statistician that he might join his team. Vaughan and others were appalled by the attempt, as Stewart presented it, at poaching. Although Stewart soon apologised, saying she had been 'thoroughly frightened', opinion hardened, and Veale wrote telling Stevenson he would not be welcome.

Himsworth swiftly said that Stevenson was a consultant to the World Health Organization and highly thought of by the Rockefeller Foundation, so Oxford by this action might damage its international reputation. As a result, the Vice-Chancellor offered him accommodation through the ORHB and suitable hospitality from the university. Vaughan presumably recognised her own over-reaction, and Stevenson soon had good relations with his Oxford colleagues. Two years later, Stewart suggested amalgamating her own department with his, having forgotten the whole incident, and was shocked when he demurred.[29]

Vaughan took great care to avoid any public appearance of favouring women. In 1965, it was decided to strengthen the SMU and co-opt Stewart to the medical faculty board. Vaughan asked a male colleague to second, or even propose the co-option, saying that she did not want this to look like 'girls hanging together'; but it would be sad if this unit broke up, and not good for Oxford's reputation.[30] She continued thereafter to protect Stewart's interests, however, as when in 1966 she urged considering together the statistics posts needed for social medicine, biomathematics and population genetics/epidemiology. Three were agreed, and Stewart at Vaughan's suggestion was steered into a closer association with biomathematics.[31]

Medical affairs 1958–67

Vaughan was always a close ally of Pickering, calling him 'the Beloved Regius'.[32] Gradually, as economic conditions improved and more government money was released to science, medicine and higher education, she saw her core objectives for Oxford medicine being realised. Her national stature was indicated by an internal UGC note in 1959, which concluded that decisions on new medical schools were still based on the Goodenough criteria.[33] After the UGC advised the health ministry to site a new medical school at Nottingham, she was the lone woman on a 19-member advisory group set up by the university there in 1964, with Pickering as chair.[34] They recommended, among other things, that most students take an honours degree in medical biological sciences, and most teaching staff be full-time.

Through the UGC she took part in the late 1950s and early 1960s in considering building plans from the London Hospital, Cambridge, Sheffield, Hammersmith and, in January 1963, for the Liverpool medical school. In one case, she queried the absence of a professor of psychiatry, especially given that over 40% of GPs' patients probably had psychiatric rather than medical problems. 'Deadly silence' ensued. Driving to the Maudsley (Psychiatric) Hospital on their next visit, the committee chair asked if her figure had been correct and she answered yes. Fortunately, over lunch the chair of the hospital management committee gave figures of the same order, unprompted by her.[35]

In Oxford, the university and the UOH governors were now allies. In 1960 the UGC reported favourably on progress and plans for medical teaching, and by 1961 applications exceeded places for the first time. Action followed to better co-ordinate pathology with clinical subjects, ensure more rigorous standards generally, and agree on developing a full clinical and postgraduate medical school.[36]

In 1963 a national hospital planning exercise forced a decision on the future siting of the teaching hospital. Initially, Pickering and the UOH governors favoured the Radcliffe Infirmary, but Vaughan supported hospital medical staff in pressing for concentration on a far larger site in Headington. She also urged discussion with the UGC, which wanted new teaching hospitals to include academic facilities for NHS as well as university staff. These arguments won out, and by 1964 a two-phase development was planned for Headington. Vaughan was fully involved in deciding staffing, teaching and research needs across preclinical, clinical and postgraduate education, and advised on funding issues. Phase 1, opened in 1971, included the maternity hospital and relocated Nuffield Institute for Medical Research; and phase 2, in 1979, a 1,000-bed teaching hospital, with a clinical school and the whole of the academic centre.

Oxford had meanwhile benefited from an NPHT initiative on postgraduate medical education. At a Trust-sponsored conference in 1961, Vaughan's old Hammersmith colleague, Francis Fraser, quoted a UGC report on the correlation found between standards of teaching and research and the number of full-time (university-appointed) staff. More professorial units were needed in subjects like paediatrics, radiology, chemical pathology and radiotherapeutics, which were not yet generally recognised as relevant to medical training; and expansion must continue to meet more such new demands. All these points came from Vaughan's note of two visits to the Postgraduate Federation in London in 1955.[37] Fraser urged universities to apply to postgraduate education the same high standards as had, following the Goodenough Report, brought about great advances in clinical training and medical knowledge. An NPHT grant later enabled Oxford to collaborate with the regional hospital board and involve the medical school in developing postgraduate medical centres in the region.[38]

The retirement of Burn, Florey and four Nuffield professors between 1960 and 1967 gave an opportunity to rebalance the use of the Nuffield Benefaction and the configuration of medical teaching and research. In January 1963, Vaughan drafted a letter, cast at her suggestion in open terms, seeking advice on the legal position regarding use of the Benefaction. This elicited a green light for the changes she, Pickering and the chair of UOH wanted: the new professors were made clearly responsible for clinical as well as postgraduate education and training, and the teaching hospital was seen as a unitary whole, dedicated to the care and cure of patients and the advancement of knowledge. The preclinical departments were enlarged in the 1960s, and the haematologist Macfarlane appointed professor of clinical pathology in 1964.[39] A good UGC report two years later resulted in increased funding for a larger intake of preclinical and clinical students.

***

Oxford science was hampered until the mid-1960s by a paucity of senior scientific posts. In her oral evidence to the Franks Commission in 1964, Vaughan pointed out that the university had eight professors of divinity, compared with four in biology. Science and medicine faculty boards had tried in vain to secure new departments, but the balance of provision must now be changed to reflect current needs. It was true that scientific departments cost more than the humanities, but this would have to be faced. After all, the university had since the war raised plenty of money to restore its ancient buildings. Expanding its science provision should have the same priority.[40]

Action was soon in hand. The medicine board asked Vaughan and two others to suggest new subjects for the five years from 1967, and in February 1965 they proposed psychiatry, virology, biophysics, therapeutics and clinical pharmacology.[41] In June that year, she negotiated with UOH provision of a department of medical physics, with adequate workshop facilities. When the Nuffield Benefaction Trustees agreed to fund the psychiatry chair, Vaughan was one of those deputed to organise its 1967 establishment. A new professor of clinical biomathematics was in place by the end of 1966. The clinical school intake improved in quality and reached about 50 by 1968.

The picture of British medical education Vaughan painted for an American audience in June 1964 was optimistic.[42] She expected an unofficial cap (at around 25% of the total) on women medical student numbers, attributed to 'unpredictable wastage' after marriage, to be eroded as part-time work increased. This should also help redress the imbalance between women's employment in public health and laboratory services and general practice, as opposed to hospital consultancy. Selection on A level results drew on good school science teaching, soon to be improved by the Nuffield-sponsored science curriculum. Most preclinical courses encouraged students to take an honours degree in physiology or anatomy, and the need for academic control of teaching was well recognised. Many offered an elective three months' study of a particular subject, and psychiatry was especially popular. Medical practitioners could increasingly access continuing education at regional postgraduate centres.

Finally, the day of an Oxford student health service arrived. In 1966 a student committee, with Vaughan's support, urged on the UGC the need for a student health centre, with a psychiatric and counselling service.[43] Students had mental health and drug-taking problems and a need for contraception and sexual health advice, as well as normal health issues. Hebdomadal Council deputed Vaughan and others to plan the service, and they recommended in 1967 that colleges provide uniform arrangements, with a college nurse and an adequate sick bay. College doctors or, if unwilling, a named alternative should offer contraceptive advice. All this was in line with provision already made at Somerville. They also recommended a university health centre, and reorganisation of Oxford psychiatric services; and urged pressure for a national inquiry into the dangers of drugs.[44] Vaughan could be well-satisfied with her contribution to all aspects of Oxford medicine.

Meanwhile, in parallel with these multifarious activities, she was continuing with her scientific research.

Endnotes

[1] JA, 133 and 142.

[2] TNA, MH 90/9, Socialist Medical Association letter, 12.3.1947. Leslie Witts and Richard Doll (the epidemiologist who became famous for studies linking tobacco smoking with lung cancer) were on the same list.

[3] This innovation was approved by the General Nursing Council. Vaughan believed they were the first Board to appoint a Chief Nursing Officer and first to employ married women part time, as both doctors and nurses. (JA, 134.)

[4] Oxfordshire History Centre, ORHB files detail the board's history.

[5] OUA, FA 4/9/2/11, Board of the Faculty of Medicine minutes and papers 1949–50, meeting on 1.2.1950.

[6] OUA, minutes of NCAM (Nuffield Committee for the Advancement of Medicine) meetings, FA 6/5/36. Vaughan must have been pleased when the appointment went to Trueta, who had made his name during the Spanish Civil War.

[7] JPP, Irene M Farmer (formerly Irene M James OBE), letter of 14.1.1993.

[8] JA, 134.

[9] JA, 135. She does not say whether her tactic led to increased funding.

[10] TNA, MH 90/20, Vaughan to Bevan, 16.2.1950.

[11] BLSA, F5512–F5522, Philip Powell. Tape 4, side B.

[12] Vaughan had early urged the Board's CMO to look at international comparators, as well as ensuring that both architects worked with the NPHT.

[13] Douglas Veale, The Nuffield Benefaction and the Oxford Medical School, in K Dewhurst (Ed), *Essays on the Evolution of the Oxford Clinical School to Commemorate the Bicentenary of the Radcliffe Infirmary 1770–1970* (Sandford Publications, Oxford, 1970), 143.

[14] Florey's work on penicillin, for which he and Ernst Chain won the Nobel Prize in 1945, was rescued by money from the Rockefeller Foundation.

[15] OUA, UR 6/MD/16 File 2, minutes of committee on hospital development in Oxford, 12.12.1947.

[16] OUA, UR 6/MD/16 File 4, development of clinical school, May 1953–February 1954 gives the story.

[17] Veale had been advised that this was reasonable, because the NHS Act required governors to provide the university with facilities for clinical teaching and research 'as appear to the Minister to be required'.

[18] OUA, UR6/MD/16/file 4. Veale note of 15.2.1954.

[19] Wellcome Collection, G W Pickering PP/GWP A.19–21. Vaughan had by this time joined Pickering on the UGC's Medical Advisory Committee, and no doubt played some part in persuading him to become Regius professor.

[20] OUA, UR 6/MD/16 File 5, note of meeting on 14.10.1954. The previous Regius professor had been a bacteriologist, so posed no threat to the scarce clinical resources at the Radcliffe Infirmary.

[21] OUA, UR 6/MD/16 File 6, notes of 27.11.1954, and 15 and 17.12.1954.

[22] E J R Burrough, *Unity in Diversity: The Short Life of the United Oxford Hospitals* (London, privately printed, 1978).

[23] Veale, The Nuffield Benefaction and the Oxford Medical School, 148.

[24] Charles Webster, Medicine, in B Harrison (Ed), *The History of the University of Oxford: Vol VIII: The Twentieth Century* (Oxford, Oxford University Press, 1994), 317–43.

[25] The medical records bureau covered Berkshire, Buckinghamshire and Oxfordshire.

[26] Dr Alice Stewart (1906–2002). A physician at the Royal Free Hospital in the 1930s, she had in Oxford developed an interest in epidemiology.

[27] For Faculty of Medicine decisions, see OUA, FA 4/9/2/12 1951–54; and for the Institute, ISM UR6/MD/13/10, files 1–5. Witts said that if Stewart had busied herself in medical politics rather than research, there would be no question of abolishing the Institute (ISM UR6/MD/13/10, file 5, Vaughan report of conversation with Witts to Vice-Chancellor, 28.5.1952).

[28] TNA, FD 23/1311, Leukaemia: Survey by Dr Alice Stewart 1955–56.

[29] TNA, FD 7/1034, Pickering/Himsworth correspondence 28.10–17.12.1957; and Himsworth correspondence and file notes, 20.12.1957–26.1.1960.

[30] Wellcome Collection, W D Paton PP/WDP/B/1/46. Vaughan to Paton, 26.6.1965. She was in fact the proposer in 1966.

[31] OUA, Nuffield Committee for Medical Research and Postgraduate Training, FA 6/6/2, Vol XXIV. Also FA 6/6/24 and 25, meetings on 22.3, 6.5 and 22.5.1967.

[32] SCA, Vaughan personal file, letter dated 15.3.1973 from Barbara Craig to the University of Liverpool.

[33] TNA, UGC 7/660, meeting on 29.6.1959.

[34] This was the first entirely new medical school in Britain since 1893.

[35] JA, 123.

[36] The story of these and later developments, and Vaughan's part in them, is in the records of the Nuffield Committee for the Advancement of Medicine (going through various changes of name and functions over time): OUA, Nuffield Medical Benefaction, FA 6/2–6/4; and Nuffield Committee for Medical Research and Postgraduate Training, FA 6/6/2–6/6/25.

[37] TNA, UGC 9/179, meeting of 4.7.1955.

[38] OUA, NCAM 5.5.62. Vaughan helped to draft the grant application letter.

[39] Vaughan was one of those backing an ad hominem appointment for him, so as to bypass the much more expensive option of an endowed chair.

[40] OUA, Franks Commission, HC 4/50/27, Vaughan oral evidence.

[41] OUA, Franks Commission, FA 4/9/2/16, BFM minutes, 3.2.1965 and 24.11.1965 (see Med (65) 34 for February report).

[42] D J Vaughan, The training of the physician. The recruitment and medical training of men and women in England in 1964, in *New England Journal of Medicine*, (6.8.1964), 271, 294–97. (Paper for a symposium, part of the Boston City Hospital Centennial Program commemorating the fortieth anniversary of the Thorndike Memorial Laboratory.)

[43] Importantly, the UGC would now give money towards central university services.

[44] OUA, Committee on Student Health, 1966–67, HC 17/1–3. Also JA, 122–23.

CHAPTER 13
Research: what happens if you irradiate bone?
1946–67

Getting started: 1947–52

The context

Vaughan's passion for research remained central to her life. The main question for any observer was how she managed to fit this in alongside all her other activities during the Somerville years. The superficial answer is that this was one more aspect of her working life to be programmed into each day, subject to flexibility of focus and priorities. More important, however, is the difference between scientific research and the other, largely administrative, calls on her time. It was different both in the nature of its intellectual and practical demands and in the comparative informality of the laboratory setting. Here she was able to be most fully herself, absorbed in her most satisfying work. She could enjoy the same kind of warm relations with scientific colleagues that she had been used to in the 1930s, and with those overseas even more so, given the relative ease of international travel from the mid-1950s. Real friendships were forged, providing emotional as well as professional support, free from the stress of rules, conventions and personal politics so prevalent in university and college life and in outside committees. Research offered her relief rather than added burdens, and a virtual free hand in deciding how to manage it.

During her first term at Somerville, Vaughan obtained useful academic status and basic research facilities from Witts at the Nuffield Institute and Burn in the pharmacology department's basement. What, then, should she do? She had lost her leading status in studying the anaemias, but knew from experience the value of entering a new research field, with few vested interests in place. Circumstances favoured her. The atomic bombs which ended the war with Japan created new hazards to human health, which no one as yet fully understood. The United States virtually stopped sharing its knowledge in this field after President Roosevelt's death in 1945, and made it illegal to do so from August 1946.[1] The potential hazards arising from atomic fission and the threat posed by the Cold War persuaded successive British governments to prioritise research spending in this area.

The Atomic Energy Research Establishment (AERE) was established at Harwell, 15 miles from Oxford, in October 1945. In November, the MRC set up a committee on the medical and biological applications of nuclear physics, with a sub-group focusing on how to protect people from the effects of radiation. Vaughan was on that sub-group, thanks to her 1930s studies of bone and bone marrow, and experience of analysing data on the blood picture in cancer patients treated with radium.[2] She was entering a field in which few medical scientists had even made a start on the problems involved, but through the sub-group she was in touch with the leading UK experts.[3]

Before 1939, the only radioactive materials in (almost entirely medical) use in Britain were tiny amounts of radium; but the work with atomic fission produced large quantities of new ones, including strontium and plutonium. The dangers were instantly realised, given the well-documented fate of people who had ingested radium by licking their brushes while painting watch dials during the First World War. It was the radioactive decay of the radium in the paint that made the dials luminous, and many dial painters later died with bone cancer and various anaemias. In May 1946, Vaughan proposed setting up a team to test workers dealing with radioactive materials, and in October she agreed both to test Harwell physicists' blood and to study the effect of irradiation on the blood and bone marrow of rabbits.[4] In practice, the rabbits soon took centre stage.

Burn, who took to calling her 'our radioactive principal', was very supportive.[5] In 1947, he arranged with AERE for a year's grant from the Ministry of Supply to cover most of her staffing and equipment costs, including a new animal house. Loutit, her colleague from blood transfusion days, was by then director of the MRC's Radiobiological Research Unit at Harwell, focusing on studies relating to human beings. In 1948 he prompted the MRC to take over the funding of her work.[6] In the post-war climate of austerity, Vaughan had to go cannily to avoid appearing to threaten the resources of others. Her bids for funding always centred on what was essential rather than only desirable, reflecting her wartime habits of make-do and mend, including sharing and 'scrounging' equipment wherever possible. A modest base was also easier to fit in alongside her other commitments.

Trial and error

Vaughan immediately saw the need for a multi-disciplinary team, which her experience as a general pathologist had prepared her well to manage. The MRC grant covered a graduate physicist and senior technician, and a graduate chemist was funded through a fortuitous 10-year Nuffield Foundation grant to Witts for a haematology research unit.[7] Initially Vaughan herself supplied the biological knowledge. A replacement physicist who started in 1949 had to learn 'something of the chemical and biological side ... in order to understand what we need of her physics'.[8] The learning process was three-way for all. For the most part she employed young graduates who were studying for a postgraduate qualification, and there was a steady turnover as they moved on, often to permanent posts. MRC funding was personal to Vaughan, and on a yearly basis only.

With no advice available from the United States, the new team had to begin by confirming published research findings while learning the necessary techniques. Basic definitions came first, especially for non-physicists. An *isotope* is the form of an element (not always radioactive), such as strontium, numbered according to the number of protons and neutrons in its nucleus – hence strontium-90. This particular isotope is radioactive, which means that it decays and, in the process, emits radiation. The rate of decay of a given isotope is measured in terms of its 'half-life': that is, the interval of time required for one half of the atomic nuclei of a radioactive sample to decay. This is an iterative process that continues indefinitely. Strontium-90 has a half-life of 28 years, and also produces a daughter isotope called yttrium, whose half-life is shorter but which produces more potent emissions.

As to the meaning of 'more potent': the type and energy of radiation vary with different isotopes. Radium and plutonium produce alpha particles, which have a short straight range and are potentially the most dangerous in their effect on individual cells in the body. Beta particles, produced by strontium and yttrium, have a long irregular range and do less damage. They can, however, vary in energy, as exemplified by yttrium's greater potency.[9]

If minute quantities of radioactive materials are breathed in or ingested with food or drink, they can stay in the body, irradiating it and potentially causing serious long-term damage. Some decay in hours, others in more than a lifetime. To begin with, scientists focused on the detection and measurement of radiation, its biological effects (usually cancer), the establishment of safe levels of exposure, and finding effective means of protection.[10]

The team were able to share equipment with the pharmacologists and with Witts' department, and Vaughan liaised with a colleague in the department of rural economy who was then the only other Oxford scientist working with radioactive isotopes. Harwell staff helped her design and master new apparatus and techniques.[11] It was probably at this time that she sought tutoring from the biochemist Florey, and her contact from Hammersmith days, the cell biologist Fell at the Strangeways Laboratory.[12]

She started by investigating radioactive strontium, a fission product of the first atomic bombs which had caused worldwide contamination of food and water. It lodged primarily in bone, and had been shown to produce bone cancer in small rodents. Vaughan wanted to confirm those findings, and find out how best to measure the amount of radioactivity retained and for how long, its effects on animals of different ages, and the rates of excretion in urine and faeces. She chose rabbits because they were the smallest animals (the main alternatives being dogs and primates) with a bone structure and growth pattern similar to those of humans.

Progress was slow as the team learned the techniques involved. They handled often tiny rabbits so as to inject substances into veins in their ears; ashed faeces in a special furnace so that strontium in the dry ash could be measured with a Geiger counter; boiled carcasses before dissecting the bones and storing them in alcohol; measured strontium in urine and bones, and in samples of internal organs, skin and flesh in solution; all whilst estimating degrees of error until they could devise more satisfactory methods.

Remarkably, they presented their first paper in December 1948, little more than a year after starting work.[13] It confirmed the published findings, but Vaughan went much further in a note for the MRC protection group, pointing out that the amount of strontium retained was related to the rate at which calcium was being laid down in the bone, meaning that the risk of tumours was considerably less for old than for young rabbits, whose bones were still growing. It would be worth exploring the effects of feeding as well as injecting the strontium, and of diets varying in calcium and vitamin D content; how much was retained at different timescales; and the rate of excretion in milk.

Early in 1949 she managed, with support from Harwell and other colleagues, to secure the costly autoradiographic equipment needed to study images of radioactive emissions. She also gained more lab space from Witts, another technician from the MRC and, later that year, a zoology graduate to develop the autoradiography techniques needed to study bone sections.[14] In her view, 'After a long and weary period of perfecting techniques we are ... obtaining results of very considerable interest.'[15]

Nonetheless, her position was not secure. In March that year, the MRC expressed concern that she was building a larger research team, 'with no evidence among them of any special knowledge or aptitude for such work', urging her to call in expert advice at every stage.[16] Vaughan replied that she was talking to experts at Harwell, Oxford's Clarendon Laboratory, the British Postgraduate Federation at Hammersmith and the rural economy department. Loutit added that her group, 'the only nucleus of radiobiology at Oxford', was producing useful results and serving as a training school for young graduates. It was not easy 'to pick ripe radiobiologists ... Dr Vaughan's team ... is like ours, learning the hard way by trial and error'.[17]

Early progress
By April 1952, they had broken new ground by examining in a consistent way the effects of age, diet, pregnancy and lactation on rabbits' absorption and excretion of strontium; by differentiating between strontium and yttrium; and starting to use autoradiographs of thin sections of bone to show more precisely where the isotopes had lodged.[18] At first it was difficult and time-consuming to cut sufficiently thin sections of bone with a milling machine; but they were able to use the Nuffield Institute's

microradiography equipment (concentrating on minute internal structure) so as to compare microradiographs and autoradiographs of the same sections. This was the first such application of these combined techniques, aimed at seeing more clearly what was happening in the cells and other materials of the bone tissue.[19]

Also in 1952, Vaughan asserted her growing authority by reviewing current knowledge on the biological hazards of strontium. Her team in particular had found that strontium was most concentrated in sites where active bone growth was taking place, explaining why young animals, still building up bone, were most at risk of developing tumours; and that retention of yttrium – more worrying because of its high intensity rays – was greater, more persistent and less affected by age than that of strontium. Yttrium was concentrated in only one site, suggesting that some localised element could bind it differently from strontium.[20] Vaughan seized on the significance of this observation, and resolved to explore it further.

The MRC, still doubtful about this small and changing team, reviewed her work later that year, when Vaughan took the opportunity to ask for improved cutting equipment which a contact in London had developed. A greater volume of thinner sections would enable more detailed examination, and help them to estimate dosage to different parts of the bone. The review group were impressed. They recommended funding the cutting machine, or microtome, as an emergency measure, with one of them advising that her work was 'important, is not being done elsewhere, and must ... go on'.[21]

***

Vaughan's habit of making links between different activities extended to her Nuffield Foundation work. In the early 1950s, the trustees were encouraging fundamental research in biology. Typically, after taking advice from an expert panel, they would invite a broader group to a conference to discuss how best to direct funding. Those attending the first two conferences, in November 1950 and March 1952, included the crystallographer Hodgkin, the cell biologist Fell, and others eminent in the field. Vaughan, chairing the first session in 1950, suggested a symposium of physicists, chemists and biologists, partly to find ways of tackling a shortage of biochemists and of non-medical biochemical teaching. This resulted in Nuffield-funded biology scholarships, aiming to attract those trained in chemistry, physics and maths into biology. The 1952 conference agreed her suggestion that botany, in line with then-current thinking, needed a stimulus, and one solution would be to take on biochemists who would learn it 'on the job'.[22] She clearly brought her own experience to all this.

Life inside the lab (i)
The atmosphere in the lab was informal, and Vaughan was known to all as simply JV. Safety precautions were still crude in the early years. The main protective rules included wearing rubber gloves and, after exposure to radioactive materials, washing them on the hands with soap and water; testing the hands with a Geiger counter; using thick glassware; using tongs or tweezers where possible to handle vessels containing radioactive materials; and wearing thick clothing, and goggles or a Perspex shield to protect the eyes. There were special arrangements for cleaning equipment and disposing of waste, and smoking and eating in the lab were forbidden.[23]

Vaughan handled all the injections and concentrated solutions herself since she believed her age protected her from harm. An impatient temperament and ingrained habits could, however, militate against caution. Barbara Kidman, an Australian graduate physicist who was on the team from January 1949 until summer 1951, remembered that facilities were primitive. There was no proper fume cupboard (a localised fume extraction system to protect against inhaling harmful substances), one of the technicians smoked and there were sometimes spills. Also 'JV … had a habit of adjusting the dose by ejecting drops from the syringe into the air …'. They used conventional glassware for chemical measurements and the cumbersome Geiger counters frequently malfunctioned.[24] Equipment and habits did improve over time, but in these early days there may well have been health and safety advantages in the group's high turnover of young graduate workers.

The team mixed well, with a lot of social contact outside the lab. They worked hard, with hours from about 9.30am till 6pm and

Saturday mornings, but Vaughan was reasonable about holidays and personal plans. The graduates were research assistants, but Vaughan 'discussed everything with us and ... respected our opinions ... [we] knew more Chemistry and Physics ... [but] I felt I was working in a team. All the research papers ... were in joint names; JV wrote the draft, but we had our say.'[25] When Kidman married in 1952, Vaughan advised on the wedding dress and lent Radcliffe House for the reception. More importantly, Kidman was inspired by her example to continue her scientific work after her marriage, and keep her maiden name for work purposes: both then rare occurrences, especially in Australia.

Becoming established: 1952–58

Continuing progress 1952–56

The International Commission on Radiological Protection (ICRP) was restructured and given its present name in 1950 by scientists and doctors from the USA, Britain, France and Scandinavia, to issue worldwide safety standards. In the context of Vaughan's work, this took the form of 'maximum permissible body burden' of a given substance, and was perforce based on what was already known about radium. The number of scientists researching radiation effects gradually increased over the next decade, as did the international involvement of US scientists.[26]

The first agreed 'danger levels' of exposure assumed that internal radioactivity was always evenly distributed in bone, and that this was true whatever an animal's age. By 1952, Vaughan's team had shown that both these assumptions were false; but no changes could be agreed without more precise information about what dose of radiation produced what outcomes and in what circumstances. For that they needed a better understanding of the make-up of 'normal' bone and how it was produced. These fundamental questions now underlay her team's research. The physicist Maureen Owen joined them in that year: married to another physicist working in Oxford, she became a permanent member of staff. The work intensified.

Vaughan's enthusiasm and occasional joy in her research could spill over into college concerns. A modern languages candidate waiting for interview in 1953 was prevented from entering her room when her secretary, Hilda Bryant, flew across the landing, told the girl to wait and shot in first to report the results of some experiments. The candidate then found the Principal in a state of euphoria. Having no scientific knowledge at all, she used her listening skills (and banked up the fire) while Vaughan told her at length about the experiments. There were then some questions directed at her own interests, but she felt already that they were good friends.[27]

The team were by this time comparing the effects of continuous feeding of strontium with those caused by a single large injection; and also pursuing Vaughan's hunch by trying to isolate the substances in bone which might combine with yttrium. They examined the growth and structure of 'normal' (unirradiated) rabbit bone, and demonstrated the need to compare damaged bone at a given level and age with corresponding 'normal' bone. Findings in one species or one bone could not be transferred to a different one. They also found that strontium, after lodging in areas of active bone growth, lingered because of the slow natural process whereby the existing bone was broken down (a process called resorption) so that new bone could be laid down in its place. Yttrium, meanwhile, was concentrated on particular bone surfaces where resorption was taking place, and where substances called sugar proteins (glycoproteins) were known to be present. Significantly, this pattern was similar to that of plutonium.

In her next review of current research, Vaughan again insisted on the need to know more about the make-up and behaviour of normal bone, and the fundamental effects of radiation on living cells. She had become by 1955–56 an internationally recognised authority.[28]

Development and expansion 1956–58
The political background to nuclear research changed dramatically in the mid-1950s. The British government, worried about diminishing coal supplies, approved an ambitious programme of building nuclear power stations. By then the United States and the Soviet Union had tested thermonuclear devices, and an intense public debate began on the hazards of nuclear fallout, with growing opposition to weapon tests. In October 1957 there was a major

accident at one of the two Windscale reactors built to produce bomb material. Interest in protection intensified around the world.

The level of threat posed by strontium was by then better understood. Studies of the amount of calcium and stable strontium passing through the food chain from soil and plants showed that both cows and humans discriminate in favour of calcium and against strontium when absorbing and excreting them, and so are quite effectively protected. Vaughan's team had shown, however, that if radioactive strontium reached a rabbit's bloodstream by intravenous injection – the equivalent of sudden accidental inhalation – it rapidly became lodged in the skeleton.

By the mid-1950s the whole team were located in renovated brick huts at the Churchill Hospital site, 15 minutes' drive from Somerville. Burn had reclaimed his basement in 1954, and Owen moved from the Nuffield Institute in 1956. Vaughan, who had been 'most anxious' not to try to create a department for herself, was pleased.[29] After a particularly rapid turnover of graduates in that year, she remarked that it was sad to lose good people, but satisfactory to train research workers 'who win awards and are welcome in other labs'.[30]

Their studies extended and diversified, often in collaboration with others, including Hubert Sissons, then in charge of morbid anatomy at the Royal National Orthopaedic Hospital and a specialist in bone tumours.[31] With a dental specialist, the team found that strontium's long-term concentration in teeth represented a threat to the surrounding bone and tissues.[32] Staff in Oxford's biochemistry department helped them investigate sugar proteins in bone, and one of those staff, the biochemist Geoffrey Herring, joined Vaughan's group in 1956 to work on finding which substances might bind yttrium and plutonium. For the first time, there was a man on the team.[33]

Her quest for precision in measuring radiation dose in relation to bone damage led to close collaboration with physicists, in particular W S (Bill) Spiers, professor of medical physics at Leeds. By 1956 her team had tested the use of microradiographs and autoradiographs for this purpose, and their estimates compared well with those of researchers using other methods.[34] After that Vaughan, Spiers and a colleague from London's Cancer Research

Institute compared the effects of strontium and radium on bone, concluding that strontium would be more evenly distributed than radium.[35] They were also turning their attention to plutonium, which was produced by the nuclear power plants being built in Britain.[36]

Vaughan's standing was confirmed when, in July 1957, she was invited to read a paper at the Gordon Conference, a prestigious event held annually in Vermont. This was her first visit to the USA since 1930, and she found it 'tremendously exciting' to be able to talk at last to researchers outside the small group she knew in England.[37] She made lifelong friends on that trip, visiting labs at the Massachusetts Institute of Technology (MIT), and at the Universities of Utah and Chicago. She already knew Hermann Lisco of Chicago's Argonne Laboratory. Having seen her work during a visit to England in 1954, he had secured her invitation to the conference. His colleague Robert (Bob) Hasterlik also became a good friend. Vaughan almost missed out, however, thanks to admitting in her visa application her brief former membership of the Communist Party. She later realised that she had been kept under surveillance in the MIT labs. And she was only ever granted a short-term visa for her future, very frequent, visits to the States. By contrast, a British colleague who went there in 1958 had a visa valid for limitless visits over four years.[38]

The 1956–57 MRC Annual Report included a long account of the team's work, and from 1958 the Council supported them as an official research group, under Vaughan as Honorary Director. The new unit had six scientific staff, five technicians and a part-time secretary. Funding was on a three-yearly basis and scientific staff had five-year renewable contracts, including pensions. Vaughan was relieved of her previous unease about the insecurity of tenure of 'my very excellent young workers'.[39]

Life inside the lab (ii)
Vaughan never publicly referred to the fact that her staff were predominantly female, as shown by the reaction of a Polish scientist who arrived in 1960. At the introductory meeting he was shifting on his seat and seemed distracted, before exclaiming to his neighbour, 'you are all women!'.[40] Vaughan simply treated this

as a natural state of affairs, making actual the imagined world of Woolf's 'Chloe and Olivia' story in *A Room of One's Own*. She gave female staff scope to develop their own lines of research. When they had children, she kept their jobs open, which was unusual at the time; and she offered part-time arrangements to help them juggle home and research responsibilities. She also encouraged them to take opportunities for career development, including periods of up to a year working in other laboratories, often abroad.

One young graduate, Lorna Lea, remembered how Vaughan would breeze through the lab, arms full of relevant papers, admiring a new dress or hairstyle and excited to hear about the research. If Lea encountered a tricky problem, Vaughan would summon senior researchers from their Oxford labs to help this very junior research assistant. The following year, Lea visited the Bloomsbury flat, where Vaughan was writing up the findings, and used a microscope there to check some results. She was most grateful to have that first publication under her belt.[41]

With advice, support and a generous reference from Vaughan, Lea went on to spend a year in a lab in Belgium on a British Council scholarship; followed by three years working on a PhD in London under Sissons, to whom Vaughan had introduced her. Six years and three children later, armed once more with a glowing reference from Vaughan, Dr Lorna Secker-Walker, as she now was, applied for a laboratory post in cytogenetics. When the application failed, Vaughan told the professor concerned that he had been a fool not to take her; and went on to direct her towards research into the genetics of leukaemia with a distinguished haematology consultant.[42]

Others remembered weekly meetings to share information and papers, and going to seminars and other gatherings, usually in London. If giving papers, they had to practise their delivery beforehand and meet stringent standards. When Vaughan was in the lab, everything had to be done at speed because she usually had an appointment somewhere else. One collaborator spoke of 'the usual rush to get things out'; and later, 'As usual, everything desperately urgent'.[43] That pace enabled the team to publish more than 60 substantial papers in the 20-year period from 1947. But she was also considerate, visiting anyone who fell ill and in one case of bereavement advising that the staff member take time off.

Vaughan was of course a role model in combining a research career with marriage and a family. To do this she rose at five in the morning if necessary, or left committee meetings for the short time needed to visit the lab and ensure that rabbits were milked and work was on track. She often worked there late in the evening, and had a secretary, funded by the MRC, to type up official letters and publications. Conferences usually took place during vacations, she could fit in MRC meetings alongside other meetings in London, and the short Oxford terms allowed her to work on reports and articles outside term, including at the London flat. There is no record of her working at Plovers Field, which seems to have been kept sacrosanct for relaxation and the family.

The Bone-Seeking Isotopes Research Unit 1958–67

By 1959 the team had shown that it was possible to correlate radiation dose with radiation damage: very localised after a single large dose, more widespread after continuous feeding, with the strontium more evenly distributed in the bone. The bones of people who had died of radium poisoning showed the same pattern: those with a heavy initial body burden, like some dial painters observed in the 1920s, died young; whilst in those receiving a lower dose there was a long latent period between ingestion and the development of bone injury.[44]

Loutit commented that Vaughan's work so far had been extremely valuable and its by-products, such as that with the physicists on measuring dose, had markedly influenced all others working in the field.[45] Her international standing had grown. She visited Vienna twice between 1958 and 1961 to advise the International Atomic Energy Authority (IAEA) on strontium, and in April 1960 the Unit hosted a three-day international conference, funded by the IAEA and the MRC. Visitors stayed at Somerville. The resulting report to the relevant UN scientific committee concluded that more sensitive methods of detecting subtle cellular injury were needed in order to understand how radiation transforms a normal cell into a malignant one.[46] Vaughan noted of this conference that 'the great advantage of the study in detail of a small group of animals by physicists, chemists and biologists working together in this Unit' stood out.[47] The multi-disciplinary approach was still not typical.

By 1962 they knew that the part of bone at risk of tumours was probably the inside surfaces of bones which border the bone marrow cavity. The most comprehensive study of the relation of dose to damage had been made on young rabbits, by her own unit; and the priority in future must be fundamental study of the biochemistry of the make-up of bone and the behaviour of cells in the tissues involved. These were precisely the objectives set for Herring and Owen.[48] Herring had encountered considerable technical difficulties in isolating possible binding substances; but 1961–62 brought a major breakthrough. Yttrium seemed to be bound differently from plutonium, despite being located in similar sites; and the team had identified some promising substances, including a group of sugar proteins which might well bind metals. As Owen later said, this was a very significant contribution to the start of a 'vast area' of research into these proteins.[49]

Life inside the lab (iii)
After the Unit was established, Himsworth visited from the MRC and noted that the 'peculiar' arrangement 'in which four out of the six scientific staff are mothers with young children' was working very well. Most of the work was being well done and extremely interesting, with that on dosimetry promising to be 'some of the best that had yet been done ... It was evident ... that Dr Vaughan's drive and enthusiasm was the probable motive force.'[50]

A second physicist, Elizabeth Lloyd, appeared providentially in spring 1958, given that Owen was due to take three months' maternity leave from 1 July.[51] She stayed on, and in 1961 Vaughan complained to the MRC of overcrowding. The most pressing need was for bench space for one of the two visiting foreign workers; and two more institutes wanted to send men for training in the unit's methods. Besides this they needed a lab for Lloyd and her technician and a room for the secretary and files. The MRC provided an additional hut. According to Vaughan, overseas workers who came to visit or work in the unit 'were aghast when they first saw our laboratories … but … had to admit that the equipment was good' and the work of 'excellent quality'.[52]

When the technician Mike Davies, the second man to join the team, arrived in 1964, Vaughan agreed that he should enrol on a Higher National Certificate (HNC) course, taking for granted the need for further training in a way he thought not typical of the time.[53] A year or so later, she sent him to a Harwell course where fellow students had doctoral qualifications, but he could hold his own thanks to his experience in the unit. Her confidence in him bolstered his own. Scrupulously fair, she once had her name removed from the authors' list heading an article and replaced by an acknowledgement of her support at the end: this at a time when many department heads insisted on being included, regardless of level of contribution, and often as the first name.

Davies found that 'JV' treated everyone equally, and the atmosphere was informal. Staff entered their agreed leave dates on a sheet pinned to the noticeboard, and he was in Germany when someone phoned his mother to ask when he would be back: the holiday list had blown away. Another time he was given an unofficial day off to go to a racing car show; but he also once stayed overnight to count short-lived strontium and calcium radioactive samples every hour, as there was no automatic sample counter and they could only afford the one sample run.

As to her driving, visiting American scientists had been told that they must be driven by Vaughan once, but only once. She rang Davies at least twice asking to be picked up because of car 'incidents', and on one occasion she was stopped for speeding through a small Oxfordshire village. In court the constable read from his notebook, 'When I asked the defendant what speed she had been doing … she replied "Young man, don't you have anything better to do than stop harmless old ladies going about their lawful business?"' There was fellow feeling when Davies, leaving late one evening, bumped into another car. He returned to call the RAC and Vaughan, who was still working, opened a cupboard and poured him a whisky.

Rules and attitudes regarding the use and treatment of laboratory animals have changed much since the post-war period up to the 1960s. It is clear, however, that the rabbits used by the Unit, and looked after by the technician Fae Schofield, were treated as humanely as was then possible. Davies got on well with Schofield, who was

> not the most tolerant lady ... she was on holiday when her favourite buck rabbit developed snuffles (we all had our favourite buck rabbit – you talked to them and spoilt them) ... someone had to do the deed to prevent it wiping out the colony and I was ... nominated on the grounds that I would be forgiven – which I was.

Last years of the Unit: 1963–67

Vaughan's personal life and plans changed drastically in 1963. First she faced the blow of Gourlay's death in January; and then, in the autumn, the onset of severe mental illness in her daughter Cilla. Her own health was shaken that year, but work gave some refuge from grief, and the MRC confirmed that she could continue as director until 1967.[54] One happy event, in April, was the first European Bone and Tooth Symposium. Vaughan was instrumental in planning it, on the lines of the Gordon Conferences, and Somerville hosted. American and Indian scientists joined the Europeans, and 60 non-residents joined the 100 who stayed in college.[55]

Thinking on radioactive strontium was changing. In May 1965, Vaughan pointed out that in the case of single injections, parts of the marrow were spared; but with an accumulating radiation dose, as would be caused by fallout, contamination was uniform and therefore severely damaging to the blood-forming process. The few animal leukaemias observed had resulted from continuous feeding experiments. The Leeds physicist Spiers had also concluded that bone marrow rather than bone was most at risk from strontium and yttrium, and shared his paper on the subject with an ICRP Task Group looking at the radiosensitivity of the tissues in bone. Loutit chaired this group, and Spiers and Vaughan were members.[56] She recalled later that the seven international experts 'met in the Vaughan Common Room where we set up a blackboard to enable the physicists to do their calculations, and ... had our meals in Radcliffe House ... before producing ... one of the important contemporary documents of the radiation world'.[57]

She would go on to contribute to three publications and provide one unpublished paper for the ICRP by 1972.[58]

Also in 1965 Betty Bleaney, physicist wife of the head of Oxford's Clarendon Laboratory, joined the Unit at her own request. She was soon helping to investigate plutonium. Vaughan was impressed:

> She gains from living in a lab [the Clarendon] – where cells are as important as dosimetry!! What worries me about so much ... work on [measuring dose] is that it is done by people who know nothing ... about cells & tissues. This is part of the trouble at the Argonne & at Utah.[59]

Their findings, published in 1967, showed that plutonium posed a much greater leukaemia risk than any other bone-seeking isotope. This was very important for protection. Plutonium's alpha particles could reach the bloodstream, and hence the bone marrow, following skin abrasion and wounds that might occur in industrial and lab work.[60]

***

Discussion of the Unit's future began in early 1963, when Vaughan's retirement was set for 1967. At first she wished Owen to replace her as director, but MRC doubts were confirmed in discussion, including with Owen herself. Vaughan had to acknowledge the divergent research interests within her team. Owen concentrated on basic bone research, through Herring's work on chemical composition and her own studies of the behaviour of cells. Others, notably Lloyd, focused on the effects of radioactive isotopes. The unit would have to be split. The fact was that Vaughan's breadth of experience and vision, combined with her medical knowledge, were extremely hard to replicate in one person.

Vaughan said Bleaney, who had developed a new, more precise method of fission track counting for the plutonium studies, must be enabled to continue, since no one else was known to be working on detailed measurement of the kind and significance that she undertook. The MRC funded her to work alongside Owen's team, but attached to Loutit, from August 1967. Owen and her team would be attached to the Nuffield department of orthopaedic surgery under Professor R B Duthie.[61] From 1967 they continued to work in the Churchill Hospital huts, with Duthie as their 'Honorary Consultant'. Owen was responsible to the MRC for their scientific programme, but would discuss administrative matters and new proposals with him before submitting them.[62] The arrangement proved a happy and fruitful one, and the team moved into the Nuffield Orthopaedic Centre in the mid-1970s.

The MRC offered Vaughan a personal grant to continue her research if she so wished; but she decided instead to 'take stock after some very strenuous years. I go out as a Visiting Professor to the Department of Medicine in ... Chicago until Christmas [and] feel at the moment that it is better to be ruthless with oneself and slam the lab door.'[63] In the event she never did take up the MRC offer, continuing instead to work with the unofficial co-operation of her old colleagues, and specific grants for particular purposes.

She still had plenty of research ideas. This account has focused on the highlights of her group's findings, without dwelling on the ever-increasing stream of questions, discussion and actual and possible lines of research which tumble out in her reports to the MRC. There must have been various reasons for her decision, but the most crucial had to be Cilla's continuing illness and its inevitable, and unpredictable, demands for her care.

The significance of her group's work had long been internationally recognised. Of particular contributions, she herself placed most emphasis on the isolation and study of relevant sugar proteins in bone, and the demonstration of the danger of leukaemia from ingested plutonium and strontium. Science is, however, a collective endeavour, and a sense of her team's input emerges in her general surveys of current research. In 1965, for example, she published a critical commentary on then-current ICRP guidance, citing over 100 papers. More than one in five of those papers were by herself or her team.[64]

She had also demonstrated that women scientists could achieve at a high level even while working part time and raising families. At least 20 (named) female scientists and technicians worked in her team during these 20 years.[65] The majority continued in worthwhile, and sometimes distinguished, scientific careers. The fact that Hodgkin too favoured female graduates in her team made Oxford, and Somerville in particular, outstanding in this respect.

Himsworth had known Vaughan since she taught him pathology at UCH in the 1920s. He now wrote to thank her on behalf of the MRC

> most warmly for all that you have done ... as [Unit] Director ... [and] before that for medical research. I know ... you will only say that you were enjoying yourself; but ... you have made not only substantial contributions to knowledge, but ... been most helpful in tricky areas of public service. You don't know ... the reassurance it is [to have] a small group of people any one of [whom] ... will see that standards and a sense of responsibility are maintained. And as the ... Secretary of a Research Council knows better than anybody else what this means to the whole organisation, can I add my personal expression of indebtedness?

She replied in December on her return from Chicago: 'I count myself fortunate to have been associated ... with the MRC ... [It] left one in peace to get on with one's work giving one support & advice & what more can a scientist ask for ... What fun we have had & thank you.'[66]

The fun would of course continue, though the context would change.

Endnotes

[1] Lorna Arnold, *My Short Century. Memoirs of An Accidental Nuclear Historian* (London, Cumnor Hill Books, 2012), 141.

[2] JA, 144, and AICL (BPMS), BPMS Annual Report for 1937–38. The latter shows work requested by Gask for the 'Radium Institute', but Vaughan may also have done analyses for Sir Ernest Rock Carling, the chair of this sub-group, who had pioneered the medical use of radium at London's Westminster Hospital. See transcript of conversation between David K Hill and Dame Janet Vaughan, 10.11.1980.

[3] As late as 1954, the secretary of the MRC said the number of medical people competent to advise in the field of atomic energy was 'very limited indeed'. There was a need to limit the time they spent on committees so as to leave more time for the research on which their advice was based. (TNA, FD 7/641, Himsworth letter, 9.9.1954.)

[4] TNA, FD 1/463, meetings of 10.5.1946 and 11.10.1946. Also TNA, AB 6/37 (Ministry of Supply) and TNA, FD 1/481.

[5] OBL, Hodgkin papers, MS Eng. C.5642, file C.177, draft article 'The Retiring Principal of Somerville' by Hodgkin and Henderson, 1967.

[6] TNA, FD 1/463 and 481.

[7] NF meeting, 22.4.1947. This funding was later used instead for the graduate physicist on the team.

[8] TNA, FD 1/481, Vaughan to MRC, 29.1.1949.

[9] X-rays are more damaging than either alpha or beta particles, because they pass straight through the body, damaging cells along the way. Alpha and beta particles can be blocked by various materials including skin, so are most damaging when absorbed internally.

[10] Arnold, *My Short Century*, 141.

[11] JA, 146. UOA, FA 6/5/33, departmental reports 1946/47 and 1947/48.

[12] For Fell, see Vaughan's Royal Society biographical memoir, 249–50.

[13] TNA, FD 1/481, Tutt, France and Vaughan, The metabolism of Sr89 in the healthy rabbit. Presented to the Pathological Society on 31.12.1948.

[14] TNA, FD 1/460, 463 and 481, meetings in 1947–49. A technician, Claire Grierson, was taken on in May 1949, and a zoologist, Miss G J Goodfield, from September.

[15] TNA, FD 1/481, Vaughan to MRC, 25.1.1949. Interestingly, in 1948 another member of the Protection sub-group, Dr Joseph Mitchell of the University of Cambridge, suggested (unsuccessfully) to Oxford's medical faculty board that the university should set up a department for radiotherapy, radiobiology and biophysics, given the proximity of Harwell and the expertise of Florey and others. (UOA, BFM FA 4/9/2/10; agenda and papers 1948–49, MD/30.)

[16] TNA, FD 1/481, Mellanby to Vaughan, 25.3.1949.

[17] TNA, FD 1/481, Loutit to MRC, 12.4.1949. Professor Witts in May 1949 explained to the Nuffield Foundation that Vaughan's group 'have for the moment been led away from the precise field of haematology'. But work in the next year should 'clarify many problems in the metabolism of strontium and incidentally throw light on the processes of calcification and decalcification in bone'. (NF meeting 11.5.1949, progress report F.28/1.)

[18] Barbara Kidman, Margaret L Tutt and Janet Vaughan. Articles in *J Pathol Bacteriol*: The retention and excretion of radioactive strontium and yttrium (Sr89, Sr90 and Y90) in the healthy rabbit (1950), 62(2), 209–27; and The retention of radioactive strontium and yttrium (Sr89, Sr90 and Y90) in pregnant and lactating rabbits and their offspring (1951), 63(2), 253–68.

[19] Maureen Owen, Dame Janet Maria Vaughan DBE, 18 October 1899 – 9 January 1993, in *Biographical Memoirs of Fellows of the Royal Society* (1995), 41, 483–98.

[20] J Vaughan, M Tutt and B Kidman, The biological hazards of radioactive strontium, in A Haddow (Ed), *Biological Hazards of Atomic Energy* (Oxford, Clarendon Press, 1952), 145–70. (Updating of a 1950 conference paper.)

[21] TNA, FD 10/530, Vaughan to MRC, 13.11.1952; and internal MRC memo 5.12.1952. Also FD 14/183, minutes of panel meeting on 4.12.1952.

[22] NF minute books, meetings on 24.1.1951 and 11.6.1952. Also OBL, Dorothy Hodgkin papers, MS.Eng.C.5635/11–14, C.97, Farrer Brown to Hodgkin, 24.1.1951.

[23] TNA, FD 1/461, June 1948 paper for MRC Protection Sub-Committee.

[24] Email to the author from Barbara Kidman, March 2007. She was by then 'nearly 80' and had suffered no ill effects from her time in the lab. According to a 1955 article, there was a fume cupboard at least by 1954.

[25] Email to the author from Barbara Kidman, March 2007.

[26] Arnold, *My Short Century*, 143–44. The ICRP's sister organisation, the International Commission on Radiation Units (ICRU), developed improved ways of measuring radiation.

[27] Telephone conversation with Jennifer Everest, 23.11.2006.

[28] Janet M Vaughan, Radiation injury to bone, in *Lectures on the Scientific Basis of Medicine, Vol 4* (London, Athlone Press, 1955), 196–223; and The effects of radiation on bone, in Geoffrey H Bourne (Ed), *The Biochemistry and Physiology of Bone* (New York, NY, Academic Press Inc, 1956), 729–65.

[29] TNA, FD 10/530, letters between Vaughan and MRC, 30.4–24.5.1956. The Nuffield Foundation grant for Witts' haematology research, which had been funding Owen, ran out at the end of the 1956/57 academic year.

[30] TNA, FD 10/530, Vaughan to MRC, 10.10.1956.

[31] Hubert A Sissons (1920–2008). He moved to a post in New York in 1979, returning to the UK in 1990.

[32] Letter to the editor, *Nature* (8.11.1958), 1294–95. A new collaboration followed, with the Professor of Dental Medicine at Guy's Hospital (M A Rushton), to follow up this work in more detail.

[33] TNA, FD 10/530, Vaughan to MRC, 10.10 and 22.11.1956.

[34] Margaret Hindmarsh and Janet Vaughan, The distribution of radium in certain bones from a man exposed to radium for 34 years, in C B Allsopp (Ed), *The Measurement of Body Radioactivity* (London, Br J of Radiology, 1957, Supplement 7): Papers read at a conference held at Leeds, 16–17 April, 1956, 71–80.

[35] Margaret Hindmarsh, Maureen Owen, Janet Vaughan, L F Lamerton and F W Spiers, The relative hazards of strontium 90 and radium 226, in *Br J Radiol* (1958), 31, 518–33.

[36] TNA, FD 14/204, Minutes of meeting on 23.10.1958.

[37] JA, 147–48.

[38] Sissons diaries, 11.3.1958.

[39] TNA, FD 10/530, Vaughan to Himsworth, 22.5.1958.

[40] Owen's speech in 'appreciation' of Dame Janet Vaughan at the 1981 Gordon Conference. Copy given to the author by Owen.

[41] Lorna Lea and Janet Vaughan, The uptake of 35S in Cortical Bone, in *Quarterly Journal of Microscopical Science* (1957), 98, 369–75. Lea worked in the lab in 1955–56.

[42] Conversation with Professor Lorna Secker-Walker, 1.5.2007; and email exchange, 1–2 November 2023.

[43] Sissons diaries, 10.6 and 28.11.1958.

[44] Dame Janet Vaughan, The effect of radiation on the skeleton, *The Newcastle Medical Journal* (1959), 25, 309–14.

[45] TNA, FD 23/696, Loutit to MRC, 19.11.1959.

[46] *Radiation Damage in Bone*, report and summarized papers of a Conference on the Relation of Radiation Damage to Radiation Dose in Bone held at Oxford, 10–14 April 1960 (Vienna, IAEA 1960). The relevant committee was the UN Scientific Committee on the Effects of Atomic Radiation. Vaughan seems also to have attended an IAEA meeting in Moscow in 1961, when problems of strontium-90 burdens in humans were discussed (TNA, FD 14/212, minutes of meeting on 23.2.1961).

[47] TNA, FD 12/86, progress report for Unit to MRC, March 1961.

[48] Janet Vaughan, Bone disease induced by radiation, in *International Review of Experimental Pathology* (1962), 1, 244–369. Also TNA, FD 12/86, Unit plans for future work, March 1961.

[49] Owen's speech at the 1981 Gordon Conference.

[50] TNA, FD 23/696, File note by Himsworth, 4.2.1959.

[51] TNA, FD 10/530, Vaughan to MRC, 2.5.1958. Lloyd came from the radiology department at Barts Hospital in London after her husband had moved to work at Harwell.

[52] JA, 149. Also TNA, FD 12/86, Unit progress report, March 1961. The two visiting workers were Dr Julian Liniecki of the Institute of Occupational Medicine at Lodz, in Poland; and Dr Vladimir Volf of the Institute of Industrial Health and Occupational Diseases in Prague.

[53] Mike Davies gave his recollections in emails to the author dated 8.6 and 13.6.2006.

[54] TNA, FD 12/87, MRC office note, 9.3.1961. Vaughan had told the MRC in early 1961 that she would retire in 1964, but discussion of the Unit's future seems only to have begun when her 1967 retirement date was confirmed.

[55] H J J Blackwood (Ed), *Bone and Tooth* (London, Pergamon Press, 1964). The success of this event led to the establishment of a regular series, held at different European venues. Owen, Gordon Conference speech.

[56] TNA, FD 14/122 and 123, minutes of 11.5.and 13.7.1965 meetings. It began its work in 1964, and Vaughan spent a week in Madrid with them in November (Unit file 19.11.1964).

[57] JA, 151. This was ICRP publication 11, 1968. The group met twice in the Vaughan building, for a week in the summer term of 1966 and two days in October that year.

[58] Email 25.8.2015 from Nobuyuki Hamada, ICRP Assistant Scientific Secretary, lists the publications as: Publication 11: *A Review of the Radiosensitivity of the Tissues in Bone*, 1968 (report prepared for Committees 1 and 2 of ICRP, Pergamon Press); Publication 14: *Radiosensitivity and Spatial Distribution of Dose*, 1969 (reports prepared by two Task Groups of Committee 1 of ICRP, Pergamon Press); Publication 19: *The Metabolism of Compounds of Plutonium and other Actinides*, 1972 (a report prepared by a Task Group of Committee 2 of the ICRP. Adopted by the Commission in May 1972. Published for the ICRP by (Oxford) Pergamon Press. Vaughan mentioned the unpublished paper, titled Temporal non-uniformity of radiation dose, in the personal information she submitted to the Royal Society in 1979.

[59] TNA, FD 12/87, Vaughan to Himsworth, 27.9.1965.

[60] Janet Vaughan, Betty Bleaney and Margaret Williamson, The uptake of plutonium in bone marrow: a possible leukaemic risk, in *British Journal of Haematology* (1.4.1967), 13(1), 492–502.

[61] TNA, FD 12/87, meeting on 9.8.1966; the fate of other staff is in later papers on same file. Duthie had succeeded Trueta in this post. Lloyd, meanwhile, decided in 1966 to return to the Argonne Laboratory where she had previously spent a year.

[62] TNA, FD 12/87, MRC 67/434, dated 18.4.1967, on future of the Unit.

[63] TNA, FD 12/87, Vaughan to MRC, 7.7.1967.

[64] Janet Vaughan, Non-uniformity of radiation dose in space with special reference to radiological protection, in *International Journal of Radiation Biology* (1965,) 9(6), 513–43.

[65] 'Technicians' in this sense are now known as Medical Laboratory Scientific Officers, but I have throughout this book used the name then current.

[66] TNA, FD 12/87, Himsworth to Vaughan, 9.10.1967; and her reply dated 4.12.1967.

HOW TO RETIRE AND KEEP ON WORKING

CHAPTER 14
How to go on serving science
1967–89

The first eight years 1967–85

When asked in old age how she wished to be remembered, Vaughan said 'As a scientist'; but a scientist with a family.[1] No man would have thought of adding that modifying statement. It reflects her enduring determination to show that women could and should combine useful and high-achieving careers with child-rearing, so that eventually their right to do so, alongside that of men, would be taken for granted.

For both men and women, the needs of a loved one can thwart the best-laid plans. Vaughan had at the start of her career placed her mother's needs before her wish to become a consultant physician. Having retired from leading her research unit, the need to think first of Cilla meant that she could not go on with MRC-funded research in the way friends like Loutit and Spiers chose to do. It was, however, unthinkable not to go on using her experience, knowledge and talents to help in the advance of science for as long as she could; so she used every means available to make her contribution.

First, she still had her extensive networks of contacts. Although retired from the Nuffield Foundation after 24 years as a trustee, she was still fully involved in the Commonwealth Scholarships Commission as well as the four ICRP task groups and MRC committees. From 1967, Owen's team gave their location as the 'Bone Research Laboratory' at the Churchill Hospital. Vaughan still managed a small amount of personal research work, especially with Bleaney, Loutit and Spiers, and gave the same address in her published articles. She kept in close touch with her old team. One young doctor at the Nuffield Orthopaedic Centre, with which they were now associated, found her enthusiasm and knowledge inspiring: she was a regular attender at their seminars and always arrived first, even for Saturday 8.30am lectures.[2] Mainly through the MRC, she continued to travel to conferences in the UK and abroad, and her expenses were also met by grants and payments from a variety of sources.[3] Fae Schofield, still working at the lab, stayed in a small self-contained flat in the new house and was a companion for Cilla when Vaughan was away.

Vaughan's energy was mainly turned to writing books as well as extended articles and book chapters for others. The conferences, meetings and seminars she attended, and time spent reading in the Radcliffe Science Library as well as frequent visits to the lab, helped her to keep up to date with developments and enabled her published work. Between 1968 and 1986 she produced two significant books, one of which ran to three editions; as well as 13 book chapters, two of them joint productions and four resulting from symposia. Her aim was not only to inform the widest possible scientific audience, but to encourage younger researchers into all the fields of study involved, and build bridges between different disciplines as well as research teams. In the period up to 1989 she also wrote or contributed to nine generally quite brief articles.

Having lost the storage space provided by the unit, she kept her papers in filing cabinets at home and usually worked there and in the science library, still paying her former lab secretary to do her typing after the secretary retired. Scholarship funding was useful in enabling the writing of her books.

***

Vaughan's first foreign trip after retirement gives an indication of her continuing energy. After settling in with Cilla at the new house and spending a beach holiday with the family, she left in September 1967 for Sun Valley, Idaho, where she gave a paper for the annual University of Utah symposium.[4] After that she was in Chicago, giving a series of lectures on radiation and the skeleton as a visiting professor. Living at the university's graduate club, she enjoyed a busy social life and also the vitality of the city itself, especially in its art galleries. At the last conference she attended, news of her 18 October birthday (her sixty-eighth) leaked out, giving rise to 'parties & finally the whole conference sang Happy Birthday when out of the air came a splendid cake covered with sparklers!! I have felt … enormously cherished.'[5] A generous Somerville travel grant enabled her to visit laboratories across America and see for herself work on dogs and pigs which had not yet been published. Her politically suspect past meant that she was denied a pass to the Hanford labs; but the staff there took a room at the Holiday Inn for the day and arrived 'in a large van complete with … slides, microscopes and lamps. We had a wonderful time.'[6] She was still enjoying the benefits of the friendships forged in the 1950s, as well as keeping in touch with the Castles and with Minot's wife and family.

On her return, she reported on the blood disorders induced by strontium, yttrium and other radioactive isotopes in the Hanford pigs; and in beagle dogs at the University of California, Davis, and Chicago's Argonne National Laboratory. The work at Hanford and Davis, still unpublished, was unknown in Chicago, and Vaughan quickly put all in touch with each other. The blood disorders had been given a variety of names, but in her view the underlying aetiology was in all cases irradiation of bone marrow stem cells.[7] Vaughan also saw comprehensive material in Chicago and at MIT on patients suffering from radium contamination, and could compare it with the findings for animals. 'It has always been important to me to see things myself down a microscope, to see actual patients, and to see radiographs rather than just read about them.'[8] The material seen on this extended North American visit informed all her subsequent work.

Turning her Chicago lectures into a monograph on the effects of irradiation of bone, she took account of recently available results from studies of large groups of human beings: survivors of the atomic explosions in Japan, and American and British radiologists and ankylosing spondylitis patients exposed to external irradiation; plus the smaller group of dial painters and radium chemists subject to internal irradiation. These tended to confirm what she knew from research with animals about which tissues were most at risk of developing cancer through both types of radiation.[9] There was also increasing evidence that the effects of external irradiation in the fetus and very young children might be owing to damage to pluripotent stem cells in the marrow or blood. She and Loutit took this forward in 1971, explaining that in experimental animals some tumours might arise in such cells in the bone marrow, which were destined for different organs and parts of the body.[10]

Ten years later, in a review of recent work in this field, she revisited her 1930s subject of leuco-erythroblastic anaemia, and concluded that in certain circumstances there was a complex interaction between the processes of bone and blood formation. A failure in one step in the differentiation, development and functioning of the cells involved in either might result in some failure in the other, causing abnormalities of both blood and bone.[11] The related disorders are now known as the 'myeloproliferative disorders', which may transform from one to another or to acute myeloid leukaemia. In 1982 she, Loutit and others went on to examine whether there was a single pluripotent blood-forming stem cell or a variety of stem cells each with a capacity for self-replication. They concluded (rightly) that both types of cell exist in the marrow.[12]

***

Vaughan began writing a major book on the physiology of bone in summer 1968, with the aim of synthesising a wide range of information so as to bridge the divide between experimentalists and physicians: she believed they had much to learn from each other, though lacking a shared language.[13] Having since the early 1950s been urging the need to find out more about 'normal' bone, she must have taken immense satisfaction in doing this. She was celebrating both the rewards gained through scientific discoveries, and the joy of the endlessly renewed quest for greater knowledge and understanding.

Published in 1970, the book was dedicated to H M Turnbull, who had contributed so much to the 1930s anaemias monograph and had inspired her long fascination with bone.[14] The *BMJ* reviewer praised its organisation and excellent microscope photographs and autoradiographs, although the specialised language did make it a difficult read for the non-specialist. Though large, it was not comprehensive: readers should treat it as an inspiration to fill up the gaps by further reading.[15] Vaughan, wishing as she said in the preface to give 'a bird's eye view of an exciting and expanding subject' for medical students and teachers, would have echoed that sentiment. The book's popularity is shown by the fact that she was asked to write two further editions.

***

Still in 1970, Vaughan and Bleaney took forward their investigation of the uptake of plutonium, concluding that in future, the term 'bone surface' would have to be more precisely defined as to which of its constituents were being referred to. Partly because of the more sophisticated equipment available, studies were becoming ever more detailed.[16] Vaughan believed more work on these lines was needed, but the disbanding of her unit made that impossible: there was no longer a dedicated team and resources for the work. The paper was sent to the ICRP task group on plutonium, of which she was a member. The National Radiological Protection Board (NRPB), created by legislation passed in 1970, was then expected to look into multi-disciplinary problems of this kind.[17] In the event, that did not happen, so the work was not taken forward as Vaughan wished.

In 1973 she wrote or contributed to three chapters on plutonium in a *Handbook of Experimental Pharmacology*, published in Germany and the United States.[18] Interestingly, the first and longest chapter featured the use of gendered pronouns to refer to team leaders, making it easier to identify how many women were involved. Of the 309 published papers cited, 85 (based in part on the form of Russian names) have women as contributors. Of those women, only one, at 16 papers, exceeds Vaughan's total of 15; whilst all except one (a haematologist) of the 12 British women contributing to a total of 28 papers had been in her research unit or the team now led by Owen.

***

Vaughan was meanwhile attempting to summarise current work on the effects of radiation on bone, having won a two-year Emeritus Leverhulme fellowship in 1971 to produce a book. *The Effects of Irradiation on the Skeleton* was published in 1973 and dedicated, 10 years after his death, to 'D G and the Lands of Summer'.[19] An American reviewer highlighted her doubts about the ICRP's acceptance of a linear relationship between radiation dose and radiation malignancy as a working hypothesis; her emphasis on the need to understand precisely how radiation induces cancer; the particular dangers of plutonium; and the difficulties of extrapolating from one species or age group to another. 'The last of 11 conclusions in this excellent monograph is that determination of doses to the sensitive tissues in different species and in man should make it possible to extrapolate radiation toxicity in animals to man with more confidence than when average dose to bone is used.'[20]

Spiers described the book as 'the first major synthesis of its kind', with the unusual merit of trying to relate biological findings to the physical properties of the radiation, so benefiting both biologists and physicists. Besides its high value to those working on bone, it would appeal to researchers in fields including nuclear medicine, radiotherapy, cancer research and radiation protection. 'Elucidation of all the problems of bone irradiation cannot be expected … in this or any other book, but the synthesis … will enlighten many and be an authoritative guide to long-term researchers'.[21] There would be no second edition. The rapidly expanding field was becoming too specialised and fragmented for a biologist to attempt such a synthesis again.

Vaughan visited the US many times in these years, and tried in February 1973 to shed the stigma of her 'communist' past. She was invited as a scholar in residence at the John E Fogarty International Centre for Advanced Study in the National Institute of Health at Bethesda, and would visit other research centres while there. It would be useful to be eligible for a salary as well as expenses, and for this the US visa department advised her to seek political clearance. This turned out to be conditional, however, on demonstrating that she had not only dissociated herself from communist activity for at least five years, but also shown 'active opposition' to it. In practice, she had never been moved to speak or write either for or against communism, and the American Consul advised that the clearance was not worth pursuing.[22]

The main purpose of the three-month scholarship, in autumn 1973, was to work on the second edition of *The Physiology of Bone*. This time her work was affected by contemporary politics. As a result of the Watergate scandal and his efforts to rein in public expenditure, people were calling for President Nixon to resign. At the National Institute, budget cuts meant that doctors were washing up their own glassware, she had to save her typing to be done in England, and Xerox machines were constantly out of order. Her faith in American efficiency was shaken, but still the autumn countryside was beautiful. Among other trips, she visited the University of Delaware to speak about the National Health Service, while making good progress in drafting the book.[23]

She also enjoyed the 'odd communal life' lived with the other scholars, including especially the Finnish neuroscientist, Olavi Erankö, cultural anthropologist Margaret Mead and Junnosuke ('J') Nakai, professor of anatomy at the University of Tokyo. 'J Nakai & I became great friends, cooking our breakfast together every morning & accused by MM of not cleaning the frying pan properly.' After Erankö had a heart attack, she went with him for his tests and follow-up and brought him back in the evening. The communal house 'was ruled by a fearsome female housekeeper' and there was no comfortable armchair in Olavi's room, 'so N & I stole one from some communal sitting room … oh such a row!! Then N & I took what care we cd of O …'. Erankö and his wife stayed with her in England afterwards, and they all kept in touch with Nakai.[24]

***

Back in Britain, in July 1974 she chaired a two-day International Parathyroid Conference in Oxford, with hospitality provided by Somerville.[25] The relevance of this is clear in the second edition of *The Physiology of Bone*, published a year later. Some sections were completely re-written to take into account the 'amazing rapidity' with which knowledge had advanced. This was 'particularly true of our understanding, still incomplete, of the behaviour of vitamin D and … the effects of parathyroid hormone … on calcium homeostasis [equilibrium]'.[26] One reviewer thought this 'Herculean undertaking' should be 'welcomed by all in the field of skeletal biology', and would be of significant value to medical and basic research scientists in numerous disciplines.[27]

Vaughan's publication rate slowed after 1976, but she produced a significant paper on bone growth and modelling in 1979.[28] The lifelong process of resorption and renewal in bone was now much better understood, including the origins of the cells involved. Bone was not an isolated organ. Its proper growth and maintenance were essential not only to its function as a scaffold, but also to the maintenance of mineral equilibrium in the body, through its high content of calcium and other minerals such as phosphate, magnesium and sodium.[29] As always, she stressed the need for more work to add to understanding.

She dealt with all this at greater length in the third edition of her physiology of bone book, begun in August 1979 and published in 1981 with a dedication to Somerville College. Once again she was excited by how much had been learned since the second edition. Indeed, Owen believed these three editions were effectively three different books.[30] A *BMJ* reviewer found only one 'obvious error': the quotation on the flyleaf was not, as claimed, from the Book of Daniel. Cicely Williams soon pointed out that her own Authorised Version of the Bible showed the quotation, 'Many shall run to and fro and knowledge shall be increased', precisely as stated.[31]

Late honours

In March 1979 Vaughan won her most prized honour when she was elected a Fellow of the Royal Society as being 'Distinguished for her contributions to radiobiology … and for her general services to science.' The citation highlighted her career as one of the first laboratory-based haematologists, 'a pioneer in integrating clinical and pathological observations with blood pictures and measurements of blood cells … and her formation of a "school" investigating the metabolism of nuclear fission products … developing radio-autography and introducing fission track autography. Now a world authority on the pathological effects of plutonium, she was the first to recognize the potential effects on bone marrow resulting in leukaemia and allied dyscrasias [blood disorders].'[32]

Proposers are likely to have included long-term colleagues such as Hodgkin, Doll and Fell. Hodgkin had written in 1972 of her 'gloom' about the Royal Society, saying she was 'really keen on having a blitz and electing about 50 or more of those I feel most strongly about having been left out'.[33] It seems safe to assume that Vaughan was one of those she had in mind. For Vaughan it was 'the most exciting thing that's ever happened to me', especially the act of signing the same vellum book as Samuel Pepys and Sir Christopher Wren.[34]

Two years later she was honorary chairman of the 1981 Gordon Conference in New Hampshire, on the Physiology of Bones and Teeth. This was a substantial tribute from her colleagues in the United States and around the world, and Owen surveyed her life and work in an after-dinner speech, stressing the way she enriched the lives of those who worked with her and was 'always such fun'. There were other tributes, as when in 1980 she was asked to cut the birthday cake at the celebration of the twenty-first birthday of the British Haematology Society. In 1985 she became a fellow of the University of London Royal Postgraduate Medical School on the fiftieth anniversary of its opening. Her former assistant John Dacie, who had retired as professor of haematology there in 1977, gave the tribute speech. Among other things he mentioned how widely liked and respected she was in Oxford, where her ability to get things done earned her the title 'the active principal'. This added to the list of her nicknames: 'JV' in the lab, 'the radioactive principal' according to Professor Burn, 'the Red Queen' according to more right-wing colleagues; and now 'the active principal', punning on the idea, in medicine, of the main ingredient that causes the desired effect. It is significant, too, that all these titles imply respect, and some degree of affection.[35]

Advice to the Royal Commission on Environmental Pollution (RCEP) 1975
Vaughan and Spiers began their final collaborative work, on plutonium and leukaemia, in 1975, when there was public concern about this potential threat to the health of workers in the nuclear industry. Very few cases had been identified, but the National Radiation Protection Board (NRPB), established in 1971, was trying to improve its record keeping for workers found to have a significant body burden of plutonium.

The RCEP was assessing radiological hazards in light of the projected nuclear power programme, and asked Vaughan and Spiers in January 1975 for an independent assessment of papers on plutonium produced by the MRC and the NRPB.[36] The MRC paper concluded that the existing UK safety standards for plutonium met the intentions of the International Commission for Radiation Protection (ICRP), subject to possible small adjustments. Unaccountably, however, neither document, nor a third by the

NRPB on research, mentioned the leukaemia risk of plutonium uptake in the bone marrow. And this despite Vaughan's 1967 paper, the 1972 ICRP task group report on the metabolism of plutonium, and the fact that her Harwell colleagues were 'preparing beautiful autoradiographs of 239Pu in the marrow of mice that are developing L[eukaemia]!!'[37]

She suggested that the NRPB provide a more detailed statistical analysis of recorded cases; but a meeting she attended in February was both illuminating and depressing: '… the Atomic Energy [Authority] Medical Director is clearly a very stupid man. The authority have destroyed all records of radiation workers except for the last ten years.' Windscale had good records, but not for workers who had left the industry.[38] Vaughan was still exercised about this in April: 'Really the idea of those responsible about how records should be kept is terrifying!!' The resulting lack of information led her to doubt that workers seeking compensation could prove their case.[39] Her indignation was understandable. As early as 1962, she had urged on the MRC the need to investigate all cases of human contamination: 'if necessary the man … must be hospitalised for … investigation over long periods, his wages etc paid and his future employment ensured … Data from one man is … worth data on thousands of rats and mice.' The MRC did follow this up, but, perhaps because of the number of organisations involved, no central register of contamination cases was set up.[40]

There had also been no effective action by the NRPB to take forward her own and Bleaney's cross-disciplinary work on the effects of alpha-emitters like plutonium. Vaughan, having put much time and effort into checking the data from animal experiments, told Spiers when sending him her draft for the report of her enormous relief 'to have escaped those Utah dogs!'[41] She was concerned about possible reputational damage to the MRC, but fortunately the balance of the evidence led them to agree with that body in endorsing the existing ICRP/UK standards.

They confirmed in oral evidence that Vaughan's 1967 paper showing that plutonium was absorbed into the bone marrow was 'the first substantial reference' to a connection between plutonium and leukaemia, and was reinforced by the 1972 ICRP report. For the future, medical checks should be conducted on all plutonium workers, as had been done in Boston and Chicago for people working with radium. Each case going to autopsy should be checked for retention of plutonium in marrow and skeleton, but such checks had only begun in August 1974. The main additonal need was to monitor those who might acquire a body burden of plutonium, or who might have been excessively exposed; and this should continue for those who retired or moved house.

The RCEP report reflected their advice. By December, arrangements were almost complete for establishing a national registry of radiation workers, to be operational from 1 January 1976. Vaughan and Spiers then wrote an article for *Nature*, putting the facts as plainly as possible in the public domain.[42] Plutonium was more carcinogenic than radium, and it was important to estimate the risks involved, especially for nuclear industry workers. These had to date been based on the outcomes of animal experiments; but Spiers and a colleague had developed a new method for calculating radiation dose, taking into account Bleaney and Vaughan's work on the marrow and Vaughan's knowledge of the effects on the cells at risk. The results in broad terms accorded well with the values of maximum permissible body burdens arrived at by the ICRP in 1959. Vaughan had also presented these findings at the annual Sun Valley symposium, in October 1975.[43]

Legal work and cataracts 1974–85
Thanks to her expertise on plutonium, Vaughan acted from late 1974 as expert consultant in legal cases brought by trade unions on behalf of workers at various nuclear sites. This was an important source of income as well as being interesting in itself; but she was hampered by the lack of proper records, which compounded the theoretical uncertainties so often preventing definitive decisions about cause and effect. In May 1975 she was working with 'a tough little solicitor' on three cases of plutonium workers who had died. 'He has left me piles of documents but I fear I shan't be able to make out a very good case for him.'[44] The work continued until the mid-1980s, involving five sets of solicitors on up to 28 cases, relating mainly to workers at Dounray, Aldermaston and Windscale.[45] A 1985 letter gives some indication of her fee income. It enclosed cheques for two cases, totalling £327.30: equivalent in

2021 to £1,055 in terms of purchasing power.[46] One solicitor recalled meetings at her home, often with other medical specialists, when she would 'provide a splendid cold buffet to which I would add … anything from Champagne to Newcastle Brown Ale! … I … enjoyed her company so much: it was invigorating to go out for a meal with her.'[47]

One case, in which the client won compensation for a cataract, led to an article with Pirie which Vaughan regarded as her swansong. She had drawn the ophthalmologist into MRC-funded research on the effects of radiation in 1952, when the problem of cataracts caused by irradiation was under discussion. In 1959 they published the finding that all parts of a rabbit's eye, except the lens, accumulated radioactive strontium. There was, however, a different pattern for retention of yttrium. The results might be applicable to humans.[48] In 1985 they suggested that the cataract in the legal case might have been caused, at least in part, by alpha particles deposited in the eye as a result of plutonium circulating in the blood. There were no previous reported cases of this kind, but the risk could be deduced from various experimental findings, including their own as reported in 1959.[49]

Vaughan wanted to put their findings on record, since she had long been concerned about cases of cataract in Germany where she suspected treatment with radium to be the cause. She and Pirie had seen a specimen of a cataract removed from a German child injected with radium and thought it very suspicious. (Fortunately the German surgeon involved had suggested the diagnosis and kept the cataract.) 'Now … though they still use 224 Ra to treat ankylosing spondylitis in Germany, they don't give it to children & … have reduced the dose. So probably we shall never know the answer.'[50] Soon afterwards, however, she rejoiced that 'after nearly 20 years of fuss on my part', German ophthalmologists had looked at the cataracts in people who had received large doses of radium-224 'and they are classical radiation cataracts. They even say they are grateful to J-V- for having fussed!!' Even better, she heard the following year that the ICRP had decided to look into the problem.[51]

Last scientific work 1985–89

After 1985, Vaughan often lamented her failing physical and mental powers. In February 1986, she went to Harwell 'for haematological gossip & a seminar – & found the gossip hard to understand & the seminar 'Molecular aspects of mutation in animal cells' – left me bewildered.'[52] In the same month, Hubert Sissons on a visit to Oxford found she had completely forgotten their arrangement to meet at the Science Library. Eventually he found her at home, where she said she was constantly forgetting things. He thought her much aged, but still able to laugh at herself.[53]

She agreed nonetheless to take on the task of writing the Royal Society Biographical Memoir of Honor Fell, starting in July 1986 and clearing the final proofs in February 1987. Her determination to do this quickly perhaps sprang in part from fears about her own declining powers. It involved reading Fell's many papers, and she found the science of the last years very difficult.[54] The result, however, is a model of brevity and clarity, and she felt lucky to have lived during the work with 'a lovely happy fulfilled biologist with no enemies dying at her working bench at 86'.[55] There is a note of envy here, and in a letter to a friend she mentioned the same absence of enemies in Hodgkin's case, despite her politics. She was too wise to think she herself could shed her faults of impatience and sarcasm; but her own comparative lack of real enemies speaks to her success in reining in those faults.

***

Vaughan's last article was written with Spiers. In 1986 he sent her an early draft of a lecture on radiation dose and leukaemia, and in January 1987, having considered again the Utah data on blood cancers in beagles, she sent some pertinent thoughts and questions. For him the main issue was the apparent protection given by partial irradiation, the issue they had raised at a meeting in 1965.[56] He wanted her to explain in what respects a blood-forming cell was more sensitive to radiation than a bone-forming one. Vaughan consulted Loutit and a series of drafts and comments followed, before a meeting in Spiers' home in Leeds in August made him much more confident that he understood. Vaughan had previously seemed confused at times, sending muddled messages to Owen, whom she was also consulting. Her increasing deafness made her more comfortable with face-to-face discussion.[57]

Spiers turned the lecture into an article, for which Vaughan helped him sort the beagle diagnoses into true bone tumours and the difficult (to him) category of tumours and disorders arising from the marrow. When Doll suggested expanding the section on leukaemia for the journal *Leukaemia Research*, Spiers said this paper, published as an editorial in June 1989 and concentrating on biological findings and discussion, should be joint.[58] Since, in humans and animals, tumours of the bone marrow arose when all of it was irradiated by bone-seeking alpha emitters, but not when only part was so irradiated, isotopes like radium and plutonium might not after all be certain causes of leukaemia. The reasons were not yet clear. Thanks went to colleagues in Utah and California for providing the full data of the beagle investigations.

The effort for Vaughan had been challenging, but she had again the pleasure of working with long-term friends and colleagues, and inching the radiation story forward. As she said, those relatively few people working on radiation protection problems in the 1940s and 1950s became friends in a very real sense. She, though no physicist or mathematician, knew the questions to ask and the physicists could answer them.[59] This was a characteristic piece of understatement, as shown by the words of one obituarist:

> Those who knew her professionally … admired the precision and lucidity with which she attacked a problem, and the careful way she would avoid comment [if] she felt she had insufficient knowledge … always watchful and sympathetic, she could be sharp with those who tried to push a point of view without scientific evidence. In a world in which radiobiology usually depends on people who lack a full medical training, she is seriously missed.[60]

Many old friends, of whom Fell was one, had died by this time. Vaughan was still writing to the Liscos and the Castles in America, and in touch with Minot's children, but Chuck Mays at Utah died in August 1989. Spiers and his wife sympathised with her in Chuck's loss; but, on a more upbeat note, he reported 12 requests for reprints of 'our paper', from the USA, Canada, Europe and Australia.[61] When Sissons visited the flat in 1990, he obeyed the notice on the door saying 'Enter and shout', to find Vaughan, Mary and Cilla finishing their tea. He was glad she remembered him and had much to talk about, though she was very deaf and her memory poor.[62]

***

Vaughan maintained to the end her belief that women must succeed on a basis of strict equality with men, even if that meant working twice as hard. While working on the Fell biography, she consulted Dr Audrey Glauert, a colleague of Fell at the Strangeways Laboratory. Glauert told her she agreed 'with so much ... you stand for, and particularly ... the role of women. We must gain respect by doing the job well ... I dislike being a "madam chairman" or a "chairperson". We are all men and part of mankind.'[63] In practice, Vaughan had not only been inspirational, but had gone many extra miles to help women advance in all walks of life, including science. Of the many letters from Somervillians over the years, one which must have given particular pleasure came in April 1990 from the molecular biologist Louise Johnson, who had come to Somerville as a lecturer in biophysics in 1967 and had just been elected to the Royal Society alongside the astrophysicist Carole Jordan: 'It is nice to think that the election of Carole Jordan and myself will help to foster the image of Somerville as the important college for Science – the image that you and Dorothy created.'[64]

Endnotes

[1] Television interview with Polly Toynbee in *Women of Our Century* (BBC documentary series), originally broadcast on 3.8.1984. Interview clip available at: https://www.bbc.co.uk/archive/janet_vaughan/zhwht39 accessed 14.6.2023.

[2] JPP, letter from Martin Francis, Wolfson College, 13.1.1993.

[3] JPP, letters from Webster Jee at Utah dated 25.7–20.8.1975 show that Vaughan received a grant from the University of Utah towards her expenses in attending a symposium, and friends at other leading US laboratories paid her expenses and honoraria so that she could visit them.

[4] Janet Vaughan and Margaret Williamson, 90Sr in the rabbit: the relative risks of osteosarcoma and squamous cell sarcoma, in Charles W Mays, Webster S S Jee, Ray D Lloyd, Betsy J Stover, Jean H Dougherty and Glenn N Taylor (Eds), *Delayed Effects of Bone-Seeking Radionuclides* (Salt Lake City, UT, University of Utah Press, 1969), 337–55.

[5] JPP, Vaughan to Griffiths, 21.11.1967.

[6] JA, 152–53. She also visited poets she knew at Riverside, part of the University of California, and Hubert Schueller at Wayne State University, Detroit, who was editing the letters of John Addington Symonds.

[7] TNA, FD 14/126, PIRC/PL/68/8, Janet Vaughan: a radiation induced haematopoietic dyscrasia as seen in the USA September–December 1967.

[8] JA, 154. After the First World War, before the dangers were appreciated, it was fashionable to give radium by injection or as a tonic by mouth for a wide variety of ills, especially in Chicago. Vaughan saw some of these patients with the bone tumours which had arisen many years later.

[9] Janet Vaughan, The effects of skeletal irradiations, in *Clinical Orthopaedics and Related Research* (January–February, 1968), 56, 283–303. Ankylosing spondylitis is a long-term condition in which the spine and other areas of the body become inflamed.

[10] J F Loutit and Janet M Vaughan, The radiosensitive tissues in bone, in *Br J Radiol* (1971), 44, 815. Pluripotent stem cells are able to develop into many different types of cells or tissues in the body.

[11] Janet Vaughan, Osteogenesis and haematopoiesis, in *The Lancet* (18.7.1981), 2(8238), 133–36.

[12] J F Loutit, N W Nisbet, M J Marshall, Janet M Vaughan, Versatile stem cells in bone marrow, in *The Lancet* (13.11.1982), 2(8307), 1090–93.

[13] HMLC Lisco, Vaughan to Lisco, 29.7.1968.

[14] Janet M Vaughan, *The Physiology of Bone* (Oxford, Oxford University Press, 1970).

[15] R A McCance review of *The Physiology of Bone* in *BMJ* (18.7.1970), 3(5715), 154.

[16] Betty Bleaney and Janet Vaughan, Distribution of 239Pu in the bone marrow and on the endosteal surfaces of the femur of adult rabbits following injection of 239Pu (NO3)4, in *Br J Radiol* (1.1.1971), 44, 67–73.

[17] TNA, FD 14/134, Meeting on 2.6.1970.

[18] Janet Vaughan in collaboration with Betty Bleaney and David M Taylor, Distribution, excretion and effects of plutonium as a bone-seeker, in H C Hodge, J N Stannard and J B Hursh (Eds), *Handbook of Experimental Pharmacology, New Series, 36, Uranium-Plutonium Transplutonic Elements* (New York, Berlin, Heidelberg, Springer-Verlag, 1973), 349–450. Two further chapters by Vaughan are at 451–71; and 471–502.

[19] Janet M Vaughan, *The Effects of Irradiation on the Skeleton* (Oxford, Clarendon Press, 1973).

[20] John H Marshall, review of *The Effects of Irradiation on the Skeleton*, in *Science* (23.11.1973), 182(4114), 818.

[21] LULSC, Spiers's personal file 11, draft review (longhand) of Vaughan's book.

22 JPP, letters from solicitors dated 23 and 26.2.1973, responding to Vaughan letter of 5.2.1973.

23 JPP, Vaughan letter to the Parks, 4.11.1973.

24 Wellcome Collection, M L Vogt PP/MLV/C/22/6/1–10, Vaughan to Marthe Vogt, 7.1.1985.

25 SCA, Vaughan personal file, 11.3.1974.

26 Preface to second edition, May 1975. Maureen Owen's team had long been investigating the effect of parathyroid hormone on stem cells.

27 E A Tonna, review of *The Physiology of Bone*, in *The Quarterly Review of Biology* (December 1976), 51(4), 547.

28 Janet Vaughan, Bone growth and modelling, in T L J Lawrence (Ed), *Growth in Animals*, (London, Butterworth, 1980), 83–99.

29 These and other minerals help move nutrients into and waste out of cells, and help nerves, muscles, the heart and the brain to work the way they should.

30 Janet Vaughan, *The Physiology of Bone*, 3rd edition (Oxford, Oxford University Press, 1981). Owen speech at the 1981 Gordon Conference.

31 Review in *BMJ* (23.1.1982), 284(6311), 263. Williams's response in *BMJ* (27.2.1982), 284(6316), 669.

32 RS, EC/1979/37, citation of candidate for election, 1978.

33 OBL, Hodgkin papers, MS Eng C.5669, E190, letters of 2.3.1972 and 16.5.1972.

34 BL, NP 7705WR TR1, Joanna Richardson interview with Vaughan (1984).

35 JPP, certificate of admission as fellow and printed copy of Dacie speech.

36 LULSC, Spiers, Frederick William LUA/PER/057 Box 10, RCEP 1. RCEP to Spiers, 7.1.1975. The MRC paper had been produced following a PQ on subject. The NRPB report, published in October 1974, was on 'Radiological Problems in the Protection of Persons Exposed to Plutonium' (NRPB – R29).

37 LULSC, Spiers, Frederick William LUA/PER/057 Box 10, RCEP 1, Vaughan to Spiers, 21.1.1975.

38 LULSC, Spiers, Frederick William LUA/PER/057 Box 10, RCEP 1, Vaughan to Spiers, 10.2.1975.

39 HMLC Castle, Vaughan to Castle, 5.4.1975.

40 TNA, FD 23/748, Vaughan to Himsworth, 4.6.1962, and later correspondence on file.

41 LULSC, Spiers Box 4, file 24, Vaughan to Spiers, 14.3.1975.

42 F W Spiers and Janet Vaughan, Hazards of plutonium with special reference to the skeleton, in *Nature* (19.2.1976), 259, 531–34.

43 Janet Vaughan, Plutonium – a possible leukaemic risk, in Webster S S Jee (Ed), *The Health Effects of Plutonium and Radium: Proceedings of the Symposium Held at Sun Valley, Idaho, on October 6–9, 1975* (Salt Lake City, UT, J W Press, 1976), 691–705.

[44] JPP, Vaughan to James Park, 16.5.1975.

[45] JPP, Vaughan personal file. Handwritten list of cases and brief notes about opinions and outcomes in relation to some. Also a copy letter to solicitors, dated 30.11.1986, changing her previous opinion on a case in the light of recent research outcomes; and a final, handwritten one thanking them for a paper and assuming they do not expect her in Liverpool (presumably for court cases), dated October 1987. Increasingly during the 1980s, cases were settled out of court through a compensation scheme set up in 1982 by British Nuclear Fuels Limited and recognised unions.

[46] JPP, solicitors to Vaughan, 28.2.1985. Also measuringworth.com, accessed 3.10.2022.

[47] JPP, Ian Robertson of Crutes Solicitors, Newcastle, to Mary Park, 12.1.1993.

[48] R H Mole, Antoinette Pirie and Janet M Vaughan, Differential distribution of radioactive strontium and yttrium in the tissues of the rabbit's eye, in *Nature*, 21.3.1959, 183, 802–807.

[49] T P Griffith, A Pirie and J Vaughan, Possible cataractogenic effect of radionuclides deposited within the eye from the bloodstream, in *British Journal of Ophthalmology* (1985), 69(3) 219–27.

[50] HMLC Castle, Vaughan to Castle 18.6.1985.

[51] HMLC Castle, Vaughan to Castle 9.9.1985 and 5.2.1986.

[52] HMLC Castle, Vaughan to Castle 5.2.1986.

[53] Sissons diaries, 3.2.1986.

[54] Wellcome Collection, GC 186/9, Vaughan to Glauert, 8.9.1986.

[55] JPP, Vaughan to Griffiths, 20.10.1986.

[56] TNA, FD/14/122, meeting on 11.5.1965.

[57] LULSC, Spiers Box 5, file 29, correspondence from June to November 1987.

[58] F W Spiers and Janet Vaughan, The toxicity of the bone seeking radionuclides, in *Leukaemia Research* (1989), 13(5), 347–50.

[59] BL, NP 7705WR TR1, Joanna Richardson interview with Vaughan (1984).

[60] Anthony Tucker, Obituary of Dame Janet Vaughan, *The Guardian* (11.1.1993), 9.

[61] LULSC, Spiers Box 5, file 29. Spiers to Vaughan, 7.8.1989.

[62] Sissons diaries, 20.2.1990.

[63] Wellcome Collection GC 186/9, Glauert to Vaughan, 4.9.1986.

[64] JPP, Johnson to Vaughan, 14.4.1990. Jordan had come to Somerville as a tutorial fellow in 1976.

CHAPTER 15
Community, friends and family
1967–93

A process of adjustment

Vaughan did not believe in retirement. Her plan when David was alive had been to live together at last at Plovers Field, with more time for reading, travelling, gardening and all the other things they both enjoyed, while she returned to hands-on medicine as a GP. Instead, she had to grapple not only with life on her own, but Cilla's need for long-term care and support. She had to pay attention to her financial position so as to safeguard Cilla's current and future comfort; but she continued with scientific work for as long as she could, for the sake of her own mental and physical health. Coincidentally, it provided at times a welcome supplement to her income.

In 1967 she was still full of energy and still a striking woman, whose thick hair stayed black, with a greyish-white streak to one side, well into old age.[1] She would gladly have continued, if she could, to be Principal of Somerville. Since she could not, she took up other activities. The compulsion to fill every moment of the day with useful activity was both a habit and, now, a way of warding off loneliness. Besides supporting Cilla and contributing what she could to the advancement of science, she tried to be useful to her family and friends, to the young in general and the wider world.

It is clear that up to 1985, when she was 85, she broadly achieved all this. Even after that time, although increasingly subject to the physical and mental toll of old age, she fought hard to keep mobile despite her arthritis, and to take part in social activities despite increasing deafness. She was undoubtedly frustrated by her own condition as well as Cilla's illness, and bitter and angry about political developments in 1980s Britain; but her habit of seeking out the positive, giving primacy to others' needs before her own, and taking comfort from beauty in all its forms, did not desert her.

***

At first Cilla was relatively stable, and enjoyed both the new house and her job as a psychology technician at the Warneford. The house was hers, and Vaughan left her all her assets under her will. She took advice from her banker brother David or his son John in financial matters, including modest but useful investments. When the clergyman Tom Griffiths and his wife Jean visited the new house, they found the main ground floor room very like that in Radcliffe House, but brighter. The Furse painting of Madge hung on the staircase. Cilla cooked dinner, after which Tom blessed the house, feeling 'the significance of this service, with Janet … very devout'. And Vaughan felt a sense of peace after he had blessed them and their new home.[2] Photographs of Minot, Price Jones and Turnbull were pinned to the board by her bed, with those of the family and of Great Tew, St Martha's Church and Gourlay's grave. The fact that Fae Schofield, still working at the lab, had a self-contained flat in the house, made it easier for Vaughan to go away at times, leaving Cilla for periods of up to three months.

She knew the value of independence to Cilla. When in 1968 her modest salary could no longer be met from a research fund, her mother paid it instead, without her knowledge. The following year, however, she asked if the hospital could find even half the cost. It was a big commitment for someone living on a pension, and she wanted 'some sort of security for her if I had a heart attack tomorrow'.[3] The response is not known, but Vaughan was from 1970 receiving royalties from the book she published that year. Cilla's next major breakdown seems to have been in late 1974.

One friend who became increasingly important in these years was Charlotte Graves Taylor, a Somerville graduate who had, as a result of depression, spent most of her student life in the Warneford, where Vaughan had got to know her well. Graves Taylor visited soon after the move to Wolvercote, and found her feeling despondent: she had just burnt her mother's unpublished novels. Vaughan never claimed the novels had any literary merit, but she was sad for Madge and angry with her father. Typically, however, she soon focused instead on preparations for her planned trip to the United States.[4]

Local and national politics

Once retired from her Somerville post, Vaughan was free to work for the Labour Party in Oxford, and was chairman of the Wolvercote ward for a number of years. In 1973 she stood for a local council seat, where she 'didn't do well though I defeated the Liberal. The Conservative romped home about 1,400 compared to my 595. Still I had a lot of fun learnt a lot & made many new friends.' There was celebration in autumn 1974, after the second Labour general election victory of that year, when Cilla was well: 'We both worked very hard over the election & got our Labour candidate in – a marginal seat ... You should have seen me ... with a ladder & a young man putting up posters – the first time the Woodstock Road has ever had a Labour poster!!'[5]

When Ted Heath's Conservative government took Britain into the European Community in 1973, the Labour Party was deeply divided on the issue. For the referendum in 1975, Vaughan supported the Keep Britain in Europe campaign, speaking alongside Conservatives and Liberals of the same persuasion: 'We have a shop ... where we sell Tee Shirts ... etc. I go round & talk in Village Halls, stick up posters ... It is all rather fun. I think Oxford ... will vote to stay in.' She had little special knowledge on the subject, mainly expressing her conviction that Britain could not survive as 'a little offshore island'.[6] Being part of a campaign must have brought back memories of the 1930s.

The emergence of Margaret Thatcher as Conservative leader in 1975 did not please her. Although Thatcher had studied chemistry at Somerville, she lacked the warmth and humanity of Shirley Williams, her Labour rival who Vaughan always hoped would rise to the highest office. It was Thatcher, however, who in 1979 became prime minister. She attended the Somerville centenary Gaudy that summer, sitting with Vaughan and Hodgkin in the garden and discussing plutonium in the context of the nuclear power programme. Vaughan found her 'a ruthless but able woman – frightening in her certainty of her goals'.[7] She did comply, however, when Thatcher requested a briefing on the potential effects of plutonium on workers in the nuclear industry. Her friend from undergraduate days, Evelyn Irons, who was staying for a few days, helped pack up the document for the post.[8]

For her the political front became ever gloomier after that, with the Labour Party in disarray after the election of the unilateralist and anti-EU Michael Foot as leader in 1980. Vaughan still believed in the European project and also the need for a nuclear deterrent, but 'oh how I hate Margaret Thatcher & her government – destroying the Welfare State I & my friends have given our lives to building'. At the primary school where she was a governor, 'we all cut & cut … We fought hard & for the time have saved our nursery school but we have lost our school bus.'[9] After Shirley Williams helped set up the new Social Democratic Party (SDP) the following year, Vaughan very reluctantly joined it. Some time after 1983, however, when Neil Kinnock became Labour leader and it was clear the SDP was not offering a viable alternative, she decided she must rejoin and work for the Labour Party '& not just sit wringing my hands as I do at the moment'.[10] She rejoiced in Kinnock's fighting speech to the 1985 party conference, and looked forward to further action.[11]

Her hatred of Conservative government policies was completely understandable and, with hindsight, prescient. Thatcher's hostility to what she saw as vested interests included the universities as well as trade unions, and her belief in the beneficence of market forces led to their attempted introduction into the health service and higher education, as well as to denationalisation of the utilities, even including water. Vaughan and many of her peers saw the reversal of every principle which had inspired their own actions and the causes they had fought for. Her American friends' letters in these years show that they felt as bitter about President Reagan's economic policies.

She expressed her feelings about the NHS in her memoir:

When I remember what we started with in the way of buildings and trained personnel … the vested interests and prejudices that had to be overcome, the enormous imagination [involved] in planning an entirely new and … technical service to serve the whole nation … I am amazed … at what has been achieved. I only wish there were films … of the casualty departments, the country operating theatres, the old mental hospitals …. and that we had a count of the number of babies and small children who died because their parents couldn't afford a doctor's fee.… [Failings still existed in the 1970s, but] medical care is available to every man, woman and child without individual payment; a mother can expect to see her children grow up and give her grandchildren ...[12]

In the 1970s, the Royal College of Physicians (RCP) had urged a greater say for doctors in health service administration, and a non-political head of the service, to shorten lines of command and escape from short-termism. This approach was rejected by the 1980s Thatcher government, with its devotion to 'business management' ideas. In 1983 the leading endocrinologist Sir Raymond Hoffenberg was elected president of the RCP, and he became president of Oxford's Wolfson College in 1985. Vaughan and he were kindred spirits. A forthright thinker and campaigner (he had left South Africa in 1967 when his anti-apartheid activities began to make life dangerous for him and his family), he wrote in 1987 that doctors were best placed 'to shift the emphasis of managerial enquiry from ... resources and costs to health outcomes and patient satisfaction. For this reason alone medical participation in management is imperative.'[13] When in 1988 the government chose instead to introduce the concept of the internal market to the health service, he was scathing in his contempt.

Vaughan made one last campaigning speech on 5 October 1985, at the unveiling of a memorial on London's South Bank to British members of the International Brigades who had fought in Spain in the 1930s. After recalling some of her Spanish Medical Aid colleagues and friends, including Isabel Brown, Leah Manning, Audrey Russell, Richard Ellis and Julian Bell, she urged her audience to fight 'for our democratic rights, for our social services, for our health service, for our children's right to full education and full employment. We can say as the Brigades said in 1936 No pasarán.'[14] Many of those listening were moved to tears.[15]

Somerville links

Vaughan tried not to encroach on her successors' territory at Somerville, but naturally took a close interest in college affairs. In January 1969 she was guest at a dinner held to celebrate the granting to her of a University of London honorary degree, when Hodgkin made the congratulatory speech, and she attended many similar events honouring others over the years. From 1973 she was president of the ASM, and went on to organise the appeal for the

1979 college centenary. As in the local Labour Party, she 'mucked in' with tasks like addressing envelopes and making tea, as well as making any necessary speeches. Visiting old Somervillians were treated with the same keen interest, wise advice and if need be medical help as when they were in college. Vaughan was also indefatigable in supporting old colleagues who were in poor health – usually by delivering meals to the doorstep or treats of alcohol, chocolates and flowers to those in care homes or hospital. Still an early riser, she would use that extra time to do cooking and jam or cake making, before going to the science library to read the latest articles. Enid Starkie said in the last year of her life that she 'owed everything' to Vaughan, who visited her constantly at her house and saw that she got enough to eat.[16]

A faithful friend, she visited or hosted those living at a distance, and offered support in times of trouble. Janet Adam Smith remembered particularly that when her husband had a major operation for cancer in spring 1973, Vaughan was keen to know who the surgeon was, at which hospital and so on, offering by phone 'the reassurance of a professional, which counted a lot'. When the cancer recurred 18 months later, she helped in practical ways, such as sending a case of quarter bottles of champagne so that he could have a glass every day after coming home for the last fortnight: 'it was so like her to think of something practical'.[17]

Family and friends
Financial worries

Vaughan always remained true to the attitude to money that she and Gourlay had embodied, and taught their children. At one point she sent her daughter Mary a copy of a poem by Alice Walker which she felt encapsulated that view. Titled 'We alone', it began

> We alone can devalue gold
> by not caring
> if it falls or rises
> in the marketplace.
> Wherever there is gold
> there is a chain, you know,
> and if your chain
> is gold

so much the worse
for you.[18]

Mary passed the lesson on to her children, and joked that as adults they reproached her for failing to encourage them out of the arts and into more lucrative occupations.

Vaughan was inordinately proud of these grandchildren, supporting all of them in their mainly musical, literary and artistic interests. In 1975, when James, the eldest, was soon to come up to Oxford, Gavin walked out of the family home to live with a younger partner. Mary was heartbroken, and Vaughan furious on behalf of her and the children. Mary was made of strong stuff, however. She went on to support the family through her pottery, supplemented by rent from lodgers, and paid the money needed to buy Gavin's share of the house. Vaughan gave interim help in the form of a loan (as Mary insisted it should be), and gifts to the children for needs such as travel and music lessons. The inflation of the 1970s peaked at 27% in 1975, but by then she had the income from two books, and in May that year took Cilla out to dinner to celebrate the 'fat fee' received for her first legal case on behalf of workers in the nuclear industry.[19]

Cilla was at the time working in a bookshop when well, but her mother had good reason to be grateful for the legal work. Her daughter was in and out of hospital in these years, usually coming home for weekends, when Vaughan in 1976 found it 'like living with a ghost'. In that year, while she was in Carlisle giving evidence in a court case, Cilla escaped from hospital and took an overdose. Vaughan was also conscious of the stress Mary was under after Gavin's departure, and worried about the grandchildren. In November Cilla had a bad relapse: 'when she is bad there is so little one can do to help & heaven knows what will happen when I am gone'. It was impossible to plan with safety to have friends to the house, and Vaughan longed for their company, and talk of books and politics.[20]

The following year was little better and she could not get away for a holiday, 'but fortunately I have had so much work to do on [legal] cases … I enjoy the good lawyers with their acute minds & it is fun in one's old age to be an expert witness.'[21] She looked forward to a break in Tunisia with Amabel Williams-Ellis in March

1978, but in the event Amabel had to drop out after breaking her hip. Vaughan decided to go alone, taking Proust's *In Search of Lost Time*, which she had long meant to read. After enjoying the Roman mosaics in the Tunis museum she abandoned the tour party and, finding the museum at Sousse closed, claimed to have read the entire novel while lying on the beach soaking up vitamin D. This was a rare excursion into novel-reading, so quite a tribute to Proust.[22]

In July 1980 she took drastic action to improve her finances, enlisting John Vaughan's help to sell several William Blake drawings and a watercolour by Edward Lear, all inherited from Madge. She raised enough money for a new Mini car in August, at nearly £2,700, and may also have increased her investment income.[23]

Mentoring

Vaughan was still ready with advice for younger women, as when she gave lunch to an ex-Somervillian who was teaching in another Oxford college, and had just had her first child. She was worried about her depressive husband, and feeling guilty about working full time now that she had a baby. Vaughan passed on advice from one of her own peers that this, though even less conventional in her own day, gave a good example to students. Learning that the family doctor thought the young woman's success as an academic must undermine her husband's self-esteem, Vaughan said that a psychiatrist had blamed her for Cilla's problems: there was no clear answer on this but one needed to reckon with that kind of reaction. Her guest felt strengthened and reassured.[24]

Joan Crouch helped revive the North Oxford Labour Party branch, and so met Vaughan, soon after coming to Oxford at the end of 1970. She worked in the local authority education department, and Vaughan befriended her when she was expecting her first child. Her husband worked in London, so Vaughan drove her to hospital for the birth, made her two nightdresses she had designed for breast feeding, and brought gifts of nourishing food after she came home. Once Crouch was back at work, she regularly gave her lunch in mid-week, saying she had 'all the time in the world apart from looking after my old ladies'. Talking through new job possibilities and current problems, she asked rigorous questions which enabled Crouch to work out her own solutions. Vaughan stressed the importance of wearing stylish clothes, so that male colleagues would take her seriously, and was completely up to date with issues then relevant to young families. She read voraciously, always serious books about politics and international affairs, and biographies. If Crouch ever doubted her own abilities, Vaughan would say 'Of course you can do it!', and she would emerge feeling able to take on the world. Only later did she realise that this same nurturing had been available to hundreds of Somervillians from 1945 onwards.[25]

When a new young head, Anne Nelson, arrived at Wolvercote Primary School in the mid-1970s, Vaughan introduced her to Crouch so that she would have another mentor. As chair of school governors, she would provide a stiff gin in the evening when they discussed school business and, if Nelson was under strain, invite her to have supper and stay the night at the weekend. She gave her tips about what she would need to know when – not if – she took on a national role, including 'always having something on the drawing board', in case a useful pot of money turned up. Seeing education as a means to open up opportunities, she wanted to see the children's work, hear about how teachers were being helped to develop, and find out about the latest educational research. She once paid for a child from a poor family to go on a residential visit to Swanage, as well as driving down herself to see the whole party.

Always conscious of time, if she needed to raise something with a local authority officer, she would summon them to her house, saying that she didn't sit knitting (a favourite phrase), so they must say exactly when they were coming and she would have the tea or coffee ready. As the official walked away afterwards, she would stand at the gate waving her walking stick benignly in farewell.[26]

During the late seventies and early eighties, encroaching arthritis in her knee and ankle made gardening difficult and caused her to take huge tablets ('like horse pills', according to James Park), as well as sitting in the sun to soak up vitamin D for the sake of good bone health. She still walked at what Graves Taylor called a 'hurtling hobble', however, and kept up her former pace and time management. One Somerville don who went to lunch occasionally on college business noticed that, while she never felt rushed, the time lapse between entering and leaving the house was exactly one hour.[27]

Worsening health and cause for grief

As the 1980s advanced, the worst aspect of ageing, for Vaughan, was increasing deafness – a particularly cruel affliction for someone who loved 'good talk' and took so much joy in social gatherings. Nelson found that conversation became increasingly difficult, and when she left for a new job in 1983, Vaughan gave deafness as her reason for resigning from the governing body. Nonetheless the head of the Oxford High School, where she was also a governor, remembered sitting next to her at a special dinner in 1984. Vaughan had one leg in a brace, but still said how lucky she was compared with most contemporaries, physically and especially mentally.[28]

Illness and death were stalking more and more of her friends. By the end of the seventies Starkie, Bowra, Cobbe, Molly Hoyle and Minot's wife Marion were gone, while others were in nursing homes of varying quality. She was much saddened by her brother David's death in July 1982, describing him as 'a very delightful human being but we disagreed about everything as he was … a Tory of the deepest dye. Still there was a real affection between us.'[29] She was glad for him, however: his poor diet meant that he developed osteoporosis in his last years, and was miserable because he could not pursue the country sports he loved.

The following year, 1983, proved especially stressful. Mary heard in January that Gavin Park was terminally ill; but she and the children were able to care for him in the final stages of his illness, so there was a sense of reconciliation in the family. Vaughan could not go to her immediately after his death in June, as Tom and Jean Griffiths were arriving for their annual stay. The next morning, she believed she was having a heart attack and lay still until the afternoon, leaving her guests to their own devices and abandoning all idea of going to London. Alarmed, she wrote to her nephew John with instructions in case of her death. It was perhaps the first occurrence of the 'occasional cardiac irregularity' noted on a car insurance application a few years later.[30]

At Christmas that year, her friend Polly Forde, Daryll's wife, was nearing death, and Vaughan explained to Mary what a blow this was:

> [Polly] belonged to my past with David and Plovers Field. She knew all the people I & David knew. Ever since David died she gave me a home & a welcome & cared about me & my life as no one else did. I have lots of friends but none of them belong to past happiness. I was stupid on the telephone because I had one of my dotty old ladies to lunch. Her 'meals on wheels' don't come on Wednesday & so she wanders here … It is better to go like Gavin & Polly when one is still at work & still oneself so one must not mourn for them – only for oneself.[31]

Polly died in early January 1984.

A few months later Halford died after a fall. Thanks to his recurrent depressive illness and his political views, they had not been close; but he was the last of Vaughan's birth family, and his loss must have made her feel even more alone. She still admired and sympathised with his wife Dorothy, however, and saw a good deal of her in the years that followed.

In this same year, she had a recurrence of the excessive bleeding which had afflicted her after Gourlay's death in 1963; but she now knew more about it, telling her American friend Lisco that she had over a period of about 40 years had 'completely unexplained haemorrhages from both the gut & the kidney – which in spite of expert … investigation remain unexplained. No pain – no warning of onset … & as I have survived to be 84 I am very philosophical about them – & feel lucky to have fallen into the hands of Weatherall. He just happened to be [at the hospital] when my ambulance arrived.'[32] David Weatherall was Nuffield professor of medicine, having come to Oxford from the Nuffield Unit of Medical Genetics in Liverpool.

Accentuating the positive
Vaughan still sought out and enjoyed stimulating sights, people and events, including at Mary's fiftieth birthday party in November 1982, when she didn't know which she enjoyed most,

the film or the wine bar or the dinner party, or as a final bonus the lights of Oxford St … very nostalgic to be … in my old haunts of T Ct Rd & Soho … I felt very proud of my grandchildren. Thank you very very much for being such a perfect lot. Love from Granny.[33]

She must have been disappointed when none of those grandchildren became a scientist, but she believed in people following their talents, as they did: James as a writer, Vanessa a professional cellist, Henrietta a shoe and then clothes designer, and Benjamin a musician and composer. Gavin's memorial service in October 1983 was again a happy occasion, with St James's Church, Piccadilly full of family friends, a beautiful service and then a big party at the Arts Club. Mary had decorated the church, and looked 'incredibly beautiful'.[34]

Nature and new life consoled too. Her friends might be ill, and old age tragic, 'but my crocuses are splendid when the sun comes out & I am to have a second great grandchild'.[35] She still had good friends to visit, including Amabel, telling Lisco in 1984 that she was going to Wales to stay in a house looking out on Snowdon with an old lady of 90 who had all her wits about her and was good, though exhausting company.

November 1983 had brought the stimulus and excitement of two days' filming in the flat by the BBC. The hour-long interview about her life was one of six, broadcast the following autumn as *Women of Our Century*, accompanied by a book of the same title. There was also a radio interview, and a repeat of the television broadcast followed in 1988. These things provided a useful boost to her income. The interview covered the most dramatic events of her life, focusing on Bloomsbury, haematology and radiation research, campaigning against poverty and malnutrition, the Spanish Civil War, blood transfusion, Belsen and the coming of the NHS.

One of the many who watched that interview and were fascinated by Vaughan and her story was the artist Victoria (Vicky) Crowe, who lived near Vaughan's niece Ann in the Scottish borders. Not knowing of the relationship at first, she exclaimed that she would love to paint this woman's portrait. Ann wrote to Vaughan, who said she would be delighted. The sittings took place over five or six days in February 1986. When Crowe was greeted by Vaughan at Oxford station, she noticed her big hawk-like nose and headscarf, 'pan-stick' makeup and bright red lipstick. Both hearing aids were disturbed by the headscarf and the batteries were 'screaming', so Vaughan failed to hear the gears screeching while driving at a furious pace in the yellow Mini through this city Crowe had never visited before. She stayed with friends nearby, with sittings lasting from 9am or 9.30am till lunchtime, after which Vaughan did her own work in the afternoon. They met again each evening for a sociable gin and tonic.

During the sittings she reminisced to Crowe about the past, saying of Belsen how distressed she was to be unable to join in the general medical relief effort, and that she never let her husband wear striped pyjamas again. The horror she had felt was visible in her eyes, as it had been during the television interview. She also talked of the 'curse' of what she called manic depression in her family: Cilla was quite ill at that time. Conversation over gin in the evenings was by contrast relaxed and light-hearted. When the sittings were over, Vaughan showed Crowe and her husband around Somerville, of which she was clearly still proud and fond. She cooked dinner for them, and opened a 30-year-old wine which had been laid down and carefully labelled by Gourlay.[36]

Last years: 1985–93

A move from house to flat

Vaughan had a watershed moment at the beginning of 1985, when she decided to sell the house and move to a small two-bedroom flat nearby. She was increasingly conscious of her own failing health, the income from books and legal cases had more or less ceased, and she could only just keep herself and Cilla – who was now as she said unemployable – on her pensions. The flat was in Cilla's name, and she knew the cleaning lady and her husband would continue to work and look out for Cilla if Vaughan died. Friends were impressed by her swift decision-making about disposal of property to family, friends and archives as appropriate, but the move was extremely stressful. In June, when it was over, she told Bill Castle, 'Don't you move house. It is most traumatic – destructive of 6 months of life – when one sits in a sort of vacuum unable to find any relevant papers or do any work.' She claimed to be content now that she had her books to hand and could entertain friends with her own belongings around her, with a view over Port Meadow to the hills beyond. Inevitably, however, she missed her garden and having space to put up friends and family.[37]

In 1986 she still spent mornings in the library, trying to keep up with the rapid advance of research in her field. Cilla was working as a volunteer for a charity Vaughan called Victims Relief, 'an interesting & useful organization but it does not keep her really busy'.[38] She spoke more freely to Graves Taylor, saying that at times she woke in the night to find Cilla in the living room weeping and wringing her hands, and that living with her was like living with a zombie. Against this must be set her dedication to Cilla's welfare, and the fact that when in 1993 she lay dying in hospital, she kept asking to go home to look after her daughter.[39]

Daily life became more constricted after the move to the flat, with increasing deafness and lameness; but she insisted on using the stairs despite her leg braces ('use it or lose it' was the mantra), and kept open house for old friends and colleagues. In some ways Graves Taylor filled the gap left by Gourlay. At supper or over lunch in each other's flats, they talked 'ceaselessly – of clothes, politics, education, paintings, ourselves, books; above all, books'. Drink always flowed, quite often sherry as well as wine, Vaughan talked about her beloved Italy, and they sometimes had quoting conversations, featuring Housman, Donne, Keats, Tennyson and Browning among others. They both loved striking clothes. In Vaughan's more active days, she would suddenly announce that her clothes were 'Rags. I'm going to Henrietta's in Woodstock to buy something Dashing.' She was equally interested in Taylor's wardrobe, once calling at her flat to inspect a new scarlet duffle coat, which received an 'approving exclamation'.[40]

She would say 'I must go and visit my old crocks', often of people a decade younger than herself, complaining that they would insist on talking about the past; she looked forward, not back, and envied Graves Taylor for the fact that she would know what happened at the end of the century. Matter-of-fact about her own decline, she once said when going to the dentist that she had put him off for months in case she died. Her driving was as alarming as ever. '"I am not fond of your walking around Oxford in the dark," she shouted one evening, as we lurched and jolted down the middle of Woodstock Road, the gears … crashing, indicators flashing in the rain.' Her departures were still abrupt, like her suddenness on the phone: 'there would be no slowing down … no farewell, just a sudden slamming down of the telephone'.

In June 1987, after suffering a fall, she wrote to her nephew John about 'Cilla's future when I go'. She had been assured that the income from investments would enable Cilla to live in the flat as she wished, with friends in Oxford and the cleaning lady helping out. Cilla was going regularly to Warneford Hospital, was heavily medicated and slept a great deal. In August, the Mini failed its MOT, and Mary opened an account for her mother with an Oxford taxi firm. She was gently rebuffed, however, on the ground that Cilla loved to drive for long-distance trips and Vaughan could manage local driving.[41]

Reaching 90

A year or so later she appeared on television again, when Esther Rantzen was the subject of *This is Your Life*, and Vaughan was thrilled to meet the surgeon responsible for pioneering liver transplants. 'We drank gin together at a splendid party … I may be lame & deaf & stupid but I do get a lot of fun out of life.'[42] In 1989 Rantzen wrote on Vaughan's ninetieth birthday to say how important her encouragement had been, 'from the early years when I was 'ground down' by the BBC, to our recent work to create Childline. But you have always made me feel that it was worth aiming high, and that failure could be overcome.'[43]

Vaughan loved that birthday, not only for the flowers, champagne and visitors but for an 'enormous sense of affection from people all over the world – old students from Somerville & from the lab going back even further to my own student days. How lucky I have been … nothing can take away the sense of affection.'[44] Some of the champagne came from Somerville, where a Judas tree, one of her favourite trees, was planted in her honour. There was more joy when the Berlin Wall came down in November, followed by the overthrow of communist rule in Czechoslovakia and installation of the liberal Vaclav Havel as president.

In December she was as usual planning what wine and food to bring as her contribution to Christmas at Mary's house, though impeded by a cut leg which had to be kept up so that it would heal; the main drawback for her being that she could not go to the library. The leg healed, but news of her cousin Kitty's death was a sadness, since this severed the last link with her own childhood. She took it stoically, and letters to Janet Adam Smith reveal that she had not lost her old sharpness. Thanking her for a newspaper piece about Kitty, she went on to say: 'You are much in my thoughts as I read the life of Ackerley ... strange book. There is a good book to be written about homosexuals of our generation. This isn't it'. In another letter: 'Yes Kitty West – what a lot of one's past – recently I have had no real contact with her [Kitty had been happily living in a retirement home run by nuns] but at one time ... we were very close ... but how exciting the changing political world. I live for Radio 4 & wonder about my communist friends of the past.'[45] She asked Mary for Denis Healey's autobiography for Christmas.

Vaughan was now in rapid decline, however. She sent Hodgkin her love and good wishes for her eightieth birthday in May 1990: 'Alas I am too deaf & too lame for party going but I look back to happy days in the Somerville SCR when you used to ... give us the latest news from USA computers about Vitamin B12 & ... your battles with Oxford University to provide you with computers here at home.' In June she declined an invitation to the Wolfson College Foundation Dinner: 'I would love to come. I have the happiest memories of early battles ... but I am very deaf & very lame & am no good as a guest.' And not long afterwards, when her grandson James was coming: 'I should warn you that I have become senile as well as deaf so don't expect any sensible conversation. Cilla is very kind to me.'[46]

Shortly before her last visit to Graves Taylor, she announced that she was becoming infirm. 'It's extremely tiresome, Charlotte, but I am afraid ... we must get used to it.' When she came, 'she wore black. Gaunt and graceful, tall and tired, she had a crumpled elegance. She was as vital as ever; but ... untypically full of reminiscence – about David, the war, Somerville, her parents ... dead friends.' Once she recognised the impossibility of going out in future, she blessed the windows of her flat which allowed her to see trees and the sky. Often after that, she would say, 'Charlotte, I am so lucky. Look at the trees.'[47]

At some point she decided that she would prefer not to live until her ninety-first birthday. Years before, she had told Graves Taylor that she had had a wonderful life, but wanted to be in control. If she felt she was losing that, she had the means to end it. 'But not a word to Mary or Cilla.'[48] Her final will was executed on 5 August 1990. When told in that month of Castle's death, she said how lucky she was to have known him and that she would send his letters to the Countway Library to join those of Minot.[49]

Soon afterwards, she took the dose designed to end her life; but for once was thwarted. Cilla heard her fall and she was rushed to hospital, still aware enough to remove a drip, but medical staff replaced it. In the remaining time before she died, in January 1993, her mind gradually buckled, although she had some periods of lucidity up till the end. For much of the time she lived in a fantasy world, looked after by Cilla; but was horrendously upset by the television images of prisoners taken during the war in Bosnia, some of which were all too reminiscent of Belsen.[50] Vicky Crowe visited them from time to time, up to about six months before she died, when Vaughan was very confused. She felt that 'something began to balance out for Cilla', now that she could care for her mother rather than the other way round.

Vaughan's death was attributed to bronchopneumonia, ischaemic heart disease and cerebrovascular disease (bleeding in the brain). She retained to the end some appreciation of her own state. Angry to be still alive, she would spit out the pills the nurses gave her in hospital. That anger, combined with fierce sarcasm, could inflict considerable pain on her family, who also had to look on at her suffering. It was in many ways a relief to them when she died, and Cilla in particular found new happiness and better health in the years that followed. Griffiths kept in close touch, as Vaughan had wished, and after his wife Jean died Cilla reciprocated his care by driving him to see particular friends and favourite places.[51]

The family buried Vaughan's ashes with Gourlay in the hilltop graveyard of St Martha's.

Coda: the late portrait

Vicky Crowe wanted to make a record of this woman who had done such extraordinary things and was so articulate and strong, although so elderly. She found the combination of the artistic and the scientific in her intriguing. Vaughan told her that her father was very much a scientific thinker, and her mother 'the arty one'. She found the flat very feminine with its pink lustre ware and the Thornton prints which, though scientific in their careful recording of species, had to Crowe's eye mysterious and erotic overtones: very visual and romantic.

For the portrait, they moved books around and made sure Madge's portrait and the Gordine sculpture on the mantelpiece were included, as well as the Thornton print because Crowe liked it. She included the candlestick on the mantelpiece as a more masculine image, its slight lean to the right balancing the leftward slant of the tree outside the window. Vaughan wore the same rather threadbare jacket as in the television interview, and a pendant which evoked for her the Spanish Civil War. Because of her arthritis, cushions were arranged carefully on the sofa to provide support. All of the interior was an attempt to indicate the worlds of science and art which came together in Vaughan's family, and to echo the male and female forces in her life and personality.

The book titles in the picture reference Vanessa Bell and Virginia Woolf, the Strachey family and her father's great-aunt Julia Margaret Cameron, the pioneering Victorian photographer. Beside her the photographs of bone, offprint of a recent article and book on plutonium represent her post-war research field. Of some details Crowe was unaware: the jacket had belonged to Vaughan's aunt Katharine Furse, and the bright silk scarf was most likely a present from Gourlay. The Thornton print is a reminder of her early interest in botany and the stone in the pendant, which she had bought two years before, came from the Jarama valley battlefield in Spain. The ring she wore was that given to her when she retired from Somerville, while the Gordine figurine of a laughing nude woman recalls pre-war bohemian life in London and Paris, and the Wayfarers travel agency.

Vaughan liked the portrait very much, and later told Crowe that she had a sense of friendship and understanding with her that she had with few other people: 'you found in my face so much that most people never see in me & you saw it & expressed it' in such a short time.[52] Crowe believed she meant by this a certain vulnerability and slight hesitance, which she attributed to her deafness. She found Vaughan strong, decisive and intellectual, but also 'so approachable and maybe age had brought with it that confidence to question where you are at and to be unsure occasionally!'[53]

Vaughan's expression also suggests both the ability to weigh up and judge, and an element of the resignation which comes with age and experience. Her upright pose and the tailored jacket convey authority and dignity, and alertness of mind and spirit. There is still a sense of vigour and imminent activity, while the cup and saucer on the table and open, slightly smiling look suggest welcome for a guest, and curiosity to hear their news. Her eyes have an unfathomable sadness, reflective of the Belsen experience and also perhaps that of the woman deprived of her life partner and blamed by some for her daughter's illness.

The portrait captures many of the key elements of a multi-faceted life, but much is necessarily omitted. Vaughan herself was conscious of how fragmented her life had been because of her compulsion to act wherever she felt qualified to help. This is the import of the poem in the Appendix, which she thought of as her epitaph. She would have been pleased by the judgement of Sir Raymond Hoffenberg, President of Wolfson College, who wrote when she died that

> As a physician, I was especially aware of the vast contribution she had made not only to medical science but to the whole field of medicine. She was unquestionably one of the great figures in medicine of this century, and the College was proud to rank her amongst our Hon Fellows.[54]

Other tributes poured in, but she would have been most touched by those who, like two old Somervillians, called her simply 'a great human being'.[55]

Endnotes

[1] Interview with Diana Reynell. Reynell was convinced she never dyed her hair.

[2] OBL, Griffiths Diaries, Vol 79: entry for 21.8.1967. And JPP, Vaughan to Jean Griffiths, 22.8.1967.

[3] JPP, Vaughan to Davidson at the Warneford Hospital, 19.2.1969.

[4] Interview with Charlotte Graves Taylor, 22.11.2006. Graves Taylor taught English at Westminster College in London from 1970.

[5] JPP, Vaughan to Griffiths, 17.4.1973 and 19.10.1974.

[6] JPP, Vaughan to James Park, 1.5 and 16.5.1975.

[7] HMLC Castle, Vaughan to Castle, 14.8.1979.

[8] Irons in Adams, *A Memorial Tribute*, 12.

[9] JPP, Vaughan to Jean Griffiths, 22.10.1980.

[10] JPP, Vaughan to Prue Smith [undated, 1980s].

[11] Joan Crouch, in Adams, *A Memorial Tribute*, 27.

[12] JA, 135–36.

[13] This quote and background in this paragraph from Asa Briggs, *A History of the Royal College of Physicians Vol 4* (Oxford University Press, 2005), 1258 ff.

[14] JPP, notes for the speech in Vaughan's file on 'Spain'. 'No pasarán' means 'they shall not pass'.

[15] JPP, Vaughan's 'Spain' file, letter Jim Jump to Vaughan, 10.10.1985.

[16] Evelyn Irons letter in Obituary of Dame Janet Vaughan, *The Independent* (12.1.1993), 25.

[17] JPP, interview with Janet Adam Smith.

[18] Alice Walker, *Collected Poems* (London, Weidenfeld and Nicolson), 2005, 329.

[19] JPP, Vaughan to James Park, 16.5.1975.

[20] JPP, Vaughan letters to Prue Smith, 1976.

[21] JPP, Vaughan to Prue Smith, 27.12.1977.

[22] JPP, postcard to James Park, 9.3.1978.

[23] JPP, report from John Vaughan on valuations of items for sale, 23.7.1980. There is no record of the amount raised, but it was potentially between £14,000 and £22,000.

[24] Interview with Janet Howarth.

[25] Joan Crouch, in Adams, *A Memorial Tribute*, 26–27.

[26] Interview with Anne Nelson, 12.12.2006. Nelson was by then Chief Executive of the Association for Early Childhood Education.

[27] Information from Pauline Adams.

[28] Interview with Joan Townsend, 12.1.2007.

[29] JPP, Vaughan to Jean Griffiths, summer [undated] 1982.

[30] JPP, Vaughan to Griffiths, 27.6.1983; and copy of insurance application.

[31] JPP, Vaughan to Mary Park, December [undated] 1983.

[32] HMLC Lisco, Vaughan to Lisco, 1.8.1984.

[33] JPP, Vaughan to James Park, 29.11.1982.

[34] JPP, Vaughan to Vanessa Park, 16.10.1983.

[35] JPP, Vaughan to Jean Griffiths, 15.4.1983. Vanessa had her first baby, Daniel, in 1982 and was expecting her second.

[36] These paragraphs based on interview with Victoria Crowe, 10.6.2000.

37 HMLC Castle, Vaughan to Castle, 18.6.1985.

38 JPP, Vaughan to Jean Griffiths, 28.3.1986.

39 JPP, interview with Mary Park.

40 This and following paragraph based on an account by Graves Taylor in Adams, *A Memorial Tribute*, 28–31.

41 JPP, Vaughan to John Vaughan, 11.6.1987; and Vaughan to Mary Park, 22.8.1987.

42 JPP, Vaughan to Mary Park, 23.11.1988.

43 JPP, Rantzen to Vaughan, 15.10.1989.

44 HMLC Lisco, Vaughan to Liscos, thanking them for the birthday telegram, [October] 1989.

45 Professor Andrew Dunlop Roberts (son of Janet Adam Smith) papers, Vaughan to Adam Smith, two letters sent in December 1989.

46 JPP, Vaughan to James Park, 27.6.1990.

47 Graves Taylor in Adams, *A Memorial Tribute*, 30.

48 Interview with Graves Taylor.

49 HMLC Lisco, Vaughan to Liscos, 22.8.1990.

50 Interview with Julia Aglionby (Vaughan's great-niece), 11.6.2000.

51 JPP, Griffiths to James Park, 22.7.1993. (Jean had died in 1991.)

52 Vaughan to Crowe, 11.10.1987. (Copy given to author.)

53 Crowe letter to the author, 3.7.2000.

54 JPP, Hoffenberg to Mary Park, 13.1.1993.

55 JPP. One was Jennifer M Taylor, writing to Vaughan on her ninetieth birthday in 1989; and the other Ann Dummett, who wrote to Cilla on 15.1.1993: 'She was a great Principal and, more rarely, a great human being.'

APPENDIX
Epitaph

Vaughan told Diana Reynell that she first heard this poem read by her headmistress at school, and that it should be her epitaph. She could not have thought it a great poem (or song, perhaps), but it is an arresting one. At its heart is the dichotomy between the beauty of the world and its harshness; the compulsion to act and the longing for rest; and the joy and the loneliness of the perpetual traveller and explorer. She must have felt, too, its relevance to Gourlay.

The Shoes of Wandering
On the nineteenth of October my lover he was born,
His mother's gossips brought him a pale rose and a thorn.
The thorn was strong, the rose was pale, but oh her scent was sweet,
And they bound the Shoes of Wandering upon my lover's feet.

They gave him eyes of hazel, that he might surely see
The canker in the rosebud, the Dryad in the tree.
They gave to him an apple and said 'thou shalt not eat,'
And they brought the Shoes of Wandering and bound them on his
    feet.

They gave him slender fingers, more quick to pluck than keep.
They blew off from his eyelids the dreary walls of sleep.
'Dream when you wake,' they bade him, 'Say farewell when you
    meet,'
And they bound the Shoes of Wandering on his reluctant feet.

With their unlucky wisdom he reads the book of life,
And he is one with beauty, and all his soul's at strife
With weariness and languor, and yet his days are sweet
That he wears the Shoes of Wandering bound fast upon his feet.
(Anon.)

Select Bibliography

Primary sources

Interviews
Unless otherwise stated, interviews are by the author.

Archival sources
Archives Imperial College London
Beinecke Rare Book and Manuscript Library, Yale University
Berkshire Record Office
British Library
British Motor Industry Heritage Trust
British Postal Museum and Archive
Centre for Buckinghamshire Studies
Charleston Trust Archive, Lewes, East Sussex.
Clifton College Library, Bristol
Collections of the Royal Society
Companies House Archives
Dorich House Museum, Kingston University
Gloucestershire Archives
Hampshire County Record Office
Harvard Medical Library Collection, Center for the History of Medicine in the Francis A Countway Library, Harvard University.
Hull History Centre
Imperial War Museum Sound Archives
James Park papers and interviews
King's College Cambridge Modern Archives
Kingston History Centre
Leeds University Libraries Special Collections
Library of the Society of Friends
London Metropolitan Archives
Marx Memorial Library
Modern Records Centre, University of Warwick
Northamptonshire Record Office
Nuffield College Oxford Library: Special Collections and Archives
Nuffield Foundation
Oxford, Bodleian Libraries
Oxfordshire History Centre
Radcliffe Science Library, Oxford
Rockefeller Archive Center
Royal College of Nursing

Royal College of Physicians Library
Royal College of Physicians Library and Oxford Brookes University, Wellcome Medical Sciences Video Archive
Royal London Hospital Archives
Rugby School Archives and Special Collections
Somerville College Archives
Surrey History Centre
The National Archives
Trinity College Cambridge Library: Special Collections and Archives
University of Bristol Library Special Collections
University College London Special Collections; and Records Office
University of Keele Special Collections and Archives
University of Sussex Special Collections at The Keep
Wellcome Trust: Wellcome Collection
Wellington College Archives
West Yorkshire Archive

Journals

Biographical Memoirs of Fellows of the Royal Society
British Journal of Haematology
British Journal of Ophthalmology
British Journal of Radiology (Br J Radiol)
Charleston Newsletters
Clinical Orthopaedics and Related Research
Heart
International Journal of Radiation Biology
International Review of Experimental Pathology
Journal of Modern History
Journal of Pathology and Bacteriology (J Path Bact)
Leukaemia Research
National Academy of Sciences, Biographical Memoirs
Nature
New England Journal of Medicine
Notes & Records of the Royal Society (Notes Rec R Soc)
Postgraduate Medical Journal
Proceedings of the Royal Society of Medicine (Proc R Soc Med)
Quarterly Journal of Medicine
Quarterly Journal of Microscopical Science
The British Journal of Experimental Pathology (Br J Exp Pathol)
The British Medical Journal (BMJ)
The Journal of Clinical Investigation
The Lancet

Select bibliography

The Newcastle Medical Journal
UCH Magazine

Newspapers
Daily Telegraph
Manchester Guardian
Sunday Times
Surrey Comet
The Independent
The Labour Leader (organ of the Independent Labour Party), *1912–1918*
The Observer
The Times
Tribunal (organ of the No-Conscription Fellowship), *1916–1919*

Unpublished sources

Abeysekera, Manel, statement about Vaughan sent to author with email dated 18.12.2006.

Bryant, Hilda (secretary to both Helen Darbishire and Vaughan), memoir in Somerville College Archives.

Fisher, H A L, lecture on Dr W W Vaughan, delivered at Princes Risborough on 21.10.1938, in James Park Papers.

Griffiths, Reverend Thomas Wailes, Diaries, in Oxford, Bodleian Libraries.

Harvey, Barbara, written account of Vaughan sent to author on 7.7.2001, with follow-up note giving small amendment on 9.7.2001.

Harvey, Julian (née McMaster), reminiscences recorded for the Association of Senior Members in 1997. Copy in Somerville College Archives.

Lascelles, Mary, memoir in Somerville College Archives.

Owen, Maureen, speech in 'appreciation' of Dame Janet Vaughan at the 1981 Gordon Conference. Copy given to the author by Owen.

Paine, Natalie, The relief mission at Bergen-Belsen concentration camp: the medical students' story (BSc dissertation, University of London, 2003), in Wellcome Collection.

Radcliffe House visitors' book, in possession of John Vaughan.

Sissons, Hubert A, Diaries, in possession of his daughter Mary Sissons-Joshi and her husband, Vijay Joshi.

Vaughan, Janet, draft piece on her Bloomsbury friends, perhaps for a talk, in James Park Papers.

Vaughan, Janet, 'Jogging Along' (1979). Ironically titled unpublished memoir. Copy given to the author by Mary Park. Other copies held by Somerville College Oxford and the Royal Society. The Royal Society copy is titled 'Jogging Along, or A Doctor Looks Back 1899-1978.' In it p. 156 replaces the previous 156-57, and criticises then-current threats to health and social services and education, especially in the universities.

Vaughan, J M, PRC 41 Protein Requirements Committee: report on the comparative value of hydrolysates, milk and serum in the treatment of starvation, based on observations made at Belsen Camp by C E Dent, Rosalind Pitt-Rivers and Janet Vaughan, in Wellcome Collection (GC/186/7).

Vaughan, W W, presidential address to the Modern Language Association, February 1915, and address as president of the Headmasters' Association, 5.1.1916, in James Park Papers.

Vaughan, W W, visitors' book, in possession of John Vaughan.

Main published work by Janet Vaughan referenced in the text (in date order)

A complete list of her scientific publications is held by the Royal Society.

Vaughan, J, Investigation of a series of cases of secondary anaemia treated with liver or liver extracts, in *The Lancet* (26.5.1928), 1(5462), 1063–66.

Harris, Kenneth E, Lewis, Thomas and Vaughan, Janet M, Haemoglobinuria and urticaria from cold occurring singly or in combination; observations referring especially to the mechanism of urticaria with some remarks upon Raynaud's Disease, in *Heart* (1929), 14, 305–37.

Vaughan, J M, Critical review: the liver treatment of anaemias, in *Quarterly Journal of Medicine* (1930), 23, 213–32.

Vaughan, Janet M, Muller, Gulli Lindh and Zetzel, Louis, The response of grain-fed pigeons to substances effective in pernicious anaemia, in *Br J Exp Pathol* (1930), 11(6), 456–68.

Vaughan, J, The value of liver in treatment, in *Proc R Soc Med* (May 1931), 24(7), 929–35.

Vaughan, Janet M and Muller, Gulli Lindh, The effect of liver and commercial liver extract on the body weight, red blood cells and reticulocytes of normal rats, in *The Journal of Clinical Investigation* (1932), 11(1), 129–32.

Vaughan, Janet, Anaemias due to a deficiency of the principle in liver which is effective in the treatment of Addisonian pernicious anaemia, in *Proc R Soc Med* (1934), 28(5), 15–18 (whole discussion pp. 9–20).

Vaughan, Janet M, *The Anaemias* (Oxford, Oxford University Press, 1934; and 2nd edition, 1936).

Price-Jones, C, Vaughan, Janet M and Goddard, Helen M, Haematological standards of healthy persons, in *J Pathol Bacteriol* (1935), 40, 503–19.

Vaughan, Janet, Leuco-erythroblastic anaemia, in *J Pathol Bacteriol* (1936), 42(3), 541–64.

Elliott, G A, Macfarlane, R G and Vaughan, J M, The use of stored blood for transfusion, in *The Lancet*, (19.2.1939), 1(6025), 384–87.

Select bibliography

Vaughan, J M and Harrison, C V, Leucoerythroblastic anaemia and myelosclerosis, in *J Pathol Bacteriol* (March, 1939), 48, 339–52.

Vaughan, Janet, Blood transfusion, in *BMJ* (6.5.1939), 1(4087), 933–36.

Vaughan, Janet M and Saifi, M F, Haemoglobin metabolism in chronic infections, in *J Pathol Bacteriol* (1939), 49(1), 69–82.

Vaughan, Janet M, The Medical Research Council Blood Transfusion Outfit as provided for the sectors and depots in London and the Home Counties, in *BMJ* (2.12.1939), 2(4117), 1084–85.

Brewer, H F, Maizels, M, Oliver, J O and Vaughan, J M, Transfusion of fresh and stored blood, in *BMJ* (13.7.1940), 2(4149), 48–53.

Vaughan, Janet M, Cecil Price-Jones (1863–1943), *The Lancet* (18.9.1943), 242(6264), 369, obituary.

Saifi, M F and Vaughan, Janet M, The anaemia associated with infection, in *J Pathol Bacteriol* (1944), 56(2), 189–97.

Spurling, Nancy, Shone, John and Vaughan, Janet, The incidence, incubation period, and symptomatology of homologous serum jaundice, in *BMJ* (21.9.1946), 2(4472), 409–12.

Vaughan, Janet, Thomson, Margot and Dyson, Mary, The blood picture and plasma protein level following injury, in *J Pathol Bacteriol* (1946), 58(4), 749–65.

Vaughan, Janet, Anaemia associated with trauma and sepsis, in *BMJ* (1948), 1(4540), 35–39.

Kidman, Barbara, Tutt, Margaret L and Vaughan, Janet, The retention and excretion of radioactive strontium and yttrium (Sr89, Sr90 and Y90) in the healthy rabbit, *J Pathol Bacteriol* (1950), 62(2), 209–27; and (1951) 63(2), 253–68.

Kidman, Barbara, Tutt, Margaret L and Vaughan, Janet, The retention of radioactive strontium and yttrium (Sr89, Sr90 and Y90) in pregnant and lactating rabbits and their offspring, *J Pathol Bacteriol* (1951), 63, 253–68.

Vaughan, J, Tutt, M and Kidman, B, The biological hazards of radioactive strontium, in A Haddow (Ed), *Biological Hazards of Atomic Energy* (Oxford, Clarendon Press, 1952), 145–70.

Vaughan, Janet M, Radiation injury to bone, in *Lectures on the Scientific Basis of Medicine, Vol 4* (London, Athlone Press, 1955), 196–223.

Vaughan, Janet M, The effects of radiation on bone, in Geoffrey H Bourne (Ed), *The Biochemistry and Physiology of Bone* (New York, Academic Press Inc, 1956), 729–65.

Hindmarsh, Margaret and Vaughan, Janet, The distribution of radium in certain bones from a man exposed to radium for thirty-four years, in C B Allsopp (Ed), *The Measurement of Body Radioactivity* (London, *Br J of Radiology*, 1957, Supplement 7), Papers read at a conference held at Leeds, 16–17 April, 1956, 71–80.

Bloomsbury, Belsen, Oxford

Lea, Lorna and Vaughan, Janet, The uptake of 35S in cortical bone, in *Quarterly Journal of Microscopical Science* (1957), 98, 369–75.

Hindmarsh, Margaret, Owen, Maureen, Vaughan, Janet, Lamerton, L F and Spiers, F W, The relative hazards of strontium 90 and radium 226, in *Br J Radiol* (1958), 31(370), 518–33.

Mole, R H, Pirie, Antoinette and Vaughan, Janet M, Differential distribution of radioactive strontium and yttrium in the tissues of the rabbit's eye, in *Nature* (21.3.1959), 183(4664), 802–807.

Vaughan, Dame Janet, The effect of radiation on the skeleton, in *The Newcastle Medical Journal* (1959), 25, 309–14.

Vaughan, Janet, Bone disease induced by radiation, in *International Review of Experimental Pathology* (1962), 1, 243–369.

Vaughan, Dame Janet, The training of the physician. The recruitment and medical training of men and women in England in 1964, in *New England Journal of Medicine* (6.8.1964), 271, 294–97. (Paper for a symposium, part of the Boston City Hospital Centennial Program commemorating the fortieth anniversary of the Thorndike Memorial Laboratory.)

Vaughan, Janet, Non-uniformity of radiation dose in space with special reference to radiological protection, in *International Journal of Radiation Biology* (1965), 9(6), 513–43.

Vaughan, Janet, Bleaney, Betty and Williamson, Margaret, The uptake of plutonium in bone marrow: a possible leukaemic risk, in *British Journal of Haematology* (1967), 13(1), 492–502.

Vaughan, Janet, The effects of skeletal irradiation, in *Clinical Orthopaedics and Related Research* (January–February, 1968), 56, 283–303.

Vaughan, Dame Janet, The future of postgraduate medical education, in Jill Gilliland and Ian Chalmers Francis (Eds), *The Scientific Basis of Medicine: Annual Reviews 1971* (British Postgraduate Medical Federation, The Athlone Press, University of London). First published in *The Lancet* (8.11.1969), 2(7628), 995–99.

Vaughan, Janet and Williamson, Margaret, 90Sr in the rabbit: the relative risks of osteosarcoma and squamous cell sarcoma, in Charles W Mays, Webster S S Jee, Ray D Lloyd, Betsy J Stover, Jean H Dougherty and Glenn N Taylor (Eds), *Delayed Effects of Bone-Seeking Radionuclides* (Salt Lake City, UT, University of Utah Press, 1969), 337–55.

Vaughan, Janet M, *The Physiology of Bone* (Oxford, Oxford University Press, 1970).

Bleaney, Betty and Vaughan, Janet, Distribution of 239Pu in the bone marrow and on the endosteal surfaces of the femur of adult rabbits following injection of 239Pu (NO3)4, in *Br J Radiol* (1.1.1971), 44, 67–73.

Loutit, J F and Vaughan, Janet M, The radiosensitive tissues in bone, in *Br J Radiol* (1.10.1971), 44(526), 815.

Select bibliography

Vaughan, Janet M, *The Effects of Irradiation on the Skeleton* (Oxford, Clarendon, 1973).

Vaughan, Janet in collaboration with Betty Bleaney and David M Taylor, Distribution, excretion and effects of plutonium as a bone-seeker, in H C Hodge, J N Stannard and J B Hursh, *Uranium-Plutonium Transplutonic Elements (Handbook of Experimental Pharmacology, New Series, 36)*, (Springer-Verlag Berlin, Heidelberg, New York, 1973), 349–450. Two further chapters by Vaughan are at 451–71; and 471–502.

Spiers, F W and Vaughan, Janet, Hazards of plutonium with special reference to the skeleton, in *Nature* (19.2.1976), 259(5544), 531–34.

Vaughan, Janet, Plutonium – a possible leukaemic risk, in Webster S S Jee (Ed), *The Health Effects of Plutonium and Radium*: *Proceedings of the Symposium Held at Sun Valley, Idaho, on October 6–9, 1975* (Salt Lake City, UT, J W Press, 1976).

Vaughan, Janet, Bone growth and modelling, in T L J Lawrence (Ed), *Growth in Animals*, (London, Butterworth, 1980).

Vaughan, Janet, Osteogenesis and haematopoiesis, in *The Lancet* (18.7.1981), 2(8238), 133–36.

Loutit, J F, Nisbet, N W, Marshall, M J and Vaughan, Janet M, Versatile stem cells in bone marrow, in *The Lancet* (13.11.1982), 2(8307), 1090–93.

Griffith, T P, Pirie, A and Vaughan, J, Possible cataractogenic effect of radionuclides deposited within the eye from the bloodstream, in *British Journal of Ophthalmology* (March 1985), 69(3), 219–27.

Vaughan, Janet, Some Bloomsbury memories, in *Charleston Newsletter* (September 1985), 12, 20–22.

Spiers, F W and Vaughan, Janet, The toxicity of the bone seeking radionuclides, in *Leukaemia Research* (1989), 13(5), 347–50.

Vaughan, Janet Maria, Honor Bridget Fell 22 May 1900 – 22 April 1986, in *Biographical Memoirs of Fellows of the Royal Society*, (1.12.1987), 33, 237–59.

Secondary sources

Abel-Smith, Brian, and Pinker, Robert, *The Hospitals, 1800–1948: A Study in Social Administration in England and Wales* (London, Heinemann, 1964).

Abir-Am, P G and Outram, D (Eds), *Uneasy Careers and Intimate Lives: Women in Science 1789–1979* (New Brunswick, Rutgers University Press, 1987).

Adams, Pauline, *Somerville for Women: An Oxford College, 1879–1993* (Oxford, Oxford University Press, 1996).

Adams, Pauline (Ed), *Janet Maria Vaughan 1899–1993. A Memorial Tribute* (Somerville College).

Addison, Paul, *The Road to 1945* (London, Jonathan Cape, 1975); *Now the War is Over* (London, Pimlico, 1995); and *No Turning Back* (Oxford, Oxford University Press, 2010).

Arnold, Lorna, *My Short Century. Memoirs of An Accidental Nuclear Historian* (London, Cumnor Hill Books, 2012).

Aspinall, Anthony, letter: The strange case of 'Bengal Famine gruel', *The Independent* (29.11.1993), https://www.independent.co.uk/voices/letter-the-strange-case-of-bengal-famine-gruel-1481737.html accessed 22.6.2023.

Beckett, F, *Enemy Within: The Rise and Fall of the British Communist Party* (London, Merlin Press, 1995).

Bell, Edward Allen, *A History of Giggleswick School, From its Foundation, 1499–1912* (Volume 3) (Leeds: R Jackson, 1912).

Bell, E Moberly, *Storming the Citadel: The Rise of the Woman Doctor* (London, Constable, 1953).

Bennett, Mary, *Who Was Dr Jackson? Two Calcutta Families: 1830–1855* (London, BACSA, 2002).

Bill, E G W, *University Reform in Nineteenth-Century Oxford: A Study of Henry Halford Vaughan 1811–1885* (Oxford, Clarendon Press, 1973).

Blackwood, H J J (Ed), *Bone and Tooth* (London, Pergamon Press, 1964).

Bloom, Mrs Freddy, *Dear Philip: A Diary of Captivity, Changi 1942–45* (London, Bodley Head, 1980).

Bowra, Maurice, *Memories: 1898–1939* (London, Weidenfeld & Nicolson, 1966).

Boyd-Orr, John, *Food, Health and Income: Report on a Survey of Adequacy of Diet in Relation to Income* (London, Macmillan, 1936).

Briggs, Asa, *A History of the Royal College of Physicians Vol 4* (Oxford, Oxford University Press, 2005).

Brown, Andrew, *J D Bernal: The Sage of Science* (Oxford, Oxford University Press, 2005).

Bruce, M, *The Coming of the Welfare State* (London, BT Batsford Ltd, 1968).

Buchanan, Tom, *Britain and the Spanish Civil War* (Cambridge, Cambridge University Press, 1997).

Buchanan, Tom, *The Impact of the Spanish Civil War on Britain: War, Loss and Memory* (Liverpool, Liverpool University Press, 2007).

Burrough, E J R, *Unity in Diversity: The Short Life of the United Oxford Hospitals* (London, 1978, privately printed).

Caldecott, L (Ed), *Women of Our Century*, (London, Ariel Books, BBC, 1984).

Carney, Michael, *Stoker: The Life of Hilda Matheson OBE, 1888–1940* (Llangynog, Michael Carney, 1999).

Cassell, Michael, *Long Lease! The Story of Slough Estates 1920–1991* (London, Pencorp Books, 1991).

Castle, W B, for the National Academy of Sciences, George R Minot 1885–1950, *Biographical Memoirs*, (1974), 45, 337–83.

Castle, W B, Grain-fed pigeons revisited: a pioneer test for vitamin B12, in *Br J Exp Pathol* (1985), 66(4), 503–10.

Ceadel, Martin, *Pacifism in Britain 1914–1945: The Defining of a Faith* (Oxford, Clarendon Press, 1980).

Chapman, R A, *The Civil Service Commission 1855–1991: A Bureau Biography* (London, Routledge, 2004).

Clark, Ronald W, *A Biography of the Nuffield Foundation* (London, Longman, 1972).

Collis, W R F, Belsen Camp: A preliminary report, in *BMJ* (1945), 1(4405), 814–16.

Coni, Nicholas, *Medicine and Warfare: Spain, 1936–39* (London, Routledge, 2008).

Cooke, A M, *History of the Royal College of Physicians, Vol 3* (Oxford, Oxford University Press, 1964).

Craddock, Sally, *Retired Except on Demand. The Life of Dr Cicely Williams* (Oxford, Green College, 1983).

Cunningham, George J, *The History of British Pathology* (White Tree Books, 1992).

Cuthbertson, D P, in Discussion: The physiology and treatment of starvation, *Proc R Soc Med* (1945), 38, 390–93.

Dacie, Sir John, Dame Janet Vaughan DBE, FRS, DM, FRCP, in *BMJ* (30.1.1993), 306(6873), 326.

Dacie, Sir John, Dame Janet Maria Vaughan, b.18 October 1899 d.9 January 1993, *Munk's Roll: The Lives of the Fellows of the Royal College of Physicians* (London, Royal College of Physicians, 1993), IX, 541–42.

Dally, Anne, *Cicely: The Story of a Doctor* (London, Victor Gollancz, 1968).

Dent, C E, Belsen, 1945, in *UCH Magazine* (1966), 49(1), 14–19.

Dewhurst, K (Ed), *Essays on the Evolution of the Oxford Clinical School to commemorate the Bicentenary of the Radcliffe Infirmary 1770–1970* (Oxford, Sandford Publications, 1970).

Duggal, Ravi, Resurrecting Bhore, *MFC Bulletin* (November–December 1992), 188–89, 1–6 (Centre for Enquiry into Health & Allied Themes www.cehat.org/publications/pa05a8 accessed 31.7.2012).

Dunn, C L, Lieut Col, *The Emergency Medical Services, Vol 1: England and Wales* (London, HMSO, 1952), Chapter 11: The Civilian BTS.

Dyhouse, Carol, *Girls Growing up in Late Victorian and Edwardian England* (London, Routledge & Kegan Paul, 1981).

Dyhouse, Carol, *No Distinction of Sex?: Women in British Universities 1870–1939* (London, UCL Press, 1995).

Ensor, R C K, *England 1870–1914* (Oxford, Clarendon Press, 1966).

Fara, Patricia, *A Lab of One's Own: Science and Suffrage in the First World War* (Oxford, Oxford University Press, 2018).

Ferry, Georgina, *Dorothy Hodgkin: A Life* (London, Granta Books, 1998).

Foster, W D, *A Short History of Clinical Pathology* (London, Livingstone, 1961).

Franklin, *Geoffrey Franklin 1890–1930* (London, Chiswick Press, printed for private circulation, 1933).

Franks, Lord, *University of Oxford: Report of Commission of Inquiry*, Vol 1 (Oxford, Clarendon Press, 1966). Copy given to the author by Mary Park.

Furse, Katharine, *Hearts and Pomegranates*, (London, Peter Davies, 1940).

Fyrth, Jim, *The Signal Was Spain* (London, Lawrence and Wishart Limited, 1986).

Garnett, David, *The Flowers of the Forest* (London, Chatto & Windus, 1955).

Gibbon, Monk, *Netta* (London, Routledge and Kegan Paul, 1960).

Gould, E C, The Home Office Scheme, in *For His Name's Sake* (Churches of Christ publication, Heanor, W Barker, 1921).

Gourlay, David, The Wayfarers Travel Agency, in Franklin, *Geoffrey Franklin 1890–1930* (London, Chiswick Press, printed for private circulation, 1933), 103–19. Copy given to author by Mary Park.

Graham, J W, *Conscription and Conscience* (London, George Allen and Unwin Ltd).

Harcourt, G C, and Kerr, Prue, *Joan Robinson* (London, Palgrave Macmillan, 2009).

Harrison, Brian, *Prudent Revolutionaries: Portraits of British Feminists between the Wars* (Oxford, Clarendon Press, 1987).

Harrison, Brian (Ed), *The History of the University of Oxford: Vol VIII: The Twentieth Century* (Oxford, Clarendon Press, 1994).

Hennessy, Peter, *Never Again: Britain 1945–51; Having It So Good: Britain in the Fifties*; and *Winds of Change: Britain in the Early Sixties* (London, Penguin Books, 1992, 2006; and Allen Lane, 2019).

Hill, A V, *Report to the Government of India on Scientific Research in India* (London, Royal Society, April 1945).

Hinton, James, *Labour and Socialism: A History of the British Labour Movement 1867–1974* (Brighton, Wheatsheaf Books, 1983).

Hinton, James, *Protests and Visions: Peace Politics in Twentieth Century Britain* (London, Hutchinson Radius, 1989).

Hoffbrand, A Victor and Steensma, David P, *Hoffbrand's Essential Haematology* (Hoboken, NJ, Wiley-Blackwell, 2020).

Hoffbrand, A Victor and Fantini, Bernardino, Achievements in haematology in the twentieth century: an introduction, in *Seminars in Haematology* (October, 1999), 36(4), Suppl 7, 1–4.

Select bibliography

Hollman, Arthur, *Sir Thomas Lewis* (London, Springer, 1997).

Holtby, Winifred, Holtby, Alice and McWilliam, Jean, *Letters to a Friend* (London, Collins, 1937).

Honigsbaum, Frank, *Health, Happiness & Security: The Creation of the National Health Service* (London, Routledge, 1989).

Hudson, G, Unfathering the thinkable: gender, science and pacifism in the 1930s, in Marina Benjamin (Ed), *Science and Sensibility: Gender and Scientific Enquiry 1780–1945* (Oxford, Basil Blackwell, 1991), 264–86.

Huxley, Julian, *Memories I* (London, Allen & Unwin, 1970).

Huxley, Juliette, *Leaves of the Tulip Tree* (London, John Murray, 1986).

Hynes, Samuel, *A War Imagined: The First World War and English Culture* (London, The Bodley Head, 1990).

ICRP (International Commission on Radiological Protection) publications: 11: *A Review of the Radiosensitivity of the Tissues in Bone*, 1968; 14: *Radiosensitivity and Spatial Distribution of Dose*, 1969; 19: *The Metabolism of Compounds of Plutonium and other Actinides*, 1972 (Oxford, Pergamon Press).

Irons, Evelyn, The undergraduate, in Pauline Adams (Ed), *Janet Maria Vaughan 1899–1993: A Memorial Tribute* (Oxford, Somerville College, 1993).

Jandl, James H, for the National Academy of Sciences, William B Castle 1897–1990, *Biographical Memoirs*, (1995), 67, 15–40.

Johnson, Harvey and Louise, Obituary: Dame Janet Vaughan, in *The Independent*, 12.1.1993 www.independent.co.uk/news/people/obituary-dame-janet-vaughan-1478124.html accessed 7.4.2014.

Kass-Simon, G and Farnes, P (Eds), and Nash, D (Associate Ed), *Women of Science: Righting the Record* (Bloomington, Indiana University Press, 1990).

Kavadi, Shirish N, *The Rockefeller Foundation and Public Health in Colonial India 1916–45* (Pune/Mumbai, Foundation for Research in Community Health, 1996).

Klein, Rudolf, *The New Politics of the NHS* (London, Longman, 1995).

Laity, Paul, *The British Peace Movement 1870–1914* (Oxford, Clarendon Press, 2001).

Langford, Christopher, The age pattern of mortality in the 1918–19 influenza pandemic: an attempted explanation based on data for England and Wales, in *Medical History* (2002), 46(1), 1–20.

Lee, Hermione, *Virginia Woolf* (London, Vintage, 1997).

Lehane, D, Kwantes, C M S, Upwood, M G and Thomson D R, Homologous serum jaundice, in *BMJ* (10.9.1949), 2(4627), 572–74.

Lewenhak, Sheila, *Women and Trade Unions: An Outline History of Women in the British Trade Union Movement* (London, E Benn, 1977).

Lewis, Aubrey, National epidemiology, *BMJ* (8.4.1961), 1(5231), 1034.

Lewis, Sir Thomas, *Clinical Science Illustrated by Personal Experiences* (London, Shaw & Sons, 1934).

McKibbin, Ross, *Classes & Cultures: England 1918–1951* (Oxford, Oxford University Press, 1998).

Magee, H E, in The physiology and treatment of starvation, *Proc R Soc Med* (29.5.1945), 38, 388–90.

Martin, Brenda and Black, Jonathan, Dora Gordine: Sculptor, Artist, Designer (London, Philip Wilson, 2007).

Matheson, H, *Hilda Matheson* (London, Hogarth Press, 1941).

Medical Research in War. The Report of the MRC for the Years 1939–1945, Cmd 7335 (London, HMSO, 1947).

Merrington, William Robert, *University College Hospital and its Medical School: A History* (London, Heinemann, 1976).

Mollison, P L, Observations on cases of starvation at Belsen, in *BMJ* (5.1.1946), 1(4435), 4–8.

Murphy, Kate, *Behind the Wireless: A History of Early Women at the BBC* (London, Palgrave Macmillan, 2016).

Neuberger, Albert, Charles Enrique Dent, 25 August 1911 – 19 September 1976, *Biographical Memoirs of Fellows of the Royal Society* (1.11.1978), 24, 15–31.

Newman, Charles, A brief history of the Postgraduate Medical School, in *Postgraduate Medical Journal* (1966), 42(494), 738–40.

Newsome, David, *A History of Wellington College 1859–1959* (London, John Murray, 1959).

Owen, Maureen E, Dame Janet Maria Vaughan DBE, 18 October 1899 – 9 January 1993, in *Biographical Memoirs of Fellows of the Royal Society* (1995), 41, 483–98.

Palfreeman, L and Pinkerton, P H, Transfusion in the Spanish Civil War: supply and demand, the role of the 'blood transfusion officer' and British planning for the outbreak of the Second World War, *Transfusion and Apheresis Science* (December 2019), 58(6), 102671: https://doi.org/10.1016/j.transci.2019.102671

Pandya, Rameshwari (Ed), *Health, Family Planning and Nutrition in India – First 5-year Plan (1951–56) to 11th (2007–12)* (New Delhi, New Century Publications, 2009).

Partridge, Frances, *Memories* (London, Gollancz, 1981).

Pemble, John, *John Addington Symonds: Culture and the Demon Desire* (Basingstoke, Macmillan, 2000).

Pemble, John, *Venice Rediscovered* (Oxford, Clarendon Press, 1994).

Perkins, Anne, *A Very British Strike* (London, Macmillan, 2006).

Select bibliography

Plaut, G, MD, Barrow, M L and Abbott, J M, The results of routine investigation for Rh factor at the NW London Depot, in *BMJ* (1.9.1945), 2(4417), i, 273–81.

Poles, Faith C, Captain RAMC, and Boycott, Muriel, lately Lieutenant RAMC, (ABTS), Syncope in blood donors, *The Lancet* (7.11.1942), 2(6219), 531.

Porter, Roy (Ed), *The Cambridge History of Medicine* (Cambridge, Cambridge University Press, 2006).

Price-Jones, Cecil, *Red Cell Blood Diameters* (London, H Milford, Oxford University Press, 1933).

Proudfoot, Harriet (Higgens), The doctor, in Pauline Adams (Ed), *Janet Maria Vaughan 1899–1993: A Memorial Tribute* (Oxford, Somerville College, 1993), 18.

Pugh, Martin, *Women and the Women's Movement in Britain 1914–59* (Oxford, Blackwell, 1992).

Rackemann, F M, *The Inquisitive Physician* (Cambridge, MA, Harvard University Press, 1956).

Radiation Damage in Bone, report and summarized papers of a Conference on the Relation of Radiation Damage to Radiation Dose in Bone held at Oxford, 10–14 April 1960 (Vienna, IAEA, 1960).

Rae, John, *Conscience and Politics: The British Government and the Conscientious Objector to Military Service 1916–19* (London, Oxford University Press, 1970).

Rantzen, Esther, *Esther* (London, BBC Books, 2001).

Report of the Committee on Higher Education (Robbins Report), Cmnd 2154 (London, HMSO, 1963).

Report of the Royal Commission on Equal Pay, Cmnd 6937 (London, HMSO, 1946).

Robb-Smith, Alastair, *Life and Achievements of Professor Robert Gwyn Macfarlane FRS* (Royal Society of Medicine Services Ltd, 1993).

Robinson, Howard, *Britain's Post Office: A History of its Development from the Beginnings to the Present Day* (London, Oxford University Press, 1953).

Rossiter, M W, *Women scientists in America: Struggles and Strategies to 1940* (Johns Hopkins University Press, Baltimore, MD, 1982).

Rubenstein, L J, Dorothy Stuart Russell, b.27 June 1895 d.19 October 1983. *Munk's Roll: The Lives of the Fellows of the Royal College of Physicians* (London, Royal College of Physicians, 1983), VII, 510.

Saxton, R S, The Madrid Blood Transfusion Institute, in *The Lancet* (4.9.1937), 2, 1(5923), 606–607.

Schellenberg, Walter, *Invasion! Operation Sea Lion, 1940* (London, St Ermin's Press, 2000).

Second Interim Report of the Social and Preventive Medicine Committee (London, Royal College of Physicians, January 1945).

Shephard, Ben, *After Daybreak: The Liberation of Belsen, 1945* (London, Jonathan Cape, 2005).

Sherrington, Sir Charles, Biographical. NobelPrize.org. Nobel Prize Outreach AB 2023: https://www.nobelprize.org/prizes/medicine/1932/sherrington/biographical/ accessed 22.6.2023.

Sigerist, H E, *Socialised Medicine in the Soviet Union* (London, Victor Gollancz Ltd, 1937).

Skidelsky, Robert, *John Maynard Keynes,* Volumes 2 and 3 (London, Macmillan, 1992 and 2000).

Smith, H L, The politics of Conservative reform: the equal pay for equal work issue, 1945-1955, in *The Historical Journal* (1992), 35(2), 401-15.

Smith, H L, The problems of equal pay for equal work in Great Britain during World War Two, in *Journal of Modern History*, (1981), 53(4), 652-72.

Smith, H L (Ed), *British Feminism in the Twentieth Century* (Aldershot, Edward Elgar, 1990).

Smith, Prue, *The Morning Light* (Cape Town, David Philip, 2000).

Stewart, John, *The Battle for Health: A Political History of the Socialist Medical Association, 1930-51* (Aldershot, Ashgate, 1999).

Strachey, Ray, *Careers and Openings for Women: A Survey of Women's Employment and a Guide for Those Seeking Work* (London, Faber & Faber Limited, 1935).

Symonds, Margaret, *Days Spent on a Doge's Farm* (London, John Murray, 1893).

Symonds, Margaret (Mrs W W Vaughan), *Out of the Past* (London, John Murray, 1925).

Tanner, Duncan, Thane, Pat and Tiratsoo, Nick (Eds), *Labour's First Century* (Cambridge University Press, 2000).

Tansey, E M, Keeping the culture alive: the laboratory technician in mid-twentieth century British medical research, in *Notes Rec R Soc* (2008), 62(1), 77-95.

Thane, Pat, *Foundations of the Welfare State* (2nd edition) (London, Pearson Education, 1996).

Thane, Pat, The impact of mass democracy on British political culture, 1918-1939, in Julie V Gottlieb, and Richard Toye (Eds), *The Aftermath of Suffrage* (London, Palgrave Macmillan, 2013), 54-69.

Thane, Pat, The women of the British Labour Party and feminism, 1906-1945, in H L Smith (Ed), *British Feminism in the 20th Century* (Aldershot, Edward Elgar, 1990), 124-43.

Thane, Pat, Towards equal opportunities? Women in Britain since 1945, in Terry Gourvish & Alan O'Day (Eds), *Britain since 1945* (London, Macmillan, 1991), 183-208.

Select bibliography

Thane, Pat, Women and political participation in England, 1918–70, in Esther Breitenbach and Pat Thane (Eds), *Women and Citizenship in Britain and Ireland in the Twentieth Century* (London, Continuum, 2010), 11–28.

Thomas, Hugh, *John Strachey* (London, Eyre Methuen, 1973).

Thomas, Hugh, *The Spanish Civil War* (4th edition), (London, Penguin, 2003).

Thompson, F M L, *The Cambridge Social History of Britain, 1750–1950* (Cambridge, Cambridge University Press, 1990).

Thorpe, Andrew, *The British Communist Party and Moscow 1920–43* (Manchester, Manchester University Press, 2000).

Thwaite, Ann, *Edmond Gosse. A Literary Landscape 1849–1928* (London, Secker & Warburg, 1984).

Trueta, Joseph, *Trueta, Surgeon in War and Peace: The Memoirs of Josep Trueta M.D., F.R.C.S., D.Sc.* (London, Gollancz, 1980).

Veale, Douglas, The Nuffield Benefaction and the Oxford Medical School, in K Dewhurst (Ed), *Essays on the Evolution of the Oxford Clinical School to Commemorate the Bicentenary of the Radcliffe Infirmary 1770–1970* (Sandford Publications, Oxford, 1970), 143–53.

Vellacott, Jo, *Bertrand Russell: And the Pacifists in the First World War* (Brighton, Harvester, 1980).

Wadsworth, M, The origins and innovatory nature of the 1946 British national birth cohort study, in *Longitudinal and Life Course Studies* (2010), 1(2), 121–36.

Walker, Alice, *Collected Poems* (London, Weidenfeld and Nicolson, UK, 2005).

Webster, Charles, Medicine, in Brian Harrison (Ed), *History of the University of Oxford: Vol VIII: The Twentieth Century*, (Oxford, Clarendon Press, 1994), 317–43.

Weindling, Paul, *Epidemics and Genocide in Eastern Europe* (Oxford, Oxford University Press, 2000).

Weindling, Paul, Human guinea pigs and the ethics of experimentation: the *BMJ*'s correspondent at the Nuremberg medical trial, in *BMJ* (7.12.1996), 313(7070), 1467–70.

Werskey, Gary, *The Visible College: A Collective Biography of British Scientists and Socialists of the 1930s* (London, Free Association Books, 1988).

West, Katharine, *Inner and Outer Circles* (London, Cohen and West, 1958).

Whitby, Col L E H, CVO, MC, The therapeutic value of transfusion of derivatives of blood, *Proc R Soc Med* (March, 1941) 34(5), 261–66.

Williams, Eryl Hall, *A Page of History in Relief* (Sessions Book Trust, York, 1993).

Wills, Lucy, Treatment of 'Pernicious Anaemia of Pregnancy' and 'Tropical Anaemia' with special reference to yeast extract as a curative agent, in *BMJ* (20.6.1931), 1(3676), 1059–64.

Wintrobe, M M (Ed), *Blood, Pure and Eloquent: A Story of Discovery, of People, and of Ideas* (New York, McGraw-Hill, 1980).

Wintrobe, M M, *Hematology: The Blossoming of a Science – A Story of Inspiration and Effort* (Philadelphia, Lea & Febiger, 1985).

Woolf, Leonard, *Beginning Again: An Autobiography of the Years 1911 to 1918* (London, Hogarth Press, 1964).

Woolf, Leonard, *Downhill All the Way: An Autobiography of the Years 1919–1939* (London, Hogarth Press, 1967).

Woolf, Virginia, *A Room of One's Own* (London, Hogarth Press, 1929).

Woolf, Virginia, *Three Guineas* (London, Hogarth Press, 1938).

Woolf, Virginia and Nicolson, Nigel (Ed), *The Letters of Virginia Woolf*, Volumes 1–6 (London, Hogarth Press, 1975, 1976, 1977, 1978, 1979 and 1980).

Woolf, Virginia and Anne Olivier Bell, *The Diary of Virginia Woolf*, Volume 1 (London, Hogarth Press, 1977); and also with Andrew McNeillie, Volumes 2–5 (London, Hogarth Press, 1978, 1980, 1982 and 1984).

Zallen, Doris T, From butterflies to blood. Human genetics in the United Kingdom, in Michael Fortun and Everett Mendelsohn (Eds), *The Practices of Human Genetics* (Kluwer Academic Publishers, Dordrecht, 1999), 197–216.

Zallen, Doris T, The Nuffield Foundation and medical genetics in the United Kingdom, in William H Schneider, *Rockefeller Philanthropy and Modern Biomedicine: International Initiatives from World War I to the Cold War* (Bloomington, IN, Indiana University Press, 2002), 224–26.

Zetzel, Louis, *Memoirs* (private publication, December 1990).

INDEX

Index

Index

Index

Index

Index

381